**Association for
Computing Machinery**

Advancing Computing as a Science & Profession

SIGUCCS'17

**Proceedings of the 2017 ACM Annual Conference on
SIGUCCS**

Sponsored by:

ACM SIGUCCS

Supported by:

HDI, Ink, Software2, PDQ.com, JAMF, Wēpa, & LabStats

**Association for
Computing Machinery**

Advancing Computing as a Science & Profession

The Association for Computing Machinery
2 Penn Plaza, Suite 701
New York, New York 10121-0701

Notice to Past Authors of ACM-Published Articles

ISBN: 978-1-4503-4919-2 (Digital)

ISBN: 978-1-4503-5613-8 (Print)

Additional copies may be ordered prepaid from:

ACM Order Department
PO Box 30777
New York, NY 10087-0777, USA

Phone: 1-800-342-6626 (USA and Canada)
+1-212-626-0500 (Global)
Fax: +1-212-944-1318
E-mail: acmhelp@acm.org
Hours of Operation: 8:30 am – 4:30 pm ET

WELCOME

On behalf of the SIGUCCS Board, welcome to Seattle and the 45th annual SIGUCCS conference! Grab a mug of your favorite beverage and join your colleagues from around the world as we Connect | Discover.

The 2017-2020 board recently took office, and we are looking forward to working together for the next three years! We encourage your comments and ideas—please join us for an Open Board meeting on Tuesday at 7:30am in Emerald 2 or chat with us during any networking event.

Enjoy SIGUCCS 2017 and Seattle!

LAURIE FOX
Chair, SIGUCCS

Chair
LAURIE FOX
SUNY Geneseo

Vice-Chair
(Conference Liaison)
DAN HERRICK
University of Colorado - Boulder

Treasurer
LISA BROWN
University of Rochester

Secretary
KRISTEN DIETIKER
Menlo College

Past Chair
MAT FELTHOUSEN
Cleaveland Institute of Art

Connect | Discover
Thank you to Cate Lyon and the 2017 conference planning committee for their hard work over the last 18 months!

CONGRATULATIONS
Congratulations to our award recipients - the Penny Crane Award for Distinguished Service recipient Tim Foley; our recent Hall of Fame Inductees Melissa Bauer, Allan Chen, Beth Rugg, and Kelly Wainwright; and the Communications Awards winners. We will celebrate their contributions and achievements during the General Session on Tuesday at 10:30 am in the Seattle Ballroom.

Join
us in 2018 at Disney's Coronado Springs Resort on October 7-10, 2018 See you there!

COMMUNITY
Extend your collaboration beyond the annual conferences by participating in one or more of our SIGUCCS online communities! Join the SIGUCCS-L email list, Slack channel or Facebook Community group. Watch for information about participating in the Mentoring Program and upcoming SIGUCCS Webinars. More information can be found on our website siguccs.org

VOLUNTEER
Please consider volunteering with SIGUCCS. It's a great way to give back to our community and an opportunity for professional and personal growth. Planning for the 2018 conference has already begun and there are many ways you can join the team! We also welcome volunteers in our marketing efforts, mentoring program, and award selection programs. Let a Board member know if you're interested!

iii

CONFERENCE CHAIR WELCOME

Welcome to Seattle - pull up a seat, grab a cup of coffee and let's talk!

Seattle is a perfect reflection of the SIGUCCS 2017 conference - it is a city of innovation, boldness, collaboration and inspiration. This is where Starbucks was first brewed, where Microsoft made its mark, and where Pike Place Fish Market, approaching bankruptcy, decided to become world famous and began throwing its product at its customers!

The core planning committee kicked off SIGUCCS 2017 by throwing our own fish at the General Session in Denver during SIGUCCS 2016. And we've since spent the past year hard at work to make this conference the best of what SIGUCCS does for its members. Special thanks goes out to the team that helped shape this year's conference - all the volunteers who are serving on the planning and conference committees, the presenters who are providing the content and offering new ways to Connect | Discover, and everyone who participates in SIGUCCS—not just at the conference but year round.

Connect | Discover is not just the theme, but the embodiment of this year's conference. Opportunities abound for professional development and networking with your peers. I invite you to kick off each morning at breakfast to "Begin the Conversation" and share ideas about the day's topics, don't miss attending the exciting and inspirational plenary and general sessions, drop by the poster session to grab some snacks and help determine the winner of a "major award", and end each day by "Continuing the Conversation" in which you will have the opportunity to discuss the day's topics with presenters and your peers.

This is YOUR conference, created by your peers, presented by your colleagues and your engagement will power it. Connect with the other attendees and speakers and discover that next new technology, smart solution or growing trend. We are throwing a big fish at you - step up and catch it!

CATE LYON
2017 SIGUCCS Conference Chair

PROGRAM CHAIRS WELCOME

As Program Co-Chairs, it is our great pleasure to welcome you to SIGUCCS 2017! We are thrilled to be here in Seattle and we look forward to sharing this year's program with you.

Our conference begins with our Opening Plenary, where three current and former CIOs, Marty Ringle, Lois Brooks, and Chris Ferguson, will discuss "Apocalypse Deferred: Wreaking Order in the Service Environment Through Effective Leadership". This session promises to be an engaging and fun discussion about the challenges of Higher Ed IT. Regardless of your role, it will get you thinking about how to address the challenges you face in your job. At the end of our conference, Amanda Messer from Because I Said I Would delivers our Closing Plenary. In Because I Said I Would, Amanda will share her insights on the importance of accountability, fulfilling commitments, and doing what you say you will do.

One of the hallmarks of SIGUCCS is that we are a volunteer organization. As such, many individuals have contributed a great deal of hard work and dedication toward the success of this conference. We received 80 submissions to our Call for Proposals, and many quality proposals had to be turned away. We accepted a mix of sessions. Presentations and posters each required writing and publishing a paper, which are now available online in the ACM Digital Library. Other sessions we are offering this week include panels, lighting talks, and facilitated discussions. Our excellent authors and presenters developed strong papers, posters, and presentations, guided by our Readers and Track Chairs. All told, over 100 people were involved in writing, editing, and presenting the program content you are accessing here in Seattle. We could not have developed this year's program without their efforts, and we thank them for volunteering their time.

From the very earliest stages of planning this conference back in June 2016, the conference committee reflected on SIGUCCS conferences, what they mean to us individually, and what we hope to achieve this year. Our conference theme Connect | Discover was developed as a result of our discussions. We are confident that over the next several days, you will connect with amazing colleagues from other institutions across the US and the world, and discover new ideas and solutions to bring back to your home institution.

KRISTEN DIETEKER & CHRIS WIESEMANN
2017 SIGUCCS Conference Program Co-Chairs

Table of Contents

Paper Session - Tuesday, 1:15pm

Paper Session - Tuesday, 2:30pm

Paper Session - Tuesday, 4:00pm

Paper Session - Wednesday, 9:00am

Paper Session - Wednesday, 10:30am

Paper Session - Wednesday, 1:15pm

Paper Session - Wednesday, 2:30pm

2017 SIGUCCS CONFERENCE COMMITTEE

Conference Chair
CATE LYON
Whitman College

Program Chair
KRISTEN DIETIKER
Menlo College

Program Chair
CHRIS WIESEMANN
University of Oregon

Treasurer
TERRY RUGER
Ithaca College

**Incoming Board Liaison &
Track Chair**
DAN HERRICK
University of Colorado Boulder

**Outgoing Board Liaison &
Photography Coordinator**
MELISSA BAUER
Baldwin Wallace University

Communication Awards
LISA BROWN
University of Rochester

Exhibitor Chair
ALLAN CHEN
Muhlenberg College

First Timers Coordinator
Dinah Logan
Texas A&M University

Graphic Designer & Posters
Becky Cowin
Washington University in St. Louis

Hospitality Room Coordinator
Eric Handler
Macalester College

Poster Session Chair
LISA BARNETT
NYU School of Law

Pre-Conference Seminars
BETH RUGG
UNC - Charlotte

Publications & Track Chair
KELLY WAINWRIGHT
Lewis & Clark College

Publicity Chair
ALEXA SPIGELMYER
Penn State University

**Registration Chair &
Mobile App Coordinator**
SHAWN PLUMMER
SUNY Geneseo

Social Coordinator
ROBERT FRICKE
Whitman Collge

Social Networking Chair
MO NISHIYAMA
Oregon Health & Science University

Volunteer Coordinator
KENDRA STRODE
Carleton College

Webmaster & Reader
MIRANDA CARNEY-MORRIS
Lewis & Clark College

Track Chair
MELISSA DOERNTE
Stanford University

Track Chair
CHRIS KING
State of North Carolina

Track Chair
MATTHEW MADEROS
Boston University

Track Chair
JOHN TYNDALL
Penn State University

Program Readers

JULIO APPLING, *Lewis & Clark College*
PATRICIA CIUFFO, *Touro College And University System*
MICHAEL CYR, *University of Maine*
MARIANNA DOHERTY, *Dickinson College*
LAURIE FOX, *SUNY Geneseo*

KATE GILBREATH, *The Ohio State University*
BOB HARING-SMITH, *Retired*
CHERYL TARBOX, *Binghamton University*
DAN VANDER PLOEG, *University of Illinois*
RACHEL WEAVER, *Macalester College*

SIGUCCS 2017 · SIGUCCS.org · #siguccs17

THANKS TO OUR EXHIBITORS

The 2017 SIGUCCS Conference is made possible largely due to the generous support of our exhibitors. On behalf of the conference, we would like to extend our sincere thanks for your support and presence, both which enhance the entire conference experience.

Attendees face similar challenges and needs at their respective institutions. They come to SIGUCCS knowing there will be opportunity to engage with exhibitors in a significant dialogue. Many of our exhibitors already have relationships with participating institutions which provides an invaluable foundation for meeting new potential clients.

We hope you enjoy the experience and we appreciate your support.

— The 2017 SIGUCCS Conference Exhibitor Team —

PLATINUM EXHIBITORS

GOLD EXHIBITORS

SILVER EXHIBITORS

Creating, Implementing, and Maintaining Successful Classroom Design

John Anderson
Director, Client Support and Technical Services
Library and Academic Technology
Washington College
Chestertown, Maryland
janderson5@washcoll.edu

Adrian Peterson
Director, Innovative Learning Spaces & Special Projects
Library and Academic Technology
Washington College
Chestertown, Maryland
apeterson2@washcoll.edu

Robert Bishop
Technical Services Technician
Library and Academic Technology
Washington College
Chestertown, Maryland
rbishop2@washcoll.edu

ABSTRACT

In the course of 3 years, Library and Academic Technology (LAT) at Washington College (WC) managed to create successful academic learning environments that benefit both teachers and learners. Our existing classroom audio/visual (A/V) systems were old, convoluted and unreliable. Additionally, the furniture was designed for utility and cost efficiency as opposed to student creativity and collaboration.

The Center for Teaching and Learning at WC funded a pilot updated classroom designed with modern, reliable A/V and student collaboration as the focus. This update included bring-your-own-device (BYOD) capabilities, updated projection equipment, and a simple-to-use control interface. We also removed the old armchairs which had small flip-up writing surfaces and replaced them with Node Chairs which have larger writing surfaces in addition to a wheeled base and a storage area for bags or books. The room redesign was an overwhelming success.

Following the pilot, the new classroom design was adopted as the standard and implemented campus wide. Classroom installations were completed during breaks in the academic year, so as to not to disrupt instruction. Performing most technology installations in-house helped keep labor costs to a minimum. Furniture updates in learning spaces are moving more slowly due to budget constraints and coordination difficulties with other campus departments. Over 80% of the 53 learning spaces on campus have been updated. Five spaces have received a furniture redesign with a focus on active learning.

Future updates and plans for this series of projects includes incorporating wireless presentation capabilities as well as working with the finance office to establish a replacement cycle for classroom furniture and technologies.

CCS CONCEPTS

• Applied computing~Collaborative learning • Applied computing~Interactive learning environments

KEYWORDS

Classroom design; Audio/Visual design; Learning spaces

1 INTRODUCTION

Founded in 1782 under the patronage of George Washington, Washington College is a private, independent college of liberal arts and sciences on Maryland's Eastern Shore, Washington College's student enrollment totals just over 1,400 undergraduate students. The student to faculty ratio is 12:1, offering small, intimate classes, where collaborative teaching and learning transpires.

2 STATE OF THE CLASSROOMS

Learning spaces on campus prior to 2014 were quite outdated, difficult to use, and far from most A/V standards of today. Academic buildings on the main campus were renovated or built between 1916 and 2004. Most classrooms on campus were last renovated in the late 1990s or early 2000s with little attention given to instructional technology. The Technical Services team at Washington College began retrofitting classrooms with InFocus projectors and an instruction station for a Macintosh and/or Windows computer in the late 1990s. These installations frequently coincided with building renovations, but also occurred during winter and summer breaks when classes were not in session. Retrofitting classrooms for A/V equipment was frequently performed in house, by the A/V technician. Due to IT budget constraints, the cheapest solutions possible were consistently implemented.

Figure 1: Before renovations, old classroom wiring

Through the years the projectors and classroom computers were updated and replaced as they failed. However, the original room infrastructure remained the same. All of the sources and cabling were analog in the original systems, making it impossible to display high definition digital devices properly in our classrooms. Connections for BYOD were not available and instructors who wanted to use their laptops or tablets would disconnect the instructor computer, and connect their own. This created a nightmare for the HelpDesk support team. As more and more instructors insisted on using their own devices, the number of calls and complaints for classroom A/V increased drastically. Due to the difficulty and fickleness of the classroom A/V, the instructor stations were very frequently left disconnected or connected improperly. The next professor using the room would then lose valuable class time fixing the A/V issues in the room, or waiting for a HelpDesk technician.

The original classrooms' A/V installations also didn't include adequate audio solutions. The systems relied on the small internal speaker included with most large venue projectors. Academic courses that include or require audio were simply not possible with this solution. Sometime after the original A/V installation, small desktop speakers were installed on the projector mounts in most classrooms. This solution did provide more volume, though still inadequate, especially in some of the larger classrooms on campus.

Classroom furniture in most spaces consisted of the standard flip-up tablet arm chairs or heavy tables and chairs. Neither solution fostered collaboration.

3 DEPARTMENT REORGANIZATION

In 2013, the resignation of the CIO and the impending retirement of the College Librarian caused the President and Chief of Staff at Washington College to question the organizational structure of the Library and Information Technologies departments.

The review team consisted of three individuals: a Library Director, a VP of Libraries and Information Technology and a VP for Information and Library Services, each from a different higher education institution. The conclusion of the review was that Washington College could benefit from unifying leadership in library and information technology. The review states that there is "obvious fruitful joint planning – library instruction, technology instruction, information literacy, and multimedia production training." It also states that a "strong, capable and engaging new leader working with existing OIT and Library leadership will be important for achieving this."

In May of 2014, the Academic Computing and Support Services group within OIT merged with the library staff. This group included the Associate CIO for Academic Computing, Educational Technology, Digital Media Services, the HelpDesk and the Senior Project Manager. The HelpDesk and the Senior Project Manager were originally excluded from the merger, but they advocated for inclusion due to the close working relationships within the department. The reorganization inspired greater focus on academics within the departments that supported technology on campus. Learning space technology was one of the first items tackled by this newly formed and reinvigorated department.

4 IDEAL COLLABORATIVE PILOT CLASSROOM

In the fall semester of 2014, a discussion began around the possibility of using a pilot classroom to test some ideas for creating a highly collaborative classroom that promoted student engagement and critical thinking. The Center for Teaching and Learning (CTL) at Washington College was interested in what might be accomplished and was willing to put forth funding to transform one of the classrooms on campus. After many discussions, a possible room was identified. It was a smaller classroom with tablet arm chairs, used by a variety of departments. One major obstacle was the classroom capacity. The project manager had researched the generally agreed upon standard for square footage of space, per person, using individual desks and found it was around 15 square feet per person. The space was previously capped at 22 students, which was far too many for the size of the room. In working with the Registrar's Office, the cap was lowered to 16 students for the spring 2015 semester to allow the pilot to take place with the appropriate space ratios.

The classroom was equipped with a new A/V layout as part of the pilot. In looking at past HelpDesk tickets involving classrooms, the largest barrier to using the technology in the space was around connection issues and unreliability of the system. Audio issues and poor picture quality were also areas of concern and frustration. Given these issues, a new system of connections and controls was designed.

Figure 2: After renovations, new classroom wiring.

There were some existing factors that needed to be considered during the design process. A DVD/VHS combo deck was still in use in the classroom. Also, some professors were still using VGA/Audio connections to hook up their own devices. Because of this, a two-part connection system was put in place, using a blend of digital and analog connections. The first wall-mounted connection box was to be used by equipment that was housed in the room permanently, which included an instructor machine (dual-boot iMac) as well as the previously mentioned combo deck. This box was designated the "do not touch" box, because there was no need to connect or disconnect anything to or from this box. The second connection box was our "BYOD" box. This had an HDMI, a VGA, and a 3.5mm audio jack. This would allow anyone wishing to connect their own device to have easy access to the appropriate connections without having to unplug any of the in-room equipment.

Figure 3: BYOD connections

This connection system was complemented by a Pixie Plus control system, removing the need to use the projector remote for basic functions (On/Off, Source, and Volume up/down). This control

device was installed with the hope of limiting the confusion that often comes with trying to use the projector remote.

Figure 4: Pixie Plus Control System

Finally, a new projector with a brighter, clearer image was installed, as well as new speakers, positioned directly in the front of the room to improve clarity and audibility. A training video was also created and distributed to help faculty teaching in the space to learn how to use the new set-up.

Figure 5 – Epson Powerlite 4770

In regards to the furniture, Washington College used an existing consortium purchasing agreement to obtain competitive pricing for 16 Node chairs (Picture 6) as well as a nesting instructor's table. However, due to miscommunication, the chairs arrived without work surfaces. This made the chairs unusable for the pilot. Fortunately, the work surfaces could be ordered, delivered, and installed on site. However, this delayed the start of the pilot. The chairs were not ready to be put into place until half way through the spring semester.

Figure 6: Node Chair

This mistake ended up providing valuable data. Because the students used the old desks for half of the semester, and then switched to the Node chairs, data could be gathered that made direct comparison on the effect the change had on both students and faculty in regards to teaching and learning. Had the mistake not been made, this comparison would not have been possible.

Both quantitative and qualitative data were collected from the pilot. A short survey was administered to students in person during class time. Qualitative questions were then asked and responses recorded. The instructor was not present for the data gathering in an attempt to get the most accurate information. A survey was also sent to faculty to gather both quantitative and qualitative data, as their schedules made in-person meetings difficult. (Figure 7)

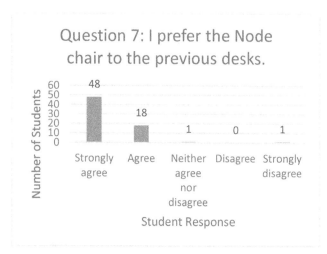

Figure 7: Results from pilot classroom student survey, Question 7: I prefer the Node chair to the previous desks.

One of the main focuses of the survey was to find out if students wanted to have more spaces on campus equipped with Node chairs. (Figure 8)

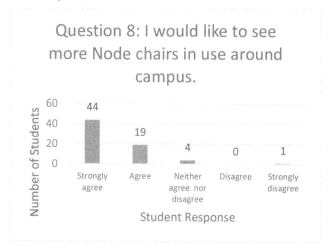

Figure 8: Results from the pilot classroom student survey

Over 90% of the students and over 80% of the faculty responded that they would like to see Node chairs in more classrooms around campus. Qualitatively, students shared feelings such as "10,000 times better than the old desks" and "I have so much more room to work" and consistently asked the surveyor, "You aren't going to take them away from us, are you?" The students had a genuine excitement about the new desks. It is important to point out that college-aged students being excited about desks is a bit of an unusual situation. The CTL was pleased with the results. The Help Desk also received far fewer complaints and issues in regards to the A/V in the room, and it was widely acknowledged that these changes were a step in the right direction.

5 CAMPUS-WIDE IMPLEMENTATION

Following the successful pilot, we began the long process of converting the remaining campus classrooms to our new standard. The process was slow due to limited access to classrooms throughout the year. During the summer Washington College hosts a wide variety of camps, clubs, and festivals. There are roughly two and half weeks in that time that classrooms are free. Aside from that time, we utilized our fall, winter, and spring breaks to convert classrooms to our new standard.

We began our implementation with William Smith Hall, our oldest academic building. Due to the block construction of the interior walls we need to use conduit to get our speakers to the appropriate areas. We used 2900 Legrand Raceway conduit, which we found to be the least obtrusive for a classroom because of the flat rectangular shape and that it can be painted. While metal conduit can also be painted to match the walls, the flat Legrand conduit still drew less attention from the eye. The building gave us an opportunity to learn several lessons. We realized during these installations that the projector we had chosen (the Epson Powerlite 4650) had a 4:3 native aspect ratio which did not match our current computer ratios. In the subsequent buildings, we changed our standard to an Epson Powerlite 4770w which rectified that issue. In this first building we also used Star Tech active HDMI to DisplayPort converters. These units require resetting from time to time and have been installed on the projector end of the cabling. Troubleshooting them requires a ladder as well as an open classroom time so that students are not in the way. We have since switched to DisplayPort-only cables and connect our computers using a Mini DisplayPort/Thunderbolt to DisplayPort cable. We plan on returning to William Smith Hall to swap out the converters.

Our next buildings held fewer issues and lessons for us. A number of the classrooms were simultaneously going through a furniture and learning space upgrade as well. Our faculty were looking for a solution to provide a much wider uninterrupted writing surface for their instruction. After some research, we found that using IdeaPaint dry erase paint was our preferred solution. We tested our standard projectors with the paint and found that while the image quality was good, the projector produced a very pronounced reflection and hotspot for some viewing positions. Needing a solution to the issue, we decided to test the Epson 585W ultra-short throw projectors. These projectors worked quite well and, since the lens was close to the wall, there were no hot spots from any of the student viewing areas. This solution worked well for rooms that were planned for the furniture updates prior to our A/V refresh. The IdeaPaint treatment was requested for a few rooms after a new projector had been installed. In those cases, a traditional pull down screen was still used.

A few of our remaining buildings posed some new challenges. The science building, which was the last full academic building to be redone, utilized stationary computer stations which were situated away from a wall. These stations had core drills through the concrete flooring for conduit to run to the ceiling. The positioning of these conduits in one of the rooms required the use of cable extensions to cover the increased distance. The contractors in charge of running the conduit found it necessary to place the openings in the most crowded part of the instructor station. Similar situations were found at the other end of the pipes in the ceiling. Running wires in those conditions was certainly not impossible, but it was far from pleasant.

We also refreshed a few non-classroom spaces on campus. The Faculty Lounge, a space that hosts several events every month, had no A/V components installed in the space previously. If an event needed video a portable screen and projector on a cart were brought in. Similarly, portable speakers were used for any audio needs. Due to the labor involved each time as well as the unsightly nature of a portable setup we decided to add a dedicated A/V system to the room. There are 12 ceiling-mounted speakers divided into 3 zones in the room as well as an iMac and Epson 4770w projector which is recessed into a lower portion of the ceiling that encases HVAC duct work. The dinners hosted in the space no longer have to contend with wires along the floor or large ugly speakers sitting in the corner.

At the time of writing, we have installed new A/V in 43 of the 53 presentation spaces on campus. They will be completed over the summer, which will give us some breathing room before we revisit spaces for technology updates again. The college is instituting a refresh cycle on our classrooms which is something that to date had not been done. We are hoping that this will keep our academic spaces from becoming as technologically dated as they were prior to this project.

6 FUTURE STEPS, LESSONS, AND POTENTIAL ISSUES

At this time, we've received several requests for wireless presentation and group collaboration capabilities in our classroom spaces. Wireless video was not something that was originally planned in our replacement A/V solution. Going forward we anticipate a growing demand for this capability. In the past year, we evaluated a few different wireless presentation solutions, specifically Apple TV, Arrive AirPoint, Crestron AirMedia, and wePresent. The primary reason for choosing the wePresent over the other options, was its ability to broadcast full mirroring of most devices, including Android, iOS, MacOS, and Windows. The wePresent WiPG-2000 unit connects to the network wirelessly or with an RJ-45 connection, and to your projector via VGA or HDMI. Adding the wePresent unit to the standard classroom A/V solution will require some reconfiguration, but will ultimately give us more flexibility with BYOD.

Moving forward with furniture needs, we hope to establish a working committee whose main charge is to evaluate our classroom spaces and make suggestions for improvements and changes that will better facilitate the kind of 21st-century teaching and learning we want to offer. This group would ideally consist of Library and Academic Technology, the Registrar's Office, Facilities, and members of the faculty. This group would hopefully meet regularly to discuss needs and strategies to address those needs. Any updates must address issues with classroom caps, furniture costs, and funding models for these changes.

Writing surfaces also play a major role in classroom maintenance and, so far, a consensus has not been reached on what surfaces best serve the faculty and students. While IdeaPaint offers a great writing area onto which you can project, the expensive prep work and cleaning issues are hindrances to its proliferation across campus. Blackboards have severe dust issues that negatively affect technology and cannot not be used as a projection surface. Quality whiteboards are expensive and have a limited writing area. Some mixture of solutions will almost certainly be where we move. Finding the right solution will involve more data gathering.

Even with the ability to project on some writing surfaces, we found that most classroom instructors prefer to project onto standard Da-lite or Draper pull-down screens. We're currently in the process of updating many of our classroom screens on campus from the 4:3 standard to the new 16:9 or 16:10.

Until now classroom A/V technology was replaced or updated on an as-needed basis. To change this practice after undertaking a whole campus refresh Washington College has committed to replacing all classroom A/V on a six-year cycle. We hope that this will keep our learning spaces up to date and less prone to technical or physical issues that can take up valuable instruction time.

The Power of PowerShell:
Examples of how PowerShell Scripts can Supplement a Patch Management System to Solve Unusual Problems

Timothy Palumbo
Lehigh University
8B East Packer Avenue
Bethlehem, PA 18015
tip204@lehigh.edu

ABSTRACT

Lehigh University currently utilizes the Flexera Corporate Software Inspector (CSI, formerly Secunia CSI) application to patch faculty/staff computers on campus. This system patches third-party applications on all currently supported Windows operating systems by leveraging the Windows Server Update Service (WSUS). This presentation is not meant to focus on a particular patch management product or system, but instead it will discuss how such a system can be used to solve unusual problems when coupled with a powerful scripting language such as PowerShell.

This presentation will focus on specific scenarios that PowerShell solved when combined with our patch management system. The scenarios it will present include: an update to our internet browser software, Mozilla Firefox, which when updated disabled our ad-blocking extension, an issue of unknown origin which caused all of our Windows 7 systems to no longer activate utilizing our Key Management Service (KMS) (this included Microsoft Office products), a glitch in Windows 7 which caused garbage files to generate non-stop and completely fill end user hard drives, and our rather unusual implementation of Java. PowerShell saved us immeasurable time in resolving these issues across our entire campus. Using PowerShell with our patch management solution allows us to resolve almost any issue, campus-wide, with the push of a button.

CCS CONCEPTS

• Software and its engineering → Software notation and tools → Context specific languages → Scripting languages.
• Social and professional topics → Professional topics → Management of computing and information systems →System management.

KEYWORDS

PowerShell; troubleshooting; patch management; remote support.

1 INTRODUCTION

Lehigh University is a small university located in Bethlehem, PA, and is well known for engineering and business. Technology support at Lehigh has historically operated in a decentralized manner, with each college or administrative unit having separate computing consultants to manage their hardware, software, and other needs. Until early 2015, machine updating and patching was handled in a piecemeal manner, done either during routine visits or as a part of machine upgrades. During 2015, Lehigh adopted a patch management tool (a presentation was done on this tool for SIGUCCS 2015 [1]) to centrally manage application updates. This tool greatly enhanced the security posture of Lehigh, but also came with extra, unplanned benefits.

Our original intent with patch management was to simply patch third-party programs, but thanks to the ability to construct custom packages and the power of PowerShell, we expanded its use to solve campus-wide problems, gather information, and install software.

To install software in a more secure manner, however, we purchased a digital certificate from DigiCert so we could sign all custom created packages and code. The signing allows us to set the PowerShell execution policy to remote signed and enforces signature verification. This also allows all of our PowerShell scripts to be run directly on user machines if a manual patch is required. The certificate was pushed out via group policy to all active directory joined computers.

2 THE FIREFOX ADD-ON ISSUE

2.1 The Problem

In early 2016, Mozilla Firefox performed an update that added additional checking on signing add-ons [2]. This additional checking caused an add on to be disabled without warning the add-on failed the Mozilla Firefox check. At the time, Firefox was our default browser with the ad-block plus tool enabled. We found that ad-block plus greatly reduced the number of viruses, malware infections, and browser hijacks we experienced. After implementing the Firefox update, we found it disabled ad-block plus on numerous computers, thus some users were running an unsigned version. Finding these users and fixing the issue was necessary in order to decrease our vulnerability footprint.

2.2 The PowerShell Solution

Utilizing PowerShell, I created two scripts to solve this issue. The first script was purely for data gathering, as we needed to know how many users and PCs were impacted. More specifically, it enumerated all user profiles on any given machine and then searched for the AppData\Roaming\Mozilla folder to see if this user had a Firefox profile. If they did, it looked at the extensions.json file for the GUID of the ad-block plus add on. It then further parsed the line containing the GUID to determine if the add-on was enabled or disabled. These results were reported by machine name and user name to a remote database. The second script installed ad-block plus as a program add-on, located within the Firefox installation directory. If the add on already existed, it was removed. The script also utilized the mozilla.cfg file to silently install the add-on and lock it to enabled. Please see appendix 1 for a snippet of the code used for this solution.

2.3 The Result

We discovered the majority of our PCs had ad-block plus disabled (about 2,500 of around 3,000) across multiple user profiles. Anecdotal data seemed to indicate an increase in virus and malware related issues coming in from our clients. We thus decided to push the fix campus-wide. This allowed us to remotely re-install and re-enable this highly important add-on.

Note: Unfortunately, a subsequent newer update to Firefox later rendered our fix as useless. We could not identify an alternative fix to use with the upgrade and thus, we switched to Google Chrome as our default browser.

3 THE WINDOWS 7 ACTIVATION ISSUE

3.1 The Problem

For many years, Lehigh, like many other schools, utilized a Key Management Server (KMS) to handle Windows operating system activation and Microsoft Office activation. However, in late 2016 we began getting reports from users that their PCs were failing genuine validation and no longer activated. We also received reports of activation failures with doomsday sounding messages about having only thirty days to act. Users were concerned these messages were fraudulent. Manually checking these machines into the KMS resolved the issue, but only temporarily, as we discovered the same machines would fail activation again after about seven days. We re-built our KMS and tried numerous other fixes, but decided to take an alternate approach and call Microsoft for assistance. After lengthy support calls with Microsoft, no solution was offered. Microsoft granted us a near limited number of Mass Activation Keys (MAK) to manually activate our Windows 7 and Office 2010/13/16 products. Windows 10 activation is handled via AD and thus was not problematic for us.

In order to stem the increasing calls into our help desk, we needed to expeditiously deploy the MAKs to the entire campus.

3.2 The PowerShell Solution

Utilizing PowerShell, I created a rather simple script to handle the activation process. The script first determined the PC operating system – if it was anything but Windows 7, it stopped immediately, as this was our only OS that had issues. The script then detected which Office products, if any, were installed. After determining what we needed to activate, the script ran the activation using our MAK. However, the process did not stop there. Since many PCs failed genuine validation, we also needed to run Microsoft's genuine validation tool. I had the script run this tool three times, as we found it failed in testing on occasion for unknown reasons. The user received no visual indication that the tool ran. After a reboot, if the tool was successful, the user no longer received warnings from Microsoft about counterfeit software.

3.3 The Result

Over 2,500 Windows 7 PCs were activated using our MAK, along with a similar number of Microsoft Office products. This update is pushed via our patch management system, so any freshly imaged Windows 7 PC is automatically activated using the MAK. Implementing this approach manually would have taken countless hours, so this particular patch saved us a lot of time.

4 THE FULL HARD DRIVES ISSUE

4.1 The Problem

In early to mid 2016, we began receiving multiple reports of full client hard drives. After analyzing several computers, we noticed the machines experiencing this issue had 1,000s of files named cab_#### in C:\Windows\Temp and extremely large CbsPersist*.log files under C:\Windows\Logs\CBS. Deleting these files remedied the issue and the files did not seem to return. We were unable to determine the root cause of these files appearing (Windows Resource Monitor and System File Checker were tied in, potentially to a bad update dating as far back as January 2016). Manually resolving this issue would have taken quite a number of man hours.

4.2 The PowerShell Solution

I created a very simple PowerShell script to delete the cab files and the CBS log files. In order to determine the impact, I did a disk space analysis before and after the tool ran. This data was reported to a central database and included machine name, disk size, utilization before and after, and percent utilization before and after. Please see appendix 3 for a snippet of the code used for this solution.

4.3 The Result

The tool ran on just over 3,000 machines over a period of a week. The database report showed we recovered a total of about 15 terabytes of disk space across the campus. Approximately 400 machines were in a critical hard drive state, with more on their way to filling up. We still needed to manually address a handful of machines, as machines with completely full hard drives were unable to download and run the fix even though it was a mere 300 KB. In those cases, we would manually delete a few small files and then run the fix as an EXE.

5 THE JAVA x86 CUSTOM SETUP ISSUE

5.1 The Problem

Lehigh utilizes Internet Native Banner (INB) for multiple functions across campus. This product requires the standalone Java installer on a client PC and has user specific settings that must be configured for it to work. This is a per user setup, thus the settings do not carry if a new user logs in to a machine. Upgrading or installing Java also requires that Java not be in use and that all browsers are closed. Thus, pushing this update out in a more standard way would not work, as user browser sessions could close unexpectedly causing data loss. Data loss is simply unacceptable.

Manually installing and configuring Java on a user PC takes about fifteen minutes based on our setup, so automation is highly beneficial. We needed the following items addressed by PowerShell:

1. Remove Java and install the latest version.
2. Setup Java with our specific settings, including disabling updates, setting Transport Layer Security (TLS) to 1.0 only, hiding warnings, creating site exceptions, and automatically accepting dialogs INB produces on first run.
3. Create the INB link on the desktop for all users.
4. Do this without interrupting our users in any capacity.

5.2 The PowerShell Solution

This particular PowerShell script is a bit more detailed, as it required handling all of the issues noted above. With that in mind, I created a script that does as follows:

1. Downloads the latest custom installer to the user's hard drive from our server.
2. To prevent issues with the program being in use I created a scheduled task that runs this executable at next reboot. This scheduled task runs with system level privileges, thus the user does not need to be an administrator for it to run.
3. At boot, the user is informed of the on-going update. If they close this window, it will continue to run. The user cannot cancel this update.
4. The status window has a persistent notice that refreshes so the user is aware and the user can tell it is not frozen.
5. The installer runs, first removing all old Java versions (utilizing JavaRa), installing the latest version silently, and implementing all of our custom settings for all current and future users of the PC (this is done by enumerating existing user profiles and also adding the Java settings files to the Default profile).
6. When it is finished, the window disappears and the PC proceeds to boot into Windows.
7. In the background, the scheduled task we created is deleted to prevent the installer from running at every reboot.

5.3 The Result

We are able to maintain Java at the latest version easily and without interrupting end user work. This patch can be applied regardless of user privileges. A non-silent variant is also available on our website as an executable that users can run on their PC manually. This variant has additional warnings but performs the exact same sequence. It is good for troubleshooting or for new job duties that require Java to be installed.

6 ADDITIONAL ISSUES

The above represent just a small handful of issues we have resolved with PowerShell in tandem with our patch management solution. We were also able to address the following additional issues:

1. eVisions Launcher – I created a simple PowerShell script to silently install and/or upgrade this software across all PCs on campus. Upgrades required removal of the old version.
2. Office 2016 Upgrade (non-deployed) – I created a script and generated an EXE that installs the latest version of Office (with help from the Microsoft tool) including updates to a user PC. All prior versions are removed before the upgrade (the built-in removal from Microsoft was unreliable for this). Previous version icons are removed from the user's desktop. The software is also activated.
3. Maple Install Status – I created a script that simply checked what version of Maple was installed on our systems. Due to a vendor issue, our patch management product could not detect this data natively. This script grabbed the version and machine name and reported it to a database.
4. Client Excel Macro – one of my clients had an Excel macro that needed to be deployed to specific users. She had a one page document to help her users place the macro into a specific folder, unblock it, and make it read only. I generated a simple script for her to have her users run instead.

7 FUTURE PLANS

We have plans to continue utilizing PowerShell, both within client support and to aid in our antiquated imaging process. For example, we intend to create and deploy a script to check BitLocker status and Trusted Platform Module (TPM) status on our machines in order to generate lists of machines that need addressing in this capacity. We also are working on automating pieces of our image, which is a manual process despite utilizing SYSPREP. We plan to create PowerShell functions that can be called as tasks to install software with our settings, modify system settings, add Open Database Connectivity (ODBC) connections, and more. While systems like System Center Configuration Manager (SCCM) are on our radar, simple PowerShell functions can help save us countless hours until we get to that point.

REFERENCES

[1] Patch Management: The Importance of Implementing Central Patch Management and Our Experiences Doing So
https://dl.acm.org/citation.cfm?doid=2815546.2815561
[2] Firefox Add-ons/Extension Signing Timeline
https://wiki.mozilla.org/Add-ons/Extension_Signing#Timeline

Appendix 1

```
11    $driveLetter = $pwd.drive.name
12    $userPath = "${driveLetter}:\Users"
13    #Retrieves the first level sub-folders of C:\Users, minus a few.
14    $userFolder = Get-ChildItem -Path $userPath -Exclude 'All Users','Administrator', 'Public' |
15        Select -ExpandProperty FullName
16  ┌ foreach($User in $userFolder){
17          $path = "$User\AppData\Roaming\Mozilla\Firefox\Profiles"
18          $Profile = Get-ChildItem -Path $path -Exclude 'All Users','Administrator', 'Public' |
19              Select -ExpandProperty FullName
20  ┌         foreach($file in $Profile){
21  ┌             if((Test-Path -Path $file\extensions.json)){
22                    $extensionFile = "$file\extensions.json"
23                    $extensionContents = Get-Content "$extensionFile"
24  ┌                 if ($extensionContents.contains("d10d0bf8-f5b5-c8b4-a8b2-2b9879e08c5d")){
25                        $adblockstring = "{d10d0bf8-f5b5-c8b4-a8b2-2b9879e08c5d}"
26                        $index = $extensionContents.IndexOf($adblockstring)
27                        $test = $extensionContents.Substring($index)
28                        $index2 = $index+1
29                        $textsnippet = $test.Substring(0,2300)
30                        $versIndex = $textsnippet.IndexOf('"version":"')
31                        $versionText = $textsnippet.Substring($versIndex)
32                        $version = $versionText.Substring(11,5)
33                        $installed = "1"
34                        $modified = (Get-Item $extensionFile).LastWriteTime.toString("yyyy-MM-dd")
35  ┌                         if($textsnippet.contains('"softDisabled":true')){
36                                $softDisabled = "1"}
37                            else{$softDisabled = "0"}
38  ┌                         if($textsnippet.contains('"active":true')){
39  ├                             $active = "1"}
40                            else{$active = "0"}
41  ┌                         if($textsnippet.contains('"userDisabled":true')){
42                                $userDisabled = "1"}
43                            else{$userDisabled = "0"}
44  ┌                         if($textsnippet.contains('"appDisabled":true')){
45  ├                             $appDisabled = "1"}
46                            else{$appDisabled = "0"}
47  ├                 }
48  ┌                 else{$installed = "0"
49                        $version = "0"
50                        $softDisabled = "0"
51                        $active = "0"
52                        $userDisabled = "0"
53                        $appDisabled = "0"
54                        $machineName = $env:computername
55                        $modified = (Get-Item $extensionFile).LastWriteTime.toString("yyyy-MM-dd")
56  ├                 }
57                    $username = $User.Substring(9)
58                    $machineName = $env:computername
59                    $url = "http://[REDACTED]=
                      $machineName&Modified=$modified&ABPinstalled=$installed&ABPversion=$version&ABPsoftDisabl
                      ed=$softDisabled&ABPactive=$active&ABPuserDisabled=$userDisabled&ABPappDisabled=$appDisab
                      led&Username=$username"
60                    (New-Object System.Net.WebClient).DownloadString("$url");
61  ├             }
62  ├         }
63  └ }
```

10

Appendix 2

```
19    $driveLetter = $pwd.drive.name
20    $TranscriptLocation = "${driveLetter}:\[REDACTED]\ActivationTranscript.log"
21    start-transcript -path $TranscriptLocation -append
22
23    #Set and create our tools directory.
24    $tools = "${driveLetter}:\[REDACTED]"
25    New-Item -Path $tools -ItemType Directory -Force | Out-Null
26
27    #Check OS version - if it isn't Windows 7, exit.
28    $os = Get-WMIObject Win32_OperatingSystem | select-object -ExpandProperty BuildNumber
29    if ($os -ne '7601')
30        {Write-host "This is not Windows 7. Terminating."
31        exit}
32
33    #Download a copy of the legitcheck.hta file to the local PC.
34    $source = "http://[REDACTED]/legitcheck.hta"
35    $destination = "$tools\legitcheck.hta"
36    $client = New-Object System.Net.WebClient
37    $client.DownloadFile($source,$destination)
38
39    #Run the ACTIVATE.bat file. This file does two things:
40    #1) CSCRIPT //I "%windir%\system32\SLMGR.VBS" -IPK [REDACTED] to install the Windows 7 MAK, then
41    #CSCRIPT //I "%windir%\system32\SLMGR.VBS" -ATO to activate Windows 7.
42    #2) Checks for ospp.vbs under Program Files (x86)\Office16 and 15
43    #For whichever version is found, it runs CSCRIPT //I "C:\Program Files (x86)\Microsoft
      #Office\Office##\ospp.vbs" /inpkey:[REDACTED], which forces Office to use the MAK.
44    #Activation proceeds via CSCRIPT //I "C:\Program Files (x86)\Microsoft Office\Office##\ospp.vbs" /act
45    Start-Process .\ACTIVATE.bat
46
47    #Wait a bit for it to run.
48    Start-Sleep -s 60
49
50    #Run legitcheck.hta, which is the Windows Genuine Validation Tool.
51    #Without running this, an activated copy will still complain is may be counterfeit.
52    Start-Process .\legitcheck.hta
53    Start-Sleep -s 30
54
55    #The process never exits - force it.
56    kill -processname mshta -force -ErrorAction SilentlyContinue
57
58    #Re-run the legitcheck, which fails sometimes. This time we sleep 60 seconds.
59    Start-Process $tools\legitcheck.hta
60    Start-Sleep -s 60
61    kill -processname mshta -force -ErrorAction SilentlyContinue
62
63    stop-transcript
64    Exit
```

Appendix 3

```
11   #We acquire our drive letter and PC name.
12   $driveLetter = $pwd.drive.name
13   $machineName = $env:COMPUTERNAME
14
15   #We want to log everything that happens in case something fails.
16   $driveLetter = $pwd.drive.name
17   $LogLocation = "${driveLetter}:\[REDACTED]\DriveSpaceFix.log"
18   start-transcript -path $LogLocation -append
19   $txtLogLocation = "${driveLetter}:\[REDACTED]\DriveSpaceFix.txt"
20
21   #We acquire the disk data and convert it to GB for free, used, size, and percentages.
22   $usedBefore = Get-PSDrive $driveLetter | Select-Object -ExpandProperty Used
23   $freeBefore = Get-PSDrive $driveLetter | Select-Object -ExpandProperty Free
24   $usedBefore = $usedBefore/1GB
25   $freeBefore = $freeBefore/1GB
26   $size = $usedBefore + $freeBefore
27   $percentUsedBefore = $usedBefore/$size * 100
28
29   #We remove the offending files from the PC.
30   Remove-Item "${driveLetter}:\Windows\Logs\CBS\CbsPersist*.log"
31   Remove-Item "${driveLetter}:\Windows\Temp\cab_*"
32
33   #We pause for 30 seconds to let the PC delete files.
34   Start-Sleep -s 30
35
36   #We acquire the same data, but after deleting the files.
37   $usedAfter = Get-PSDrive $driveLetter | Select-Object -ExpandProperty Used
38   $freeAfter = Get-PSDrive $driveLetter | Select-Object -ExpandProperty Free
39   $usedAfter = $usedAfter/1GB
40   $freeAfter = $freeAfter/1GB
41   $percentUsedAfter = $usedAfter/$size * 100
42
43   #We log the data locally.
44   Add-content $txtLogLocation "
45   Name: $machineName
46   DiskSize: $size
47   Used Before: $usedBefore
48   Used After: $usedAfter
49   Free Before: $freeBefore
50   Free After: $freeAfter
51   Percent Used Before: $percentUsedBefore
52   Percent Used After: $percentUsedAfter
53   "
54
55   #And send the data to our database.
56   $url =
     "[REDACTED]?MachineName=$machineName&DiskSize=$size&FreeBefore=$freeBefore&FreeAfter=$freeAfter&UsedBefore=$usedBe
     fore&UsedAfter=$usedAfter&PercentUsedBefore=$percentUsedBefore&PercentUsedAfter=$percentUsedAfter"
57   (New-Object System.Net.WebClient).DownloadString("$url")
58   stop-transcript
```

Appendix 4

```
11   #We want to log everything that happens in case something fails.
12   $driveLetter = $pwd.drive.name
13   $LogLocation = "${driveLetter}:\[REDACTED]\MapleCheck.log"
14   start-transcript -path $LogLocation -append
15   $txtLogLocation = "${driveLetter}:\[REDACTED]\MapleCheck.txt"
16
17   $maplePath = "${driveLetter}:\Program Files\Maple*"
18   $maplePathx86 = "${driveLetter}:\Program Files (x86)\Maple*"
19   $machineName = $env:computername
20   $model = Get-WmiObject Win32_Computersystem|Select-Object -Property Model -ExpandProperty
     Model
21
22   if (Test-path -path $maplePath){
23       Add-content $txtLogLocation "Maple 64-bit detected. Submitting data."
24       $url = "[REDACTED]?MachineName=$machineName&Model=$model"
25       (New-Object System.Net.WebClient).DownloadString("$url");
26       }
27   elseif (Test-path -path $maplePathx86){
28       Add-content $txtLogLocation "Maple 32-bit detected. Submitting data."
29       $url = "[REDACTED]?MachineName=$machineName&Model=$model"
30       (New-Object System.Net.WebClient).DownloadString("$url");
31       }
32   else{
33       Add-content $txtLogLocation "Maple not detected on this machine OR it is installed in a
         non-conventional location."
34       }
35
36   stop-transcript
```

Appendix 5

```
1    #We first grab the Windows Drive letter.
2    $driveLetter = $pwd.drive.name                        .
3
4    #We get the current logged on user, removing the AD\. This will fail for non-AD
     computers.
5    $userID = Get-WMIObject -class Win32_ComputerSystem | select username -ExpandProperty
     username
6    $separator = $userID.IndexOf("\") + 1
7    $userLength = $userID.length
8    $user = $userID.Substring($separator,$userLength - $separator)
9
10   $excelFilePath = "${driveLetter}:\Users\$user\AppData\Roaming\Microsoft\Excel\XLSTART"
11
12   #We create the Excel  folder if it doesn't exist.
13       if (Test-Path $excelFilePath) {
14       }
15       else {
16           New-Item -ItemType Directory -Path $excelFilePath -Force
17       }
18
19   #We set our source and destinations for the PERSONAL.XLSB
20   $destination = "$excelFilePath\PERSONAL.XLSB"
21   $source = "http://[REDACTED]/[REDACTED].XLSB"
22
23   #Given the file is read-only, we need to remove it forcibly if it exists before
     placing the new version into the folder.
24   if (test-path $destination)
25       {Remove-Item $destination -force}
26
27   $client = New-Object System.Net.WebClient
28   $client.DownloadFile($source,$destination)
29
30   #We unblock the Internet downloaded file and set it as read-only.
31   Unblock-File -Path $destination
32   Set-ItemProperty -Path $destination -Name IsReadOnly -Value $true
```

Building an In-house Leadership and Management Development Program

Deyu Hu
Virginia Tech
735 University City Blvd
Blacksburg, VA, 24060
dhu@vt.edu

ABSTRACT

At a large public university in the U.S., managers within the Division of Information Technology (IT) were often promoted to managerial positions due to their excellence as individual contributors. Many of them, however, have not received any management education or training and are not prepared to take on supervisor roles. To support these managers to perform effectively and efficiently in their positions, an in-house leadership and management training program was established within the Division of IT. This in-house training program aims to meet the organization's leadership and management needs by identifying and preparing capable individuals through planned professional development. In this presentation, the presenter will introduce the organizational benefits of providing a leadership and management training program as well as factors that influence the decision of establishing an in-house training program versus using external vendors. Major program design processes used to create the in-house leadership and management training program, including determining the program purpose, conducting needs assessment, creating program goals and objectives, and establishing curriculum will be discussed. One training module will be demonstrated to show the various learning activities used in the hybrid training approach, which includes both online and face-to-face delivery. Feedback from a pilot study using one unit within the Division of IT will be shared. The presenter will also discuss plans for improvement and approaches for scaling-up the program to the whole Division of IT.

CCS CONCEPTS

• **General and reference** → **Document types** → **General conference proceedings**

SIGUCCS '17, October 1–4, 2017, Seattle, WA, USA
© 2017 Copyright is held by the owner/author(s). Publication rights licensed to ACM. ACM 978-1-4503-4919-2/17/10...$15.00
https://doi.org/10.1145/3123458.3123484

KEYWORDS

leadership development;; management training; leadership and management development; professional development;

1 INTRODUCTION

The promoting-from-within practice is quite common in the U.S., including in higher education, as about three-fourths of all managers are selected this way [1]. Within its Division of Information Technology (DoIT) at Virginia Tech, a large public university in the southeast of the U.S., managers are often promoted to managerial positions due to their technical excellence. Many of them, however, have not received adequate management education or training either before or after the promotion and are not well prepared to take on supervisory responsibilities. While some organizations take the "sink or swim" approach to career advancement, this kind of practice can be problematic in that technical success does not transfer to management success [2]. To help managers acquire knowledge and skills for their new responsibilities and support them to perform effectively and efficiently in their positions, an in-house leadership and management development program (L&MD) was initiated within the DoIT.

2 Benefits of L&MD Programs

Organizations sponsor management and leadership development programs for many reasons. Rothwell (1999) conducted a survey to 300 randomly selected L&MD specialists, who were members of the American Society for Training and Development (ASTD). The survey results indicated that the top two reasons that organizations sponsor L&MD programs are that such programs help organizations to implement their strategic plans and allow managers to build people management skills. Other reasons include preparing individuals for more responsibility, responding to environmental and technological change, increasing management productivity and morale, helping employees to plan their careers, and increasing opportunities for high-potential workers. Planned well, these kind of L&MD programs can also help women and members of minority groups move to management positions.

3 Rationale of In-House Development

Managers can acquire management and leadership knowledge and skills via multiple mechanisms. An examination of existing mechanisms and an analysis of their pros and cons can help establish the legitimacy of an in-house program. First, managers can pursue L&MD opportunities provided by professional organizations. For instance, Educause, a nonprofit organization that advances higher education through information technology, provides professional development programs for IT managers and leaders at different levels, including new IT managers, mid-level managers, more experienced IT professionals and CIOs. These programs are often offered at the same times each year. If there is a schedule conflict, then IT managers will not be able to participate. The program locations are also off-site from IT managers' home institutions so they must take more time off from their daily work to participate.

Additionally, since the opportunities are open to all IT managers in higher education, often only one participant from each institution can participate in a program. This greatly restricts the number of IT managers that each institution can train via this mechanism. They are expensive as well. Take Educause as an example, it will cost an institution $3,000 to $4,000 to send a manager to a five-day management institute. DoIT at Virginia Tech has more than 400 employees and around 80 to 100 managers at various levels. It is not feasible to train them all through professional organizations either financially or operationally.

A second mechanism to acquire management and leadership knowledge is through formal education. Motivated individuals can enroll in master or doctoral level management or leadership related programs. In comparison with the first method, this is even a less chosen route. Working professionals generally have work, family, and/or social commitments. Spending several years to finish a post-secondary degree out of their already busy schedule is a big decision to them and their family. Thus, not many professionals choose to pursue a higher degree in management or leadership.

The third method may not be available to some managers as it varies from institution to institution. If an institution already offers management or leadership development opportunities, IT managers may benefit from them. At Virginia Tech, faculty and staff can attend management and leadership training sessions. A major issue with these training sessions is that they are offered at topic levels, such as Delegation or Effective Communication. The topics are disconnected from each other. Even if a manager attends all the individual sessions, which is rare, it is difficult for the manager to put the fragmented pieces together to form a holistic and systematic view about management. As a result, what they gained from such training sessions are just a disconnected hodge-podge of knowledge or skills.

4 Our Program's Purposes

DoIT at Virginia Tech includes nine units and employs more than 400 full time faculty and staff. It also hires many part-time employees, emergency hires, student workers, student interns, and graduate students for various responsibilities. To meet the immediate needs of L&MD within DoIT, the purposes of this in-house program include:

- informing participants about basic management concepts, principles, and best practices;
- fostering transfer of learning to their work;
- improving participants' management performance;
- encouraging collaboration among participants through solving authentic problems; and
- informing participants various resources for acquiring management knowledge and skills.

The target audience of this program is lower to middle level DoIT managers. In the long run, this program will help identify and prepare competent individuals before they start their managerial responsibilities. It will also promote the development of succession plans within each unit for critical positons.

5 Needs Assessment

To design the L&MD program, a needs assessment will be conducted to identify the gap between the participating managers' current and desired knowledge, skills, and abilities on various management topics. The results of the needs assessment will help define the scope of the L&MD program.

To identify the participating managers' current knowledge, skills, and abilities in management, both subjective and objective data will be collected and analyzed. A free online quiz will be utilized to measure a managers' management skills in eight categories: 1) understanding team dynamics and encouraging good relationship; 2) selecting and developing the right people; 3) delegating effectively; 4) motivating people; 5) managing discipline and dealing with conflict; 6) communicating; 7) planning, making decisions, and problem solving; and 8) avoiding common managerial mistakes. In addition to the objective assessment, we have also designed survey questions that ask participants to evaluate their perceived knowledge and skills in various management topics and how important they think those topics are to them.

The characteristics of the learners, the tasks to be performed, as well as the characteristics of an organization can influence the effectiveness of training. Therefore, we will collect and analyze data on the participants, task, and organization. For the participant data, we will collect basic demographic data, including educational background, history with DoIT and Virginia Tech, preferred learning methods, and prior experience with online learning because these data will inform us the most appropriate training design and support to the targeted audience.

Organizational characteristics will also influence the training results as well as managers' performance. We plan to collect the following information about the organization: missions and goals, structure and policies, culture and values, reward and recognition system, leaders' support and expectations of training, barriers to transfer of learning, and general human resource data such as turnover and absenteeism. As to the nature of the management tasks, due to the wide variety of jobs performed by IT managers we will not analyze the duties, steps, and sequences of steps involved in each manager's daily work. Our focus will be on the list of management knowledge, skills, and abilities required for a management position and a description of mastery performance. In addition, data from the participating managers' supervisors, peers, and subordinates will be collected to see if there is any possible discrepancy between self-assessed needs and what others deem as the development needs.

6   The Program Design

This program assumes no prior leadership or management knowledge or skills. This reflects the backgrounds of many of our participants. To reach the best learning results, we will build the program based on best practices in professional development and teaching and learning, especially for adult learners.

6.1   Cohort-based Approach

We will adopt a cohort approach for our L&MD program. Cohorts are "arrangements by which groups of learners begin course work together and remain together to complete a degree, certificate, or series (Reynolds & Hebert, 1995, p. 35)". In cohort programs, learners typically go through pre-determined curriculum in fixed order while a supportive and collegial environment is formed through trust, openness, responsiveness, and respect. The cohort model was first used to train and educate medical, law, and business professions. It gained its popularity from the 1940s in educational leadership programs (Saltiel & Russo, 2001). Since then, it has been used in both student learning and professional development (Cox, 2004; Barnett, Basom, Yerks, & Norris, 2000; Saltiel & Russo, 2001).

We anticipate several benefits from the cohort format. First, it will provide structured opportunities to support group interaction in that members of a cohort are generally required to exchange ideas and provide and receive critical feedback to and from peers. Second, a cohort will offer social support to its members through shared goals and experiences, friendship, and camaraderie. Third, the cohort approach utilizes a more structured administrative framework, including focused topics, structured timelines, and positive peer pressure that keep member moving forward, remain in a program, and get things done (Dismore & Wenger, 2006; Drago-Severson, et al, 2001; Prawat, 1999; Saltiel & Russo, 2001).

6.2   Flipped Model

Educators from K-12 to higher education have adopted flipped classroom in teaching various subject matters. In a flipped classroom what generally happens inside and outside of a classroom exchanged. Lectures that are generally delivered in a traditional classroom are now part of homework prior to class while the class time is dedicated to active and engaging learning activities. While flipped classroom does not guarantee better student learning by default, research results still showed that flipped classroom is at least as effective as or more effective than traditional lecture-based classroom (Arnold-Garza, 2014; Butt, 2014; Findlay-Thomson & Mombourquette, 2014; Lage, Platt &

Treglia, 2000; McLaughlin et al., 2014). Therefore, it is promising that flipped workshop could improve professional development.

A flipped classroom model will be adopted for the L&MD program. For each management topic, participating managers will be asked to finish various activities, such as short readings, videos, online discussions, and quiz, before joining in the face-to-face session. During the face-to-face session, they will be involved in various activities that allow them to apply their newly acquired knowledge and skills. They will be engaged in small or big group discussions, case studies, problem solving, role playing, and other active learning activities. After the face-to-face session, the participants will make plans for improving relevant management practices, implement the plan, observe the results, reflect on the plan, and share their findings or lessons learned with their cohort peers. Their peers will provide feedback as to how they can further improve.

6.3   Long-term Development

Many L&MD programs are short-term based. Loucks-Horsley and her colleagues pointed out that significant hours of professional development are necessary for substantial changes in practice (Loucks-Horsley, Hewson, Love, & Stiles, 2010). Similarly, Garet and his colleagues (Garet, Porter, Desimone, Birman, & Yoon, 2001) suggest that professional development should sustain over time. They found that both the duration, i.e. the total number of contact hours, as well as the span of professional development over time, contribute to the effectiveness of professional development. Long duration provides participants with more opportunities for in-depth learning and reflection as well as greater likelihood of trying out the new practices. Specific to L&MD, Rothwell (1999, p.11) suggested that "(m)ore focused, structured, practical, and long-term developmental experiences are often necessary to build leadership and management skills." Therefore, instead of providing individual training topics that are disconnected with each other, our program will last for a year. Within the year, participants will work in a cohort through a well-planned curriculum. By increasing both the total number of contact hours as well as the span of professional development, we hope the program will greatly improve the participants' management practice over time.

6.4   Pilot Program and Scaling

Given that each unit within DoIT has distinct functions and differ greatly in size, it would be difficult to design a L&MD program that is one size fits all. Thus, we will pilot the L&MD program with one of the DoIT units. Based on feedback from participants in the pilot program, we will revise the program so that it can be either scaled up or down to fit the needs of other units within DoIT.

7   Summary

Promoting-from-within is a common practice in selecting leaders and their successors across sectors and industries, including in higher education institutions. Providing in-house leadership development opportunities to managers can help them master knowledge and skills required by managerial positions. It can also help organizations in many ways, including increasing individual productivity and organizational productivity, responding more effectively to a fast-changing environment, improving management morale, and more (Rothwell, 1999). In DoIT at Virginia Tech an in-house leadership development program has been planned and is under development. The first cohort will kick off in late summer of 2017. The overall program design, a demonstration of one of the training modules, and lessons learned from the initial delivery will provide useful insights about leadership development.

REFERENCES

[1] Patricia S. Abril and Robert Plant. 2007. The patent holder's dilemma: Buy, sell, or troll? *Commun. ACM* 50, 1 (Jan. 2007), 36–44. DOI: http://dx.doi.org/10.1145/1188913.1188915

[2] I. F. Akyildiz, W. Su, Y. Sankarasubramaniam, and E. Cayirci. 2002. Wireless Sensor Networks: A Survey. *Comm. ACM* 38, 4 (2002), 393–422.

[3] David A. Anisi. 2003. *Optimal Motion Control of a Ground Vehicle*. Master's thesis. Royal Institute of Technology (KTH), Stockholm, Sweden.

[4] P. Bahl, R. Chancre, and J. Dungeon. 2004. SSCH: Slotted Seeded Channel Hopping for Capacity Improvement in IEEE 802.11 Ad-Hoc Wireless Networks. In *Proceeding of the 10th International Conference on Mobile Computing and Networking* (MobiCom'04). ACM, New York, NY, 112–117.

[5] Kenneth L. Clarkson. 1985. *Algorithms for Closest-Point Problems (Computational Geometry)*. Ph.D. Dissertation. Stanford University, Palo Alto, CA. UMI Order Number: AAT 8506171.

[6] Jacques Cohen (Ed.). 1996. Special Issue: Digital Libraries. *Commun. ACM* 39, 11 (Nov. 1996).

[7] Bruce P. Douglass. 1998. Statecarts in use: structured analysis and object-orientation. In *Lectures on Embedded Systems*, Grzegorz Rozenberg and Frits W. Vaandrager (Eds.). Lecture Notes in Computer Science, Vol. 1494. Springer-Verlag, London, 368–394. DOI: http://dx.doi.org/10.1007/3-540-65193-429

[8] Ian Editor (Ed.). 2008. *The title of book two* (2nd. ed.). University of Chicago Press, Chicago, Chapter 100. DOI: http://dx.doi.org/10.1007/3-540-09237-4

Transitioning from Blackboard to Moodle amidst Natural Disaster: Faculty and Students Perceptions

Ajayi Ekuase-Anwansedo
Southern University and A & M
ajayi_anwansedo_00@subr.edu

Jose Noguera
Southern University and A & M
jose_noguera@subr.edu

Brandon Dumas
Southern University and A & M
brandon_dumas@subr.edu

ABSTRACT

Higher educational institutions continuously look for ways to improve the quality of their eLearning services and adapt learning solutions to suit the needs of the institution. During the 2016 Fall Semester, a university located in the Southern part of United States decided to transition from the Blackboard learning management system (LMS) to the Moodle learning management system. Typically such a transition presents a huge challenge for the University staff, faculty, and students. Additionally, on August 2016, what CNN themed "the worst natural disaster, to strike the United States since Hurricane Sandy" [47], occurred in Louisiana during the transition. This led to massive disruptions in activities throughout the state.

This paper examines the perceptions of both faculty and student on the transition from one LMS to another and also what impact, if any, the natural disaster had on the process. Faculty and students were surveyed to gain understanding of how they perceived the transitioning process, their perception of both systems, their preferences, and why. Furthermore, we identified issues peculiar to transitioning during a natural disaster. The results of this study can be used to anticipate issues that may be associated with transitioning from one LMS to the other and issues peculiar to transitioning amidst a natural disaster. It can also be used to identify areas for improvement.

CCS CONCEPTS

• **Applied computing** → **Education** → **learning management system**

• **Applied computing** → **Law, social & behavioral sciences** → **Psychology**

KEYWORDS

E-Learning; Blackboard; Moodle; Natural Disaster; Flood; PTSD; Depression; Anxiety; Technology Acceptance Model

SIGUCCS '17, October 1–4, 2017, Seattle, WA, USA
© 2017 Copyright is held by the owner/author(s). Publication rights licensed to ACM.
ACM 978-1-4503-4919-2/17/10...$15.00
https://doi.org/10.1145/3123458.3123467

1 INTRODUCTION

As information technology is being integrated into teaching and learning in our higher educational institutions [20], learning management systems (LMSs) have become the norm. This has led to the development of a variety of LMSs, both commercial and non-commercial. The non-commercial LMS are called open source and most of them allow the user to obtain the software and adapt it to suit their needs. Previous research indicated that Moodle is the most popular open source LMS [5], [21] and is preferred over Blackboard by students [8], [9], [29]. Some of the advantages of Moodle include adaptability, its design philosophy based on social constructionist pedagogy [11], absence of license and maintenance fees [11], [43], strong community of users [11], [46] and providing self-directed learning to students [26]. Even though, Moodle has rave reviews, its success is dependent on its acceptance and use by the students. [3], [24], [25], [36], [48]. Hence, there is a need to investigate the adoption of Moodle by students especially in unusual circumstances, to determine its success and if these external factors influence its adoption. The technology acceptance model (TAM), proposed by Davis, [14], has been identified by Hsu & Chang, as the most used tool for predicting technology acceptance and usage intentions [24]. In this study, a research model uses TAM as a base model and integrates the impacts of a natural disaster, in this instance, a flood, as external variables, to examine how it affects faculty and students' acceptance behavior and use intentions of Moodle.

The remainder of this paper will first review research on TAM and TAM extensions, the impact of flood, the impact of emotion on cognition in PTSD, Depression and Anxiety. An extended model of TAM that presents the impact of the flood on Moodle adoption is then developed. Finally contributions of this study and suggestions for future research are discussed.

2 PURPOSE OF STUDY

Transitioning from one LMS to another presents unique challenges of integrating and adapting to the new technology. However, when this transition takes place during or after a natural disaster, it presents a whole new challenge that includes not only accepting and using the new technology but also managing the after effects of the natural disaster.

Amidst the transition process from Blackboard to Moodle learning management system by a university in the southern part of the United States, one of the worst natural disasters in the United States occurred [47]. Thus in addition to investigating the adoption of Moodle among the faculty and students, there is a need to examine the impact of the flood on faculty and students' acceptance and use of Moodle.

Flooding impacts individuals economically, medically, socially, and mentally; which in turn impacts cognitive function and consequently behavior. In addition, flooding has been the most common type of natural disaster globally and there is a likelihood of increased flooding in the future due to rising sea levels and more frequent and extreme precipitation [1], [2]. Also, during natural disasters, where physical commute is impossible, virtual learning presents an opportunity for continued, uninterrupted teaching and learning activities [25]. Consequently, there is a need to investigate how natural disasters influences the adoption and use of technology in this case Moodle.

A similar study [25] investigated factors which may affect the intention to use Moodle by university students at a university in the Eastern Region of Turkey after an earthquake. They extended TAM to include technical support and computer self-efficacy. However, they did not examine if the psychological impact of the earthquake on the university students had any effect on their intention to adopt or use Moodle.

Thus, this study examines the psychological impact of natural disasters - flood on technology adoption and use, in this instance Moodle.

3 RESERCH MODEL AND HYPOTHESIS FOR MOODLE ADOPTION AMIDST A NATURAL DISASTER - FLOOD

In this study, the research model proposed is based on TAM with a view to investigate the acceptance and use of the Moodle by faculty and students in, the university.

In our model, we extended TAM to include external factors – PTSD, depression, and anxiety -- which are the most common impact of a flood -- to examine faculty and student adoption of Moodle in the midst of a flood event at the University. The research model, as illustrated in Figure 2, consists of six constructs: PTSD, depression, and anxiety; perceived usefulness (PU); perceived ease of use (PEU); attitude towards use (ATU); behavioral intention to use (BIU); and Actual system use (ASU).

3.1 Technology Adoption Model (TAM)

The technology acceptance model (TAM), developed by Davis [14] is the most researched model used to determine the perception of user's acceptance and use of technology [25], [40]. It is based on the premise that the success of technology is based on the user's acceptance of that technology which is dependent on the perceived use, the perceived ease of use and the intention to use the technology [3], [15]. According to TAM, an individual's

perception of the effort involved in using the technology and how much they think the technology improves their work will help them determine if they want to use the system or not [15]. In other words, the decision to use a technology is largely dependent on the individual's behavioral intention to use the technology, which is formed as a result of a cognitive process [37], [45].

The TAM is made up of six constructs (figure 1) namely: perceived ease of use (PEOU), perceived use (PU), attitude towards use (ATU), behavioral intention to use (BIU), actual system use (ASU) and external variables (EV). These six constructs help determine user's perception towards adopting a new technology. In the context of Moodle as the technology, PEOU represents the individual's belief that Moodle will require minimum effort to use, PU represents the individual's belief that using Moodle will enhance their work [15], [34]. ATU represents the individual's desire to use or not to Moodle, BIU represents the user's willingness to use Moodle, ASU represents the use of Moodle by the individual and EV comprises system design, user characteristics, environments and user involvement [10], [34], [37], [45].

TAM proposes that PEOU, PU and ATU determines individuals' attitude towards using a system, PEOU and PU has a significant impact on BIU, which influences BIU, which invariably determines the actual usage of the system [15], [21], [34], [40], [48].

Therefore, the following hypotheses based on TAM are proposed:

[H1] Perceived ease of use (PEOU) has a positive effect on the perceived usefulness (PU) of Moodle.

[H2] Perceived ease of use (PEOU) has a positive effect on attitudes toward the use (ATU) of Moodle.

[H3] Perceived ease of use (PEOU) has a positive effect on the behavioral intention to use (BIU) Moodle.

[H4] Perceived usefulness (PU) has a positive effect on attitudes toward the use (ATU) of Moodle.

[H5] Perceived usefulness (PU) has a positive effect on the behavioral intention to use (BIU) Moodle.

[H6] Attitudes toward using (ATU) have a positive effect on the behavioral intention to use (BIU) Moodle.

[H7] Attitude towards use (ATU) has a positive effect on the actual use (ASU) of Moodle.

[H8] Behavioral intention to use (BIU) has a positive effect on the actual use (ASU) of Moodle.

3.2 External variables

External variables are essential in strengthening the TAM model [24].

Several researchers have suggested that external variables influences the user acceptance of a system via the cognitive constructs (PEOU and PU) of the TAM model [3], [10], [14], [15], [45].

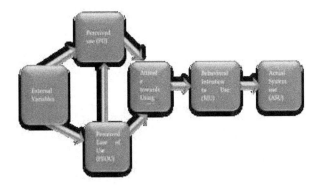

Figure 1: Technology Acceptance Model (Adapted from Davis, 1986)

3.3 Impact of the flood

Natural disasters are unintended traumatic events [27], [32]. Globally, floods are the most common natural disaster and is accountable for almost half of all natural disaster fatalities [2], [16], [19]. In addition to economic losses, other harmful impacts of flooding include mortality, mental health issues, damage to physical health, infrastructure and property [16], [19], [22]. Furthermore, post-traumatic stress disorder (PTSD), depression and anxiety, have been identified as the most commonly reported psychological effects of flooding [7], [19], [22], [31]. When compared to non- flooded areas higher levels of these psychological effects have been observed in flood affected areas [17], [41].

Also, exposure to floods have negative impacts on cognition [30]. Given that flood events are likely to increase in frequency and intensity in the future, due to climate change and exposure to flood events is likely to increase due to population growth, population proximity to coastline and increasing urbanization, there is a need to increase flood prevention and mitigation strategies [2], [16] in order to avoid been casualties of potential flood events [33].

3.4 Impact of emotions on cognition in Post-traumatic stress disorder (PTSD), Depression and Anxiety

PTSD is a mental health disorder which occurs after exposure to traumatic or stressful events, Depression is described as a feeling of intense sadness, hopelessness and worthlessness and Anxiety is the anticipation of future treat [4]. PTSD, Depression and Anxiety has been associated with some form of cognitive dysfunction such as impaired concentration, impaired decision making ability and memory impairment [4], [23], [13], [44] and has significant impact on cognitive structure –the way the individual stores information internally, cognitive operations – the individual's information processing processes and cognitive products – what information the individual recalls [1]. In other words, individuals with symptoms of PTSD, Depression or anxiety experience bias when processing information [1]. For instance, when given a task such individuals, focus more on task unrelated information (e.g. fear, worry) and this reserves a small space in the working memory for task related information [18]. In the context of adopting a new technology, in this instance, Moodle, PTSD, depression and anxiety will impact negatively the cognitive processes associated with using the technology and in the TAM model, this is represented by the PEOU and the PU [37], [42].

Therefore we hypothesis that;

[9] PTSD will have a negative effect on PEOU

[10] PTSD will have a negative effect on PU

[11] Depression will have a negative effect on PEOU

[12] Depression will have a negative effect on PU

[13] Anxiety will have a negative effect on PEOU

[14] Anxiety will have a negative effect on PU

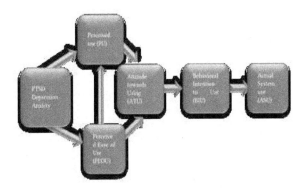

Figure 2: Extended TAM to include PTSD, Depression and Anxiety

4 FUTURE RESEARCH

In future research data will be collected by means of the following constructs, TAM (Davis, 1989), PTSD Checklist Civilian Version (PCL-C) [12], – Center for epidemiologic studies depression scale (CES-D scale) [35] and the Generalized Anxiety Disorder 7 –item (GAD - 7) scale [38], [28] and analyzed using structural equation modeling (SEM)

5 CONCLUSION

Natural disasters are inevitable with the present climate conditions in the world today. Technology presents a way to mitigate the impact of natural disasters in education, by ensuring provision of uninterrupted educational services via learning management systems. This paper examines how a natural disaster may impact the adoption and use of technology. The conceptual model and 14 hypothesis was proposed integrating PTSD, depression and anxiety as external variable into the TAM model.

REFERENCES

[1] Ahern, M., Kovats, R. S., Wilkinson, P., Few, R., & Matthies, F. (2005). Global health impacts of floods: epidemiologic evidence. Epidemiologic reviews, 27(1), 36-46.Allison, C. (2016). Technology Acceptance and Course Completion Rates in Online Education: A Non-experimental, Mixed Method Study (Doctoral dissertation, Northcentral University).

[2] Alderman, K., Turner, L. R., & Tong, S. (2013). Assessment of the health impacts of the 2011 summer floods in Brisbane. Disaster medicine and public health preparedness, 7(04), 380-386.

[3] Allison, C. (2016). Technology Acceptance and Course Completion Rates in Online Education: A Non-experimental, Mixed Method Study (Doctoral dissertation, Northcentral University).

[4] American Psychiatric Association. (2013). Diagnostic and statistical manual of mental disorders (DSM-5®). American Psychiatric Pub.

[5] Baytiyeh, H. (2011). Work in progress—Open source usability evaluation: The case of Moodle. In Frontiers in Education Conference (FIE), 2011 (pp. F4E-1). IEEE.

[6] Beck, A. T., & Clark, D. A. (1988). Anxiety and depression: An information processing perspective. Anxiety research, 1(1), 23-36.

[7] Bei, B., Bryant, C., Gilson, K. M., Koh, J., Gibson, P., Komiti, A., & Judd, F. (2013). A prospective study of the impact of floods on the mental and physical health of older adults. Aging & mental health, 17(8), 992-1002.

[8] Berg, R. D., & Lu, Y. (2014). Student attitudes towards using Moodle as a course management system. In International Conference on Recreation and Leisure Industry & Language Application (pp. 327-336).

[9] Bremer, D., & Bryant, R. (2005). A Comparison of two learning management Systems: Moodle vs Blackboard. In Proceedings of the 18th Annual Conference of the National Advisory Committee on Computing Qualifications (pp. 135-139).

[10] Chen, H. H., Lee, M. C., Wu, Y. L., Qiu, J. Y., Lin, C. H., Tang, H. Y., & Chen, C. H. (2012, August). An analysis of moodle in engineering education: The TAM perspective. In Teaching, Assessment and Learning for Engineering (TALE), 2012 IEEE International Conference on (pp. H1C-1). IEEE.

[11] Cole, J., & Foster, H. (2007). Using Moodle: Teaching with the popular open source course management system. "O'Reilly Media, Inc.".

[12] Conybeare, D., Behar, E., Solomon, A., Newman, M. G., & Borkovec, T. D. (2012). The PTSD Checklist—Civilian Version: Reliability, validity, and factor structure in a nonclinical sample. Journal of clinical psychology, 68(6), 699-713.

[13] Danckwerts, A., & Leathem, J. (2003). Questioning the link between PTSD and cognitive dysfunction. Neuropsychology Review, 13(4), 221-235.

[14] Davis Jr, F. D. (1986). A technology acceptance model for empirically testing new end-user information systems: Theory and results (Doctoral dissertation, Massachusetts Institute of Technology).

[15] Davis, F. D. (1989). Perceived usefulness, perceived ease of use, and user acceptance of information technology. MIS quarterly, 319-340.

[16] Doocy, S., Daniels, A., Dooling, S., & Gorokhovich, Y. (2013). The human impact of volcanoes: a historical review of events 1900-2009 and systematic literature review. PLoS currents, 5.

[17] Eisenberg, D., Golberstein, E., & Hunt, J. B. (2009). Mental health and academic success in college. The BE Journal of Economic Analysis & Policy, 9(1), 1-37.

[18] Eysenck, M. W. (1979). Anxiety, learning, and memory: A reconceptualization. Journal of research in personality, 13(4), 363-385.

[19] Fernandez, A., Black, J., Jones, M., Wilson, L., Salvador-Carulla, L., Astell-Burt, T., & Black, D. (2015). Flooding and mental health: a systematic mapping review. PLoS one, 10(4), e0119929.

[20] Gautreau, C. (2011). Motivational factors affecting the integration of a learning management system by faculty. Journal of Educators Online, 8(1), n1.

[21] Grabowski, M., & Sagan, A. (2016). Attitudes Towards a Moodle-based E-Learning Platform: A User Segmentation Perspective

[22] Green, B. L., Korol, M., Grace, M. C., Vary, M. G., Leonard, A. C., Gleser, G. C., & Smitson-Cohen, S. (1991). Children and disaster: Age, gender, and parental effects on PTSD symptoms. Journal of the American Academy of Child & Adolescent Psychiatry, 30(6), 945-951.

[23] Gotlib, I. H., & Joormann, J. (2010). Cognition and depression: current status and future directions. Annual review of clinical psychology, 6, 285-312.

[24] Hsu, H. H., & Chang, Y. Y. (2013). Extended TAM model: Impacts of convenience on acceptance and use of Moodle. Online Submission, 3(4), 211-218.

[25] Kilic, E. (2013). Determining factors of affecting use of Moodle by using Technology Acceptance Model: A tale of university after an earthquake. In 2013 IEEE 63rd Annual Conference International Council for Education Media (ICEM).

[26] Kotsifakos, D., Adamopoulos, P., & Douligeris, C. (2016, September). Design and Development of a Learning Management System for Vocational Education. In Proceedings of the SouthEast European Design Automation, Computer Engineering, Computer Networks and Social Media Conference (pp. 110-117). ACM.

[27] Lonigan, C. J., Shannon, M. P., Finch, A. J., Daugherty, T. K., & Taylor, C. M. (1991). Children's reactions to a natural disaster: Symptom severity and degree of exposure. Advances in Behaviour Research and Therapy, 13(3), 135-154.

[28] Löwe, B., Decker, O., Müller, S., Brähler, E., Schellberg, D., Herzog, W., & Herzberg, P. Y. (2008). Validation and standardization of the Generalized Anxiety Disorder Screener (GAD-7) in the general population. Medical care, 46(3), 266-274.

[29] Machado, M., & Tao, E. (2007, October). Blackboard vs. Moodle: Comparing user experience of learning management systems. In Frontiers In Education Conference-Global Engineering: Knowledge Without Borders, Opportunities Without Passports, 2007. FIE'07. 37th Annual (pp. S4J-7). IEEE.

[30] Merkley, R. (2015). The Impact of Trauma Exposure on Academic Performance: The Roles of Resilience and Posttraumatic Growth as Protective Factors (Doctoral dissertation, Marywood University).

[31] Norris, F. H., Murphy, A. D., Baker, C. K., & Perilla, J. L. (2004). Postdisaster PTSD over four waves of a panel study of Mexico's 1999 flood. Journal of Traumatic Stress, 17(4), 283-292.

[32] Otto, K., Boos, A., Dalbert, C., Schöps, D., & Hoyer, J. (2006). Posttraumatic symptoms, depression, and anxiety of flood victims: The impact of the belief in a just world. Personality and individual differences, 40(5), 1075-1084.

[33] Papaspiliou, K., Skanavis, C., & Giannoulis, C. (2014). Civic Ecology Education and Resilient Societies: A Survey of Forest Fires in Greece. Journal of Education and Training Studies, 2(2), 48-57

[34] Rabaa'i, A. A. (1975). Extending the Technology Acceptance Model (TAM) to assess Students' Behavioural Intentions to adopt an e-Learning System: The Case of Moodle as a Learning Tool. Journal of Emerging Trends in Engineering and Applied Sciences (JETEAS), 7(1), 13-30.

[35] Radloff, L. S. (1977). The CES-D scale: A self-report depression scale for research in the general population. Applied psychological measurement, 1(3), 385-401

[36] Sánchez, R. A., & Hueros, A. D. (2010). Motivational factors that influence the acceptance of Moodle using TAM. Computers in human behavior, 26(6), 1632-1640.

[37] Shroff, R. H., Deneen, C. C., & Ng, E. M. (2011). Analysis of the technology acceptance model in examining students' behavioural intention to use an e-portfolio system. Australasian Journal of Educational Technology, 27(4).

[38] Spitzer, R. L., Kroenke, K., Williams, J. B., & Löwe, B. (2006). A brief measure for assessing generalized anxiety disorder: the GAD-7. Archives of internal medicine, 166(10), 1092-1097.

[40] Šumak, B., Heričko, M., Pušnik, M., & Polančič, G. (2011). Factors affecting acceptance and use of Moodle: An empirical study based on TAM. Informatica, 35(1), 91-100.

[41] Svanum, S., & Zody, Z. (2001). Psychopathology and college grades. Journal of Counseling Psychology, 48(1), 72-76.

[42] Tobias, S. (1979). Anxiety research in educational psychology. Journal of Educational Psychology, 71(5), 573.

[43] Unal, Z., & Unal, A. (2011). Evaluating and comparing the usability of web-based course management systems. Journal of Information Technology Education, 10, 19-38.

[44] U.S Department of Veterans Affairs (2016). Mental Health Reactions after Disaster. Retrieved June 5, 2017, from https://www.ptsd.va.gov/professional/trauma/disaster-terrorism/stress-mv-t-dhtml.asp

[45] Venkatesh, V. (2000). Determinants of perceived ease of use: Integrating control, intrinsic motivation, and emotion into the technology acceptance model. Information systems research, 11(4), 342-365.

[46] Wainwright, K., Osterman, M., Finnerman, C., & Hill, B. (2007). Traversing the LMS terrain. In Proceedings of the 35th annual ACM SIGUCCS fall conference (pp. 355-359). ACM.

[47] Yan, H., & Flores, R. (2016). Louisiana flood: Worst US disaster since Hurricane Sandy, Red Cross says. Retrieved February 28, 2017, from http://www.cnn.com/2016/08/18/us/louisiana-flooding/index.html

[48] Yeou, M. (2016). An Investigation of Students' Acceptance of Moodle in a Blended Learning Setting Using Technology Acceptance Model. Journal of Educational Technology Systems, 44(3), 300-318.

Trying it Out with College Library: The Role of Beta-testing and the Pilot Process in Establishing Successful Services

Jeremiah Ray
University of Wisconsin-Madison
600 North Park Street
Madison, WI 53706
jay.ray@wisc.edu

Crague Cook
University of Wisconsin-Madison
600 North Park Street
Madison, WI 53706
crague.cook@wisc.edu

ABSTRACT

UW-Madison's College Library is always on the lookout for new and interesting technologies in the hope of providing access to our patrons. In recent years, we have attempted to better define our beta-testing/piloting as a process of finding, testing, and implementing new solutions to gather usage data and user feedback. Once the pilot process is complete, we decide on the future path for solutions based on collected data.

With budget uncertainty and an ever-changing technology landscape, projects that are of interest are often hard to roll out in scale in a timely fashion. The pilot process allows for relatively small upfront investment to assess a technology's success in a given setting before full investment and rollout; it also allows for data collection and feedback that may lead to better solutions in future iterations and assistance in funding procurement and partnership formation.

Focusing on successes and pitfalls of the pilot process, we will use examples from recent memory to explain the framework we have developed and provide guidance to assist in the development of such frameworks for others.

CCS CONCEPTS

• **General and reference~Experimentation** • *General and reference~Evaluation* • **Social and professional topics~Hardware selection** • *Social and professional topics~Computing equipment management* • Social and professional topics~Pricing and resource allocation • **Applied computing~Interactive learning environments** • Applied computing~Computer-assisted instruction • *Human-centered computing~User centered design* • *Human-centered computing~Activity centered design* • *Human-centered computing~Scenario-based design* • *Human-centered computing~Participatory design* • Hardware~Test-pattern generation and fault simulation • Software and its engineering~Documentation • Software and its engineering~System administration

KEYWORDS

Pilot testing; beta testing; emerging technology; technology access; technology experimentation; technology services; library environment.

SIGUCCS '17, October 1–4, 2017, Seattle, WA, USA
© Association for Computing Machinery.
ACM ISBN 978-1-4503-4919-2/17/10...$15.00
https://doi.org/10.1145/3123458.3123460

1 INTRODUCTION

The University of Wisconsin-Madison Libraries take an active interest in serving the teaching, research and scholarly activities of UW System students, faculty, and staff, as well as visiting scholars and the citizens of Wisconsin; the libraries serve over 4,000,000 visitors every year. UW-Madison's College Library [5] is the main undergraduate-focused library on campus, serving Freshmen and Sophomore students through teaching and learning, reference assistance, and emerging technological pursuits. Additionally, College Library serves the rest of the campus community and the general public with multipurpose spaces, reservable rooms, computer workstations, scanning, copying, and checkout services, which include both educational and recreational text collections, as well as technologies.

The College Library technology services team provides access to a large list of technologies for use and checkout, including desktop and laptop computers, still and video cameras, projectors, iPads, and game consoles. The technology staff is also responsible for infrastructure support throughout the building, including technology checkout services, study room reservations, poster printing, 3D printing, wireless display technologies, and active learning spaces.

The technology staff are always on the lookout for new and interesting technologies in the hope of providing access to library patrons, as well as finding creative and innovative uses of this technology with patron assistance through pilot testing. College Library is often willing and has the necessary flexibility to invest resources to try solutions in library spaces in the attempt to gather data, create partnerships, and inform those who are interested.

With budget uncertainty and an ever-changing technology landscape, projects that are of interest are often hard to roll out in scale in a timely fashion. The College Library pilot process allows for relatively small upfront investment to assess a technology's success in a given setting before full investment and rollout; it also allows for data collection and feedback that may lead to better solutions in future iterations and assistance in funding procurement and partnership formation.

2 THE IDEA

College Library has created a portable and reproducible framework by which to approach new technologies, test new solutions, assess outcomes, and share findings with partners. As technology becomes more prevalent in every facet of the work of faculty, staff, and students, as well as integral to the workings of an institution, creating a framework becomes ever more important, as it provides the aforementioned flexibility to try new things and learn from both successes and failures in measureable ways. Any such framework must define the who, what, why, and where logistical specifics of a given project; the process of gathering user feedback; and possible partnerships between campus entities to fund and propel ideas into successful services, among other things. Following a similar process with each project can then provide tools to navigate those areas that are harder to define due to the nature of the technology or the complexity of the service.

In the case of College Library, the new solutions often deal with emerging technologies that are either financially or physically difficult for library patrons to procure on their own. Otherwise, solutions can be service specific or operational in nature, as well as novel uses of established technologies. No matter the specifics of the situation, the pilot process as defined provides a pathway to better understanding the needs of patrons and the opportunities that new and old technologies provide within the library context.

Though College Library has used a pilot testing system for many years in order to provide patron access to new and interesting technologies, the process was predominantly experiential and cultural. The library was able to create a culture around trying things out and every patron and staff member knew that College Library was the place to find unique spaces, services, and technologies. A small sample of projects that have been tested and formalized using the process over the years include: services such as poster printing and 3D printing; installations such as Liquid Galaxy and Oculus Rift Virtual Reality Station; and circulating items such as a Pixelstick and GoPro video cameras.

Creating a standard process allows the library to methodically find, test, fund, present, and expand untested or fledgling technologies into successful services, while presenting a consistent way of approaching such solutions when forming partnerships across campus. In addition, regarding specific technologies or services as existing within a pilot phase allows the library to test new ideas without creating undue expectations from stakeholders that a project is a permanent installation, especially if the project is deemed to lack the academic buy-in or patron interest necessary to be beneficial within the library environment.

The pilot process also creates a culture around continuous evaluation of technologies and services offered to library patrons in the attempt to discover and correct issues, while more proactively engaging individuals who seem to express a consistent interest in a given technology or service.

3 THE APPROACH

The technology staff at College Library have attempted to better define the pilot process into manageable, repeatable, and sharable steps. As seen in Figure 1, the approach includes inlets and outlets that can lead to either project formalization or potential end-of-life, but allows for further development should an initial pilot attempt fail or need simple retooling. This section focuses on the step-by-step process between initial interest in a project and its final outcomes. In this section, unless noting behaviors within a library-specific environment, the term "patron" has been substituted with "user".

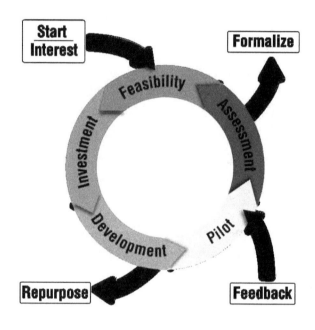

Figure 1: The Pilot Process, which includes initial interest, feasibility assessment, initial investment, solution development, the pilot phase with feedback gathering and outreach initiatives, and the assessment stage, with decision points throughout.

Interest is the logical starting point for any project. Whether due to an epiphanic moment, a conference presentation, or otherwise, all projects must begin with interest in an emerging technology or a novel use for a current technology. Though necessary to begin the process, interest feeds the pilot process loop and an institution must have both the culture and ability to sustain moving from a general interest into a fully formed pilot process. In the case of software solutions, interest may also equate to a proof of concept that will feed the team's understanding of a project's feasibility.

3.1 Feasibility

After establishing interest, a feasibility assessment is done to decide how a solution would fit into the institutional environment and how best to offer the solution to users. Though the assessment doesn't need to incorporate the very specific logistical details around the service or technology, it should provide the general ideas around pilot execution. A few of the considerations around feasibility include a project's ability to serve in support of the College Library mission, the pedagogical aims of a project, target audience, future ability for expansion, current staff availability for support, other pilots in progress, and overlap with other technologies already offered, among others.

The factors that can prevent an idea from being successful through the feasibility assessment can also include high cost, lack of support, lack of resources (staffing, space, time, etc.), or even limitations of the hardware or software currently available, especially given budgetary considerations. Feasibility assessments can be revisited at each stage of the pilot process should new information become apparent or available.

3.2 Investment

Once the feasibility of a project is confirmed, an initial investment is necessary to keep the process moving forward. The investment for a pilot project must be measured in both money and man-hours. Funds may be required for the purchase of physical items, but staff time must be considered in this investment, as some solutions include simplified plug-and-play development, while others necessitate coding or other development time. In the case of software solutions, time investment is a more integral metric to track.

Crafting a detailed budget for the pilot may be valuable at this point to ensure that development time and expected project outcomes are worth the final investment, and to completely assess the time and resource needs for a successful long-term implementation. For example, the budget may reveal that it is more logical to hire temporary, dedicated assistance for development and execution of the pilot instead of simply reallocating current staff. While this step can be considered fulfilled as soon as a product purchase is made, the majority of the time investment occurs during the development and potentially the execution of the pilot.

3.3 Development

Development allows for scenario-specific or use case testing before pilot deployment. This stage assists in discovering possible issues with the technology or service model and testing the technology or service with a small group of participants. The benefits of a closed development cycle are three-fold: it provides a timeframe to become intimate with the new service or technology; it allows time to create documentation and approaches for future support; and it provides insight during the

pilot itself should real world use cases not align with expected use cases.

The development stage requires planning the fine details for how to offer the technology or service to the target audience, and testing the solution in a small, tightly-controlled environment. Some important details to consider are staffing logistics, how and where to market the pilot, physical placement for maximum exposure, possible security risks, and the duration or timeline of the entire pilot. A deadline for deployment and a date of pilot completion are also defined at this stage.

If the project is a service, it could be offered internally to staff or colleagues in a preproduction form. The same group could also be used to trial new technologies. When testing a new technology, it's best to initially give as little guidance as possible to test a first-time user's interaction with the hardware and use such interactions as the baseline for support and documentation. This will provide an idea of the amount of guidance users will need and what types instructions or assistance will need to be provided. Any issues in usability that are discovered may require adjusting the format of the pilot, or provide the information and tools needed to solve a problem quickly when the pilot phase is active.

Creating extensive documentation will help ensure that the pilot runs smoothly. For services, this would include information on procedures for running the service, use instructions for new technologies included in the service, and troubleshooting information. While newly implemented technologies should be as simple as possible, it can be valuable to provide users with access to detailed information on use and capabilities of hardware or software. Most users will only care to use the technology in its simplest form, but some may be interested in a more advanced use, and this should be encouraged and supported whenever possible.

Periodically, working through the details of a solution reveals that the pilot isn't feasible after all. At this point, since the investment has already been made, exploring other purposes for the technology or service may be advantageous to craft a new pilot thereby restarting the process or working to find novel uses for the technology. Due to College Library's established checkout services, circulating technology to library patrons that was unable to be used in-building is often explored at this stage. In instances that have little to no monetary cost, the payoff is often in experience and professional development for the technology staff involved in the project.

3.4 Pilot

The development cycle inevitably leads to the pilot phase, though the time between start of development to start of pilot can vary depending on many and varied factors. When the pilot begins and the technology or service is rolled out to the target audience, observation, support, and outreach and feedback gathering are the main activities for support and technical staff. Adjustments to pilot criteria, timeline, marketing, and user expectations may be necessary throughout the pilot phase based on all of the above.

Marketing tends to be the first step, and can require a lot of trial and error depending on the environment. Signs can be helpful, but users tend to ignore them unless they are looking for specific information. Showcasing the service or technology in a high traffic area is of the utmost importance in situations where the value of the technology or service is not immediately apparent. If physical location is less flexible, wayfinding techniques, social media, and word of mouth tactics may be employed. Activity will draw a user's eye more than static documentation, so implementing a digital sign with a slideshow, or showing active use of the hardware are effective marketing tools. Social media may attract some users, but active and direct outreach is most effective. Send emails to or visit parties who may be interested in access or may have network opportunities that correlate to the expected use cases, and ask them to refer users.

The outreach component should also include dedicated communications with institutional parties that could provide academic or research-oriented analysis of the solution. Such insight can provide a better understanding of the market for the technology or service, and if funding partners exist, to ensure the success of a post-pilot solution. Gauging interest is another aim of such partnerships, especially for emerging technologies that have a more niche focus or more novel uses outside of the pilot scope. In a library environment, patrons may not see the broader possibilities of a given technology or service if the global marketing of the solution has focused on a specific subset of applications.

To ensure the success of the pilot, it's important to frequently monitor its state. Users will frequently test boundaries of services or technologies, which is incredibly useful but can also be a point of contention for public spaces. With hardware-based technologies, the setup may be moved, unplugged, reconfigured, or even broken. In order to provide a consistent user experience, defining a default state for the technology is useful. Daily, or after each use, the technology should be returned to the default state.

Pay close attention to the ways that users utilize the service or technology. If there are consistent behaviors and interaction paradigms with the pilot that differ from the original intended use case, consider embracing the novel use cases. These behaviors likely indicate an issue with how the pilot is being offered, or may reveal an entirely different need.

Services can require a lot more management and observation if they involve staffing. Documentation may need frequent updating as procedures evolve and change; if new issues are discovered, new documentation may be required for troubleshooting. It can be immensely valuable to offer paid services for free initially to the user base as an information gathering tactic. Free services manage expectations and provide the opportunity for staff to become familiar with providing the service without the pressure of satisfying paying customers. As a marketing tool, free services are also valuable because it generates a user base, and drives demand. In these situations, the initial state of the service may be uncertain and the quality may be diminished, so staff involved need to be aware of that and disclaimers should be used to ensure proper expectations from the user base.

Providing users with an avenue for offering feedback is always necessary and contact information should be made available if users have specific questions, suggestions, or a special use case for the technology or service. Often users don't readily offer feedback unless they are directly approached or enticed by some type of reward. Otherwise, those that offer feedback unsolicited might only be willing to do so due to a complaint about the service.

Some effective ways to solicit feedback are by offering a service for free initially and requiring the completion of survey as "payment", training staff to ask specific questions if they interact with a user before they can access technology, or including users in a drawing for a reward for completing a survey. Virtual surveys are especially convenient since they automatically track results, but never underestimate the effectiveness of short paper surveys. Offering brief paper surveys, with multiple choice questions can frequently provide more success for soliciting feedback than offering a URL or QR code to an online survey. In the end, the longer or more complicated a feedback mechanism, the less likely responses will be submitted.

If the pilot is not evolving into a permanent installation or service for any reason, communicating to users when the pilot is coming to an end is imperative. Possible options for such communication include signage, whether integrated into existing signage or at another stage of the experience, or direct outreach to interested or invested parties. Transparency can also be useful in motivating users to provide feedback or encourage them to facilitate partnerships for continuing to use the technology. Regardless of whether the pilot becomes formalized or retired, some assessment is required.

3.5 Assessment

Assessment is an integral step to formalize a pilot into a permanent installation or retire the service or technology. Formalization may just be continuing to offer the service as is, or could be the motivation for a bigger investment in the successful product. Further investments could involve redundancy, more or improved equipment, or expansion in staffing in order to make the service more effective or the technology more frequently available.

A retired pilot can also provide insight. The equipment or resources could be reused for an entirely different purpose; computer equipment especially is flexible in use and easily repurposed. Also, a new use case may have surfaced, which could result in a modified or entirely new pilot. Due to the nature of the pilot process as described, the continuation of the process is also a possibility. In the case of a pilot that included a free service to gather information, a slightly altered version of the pilot with a service cost, higher availability, and established expectations of quality is feasible. The assessment stage may provide only the information for what a formal service might look like, but may not provide enough insight to ensure service availability into perpetuity.

At a certain point, a pilot must end and be determined to be successful or unsuccessful. If it was a success, then it's time to formalize and/or expand. If the pilot is considered unsuccessful, it may be an opportunity to start the process over again repurposing new resources. Assessment of the pieces of the project that were successful or not with regards to marketing, feedback, and general management should be a focus, using that information to improve upon the future pilot processes.

4 Past Projects

4.1 3D Print Service

3D printing as a service [4] for a library without the added infrastructure provided by a full makerspace is unusual on UW-Madison's campus. However, other 3D printing shops on campus are focused on user groups with specific majors or application-specific use cases. In addition, large format printing [7] is one of College Library's most highly utilized services, so 3D printing appeared to be a natural way to expand print services within the library context. Implementation of 3D printing was complicated, and required working through the pilot framework more than once. Initial testing involved becoming familiar with the technology and offering the service to student staff for free in a very simple form. Student staff submitted a variety of print jobs and helped get a rough idea of turnaround time. This eventually led to providing a free 3D print service to the public for further testing and data gathering.

Continuing to provide the service for free assisted in managing patron expectations for turnaround time and quality of service while student staff became familiar with the technology and the new workflow. As a form of payment for a 3D print, patrons were asked to fill out a survey to help define expectations for cost and turnaround time. After offering the free service for a semester, the library transitioned 3D printing to a paid service, which required a reevaluation of feasibility.

Making the transition to paying customers meant expectations would be higher. Significant changes had to be made to the current form of the 3D print service to guarantee a more efficient and higher quality service. Reformatting the service meant that it was untested, and required its own pilot process. The information and experience gained from offering a free service made the new pilot much less rigorous and resulted in the successful implementation of a functioning, paid 3D print service.

Though the 3D print service is now officially out of its pilot process, continual assessment is necessary, as the long-term vision of the service is still in flux. Cost of staffing, support, and materials, along with patron expectations and future possibilities for expansion, are all important metrics to track. If the service becomes too costly to support for any number of reasons, the library's ability to offer it may change. In addition, changes to pricing dynamics to continue offering the service may not be well received by the main user base though pricing may need to be adjusted in the future.

4.2 Liquid Galaxy Installation

Liquid Galaxy is an immersive visual experience built on top of Google Earth that is open-source. The Liquid Galaxy installation at University of North Carolina-Chapel Hill [3] supplied the necessary interest to research the technology and begin the pilot process. Due to the open source nature of the application [1] and its ability to use any hardware that runs the Google Earth software [8], the feasibility assessment was simplified. Surplus computer hardware was used on the project and getting the software to work as desired was well-documented and required only a short amount of development time. An investment in monitors was necessary to get the installation up and running, but monitors are a technology that can be easily repurposed after the pilot process.

The technology had a seemingly obvious draw to library environments on UW-Madison's campus, where geography, cartography, or geology libraries might show interest in having an installation of their own, thereby creating a partnership with regard to support, funding, and availability. Student interest was high as well due to features such as flight simulation, visiting the moon or mars, and finding one's house in Google Earth. Liquid Galaxy simulates an immersive experience akin to virtual reality, though this installation occurred prior to the wide availability of virtual reality solutions.

The pilot execution went well, placing the installation in a well-trafficked area and noticing anecdotally that students consistently approached and tested the station. The technology staff had conversations with campus libraries believed to see the best return on such an investment. However, in the end, there was little academic interest and, while consistently used by students, the installation only had so many novel uses in a general library setting.

Feedback the library received suggested that those who used it most often missed it once it was removed from the space. However, the contacted libraries suggested that unless the functionality allowed for more tailored experiences with library-owned or collected data, the utility would be minimal even within libraries that had a more specific intent toward mapping and earth sciences.

4.2 Circulating Equipment

The technology equipment circulated by College Library [6] also goes through the pilot process, but in a slightly truncated form. Feasibility focuses mainly on expected patron interest and the logistics of circulation. The development phase simply clarifies the logistics and focuses on any security concerns that may arise in circulation. And finally, the pilot phase does not always have an end date and formalization takes a number of different forms.

Often, College Library measures the success of circulating equipment by the demand for it and the frequency with which it circulates. As an example, GoPro cameras [9] are an item the library began circulating that quickly gained popularity and high demand. Knowing the popularity that might accompany GoPros, two cameras were initially offered only through the equipment reservation system to ensure that special circumstances, specific timeframes, and project-based needs were met. The library quickly expanded the offering to include an additional four cameras available on a first-come, first-served basis. The success resulted in a larger investment in the technology to expand stock, upgrade to the newest hardware, and attempt to better meet demand.

If the pilot of a piece of circulating equipment is determined to be unsuccessful, it typically will remain in circulation unless the technology breaks or another use can be defined. An example of this would be the Pixelstick. [10] After spending several months in circulation with active marketing, it became clear that the Pixelstick appealed to a very limited market. Despite the fact it is rarely borrowed, it still remains in circulation. Equipment generally requires little special attention if it's seldom used, so keeping it in circulation is virtually effortless. Once the investment is made, any use is better than no use, and while a piece of technology may only circulate once per year, at least the library is accommodating that single individual.

5 Current Project

5.1 Oculus Rift Virtual Reality Headset and Workstation

One of College Library's current pilot projects is an Oculus Rift Virtual Reality (VR) workstation, which the library is offering to all patrons. It is a unique example of a circulating item becoming a full installation within the library computer lab. In its initial form, the library circulated an Oculus Development Kit 2 (DK2) headset, which was a version of the virtual reality headset Oculus offered prior to their retail version to allow developers to experiment with the technology and assist in building their library of virtual experience prior to full retail release. The hardware demands for computers to run the DK2 were relaxed for the sake of software development. The recommendations within the Oculus DK2 documentation [12] meant most standard computer hardware would allow experimentation with the headset. Due to the constant demand for this product, we preordered the retail version of The Oculus Rift headset to replace the DK2 when it was released.

However, the retail version of the Oculus Rift [11] required substantially higher hardware demands than its developer-focused predecessor. In fact, even the library didn't own a computer that could make use of the device. It became apparent that it was unrealistic to expect patrons to have the hardware to use the technology, and the technology staff concluded that circulating a computer with the device would require more support and management than the library was capable of or interest in providing. This led to the transformation of an already formalized pilot—the circulation of a VR headset—into something else to fit the investment that had already been made, which required an entirely new pilot process.

Eventually, the library decided to experiment with the idea of offering a computing station within the computer lab that would allow patrons to experience the technology using a customized computer specifically for the purpose of VR. Simply purchasing a new version of a VR headset evolved into investing in more

technology to support access to that device. The development of the VR station coincided with the release of the Oculus Rift Touch Controllers, which allow patrons to physically interact with virtual objects using their hands, so this technology was added to the pilot set up.

The testing portion of development involved asking staff, coworkers, and friends to try the technology. This was an opportunity to observe how a diverse group of users would interact with the VR station. Testing led to the creation of simple steps to guide first time users as well as offering suggestions for novice VR experiences. It also prompted the creation of a list of VR experiences that would require the least amount of equipment, or adjustments to the equipment provided.

Once testing was complete, an intern, Jorge Perez-Trejo, assisted in finalizing the setup, and surveyed possible locations to offer the workstation in the lab. The technology required a fair amount of space since patrons are physically interacting with the environment, so deployment required removal and repositioning of furniture and the purchase of a retractable belt barrier to create a visual and physical perimeter for the space.

In early March 2017, the workstation was installed in a high traffic area—at the entrance of the lab—for maximum visibility. To avoid computer use that was not related to VR, the computer has no connected mouse or keyboard, but a large display is utilized, so passersby can see the current experience in progress. Since the wireless Touch Controllers were difficult to secure, patrons are directed to the service desk to check the controllers out using their ID. Requiring patrons to borrow the controllers through the equipment checkout system was advantageous because it created an automatically tracked metric for how many times the controllers were borrowed. The VR station is also reservable within the library's room reservation system to allow patrons to reserve the station if they wanted to plan their use ahead of time. Reservations were advertised with a day schedule that is automatically populated and appears on a local iPad. The iPad display was a previous, successful pilot project for showing the schedules of our study rooms and classrooms.

In order to market the technology, the library generated a blog post announcing its availability and shared it via the library's and the University's social media accounts. On top of this, the technology staff have reached out directly to groups, via email, who might be interested in taking advantage of the technology for academic purposes. The workstation's signage offers simple instructions for first time users as well as a recommendation for what VR experience to try first. A survey is also advertised with a URL to allow patrons to share feedback or make requests for software or special academic use.

While still piloting the VR station within the library environment, some adjustments have already been made to the setup since deployment. The expectation was that patrons would use the station to explore a variety of VR experiences, and the library initially wanted to showcase all of the mechanics of the VR technology regardless of the content of the experience. The fact that the majority of patrons were drawn by first person shooter (FPS) style games became readily apparent, which impacted the appeal of trying the hardware, since the technology appeared to be focused on video gaming rather than a variety of experiences such as painting, building, and exploring. The library, as a general rule, attempts to make sponsored content available and welcoming to all patrons, so the FPS content was deemed too explicit to be consistently showcased within the environment, especially in such a high traffic area. This led to an adaptation of the list of software offered for a wider variety of experiences, and a complete removal of any FPS style games.

Unfortunately, the Oculus software has no tools to allow the library to prevent patrons from installing free, or already purchased software. As a result, almost daily checks for and removal of undesirable experiences is necessary and an unexpected support component. There is now a poster listing all software titles near the station that categorizes and provides brief descriptions of the adapted content list. Ideally, this informs the users and lets them pick the experience they want to try before putting on the headset.

Currently, the library is partnering with a group using the station to do a motion sickness study. The pilot will be offered through the summer, while the technology staff explore further outreach opportunities to build partnerships and encourage academic use of the technology. Success of the pilot depends on the library's ability to create lasting partnerships with groups on campus that see uses for the technology beyond gaming. The ideal outcome would see the technology introduced into curricula or research and development activities on campus to allow for further expansion.

6   Conclusions

College Library has a culture surrounding the use, reuse, and testing of interesting solutions, both inside or outside of the technology space. Use of current and upcoming paradigms in teaching and learning, reuse of old technology for novel purposes, and testing homegrown solutions for old problems are all ideas that College Library approaches with interest. The former pilot process that was more innate and experiential in nature accomplished much of what is detailed above for solutions and services, both technological and not. In short, a general interest on the part of a staff member, leads to an assessment of feasibility, an initial investment, development of a solution, and a rollout of a short-term pilot for further assessment and possible formalization and expansion.

The pilot process, as now formalized and described above, enables a better-defined approach to continuous assessment that has allowed College Library to improve the services offered to patrons, while cultivating an eye for improvement, marketing, and partnership formation. The library technology staff has started to take suggestions from other entities on campus of solutions that need to be tested. Taking suggestions allows the library to form partnerships, experiment with technologies not always directly aligned with library services, and find more sources of interest as a starting point for future pilot processes. Forming partnerships through shared investment in new and interesting technologies benefits the students, staff, and faculty of UW-Madison, as well as the general public in some situations.

The process has also created a deeper understanding of the library's services and solutions, which manifests itself in better reporting of the outcomes of pilot testing. Reports written by the College Library technology staff are shared to the general public to allow future library staff members and others on the UW-Madison campus and beyond to learn from the time and money invested by the library, as well as the pilot testing itself, in their own endeavors. [2]

ACKNOWLEDGMENTS

The pilot process idea and its continued execution within the College Library context would be impossible without the assistance the UW-Madison Libraries' institutional culture of access, research, and experimentation. In particular, Carrie Kruse, Director of College Library; Dave Luke, Technology Services Coordinator for the Libraries; and a long list of partner libraries and campus organizations have enabled the formalization of this process.

Figure 1 was created and provided by John Nannetti, College Library Technology Services Student Lead.

REFERENCES

[1]   Kiel Christofferson. 2016. Home – LiquidGalaxy/liquid-galaxy Wiki. (Mar 11, 2016). Retrieved June 23, 2017 from https://github.com/LiquidGalaxy/liquid-galaxy/wiki.

[2]   Crague Cook and Jay Ray. 2017. College Library Pilot Projects. (March 2017). Retrieved June 23, 2017 from http://go.wisc.edu/collegepilot.

[3]   Judy Panitch. 2014. Liquid Galaxy puts Davis Library on the map - The University of North Carolina at Chapel Hill. (October 17, 2014). Retrieved June 23, 2017 from http://www.unc.edu/campus-updates/liquid-galaxy-puts-davis-library-on-the-map/.

[4]   College Library. 2017. 3D Printing. (Jun 3, 2016). Retrieved June 23, 2017 from https://www.library.wisc.edu/college/services-at-college/computer-lab/3d-printing/.

[5]   College Library. 2017. College Library in Helen C. White Hall. (May 16, 2014). Retrieved June 23, 2017 from https://www.library.wisc.edu/college/.

[6]   College Library. 2017. Equipment for Checkout. (Dec 9, 2014). Retrieved June 23, 2017 from https://www.library.wisc.edu/college/services-at-college/equipment/.

[7]   College Library. 2017. Poster Printing. (Jul 3, 2014). Retrieved June 23, 2017 from https://www.library.wisc.edu/college/services-at-college/computer-lab/poster-printing/.

[8]   Google Earth. Liquid Galaxy. Retrieved June 23, 2017 from https://www.google.com/earth/explore/showcase/liquidgalaxy.html.

[9]   GoPro Official Website. 2016. Retrieved June 23, 2017 from https://gopro.com.

[10] Pixelstick. 2016. Retrieved June 23, 2017 from http://www.thepixelstick.com.

[11] Oculus. 2017. Oculus Rift. Retrieved June 23, 2017 from https://www.oculus.com/rift/.

[12] Oculus Developer Center. 2017. System Requirements. Retrieved June 23, 2017 from https://developer.oculus.com/documentation/pcsdk/0.4/concepts/dg-sdk-setup-requirements/.

[13] Ultimaker. 2017. Ultimaker 2+ 3D Printer. Retrieved June 23, 2017 from https://ultimaker.com/en/products/ultimaker-2-plus.

The Help Center of the New American University, it's IT and Beyond

Eric Dover
Arizona State University
PO Box 876312
Tempe, Arizona 85287-6312
Eric.Dover@asu.edu

Deborah Whitten
Arizona State University
PO Box 876312
Tempe, Arizona 85287-6312
Deborah.Whitten@asu.edu

ABSTRACT

This will be a behind-the-scenes look at Arizona State University's Help Center, which is part of a university that embraces a "one university" approach for many campuses. The ASU Help Center is an IT Help Desk and beyond, providing tier 1 support for other foundational services such as financial aid and parking. This will be a look at a structure in evolution, services in development, implementing a customer service focused culture, processes for onboarding new services, and the metrics that tie it all together. At its core, this will be a look at how ASU is growing its 24/7 Help Center to be the front door to all major ASU services and serve the Arizona community.

1 INTRODUCTION – THE BEGINNING

In 2007, Arizona State University made the decision to outsource its IT Help Desk operation. Certainly, cost was a major factor driving the decision, but other challenges included the expanding space needs for classrooms and faculty offices, staffing needs for a 24-hour help desk operation, and the management overhead associated with operating a central help desk. The current call center operation was not equipped to scale efficiently to the increasing needs of the university. ASU needed a well-defined, one-stop service center for students, parents, and faculty – a service center that could provide consistency in services and be flexible to support 1,800 calls daily, and up to 4,000 or more calls per day during peak periods. The service provider chosen had been currently serving another state agency and the provider was confident that they could support the ASU requirements. Shortly thereafter, however, it became apparent that the provider did not deliver on the knowledge base they committed to, could not provide the requested metrics, and their

overall service to ASU customers was not satisfactory. Near the end of the three-year agreement, ASU decided to change service providers. Another attempt failed, and two years into that second engagement, ASU President, Dr. Michael Crow, directed the Chief Information Officer, Gordon Wishon, to lead an initiative to bring the ASU Help Desk back on premise.

The purpose and justification for such a large undertaking was the overwhelming need to reinstate confidence and trust in the user community. Customer reliability and satisfaction had deteriorated with the two outsourcing initiatives. The University Technology Office (UTO) had lost its edge in being the technology resource to the ASU constituency. A support process was needed that would re-engage the customer, academic and business units with the UTO again. The new UTO Help Desk would provide a single entry point for service and support that aligned with the ASU mission to

- Demonstrate American leadership in academic excellence and accessibility
- Establish national standing in academic quality and impact of colleges and schools in every field
- Establish ASU as a global center for interdisciplinary research, discovery and development by 2020
- Enhance our local impact and social embeddedness.

The plan called for reinstating the Help Center back into the central University Technology Office administration where it had originally resided. But there were many challenges. First, the cutover date for the new installation had to align with the end of the contract with the current service provider (July 2014). The project team, under the direction of the Deputy Chief Information Officer, had nine months to develop a plan, prepare the site, hire and train staff, and be ready for a go-live date. Space needed to be found, utilities and infrastructure had to be installed, furniture and computing equipment procured, and software and systems evaluated and acquired including an integrated voice response system (IVR) and incident management ticketing system. Additionally, management staff had to be hired or acquired and trained, followed by the process of hiring and training 100+ customer service agents.

Documentation including hundreds of knowledge base articles had to be written. The deadline was tight and the aggressive project plan left little room for contingencies.

The scope of the project included plans to:

- Design and build an enterprise Service Desk that could manage 1,800 calls/day on average
- Collapse previous outsourced and internal functions into the Service Desk
- Create a knowledge base workgroup and oversight board
- Create a Student Center workgroup and oversight board
- Expand and improve the three distinct knowledge bases
- Create training teams and training curriculum
- Transition Financial Aid, Human Resources, and technical support to the Service Desk
- Continue FA and HR partnership with service provider during transition
- Continue partnership with service provider for ID account and password support
- Identify current inefficient processes and remedy

The costs for startup and ongoing maintenance were significant. The initial start-up budget was two million dollars, but as expected with most large-scale initiatives, some costs were easily escalated during project execution. Costs were high in the first year because the newly designed on-premise Help Desk had to operate alongside the service provider for the first six months to ensure a seamless transition and cutover without degrading services to the ASU community. The following chart depicts the one-time and recurring operational costs for the start-up and continuing maintenance over a three-year period.

ASU Help Desk: Projected Costs

Total Project Costs

Project	FY 2014 Total Project Budget	FY 2015 Total Project Budget	FY 2016 Total Project Budget
Contact Center-Helpdesk			
One Time Start Up Expenses	699,825	1,057,875	325,500
Ongoing Expenses	2,247,411	6,935,462	8,161,197
UTO Current BlackBoard Student	2,122,300	2,251,077	-
Total Contact Center-Helpdesk	5,069,536	10,244,414	8,486,697

The newly established ASU Help Center went live in May 2014 with a "soft launch" to gain experience and pilot new processes prior to the official "Go-Live" date of July 1. As a contingency plan, the contract with the current service provider was extended for another six months to allow for a longer transition period with the complex Financial Aid call center operation, and to ensure that a backup and overflow mechanism was in place should the onsite center experience problems. Additional temporary help was secured through a local call center operation to another level of overflow during the peak periods in the summer and between semester breaks.

The first year of the ASU Help Center;

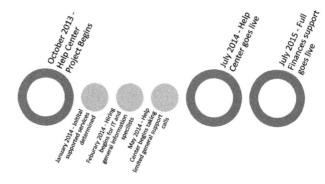

In the first year of operation, July 2014 through June 2015, the Help Center took 258,310 calls and 22,683 chats. Just two years later, the Help Center, from July 2016 through June 2017, took 481,266 calls and 73,057 chats. That equals a combined volume increase of 49% over the course of just two years.

The original management structure for the Help Center included one manager and several supervisors, each charged with supervision for calls of specific functional business areas. In June of 2015, the UTO restructured teams and aligned all customer facing units together into one centralized team called IT Customer Service and Support. This team included the new Help Center, classroom support, deskside support, training, client services, and audio/visual technology support teams across all campuses. The purpose of aligning all customer facing units together was to streamline processes, provide a seamless and transparent customer interface experience, eliminate redundancies and duplication of effort, and gain efficiencies across teams to better serve the customer needs. As part of this realignment, it was apparent that the current management structure in the Help Center needed to evolve, and a Director role for the operation was developed, posted, and filled. A national search completed in hiring a highly qualified, experienced, and customer-focused director who has brought process improvement, collaboration, and strong dedication to the institutional mission to the team. Hired in March 2016, Eric Dover brought strong leadership and customer service skills and knowledge to the team.

2 VISION/MISSION OF THE ASU HELP CENTER

The overall vision and mission of the ASU Help Center is "to become the front door for all ASU services and to provide the highest level of service and support to our ASU family and beyond." Wrapped in this vision and mission is the belief that we need to provide as friction-free of an experience as possible for our ASU students, parents, faculty and staff. By that, we mean our vision and mission is to provide as close as a one-stop service center as we can. Being able to provide tier 1 level support for multiple services beyond just IT allows for us to ask the important question at the end of an interaction ("Is there anything else we can help you with today?") and be able to answer "I can help you with that" – be it a need for parking information, question on financial aid, or anything else.

The "beyond" portion of our vision and mission is to provide assistance and resources to groups outside of ASU. We are exploring providing emergency contact center services for Maricopa County and the State of Arizona. We are also pursuing other partnerships in the community that may be able to take advantage of our 24/7, 365 days a year service to aid in after hour service or provide tier 1 services around the clock throughout the entire year.

The foundation of all of this is service. It is not just our mission to deliver the highest level of customer service possible – it is our mission to explore every possible option to get to "yes." When approached to add services, or explore new directions, we go out of our way to find "yes." As a highly flexible and nimble organization, this is critical.

3 SERVICES PROVIDED

The ASU Help Center is a multi-service tier 1 help center that is very unique within the higher education space. Rather than rely upon multiple service desks to support an individual major service, ASU has consolidated several of these major services into one Help Center. Over the last three years of operations, the Help Center has continued to advance in the mission of being the front door to all major ASU services. At present, the Help Center provides tier 1 services for almost 30 services. These services include but are not limited to:

- Information Technology
- Financial Aid
- Student Business Services (collections, account payments, etc.)
- Parking & Transit Services
- Faculties after-hours and overflow
- Pharos Print Anywhere
- Door access system
- Herberger College learning management system

- Plus Alliance partnership
- Mary Lou Fulton Teacher's College system support
- All Clear Security Response Readiness Support
- Emergency reunification
- General questions

The ASU Help Center also maintains an informal network of other service providers that allow for us to quickly and accurately transfer calls and requests directly to those units. One such informal partnership is with Housing. Although we at the Help Center currently do not provide tier 1 service for Housing related questions and/or issues, we do maintain a close working relationship with Housing staff to ensure that we can hand off students that may have questions or are experiencing issues.

One of the functions that the Help Center serves for Arizona State University is a reunification center in the case of a catastrophic event happening on any of the ASU campuses. A drill was conducted in April 2016 that involved local hospitals and emergency response personnel, and was overseen by county and state officials. The performance of the Help Center in this drill was exceptional and recognized by the State and County for the performance and professionalism that they witnessed. This drill opened the door of communication with state and local officials for the possibility of Arizona State University providing similar services for local, regional and state level emergencies.

These discussions are ongoing and Arizona State University is very interested in this partnership between Maricopa County and the State of Arizona. We are exploring several options for partnership that range from access to our unique call center environment that would be staffed with county and/or state officials in the case of an emergency all the way to using ASU Help Center staff as well as the Help Center facility to help when called upon.

3 STRUCTURE

The Arizona State University Help Center is presently staffed with 69 full-time customer support specialists along with up to 30 student staff. This makeup is highly unique in the higher education space. Many other universities will staff their tier 1 service desks mostly with student staff. To gain the highest level of proficiency, staffing schedule predictability and customer service, ASU relies upon a full-time staffing model first and then augments with student staff. In the second half of 2017, the Help Center will be adding 12 permanent part-time positions that will fill critical volume times during the heart of the day as well as provide additional coverage during peak season times.

3.1 MANAGEMENT STRUCTURE AND CHANGES

After the startup of the Help Center and the subsequent hiring of a director of the Help Center, an analysis was conducted to see if the management structure was meeting the needs of the organization and university. The new director took the time to evaluate roles, structure and develop a deep understanding of the overall capabilities of the Help Center. What they found was a passionate group of staff that were well resourced, but with a few changes, could also help de-silo and create an organization that was more agile and flexible to the growing needs of the university. To start the process of realigning the Help Center to better meet the needs of Arizona State University, the director needed to realign the management team to lead a realigned Help Center staff.

An exercise was undertaken to evaluate the management needs of the Help Center. All of the managers were asked to identify functions by writing them down on a sticky note and placing it on a wall in the Help Center. Once all of the managers had had a chance to note functions of the Help Center, a grouping exercise followed. Over the course of a week, the managers would group the functions on sticky notes. This exercise was done solo and with no discussion. It was simply a grouping exercise to identify function families.

Once the managers had completed the grouping exercise, all came together to discuss the groupings to see if there were any further groupings to complete. In the end, the managers had identified several families of functions that aligned quite well with management responsibilities. Through this exercise, they were able to determine that the following management roles were needed: Floor and Agent Engagement Manager, New Initiatives and Operations Manager, Quality Control Manager and Customer Relationship Managers.

The Floor and Agent Engagement Manager is responsible for the day-to-day management and coaching of all agents. They work to establish culture and expectations and ensure we are providing the highest level of service to our customers while also working with agents to grow.

The New Initiatives and Operations Manager works to operationalize and onboard new customers and initiatives. They also oversee the technical systems the Help Center uses such as the inContact phone system, and act as the system owner for inContact with other departments at Arizona State University that use this system.

The Quality Control Manager leads all quality control efforts. They work to establish and maintain the quality scorecards as well as review calls, chats, processes and other initiatives related to quality. They work closely with trainers to review and develop training plans.

The Help Center has two Customer Relationship Managers and they work closely with all services owners and the Help Center director to ensure that SLA targets are met, in addition to working with the Help Center director to manage the day-to-day relationships with the service owners. They also work very closely with the Help Center director in outreach, university and community engagement activities and expanding our service portfolio, which will bring us closer to our mission and goal of being the front door to all ASU services.

3.2 AGENT STRUCTURE

At present, the ASU Help Center has a siloed agent structure based around some of the major services provided. This structure is one that is in transition. Presently, the Help Center is comprised of three major teams: Information Technology, Student Services and Finances. Currently, the Finances team is largely dedicated to just financial aid and Student Business Services-related questions and/or issues. On occasion, the Finances team will aid in the overflow of general questions and Facilities related calls. The bulk of the other services are spread across the other two teams. These silos have made it a challenge to add new services as we have not been able to take full advantage of all our resources.

The agents themselves are presently structured in a very flat way. At present, there is no in-place promotional or growth path that would reward staff for knowledge and performance gain nor is there any incentive to encourage staff to stay with the Help Center longer than the typical 2 years for a tier 1 service provider. This is an area that is poised for improvement over the course of the next several months.

In looking at the siloed structure as well as the costs for the temporary seasonal staff, we have developed a plan to restructure the agents and take a more sustainable and cost-effective approach to our seasonal staffing needs. At present, we are working on an agent structure that is based on three levels and dependent on skill and performance. The three position titles that will be associated with this structure are customer support specialist, customer support specialist senior and customer support specialist lead. These changes will allow for a progression path through the Help Center that should allow us to retain talented staff longer than an average of two years. This will allow for skill growth, which adds flexibility to our service that will allow us to better accommodate shifting changes in coverage needs on a moment-to-moment basis.

A side benefit to these changes is the ability to help develop staff to better transition into other positions within UTO, as well as other ASU departments. The Help Center is becoming a key entry point for other ASU opportunities as we have had nearly a third of our agent staff move on to other opportunities within ASU over the last year.

Also, a part of the agent structure is the use of temporary contracted staff used during high volume times to help augment during the peak months of January, July and August. This has been met with varying levels of success, but it was determined after the August 2017 contract to reevaluate options for ASU peak volume staffing.

To better position itself for the high-volume periods, the Help Center has repurposed the budget line for temporary contracted staff to fund a core group of part-time staff that can be used year round rather than for only a few months in the year. By moving to part-time staff we will be able to have them train once and then go through recurring training like their full-time colleagues. The part-time staff are guaranteed a minimum of 25 hours a week during the normal volume parts of the year to ensure information currency and to help bolster the staff coverage during the busy heart of the day. This part-time strategy turns dollars spent on season staff who needed to be rehired and retrained just before each high-volume season into a sustainable year-round staffing augmentation plan for the same relative cost as the temporary contracted labor.

The overall agent structure is very much a work in progress, but a clear path has been developed with parts of it being implemented now. The other parts have leadership support, and the final stages of finding the additional monetary resources for implementation are in motion.

4 METRICS

Metrics are a key resource in planning and measuring our success at the ASU Help Center. Through our inContact system, as well as via our Salesforce environment, we have been able to collect a tremendous amount of data. For us to maximize our ability to take advantage of this data, we worked with ASU's business intelligence unit to have all data dumped into the university data warehouse where we could utilize BI tools to analyze and dashboard the data. We have identified two sets of metric data that we create dashboards for: cost metric data and performance metric data. Sometimes, these two data classifications blend and overlap, but they can be treated as separate. In this section, we will share some of the metric points we collect and report on as well as how we use the data in our process of continual improvement.

Performance metrics (value)
- Abandon rate greater than 15 seconds
- Overall customer service
- Professionalism
- Accuracy
- Escalation rate
- First call resolution

Resource planning metrics (cost)
- Average speed to answer
- Utilization
- Average handle time

Transparency of the metric data has been a key tenet of the Help Center. The desire is to make the data as open as possible for accountability and to help show the story of a growing university through the data we collect. One of the ways that the Help Center has become transparent with data has been in the creation of dashboards that are tailored for audiences at the executive level down to the service owner level. These dashboards are updated every 24 hours and provide a visual representation of performance on several key performance indicators.

Beyond the dashboard data, the Help Center has also worked to provide data for various projects that could help lead new discoveries that can help the Help Center grow and adapt faster to the changing needs of our ASU family. The data that the Help Center collects can also be used by other ASU departments to understand volume drivers to identify possible process improvements or information availability gaps that, if closed, could remove a possible friction point for ASU.

5 THE FUTURE

2016 and the first half of 2017 have been an evolutionary period for the ASU Help Center. With the hiring of the Help Center director, several observations and initiatives have been made, started and completed. Some of these we have discussed earlier in this paper, such as the management restructure, agent progression path development and the development of a part-time core. Other major changes and initiatives on the horizon include:

- Reevaluating methods that are used by our ASU family and beyond to contact the ASU Help Center for assistance. One specific area that will be looked at is the integration of support via chat and email into the current Help Center contact system.
- Formalizing agreements with Maricopa County and the State of Arizona to provide emergency contact center services in the case of a major to catastrophic event.
- Continuing to expand services supported by partnering with major service units across ASU.
- Working to formalize the ASU Help Center as a resource pool for other ASU departments to recruit from.
- Evaluating space needs to develop a plan for an expanding staff. This will include the examination of a second site for disaster recovery, growth expansion and possible staff recruiting and hiring opportunities in another region of the Phoenix area. We will also be exploring the possibility of offering permanent telecommuting options.

5 LESSONS LEARNED

Several key lessons have been learned over the years through ASU's experience with building a centralized multi-service Help Center. Some of these are:

- Don't outsource core services
- Customer service is key to university mission and goals
- Need strong leader for a project of this size
- Get everyone involved from across all service areas early
- Be sustainable with resources
- Develop expectations between service owners and the service provider

6 CONCLUSIONS

Innovation is one of the cornerstones of Arizona State University. As the university continues to transform and adapt into the new American university the Help Center will be an integral part of being able to deliver services to the broader ASU family. As we continue to celebrate, as a university, our charter principal of being "measured not by whom we exclude, but rather by whom we include and how they succeed," the Help Center will be that first stop resource for our ASU family as they work to achieve their dreams and leave a permanent and positive impact on our local and global community. Providing excellent service will continue to be the first and foremost mission for the ASU Help Center to ensure that the user experience for everyone at ASU is the very best that it can be.

A Touchless Gestural System for Extended Information Access Within a Campus

Salvatore Sorce*
Ubiquitous Systems and Interfaces (USI) group - http://usi.unipa.it
College of Engineering, Design and Physical Sciences - Department of Computer Science
Brunel University London
United Kingdom
Salvatore.Sorce@brunel.ac.uk

Vito Gentile
Ubiquitous Systems and Interfaces (USI) group - http://usi.unipa.it
Dipartimento dell'Innovazione Industriale e Digitale (DIID)
Università degli Studi di Palermo
Palermo, Italy
vito.gentile@unipa.it

Cristina Enea
Università degli Studi di Palermo
Palermo, Italy
cristina.enea@libero.it

Antonio Gentile†
Ubiquitous Systems and Interfaces (USI) group - http://usi.unipa.it
Dipartimento dell'Innovazione Industriale e Digitale (DIID)
Università degli Studi di Palermo
Palermo, Italy
antonio.gentile@unipa.it

Alessio Malizia
Human Centred Design Institute
Brunel University London
United Kingdom
Alessio.Malizia@brunel.ac.uk

Fabrizio Milazzo
Ubiquitous Systems and Interfaces (USI) group - http://usi.unipa.it
Dipartimento dell'Innovazione Industriale e Digitale (DIID)
Università degli Studi di Palermo
Palermo, Italy
fabrizio.milazzo@unipa.it

ABSTRACT
In the last two decades, we have witnessed a growing spread of touchless interfaces, facilitated by higher performances of computational systems, as well as the increased availability of cheaper sensors and devices. Putting the focus on gestural input, several researchers and designers used Kinect-like devices to implement touchless gestural interfaces. The latter extends the possible deployments and usage of public interactive displays. For example, wall-sized displays may become interactive even if they are unreachable by touch. Moreover, billboard-sized displays may be placed in safe cases to avoid vandalism, while still maintaining their interactivity. Finally, people with temporary or permanent physical impairment (e.g. wheelchair users) may still comfortably interact with the display. Here we describe an information provision system allowing for touchless gestural interactions, along with a trial implementation within our University campus to test its effectiveness in a real setting. Our system is intended for use by students, lecturers and staff members, providing a captivating way to access news, lectures information, videos and more. We also report the results of an ongoing user study, defining a set of guidelines for future designs.

CCS CONCEPTS
• **Human-centered computing** → **Field studies**; **Gestural input**; *Usability testing*; *Empirical studies in HCI*; *Empirical studies in interaction design*;

KEYWORDS
Touchless Interaction, Gestural Interaction, Natural Interfaces, Human-Computer Interaction, Information-provision Systems

ACM Reference Format:
Salvatore Sorce, Vito Gentile, Cristina Enea, Antonio Gentile, Alessio Malizia, and Fabrizio Milazzo. 2017. A Touchless Gestural System for Extended Information Access Within a Campus. In *Proceedings of SIGUCCS '17, Seattle, WA, USA, October 1–4, 2017,* 7 pages.
https://doi.org/10.1145/3123458.3123459

*Also with InformAmuse s.r.l. - Academic spin-off - www.informamuse.com.
†Also with InformAmuse s.r.l. - Academic spin-off - www.informamuse.com.

1 INTRODUCTION
Information provision systems in the form of interactive displays are increasingly available in several public contexts. They offer promising business opportunities and pose interesting research questions in different fields, due to their common physical features (spatial placement, deployment environment), and to their typical purposes (interactive advertising, information provision).

In the last two decades, there has been a growing interest in touchless gesture-based interaction with computer systems, both from the scientific and the commercial worlds [1]. Such interest, formerly driven by home gaming systems, recently had a boost due to the increased availability of interactive public displays of any size. In most cases, the touchless gestural interaction seems to be the most suitable one to address both technical, physical, social and effectiveness problems.

For wall-sized displays, such as the so-called *media façades* [2], the gestural input with no devices worn by the users is often the only feasible way to add interactivity. This is mainly due to the big size of the display, which results in a necessarily high interaction distance.

Concerning smaller interactive displays ranging from TV to billboard screens, such as the so-called *situated public displays*, they are typically placed at eye-level and within arm's reach [3]. These features naturally afford touch-based interaction, and possibly this is the main reason why touchless interaction has been rarely studied for such displays so far.

Currently, it seems there is a trend reversal, and touchless gestural interaction with situated public displays is gaining a growing interest for different reasons. Among them:

- simplify and encourage multiple parallel interactions, mainly due to the higher allowed interaction distance. In fact, the interaction distance defines the available space in front of the display for users to interact: the more the interaction distance, the more room for multiple users;
- increase the social acceptability of interactions with publicly accessible devices. Due to the growing diffusion of situated public displays in popular places, people could feel more comfortable to interact with no need to touch something that has been used by other people, for hygienic reasons;
- extend the number of prospective users, thus including people who, for some reason, temporary or permanent, may (or wish) not access a touch-based interface;
- place the display with no constraints related to the touch reachability;
- limit vandalism, as a direct consequence of the previous one.

Despite the undoubted usefulness of the touchless gestural input, there are several issues that must be taken into account when including it in general-purpose information provision systems available in public spaces. These issues are mostly related to the intended audience and the provided contents. Indeed, in the case of very specific applications, such as games or entertainment systems, they provide specific content to specific users, who are often aware of the interaction capabilities and media. On the other hand, in the case of information provision systems, a large and heterogeneous community access different kinds of information, presented in different media formats.

In this case, the design of a useful and intuitive visual interface requires the analysis of several context factors, both technical (size of the devices, place in which they are deployed, information they provide), and socio/psychological. One of these is the *legacy bias* [4]. According to this, users are affected by traditional interaction models (such as the well-known WIMP one [5]), also when interacting using completely different paradigms. Another human-related issue is the *display blindness* [6], according to which users do not look at the display, expecting uninteresting content (e.g. advertisements), or simply because it does not capture their attention.

Maybe the most relevant issue in the design of interfaces for situated public displays is the *interaction blindness* [7]. In this case, even

if people are looking at the display, they may not understand neither that it is interactive nor the touchless nature of its interactivity.

All these issues are additionally influenced by other human factors, such as the personal profile of the intended users, the influence of the possible audience during the interaction [8], the culture-related acceptability of a gestural interaction in public, and many others. The discussion above means that the definition of general guidelines must undergo some statistical analysis over a sample of actual users. The more significant the sample, the more reliable the results.

Microsoft, who first provided access to the cheap and easy development of gesture-based systems, proposed its Human Interface Guidelines (HIG) for the development of Kinect-based applications [9]. Such guidelines are not mandatory, do not cover all related issues, and are not suitable for all situations (for example, for systems based on different devices). As a result, even if there are several implementations of information provision systems on situated public displays that are HIG-compliant [10] [11] (often only partially), there are no general rules to address all the interface design questions related to the touchless gestural interaction.

In this paper we present a possible layout for a visual interface to be used in a general-purpose information provision system allowing for touchless gestural interaction. In more detail, we implemented an *avatar-based* visual interface and deployed it in an actual information provision system as a public display within a building in our university campus. We then analyzed the people's behavior during their interactions with the display, in order to assess the overall usefulness of the system and, in particular, the effectiveness of a human-shape that replays the users' movements within a visual interface in conveying the interactivity capabilities and functions.

We conducted a three-months-long observation of such installation and carried out a longitudinal study in-the-wild on it. As a result, we assessed the effectiveness of the system, and we also deduced some basic general guidelines for the design of visual interfaces for gestural interaction. These guidelines should be useful for display or space managers, to better tune their setups and maximize their revenues.

2 RELATED WORKS

The research on public displays focuses on several different issues, such as audience behavior, privacy, software and hardware solutions, and the ability to communicate interactivity to passers-by and users [12]. Focusing on the last of these issues, researchers must take into account the need of overcoming the *display blindness* and - probably more complicated - the *interaction blindness*. The first problem occurs when people do not look at the display because of their prejudice about the content, which is expected to be an advertisement. Researchers must thus overcome this issue in order to study any aspect related to the interactions, especially in-the-wild, i.e. in uncontrolled environments where many external factors affect users' behaviors. Among the proposed solutions for attracting passers-by glances, visual animation effects and/or sounds have been demonstrated to be helpful. Other factors that can mitigate the display blindness are the colorfulness, the amount of time the display is potentially visible to passers-by, and the display size [13]. However, this problem is not simple to solve and can require applying some techniques from the persuasive computing area [14].

However, the display blindness is not the main issue, especially if we deal with interactive displays. Indeed, even when users look at the display, they often do not interact with it because they simply do not know that they can. This means that there is the need to communicate the interactivity and thus entice interactions. This is the *interaction blindness* phenomenon, and it generally refers to the inability of people to recognize the interactive capabilities of the display, also when looking at it [15]. Among the many solutions described in the literature, one of the most commonly adopted is the use of explicit visual clues that suggest users to perform some gestures. In [16], Walter et al. compared different presentation modes for such visual clues, i.e. integration, temporal division and spatial division. This study showed that spatial division results to be the most suitable solution for public displays, although it implies the need of allocating part of the screen to show such clues.

Ojala et al. suggest that one way to overcome interaction blindness and entice interaction is to make the interface more natural. Proxemic interactions are emerging as a potential paradigm for realizing natural interfaces, but simple visual proxemic cue (the *Touch me!* animation) did not noticeably increase user interaction [17]. *Proxemic interactions* were introduced by Ballendat et al. [18], and they are very related to (and actually based on) a previous work by Vogel and Balakrishnan [19]. In these works, authors propose systems that react on user's position and orientation, i.e. without any implicit interaction. Such idea seems promising in solving interaction blindness since users can easily understand the display interactivity if its contents change corresponding to their movements. Indeed, proxemic interactions allow for the implementation of more sophisticated solutions than a simple Touch me! animation, and there is the need for further investigations on how they can help to solve interaction blindness.

Moreover, proxemic interactions can help users to understand the features of an interactive public display, by modeling it as a sort of mirror (i.e. one of the four mental models studied in [20]). The mirror mental model has been shown to have a strong potential in catching users' attention [21], which suggests using it also as a partial solution to the display blindness, as well as for communicating touchless interactivity. A successful application of the mirror mental model is MirrorTouch [22], where authors studied the use of touch-based interactions combined with mid-air gestures. In this application, a user interacted with her silhouette shown in a public display, and this showed how effectively the mirror model communicates the touchless interactivity. Indeed, authors underlined the need of explicit call-to-action as the only effective way to let users interact via touchscreen, instead of sticking on the gestural interaction modality only.

The use of users avatars in a visual interface can thus be seen as an implementation of the aforementioned mirror mental model, and MirrorTouch is not the only one solution that exploits this idea. For instance, Müller et al. showed that displaying the users' silhouette may help in communicating the display interactivity in Mirror-Touch. Similarly, this idea has been explored in ShadowTouch [23] and Cuenesics [24], two touchless gestural application for public displays based on users' representations in the form of avatars.

According to this discussion, in order to evaluate the overall usefulness of a touchless-based information provision system, in this work we also assess the potential for an avatar in a visual interface to communicate the touchless gestural interactivity. To this end, we analyzed the people's behavior around an actual situated public display showing an avatar-based visual interface [25]. Our goal is to check whether the presence of the avatar may attract people, and if it may help them to easily understand the purposes of the system, thus maximizing its effectiveness and its communicative and informative goals.

3 SYSTEM DESCRIPTION

The information provision system we implemented is deployed as a public display in a 150 square-meters-large indoor space inside a building within the University campus in Palermo. The display is placed next to a couple of benches where students often sit while waiting for lectures starting times. Students of different disciplines

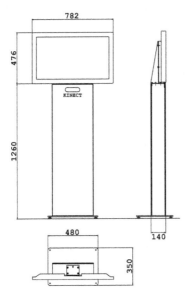

Figure 1: Physical layout of the hard case (size in mm)

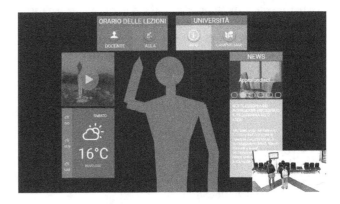

Figure 2: Main layout of the visual interface

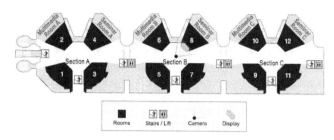

Figure 3: Map of the building and position of the display. The black dot shows the camera position; the yellow cone shows its field-of-view; the green shape represents the display

Figure 4: A view of the display and people around it from the observation camera

and ages (mostly from 19 to 35 years old), lecturers, and other University staff members usually frequent this area.

The hardware consists of a 40-inches LCD monitor placed at eye-level, with a Microsoft Kinect sensor placed right below it, and a suitable PC. A hard case encloses all the hardware for security, safety and aesthetic reasons (Figure 1).

The visual interface layout consists of a suitable number of interactive tiles arranged all around an avatar placed in the middle of the screen (Figure 2).

The avatar appears whenever a user approaches the display, and remains permanently present in the middle of the screen, continuously replaying user's movements. In particular, the avatar's arms end in two hand-shaped cursors, which represent and replay the user's hands movements. As stated in the previous Section, the presence of a predominant entity that continuously reproduces user movements should significantly contribute to reducing the interaction blindness. In other words, the main rationale behind the presence of an interactive avatar placed in the middle of the interface should be to help users in understanding both the interactivity of the system and its touchless nature.

As far the interaction is concerned, it takes place by means of in-air direct manipulations. In other words, users can mimic the direct manipulation of objects, as they would do in real life, without actually grabbing or touching them, with no need to learn specific activation gestures. The users can trigger the interaction events just by driving the avatar's hands and placing them on top of the available tile-shaped components.

For our study, we installed a Wi-Fi camera in front of the display, in a not-reachable position. This allowed us to observe the users' behavior in a quiet way, as well as to check the actual display status. Figure 3 shows the overall experimental set up, and Figure 4 shows a frame captured from the observation camera.

4 STUDY SETUP

The information system allows people to accomplish the following tasks:

- reading news;
- reading university information;
- displaying and navigating the building map;
- displaying lecture timetable;
- displaying weather data;
- displaying a video.

We conducted an exploratory study on people's behavior around the display following two different approaches. In the first one, we explicitly asked passers-by to interact with the display, and then submitted them a semi-structured interview. This study took about 20 hours across 40 days. In the second one, we quietly observed the users' behavior, for a total of about 30 hours, distributed across 40 days. During this time, we collected useful data both from our observations and from the video feeds from the camera. Also in this case, we submitted our semi-structured interview to users after we observed them, as described in the following section.

In both cases, we used the same scheme for the semi-structured interviews as follows:

Q1) Did you already know that this system is based on touchless gestural input?

Q1.1) If no, have you guessed that it was gestural?

Q1.1.1) If yes, which hints have suggested you that the system was gestural? (e.g.: display size, presence of the Kinect sensor, the avatar on the screen, etc.)

Q2) Have you ever had previous experiences in interacting with gestural systems?

Q3) Did you miss the touchscreen or other more conventional interactive modalities?

Q4) Are there some other tasks that you would like this system to accomplish?

Q5) Do you have any other suggestions or ideas to improve this system?

We also asked users for some further information to sketch a personal profile, such as gender, age, current job, and if they were right-handed, left-handed or ambidextrous.

5 RESULTS AND DISCUSSION

Here we report the details of both approaches and a summary of their outcomes regarding the effectiveness of the avatar-based interface against the interaction blindness.

5.1   Explicit Experimenter Intervention

In this first approach, we explicitly asked people to interact with the display without revealing its touchless nature. In this case, the interactivity of the system was thus well known, and the main goal was to assess the capability of the avatar to convey the touchless gestural interactivity.

We asked 17 users (10 males, 7 females) to perform a 5-minutes-long interaction session, followed by a semi-structured individual interview. We directly observed users during their interactions, and they were aware of our presence. In order to obtain the most significant results, we have chosen a diversified users sample, with different levels of technology-related skills. In particular, we enrolled students attending various courses, from different disciplines.

In the interaction sessions, we asked each participant to carry out the following tasks:

(1) find and read a specific news;
(2) find and read university information;
(3) find the timetable for a specific class;
(4) play a video;
(5) find and read the weather forecast.

Users had to perform these tasks without any suggestions or hints on how to achieve such goals, especially in terms of interaction modality.

5.1.1   Outcomes. We analyzed the semi-structured interviews we conducted at the end of each interaction session, along with our observation reports. Such analysis allowed us to deduce some interesting results about the capability of the avatar to convey the touchless gestural nature of the interactivity. We also obtained useful clues on other aspects related to the presence of an avatar in a visual interface for touchless gestural interactions.

Concerning the ability to communicate gestural interactivity, none of the users we enrolled knew that the system was based on touchless gestural input. Moreover, 13 users out of 17 claimed that they guessed the touchless nature of the interactivity thanks to the presence of the avatar. Among the remaining four users, two claimed that the main clue for understanding the touchless gestural interactivity was the presence of the Kinect, and two did not understand it at all. It is worth noting that eight users already knew the Kinect sensor. Nevertheless, six of them recognized the nature of the interactivity from the presence of the avatar.

Concerning other aspects of interaction, we found that users often perceived the presence of the avatar as annoying, confusing and useless, especially during the reading of long texts. In such case, the avatar continued to be visible in the middle of the interface (despite it became semi-transparent to let users read and see the contents through it). Four users explicitly assessed that displaying only hand-shaped cursors would be preferred in such cases.

5.2   Quiet Experimenter Intervention

With this approach, we wanted to check if the presence of the avatar in the middle of the screen is useful to overcome the interaction blindness itself.

In this case, during the observations we were around the deployment place, blended in the crowd or sat on a bench next to the display, and quietly noted down the users' behaviors. We also asked users to undergo the semi-structured interview described before, only after each spontaneous interaction session, or after we observed someone staring at the system for a while. We observed 50 users, of which 29 accepted to answer the semi-structured interview.

5.2.1   Outcomes. The analysis of the local and remote observations, along with the collected interviews, allows us to infer again some interesting results, concerning both the interaction blindness and other interaction-related aspects influenced by the presence of the avatar. As far as the interaction blindness is concerned, we had 20 out of 29 interviewed users who stated that the avatar was the main hint to understand the interactivity of the system and its touchless nature. This comes out in favor of the avatar, especially if we consider that a group of 14 users out of that 20 already knew gestural systems. Among the remaining nine users, six claimed that the main clue for understanding the touchless gestural interactivity was the presence of the Kinect, and three did not understand it at all. 25 users stated that they would have preferred to interact with a touchscreen.

Our observations confirm this quantitative result. For example, we noted down that:

A user was attracted by the avatar, and he approaches the display. He observed the screen (and, in particular, the avatar) for several seconds, being clearly curious but without interacting. He explained that he had understood the interactivity and its touchless nature thanks to the avatar, but he did not interact because of his shyness.

We also noted that the recognition of the interaction device, due for instance to previous experiences with Kinect-based applications, is another common hint to understand the gestural interactive capabilities. This is the case of the user interaction described in the following note:

At the beginning of this observation session, I noticed a user who was using the interface. He seemed very skilled, so when he finished I approached him and asked some opinions about his experience. He told me that he had previous experiences with gestural systems (he used one abroad in the past), and he immediately noted the presence of the Kinect. He [...] was definitely satisfied with the currently supported features.

Not all the users were able to understand the gestural capabilities, and some of them did not understand them correctly. In many cases, the users' prejudice about the supported interaction modality was clear: the display size probably naturally affords more touch-based interactions than touchless ones. Moreover, using gestures in public seems to be something not easily acceptable for all. In our notes, several excerpts demonstrate both this prejudice and the low acceptability of gestural interactions:

Two users interacted with the interface. The first one approached the display and tried to use it as a touchscreen. After some attempts, she figured out that the system was not responding, so I tell her that it was touchless. She did not know any similar systems and stated that touchscreens are, in her opinion, more practical. The second user interacted by means of gestures (but after having understood how to interact by observing the first one). After a brief interaction session, she explained her embarrassment in using mid-air gestures, and that she would prefer to use a more traditional touchscreen.

An interesting observation confirmed the several attempts of using the screen by means of touch interactions:

[...] I noticed a really curious fact. The backlight showed me several fingerprints on the screen surface, and this can only mean one thing: during these days, several users guessed that the display was able to detect touches, so they used it as a traditional touchscreen.

These last observations let us believe that in some cases the avatar only conveyed the interactive capability of the display, and not its touchless gestural nature.

A possible and partial explanation of such issues may be found in the screen size and the previous experiences of users in interacting with situated public displays. As stated before, such displays are most commonly equipped with touchscreens. It is plausible to believe that users' expectations about the supported interactivity are more oriented on touch-based ones than on other alternatives. Obviously, such issue should disappear if the system is deployed with bigger and/or not reachable displays, where touch-based interaction can be neither afforded nor supported.

It is also important to note that some users approached the display from the left or right almost in parallel with the screen surface, entering in the Kinect field-of-view being 10-20 centimeters away. At this distance, the avatar is not shown at all, due to the sensor capabilities.

Anyway, the avatar turned out to be the main visual element that attracted people towards the system, mainly due to its dynamic shape that moves along with recognized bodies, thus disrupting the interface steadiness.

6 CONCLUSIONS AND FUTURE WORKS

In this paper, we presented our study on people's behavior while interacting with a situated public display showing an avatar-based interface. Our main goal was to assess the usefulness of the system and the effectiveness of the avatar in conveying the interactivity of the display and its touchless gestural nature.

Here we summarize the findings gathered from the study described above, that should be useful for the design of avatar-based touchless gestural interfaces for public displays. We also attach a short discussion and motivation to each finding.

(1) *Using an avatar-based interface helps to convey the touchless interactivity, but may not be enough.*

We observed that the presence of an avatar is often considered helpful to communicate the interactivity of a system and its touchless nature. However, it should also be taken into account that, in some situations, users may be wrongly recognized by the software (or not recognized at all, thus resulting in the avatar is not displayed). Designers should thus consider using some trick to guarantee a correct recognition. For example, placing a marker on the floor to indicate the optimal interaction distance, or adding explicit instructions on the screen or next to the display.

(2) *Always take into account the actual sensorial capabilities of the devices used for gesture recognition.*

If the gesture recognition capabilities are based on the use of Kinect-like devices [26], then designers should take into account the critical approach paths. If users may arrive from sides, then the avatar may not be displayed at all because of the limitations of the device. Using multiple cameras, pointing at different directions, may instead allow for a more robust avatar visualization.

(3) *Leave the touch interaction together with the touchless one when designing for reachable screens (i.e. touchable and placed at eye-level). Opt out for touchless gestural interactions only when it is not possible to interact via touchscreens.*

According to our observations, situated public displays seem to afford mainly touch-based interactions. While several users enjoyed touchless interactions, observations have shown that some of them were more attracted by the novel way of interaction rather than its usefulness. Users appeared to feel not comfortable while interacting with gestures in public settings. Both interaction modalities could allow most users to interact as they expect, and impaired users to exploit their residual capabilities to interact as they can. The visual interactive elements of our interface and their layout allow for both type of interactions at the same time.

(4) *Try to make a touchless gestural interactive display accessible regardless of the number of users in front of it.*

Single-user interfaces could be enough in several situations. However, this does not mean that the interface may not work when more than one user tries to interact with it. Moreover, it should be clear which user is recognized as active among the detected ones.

As a overall result, in systems that afford well-known input methods, such as the touch one, the gestural input should be suitably included to enrich the interaction channels. Such multimodal input should increase the number of prospective users, extending the access to those who for some reasons cannot use the touch input. The gestural input plays a relevant social role, and the resulting *honeypot effect* [27] can be successfully exploited by the display and space owners to increment their revenues.

For the near future, we are planning to apply the aforementioned hints to improve the visual interface studied in this paper. In particular, currently we are working to implement all the suggested hints, since they may dramatically increase the number of interacting users and, as a consequence, the space owners revenues.

ACKNOWLEDGMENTS

This paper is partially funded on a research grant by the Italian Ministry of University and Research, namely project NEPTIS (Grant no. PON03PE_00214_3).

REFERENCES

[1] Fabrizio Milazzo, Vito Gentile, Giuseppe Vitello, Antonio Gentile, and Salvatore Sorce. Modular Middleware for Gestural Data and Devices Management. *Journal of Sensors*, 2017, 2017.

[2] Matthias Hank Haeusler. *Media Facades-History, Technology, Content*. Avedition, 2009.

[3] Sven Gehring and Alexander Wiethoff. Interaction with Media Façades. *Informatik-Spektrum*, 37(5):474–482, 2014.

[4] Meredith Ringel Morris, Andreea Danielescu, Steven Drucker, Danyel Fisher, Bongshin Lee, Jacob O Wobbrock, et al. Reducing Legacy Bias in Gesture Elicitation Studies. *Interactions*, 21(3):40–45, 2014.

[5] Andries Van Dam. Post-WIMP User Interfaces. *Communications of the ACM*, 40(2):63–67, 1997.

[6] Jörg Müller, Dennis Wilmsmann, Juliane Exeler, Markus Buzeck, Albrecht Schmidt, Tim Jay, and Antonio Krüger. Display Blindness: The Effect of Expectations on Attention towards Digital Signage. In *Proceedings of the 7th International*

Conference on Pervasive Computing, pages 1–8. Springer-Verlag, 2009.

[7] Vito Gentile, Alessio Malizia, Salvatore Sorce, and Antonio Gentile. Designing Touchless Gestural Interactions for Public Displays In-the-Wild. In *International Conference on Human-Computer Interaction*, pages 24–34. Springer, 2015.

[8] Vito Gentile, Mohamed Khamis, Salvatore Sorce, and Florian Alt. They are Looking at me! Understanding how Audience Presence Impacts on Public Display Users. In *Proceedings of the 6th International Symposium on Pervasive Displays (PerDis 2017)*. ACM, 2017.

[9] Microsoft. Human interface guidelines 2.0. http://download.microsoft.com/download/6/7/6/676611B4-1982-47A4-A42E-4CF84E1095A8/KinectHIG.2.0.pdf, 2013. Accessed: 2017-04-29.

[10] Paolo Cremonesi, Antonella Di Rienzo, Cristina Frà, Franca Garzotto, Luigi Oliveto, and Massimo Valla. Personalized Interaction on Large Displays: the StreetSmart Project Approach. In *Proceedings of the 2014 International Working Conference on Advanced Visual Interfaces*, pages 353–354. ACM, 2014.

[11] Vito Gentile, Salvatore Sorce, Giuseppe Russo, Dario Pirrone, and Antonio Gentile. A Multimodal Fruition Model for Graphical Contents in Ancient Books. In *Proceedings of the 17th International Conference on Computer Systems and Technologies 2016*, CompSysTech '16, pages 65–72, New York, NY, USA, 2016. ACM.

[12] Nigel Davies, Sarah Clinch, and Florian Alt. Pervasive displays: understanding the future of digital signage. *Synthesis Lectures on Mobile and Pervasive Computing*, 8(1):1–128, 2014.

[13] Elaine Huang, Anna Koster, and Jan Borchers. Overcoming assumptions and uncovering practices: When does the public really look at public displays? *Pervasive Computing*, pages 228–243, 2008.

[14] Brian J Fogg. Persuasive technology: using computers to change what we think and do. *Ubiquity*, 2002(December):5, 2002.

[15] John Hardy, Enrico Rukzio, and Nigel Davies. Real world responses to interactive gesture based public displays. In *Proceedings of the 10th International Conference on Mobile and Ubiquitous Multimedia*, MUM '11, pages 33–39, New York, NY, USA, 2011. ACM.

[16] Robert Walter, Gilles Bailly, and Jörg Müller. Strikeapose: Revealing mid-air gestures on public displays. In *Proceedings of the SIGCHI Conference on Human Factors in Computing Systems*, CHI '13, pages 841–850, New York, NY, USA, 2013. ACM.

[17] Timo Ojala, Vassilis Kostakos, Hannu Kukka, Tommi Heikkinen, Tomas Linden, Marko Jurmu, Simo Hosio, Fabio Kruger, and Daniele Zanni. Multipurpose interactive public displays in the wild: Three years later. *Computer*, 45(5):42–49, 2012.

[18] Till Ballendat, Nicolai Marquardt, and Saul Greenberg. Proxemic interaction: Designing for a proximity and orientation-aware environment. In *ACM International Conference on Interactive Tabletops and Surfaces*, ITS '10, pages 121–130, New York, NY, USA, 2010. ACM.

[19] Daniel Vogel and Ravin Balakrishnan. Interactive public ambient displays: Transitioning from implicit to explicit, public to personal, interaction with multiple users. In *Proceedings of the 17th Annual ACM Symposium on User Interface Software and Technology*, UIST '04, pages 137–146, New York, NY, USA, 2004. ACM.

[20] Jörg Müller, Florian Alt, Daniel Michelis, and Albrecht Schmidt. Requirements and design space for interactive public displays. In *Proceedings of the 18th ACM International Conference on Multimedia*, MM '10, pages 1285–1294, New York, NY, USA, 2010. ACM.

[21] Johannes Schönböck, Florian König, Gabriele Kotsis, Dominik Gruber, Emre Zaim, and Albrecht Schmidt. Mirrorboard-an interactive billboard. In *Mensch & Computer*, pages 217–226, 2008.

[22] Jörg Müller, Gilles Bailly, Thor Bossuyt, and Niklas Hillgren. Mirrortouch: combining touch and mid-air gestures for public displays. In *Proceedings of the 16th international conference on Human-computer interaction with mobile devices & services*, pages 319–328. ACM, 2014.

[23] Ivan Elhart, Federico Scacchi, Evangelos Niforatos, and Marc Langheinrich. Shadowtouch: A multi-user application selection interface for interactive public displays. In *Proceedings of the 4th International Symposium on Pervasive Displays*, PerDis '15, pages 209–216, New York, NY, USA, 2015. ACM.

[24] Robert Walter, Gilles Bailly, Nina Valkanova, and Jörg Müller. Cuenesics: using mid-air gestures to select items on interactive public displays. In *Proceedings of the 16th international conference on Human-computer interaction with mobile devices & services*, pages 299–308. ACM, 2014.

[25] Vito Gentile, Salvatore Sorce, Alessio Malizia, Dario Pirrello, and Antonio Gentile. Touchless interfaces for public displays: Can we deliver interface designers from introducing artificial push button gestures? In *Proceedings of the International Working Conference on Advanced Visual Interfaces*, AVI '16, pages 40–43, New York, NY, USA, 2016. ACM.

[26] Vito Gentile, Salvatore Sorce, Alessio Malizia, and Antonio Gentile. Gesture recognition using low-cost devices: Techniques, applications, perspectives [Riconoscimento di gesti mediante dispositivi a basso costo: Tecniche, applicazioni, prospettive]. *Mondo Digitale*, 15(63):161–169, 2016.

[27] Niels Wouters, John Downs, Mitchell Harrop, Travis Cox, Eduardo Oliveira, Sarah Webber, Frank Vetere, and Andrew Vande Moere. Uncovering the honeypot effect: How audiences engage with public interactive systems. In *Proceedings of the 2016 ACM Conference on Designing Interactive Systems*, DIS '16, pages 5–16, New York, NY, USA, 2016. ACM.

Maintaining Effective Collaboration: Supporting a Shared Library System Across 39 Academic Institutions

Ray Laura Henry
Orbis Cascade Alliance
2288 Oakmont Way
Eugene, OR 97401
rayhenry@orbiscascade.org

ABSTRACT

In 2012, the Orbis Cascade Alliance library consortium, currently made up of 39 post-secondary academic institutions in Oregon, Washington, and Idaho, began implementing a shared, cloud-based integrated library system (SILS): Ex Libris' Alma and Primo. As the process of onboarding institutions continued over a two-year period, efforts to support geographically disbursed collaborative work increased. This paper focuses on the tools and structures used by the consortium central staff to train, engage, and professionally develop staff at member libraries, who spend significant portions of their time doing the consortium's work in these shared applications. Successful approaches to relationship-building, accountability and recognition efforts, as well as how specific organizational structures and collaboration tools help address technical challenges are discussed.

CCS CONCEPTS

• **Social and professional topics** → **Computer supported cooperative work** • *Social and professional topics* → *Project and people management* • *Information systems* → *Collaborative and social computing systems and tools*

KEYWORDS

Collaboration; Knowledge Management; Human Factors.

1 INTRODUCTION

The Orbis Cascade Alliance is a consortium of 39 diverse academic institutions across Oregon, Washington, and Idaho [1].

SIGUCCS '17, October 1–4, 2017, Seattle, WA, USA
© 2017 Association for Computing Machinery.
ACM ISBN 978-1-4503-4919-2/17/10...$15.00
https://doi.org/10.1145/3123458.3123463

These include private liberal arts colleges, large research institutions, and community colleges, with student populations ranging from several hundred to tens of thousands. Some members have specialized medical or law libraries, and some have geographically dispersed campuses, among other differences. Regardless of type or size, each of the member institutions has an equal vote in the governance structure as members of the Alliance's Council, made up of the Deans and Directors of these libraries. The consortium's annual budget and strategic initiatives are approved by the full Council, and those initiatives are carried out by a small central consortial staff of ten, two of which currently work remotely. Originally housed at the University of Oregon, the consortium's Executive Director and central staff will complete a move to a stand-alone 501(c)(3) in 2017.

In 1993, one of the original motivations for forming the consortium now known as the Orbis Cascade Alliance was supporting sharing physical materials between member libraries. Any member's patrons are able to request materials from any other member, and have those materials (primarily books, CDs, and DVDs) sent via the consortium's courier service to their own institution. In the past, these requests went through a separate interlibrary loan system (ILL). As that service evolved, beginning in 2009, many consortium members adopted a "discovery layer" solution (OCLC's WorldCat Local), a cloud-based application where their local materials and other libraries' materials would be searchable in a single user interface. This positive evolutionary step was still far from seamless: to request materials from other libraries, patrons needed to have an additional, separate account in an Alliance-maintained application (Summit resource sharing).

While WorldCat Local improved the patron experience by enabling easier searching for and discovery of shared materials, the integrated library systems (ILSes), used to manage the entire lifecycle of library materials, were still siloed. Alliance libraries individually maintained their own ILSes. Some institutions maintained servers running the ILS applications locally, some had vendor-hosted options. Hardware and software versions could be divergent, and each institution managed their own relationships with those vendors for upgrades and support. What was seen as the next evolutionary step, moving to a shared ILS, was planned because "...the Alliance has concluded that improved services, cost-efficiency, and prospects for collaborative approaches to technical services may be facilitated by a move from more than thirty stand-alone Integrated Library Systems to a single consortial solution. More than simply replicating legacy systems in a shared or cloud-computing environment, we are issuing this RFI with an expectation of evaluating new options that exceed traditional ILS capabilities" [2]. A move to a cloud-based system was expected to eliminate local hardware maintenance responsibilities for library (or institution) IT staff, as well as the need for local negotiation of service contracts and other related time, personnel, and fiscal expenditures.

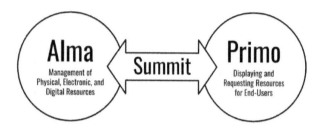

Figure 1: The relationships between the SILS applications, Alma and Primo, and the Alliance's Summit resource sharing service.

In 2012 the RFP process was completed, and Ex Libris' Alma (library resource management system) and Primo (resource search and discovery interface) products were selected as the consortium's shared integrated library system (SILS). During the implementation process, the consortium helped to steer Ex Libris' development of Alma's resource-sharing functionality. Two of the RFI's desired service improvements were reducing or removing barriers to resource sharing, and improving the discoverability of those shared resources for more than 275,000 end users. As one example of improvement in this area, after the completion of the 2-year migration and implementation process, as of 2014 Alliance library patrons no longer have to maintain a separate Summit resource sharing account for requesting consortially-owned materials; they can both discover and request materials from their institution and others in a single interface.

The support of Alma and Primo, the SILS applications, is cooperatively by multiple members of the central staff in partnership with member library staff, who in turn support hundreds of other staff at member libraries. Member library staff perform consortial work ranging from the routine to the complex, and with consortium-wide impacts that can affect the experiences of all end users directly. In one case, a configuration decision implemented by one of the Alliance's working groups allowed for significantly improved differentiation of e-books and print books in Primo compared to the default configuration. This change supported a better patron experience for every end user of the shared discovery layer across all member institutions.

The small number of SILS-focused central staff have increased support responsibilities, and do not have the capacity to fully support the SILS effort without the critical and ongoing significant contributions of member library staff. Thousands of hours of effort from hundreds of contributors annually ensure the daily business of the consortium's member libraries continues without interruption. And while the Alliance has depended on member contributions since its inception, the scope of the current work (as well as the possibilities of additional shared work that could be afforded by the SILS) requires not just a shared system, but a greater shared infrastructure of support that is both technology- and relationship-based.

2 SHARED SYSTEMS

2.1 Shared Technology

The Alliance's move to a shared ILS has had two impacts for local and central IT infrastructure. The first was identifying the level of intervention that should be performed by member library staff (including, but not limited to, systems department staff) to provide localized functionalities. While some configuration decisions must be made at a consortium-wide level (one example is resource sharing, where all partners must have SILS software settings uniformly applied to give patrons a consistent experience when they request physical materials), many diverse configuration approaches are possible with Primo and Alma. Expected user role granularity, which would allow precise control over which users could administer which pieces of Alma or Primo, and the ability to have consortium settings override local ones when desired, were not in place at the point of implementation. This could have allowed for more flexibility in deciding which partners were responsible for managing specific pieces of the software: either central management by Alliance staff, or distributed and localized management by member staff. Some of these configuration options are now possible but not yet implemented; others are still not available in the chosen products.

Additionally, it is challenging to achieve administration and support efficiencies in the Alliance's SILS without standardization. Though there were initial conversations about standardization at the Alliance's Council level before implementation began, including standardizing the Primo user interface across the consortium, or standardizing collaborative practices in the new SILS, no firm decisions came from that group in advance of implementation. This led to standardization efforts being set aside to prepare for the 2-year migration period. A re-evaluation of existing (pre-SILS) standardization efforts across program areas, including metadata for unique collections materials, records creation and maintenance, and user interfaces began in earnest in 2016.

The second impact to IT infrastructure is the challenge of doing collaborative work in a distributed environment across multiple institutions in a divergent information technology ecosystem. Across the member institutions, some are G Suite (previously called Google Apps) organizations, but their implementations vary widely in terms of what products are enabled, such as allowing Groups listserv subscriptions from outside the institution. Other institutions use Microsoft Office 365 or a similar browser-based/SAAS productivity suite. Web conferencing applications also vary, with some, but not all, institutions having their own facilities. The Alliance central office, in separating from the University of Oregon as its parent organization, also moved to G Suite as a cost-effective approach to productivity infrastructure, primarily using the Gmail, Docs, Drive, Calendar, Analytics, and Hangouts products.

For web conferencing, the Alliance's central office maintains a GoToMeeting/GoToWebinar subscription. Sessions may be as small as one-on-ones between central staff and member library staff, or as large as 100 attendees. Annually, the Alliance hosts more than 750 of these online meetings. Meetings can range from large training efforts, to panel interviews, to one-on-one calls to screen share and resolve issues. As one example, program areas, each representing one or more library functional areas (such as the author's program area of Discovery and Delivery), can opt to host regular "open calls," where anyone in the consortium who is interested in the topics presented is invited to attend. These calls focus on program area updates and work progress, as well as training issues or other shared informational needs, and use screen sharing and multiple presenters to engage and support member attendees. Open calls and other training calls are recorded for any members who can't attend those scheduled meetings, and are publicly available from the Alliance website.

In addition to other IT infrastructure and service provision, the Alliance central office maintains a public-facing website primarily updated by central office staff. The site is built in a hosted Content Management System (CMS), and has information about the organization, including SILS documentation. Some members are allowed limited access to updating pages, primarily supporting documentation efforts.

The work of the consortium relies heavily on technology-based collaboration, requiring tools that support productivity, online meetings, and information sharing. However, there are functional barriers to integrating this support system, as there is no consistently shared platform or tool across all consortium members. Member capacity for local IT support also varies widely. Some Alliance members have no library staff devoted to IT, and rely on institutional support, while others have multiple developers housed in the library. And while here is no consistent correlation between library IT resources and institution size, it is often smaller institutions that have the least in-house IT support. At the consortium office, 2.5 Alliance central staff FTE are in IT-focused positions, and they support a diverse portfolio that includes the SILS.

In this environment, technologies that support communication can also be barriers; it isn't practical to have a 50-attendee web conference with every participant's webcam enabled. Listserv emails can be too brief for accurate communication, or too long for effective communication of critical issues. Websites can become stale, lack useful search functionality, or not keep pace with organizational requirements. Shared documentation efforts can fail when future repository access isn't accounted for, and key materials can be permanently lost or made irretrievable because of asset ownership issues. However, even the best, most cohesive technology infrastructure cannot support this work alone. The Alliance's operational infrastructure must also be robust and have regular maintenance to successfully perform the required work of collaboratively maintaining the SILS.

2.2 Shared Operational Infrastructure

Perhaps the most significant barrier to performing cooperatively is understanding expectations. Shared work must be performed to a standard, and completed to a deadline. Typical academic committee work at post-secondary institutions can give some sense of what is required, but even with diverse stakeholders as participants, most committee members share a single institution, and so have broad-based institutional support structures to accomplish shared goals. At the Alliance, a different kind of collaborative infrastructure is required for the scope and reach of consortium-wide SILS-related work. Because the ratio of central staff to the end users of the SILS (both patrons and member library staff) is so small, the consortium employs Program Managers to lead program area efforts, and relies on these central staff members to bridge that infrastructure gap by empowering and supporting membership. These areas have small teams made up of staff from member libraries; these teams then form working groups to address specific goals.

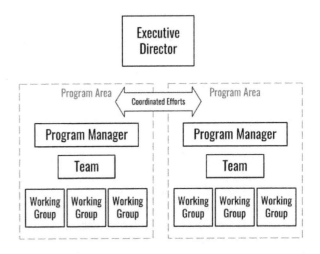

Figure 2: A schematic of the Alliance's collaborative structure

The current infrastructure (Figure 2) was created to support the initial processes of the SILS migration. The Executive Director worked with the Program Managers to anticipate what new roles might be needed, and to organize several of the program areas to more directly connect with the needs of the migration. Program Managers would then lead efforts in their program areas, including managing three key pieces of the collaboration infrastructure supporting the Alliance's Strategic

Agenda: forming teams, helping teams form working groups, and developing annual goals.

The Alliance's Strategic Agenda has three big-picture objectives: Work Smart, Design for Engagement, and Innovate to Transform [3]. In each program area, teams made up of member library staff are appointed to advance these objectives, and are charged with proposing specific initiatives they will undertake to do so each fiscal year. Teams can also create working groups (WGs) to put additional resources into an initiative. Those WGs either continue year-over-year, or have a more time-limited scope.

2.2.1 Teams. Alliance teams currently have staggered, two-year (12-month) appointments, to ensure stability, consistency, and knowledge transfer from team to team. A consortium-wide nomination process begins early in the calendar year, with the goal of forming teams before the end of the fiscal year in June. Potential team members can nominate themselves, as can their colleagues or supervisors. Once nominations close, the current team Chair and the Program Manager (PM) review the nominees, and look to create an effective group that has members from different institutions, representing multiple types of libraries, from geographically disparate locations (e.g., not all from the Portland/Vancouver metro area), and with varying levels of Alliance-wide experience. The Chair and PM work together to propose a slate of incoming members for the team. This proposal also identifies continuing members and their responsibilities, including choosing a proposed Chair-Elect.

Team Chair positions require a significant investment of time, even more than team members who are expected to put in between 2 and 7 hours weekly (and sometimes more) in support of Alliance work, which "is not seen as 'extra,' 'volunteer,' or 'as time allows,' but rather an important formal assignment" [4]. Because of that time commitment and its potential impingement on local responsibilities, and because the teams direct critical work in their program areas as led by their Chairs, the Alliance takes the team membership proposal process seriously. PMs work directly with the proposed Chairs-Elect to make sure they understand and agree to those requirements before putting their names forward.

Terms of service for team members begin and end at the close of the fiscal year, so the orientation of new members takes place during a relatively quiet part of the academic calendar. One challenge with this appointment is that important consortial work is accomplished over the summer, and the year-round service requirement is difficult or impossible for some institutions to accommodate, as their library faculty may be on 9-month contracts with summers off.

Once appointed, the teams are convened to review the next fiscal year's goals, as set by the previous team. These goals have also been shared widely after their approval by Council early in the calendar year, so incoming team members should have a clear sense of what they are agreeing to accomplish. Teams then work with their PMs to identify which additional Working Groups will need to be formed to support the team's goals.

2.2.2 Working Groups. Once a team identifies the need for a WG, they work with their PM to develop a charge for that group, then recruit their colleagues from across the consortium, in a process similar to team recruitment. The significant difference is that the team Chair and PM review the nominees, create the slate of members using essentially the same criteria as the team recruitment (with the addition of specific local functional responsibilities) and then appoint the WG members (and WG Chairs or Chairs-Elect) directly. As one example of specific functional responsibilities, a WG formed with the purpose of standardizing the Primo discovery user interface may require members to have administrative responsibilities in that area at their institution.

WG members' terms of service can vary. In Discovery and Delivery, which has a number of WGs whose work is an integral and ongoing part of the daily required work of the Alliance, members serve one-year terms, with "mutually agreeable" renewal possible for up to three years. This allows for capacity-building, as members can try out consortial work for a year, and see if they can balance those responsibilities effectively alongside their local ones. This also allows for expertise building, since in a two-year term, Chairs-Elect must always be "new" to the team, being willing to serve their first year as Chair-Elect, and their second as Chair. In contrast, an up to three-year WG term allows member library staff time to gain confidence in their abilities, and to more easily move from member to Chair-Elect to Chair. This also helps keep the same experienced members from being placed in leadership roles, leading to either perceptions of favoritism or experiences of burnout, neither of which is desirable for sustainability.

3 RELATIONSHIP BUILDING

3.1 Role of the Program Manager

This structure, where the Alliance Program Managers' portfolios are program areas, which have teams that in turn form working groups, has been a successful one for the Alliance. Three primary factors contribute to that success: availability of collaborative technologies, the engagement and willingness of member library staff, and the coordination efforts of Program Managers.

The Alliance's technology infrastructure and team/WG approach are relatively visible to consortium member library staff and leadership, especially in the area of SILS support. The Program Managers, however, play a critical (if perhaps less visible) role in successful collaboration. PMs have responsibilities to actively build membership capacity and develop member library staff, in addition to their own daily operational work. Without this attention to relationship-building, it becomes very difficult to successfully identify team members who will be able to work well together, to find and develop members who have leadership potential, or to keep members who are doing the work excited and focused on completing annual goals.

For the Alliance, the most heavily used technologies to support relationship-building across the consortium are not products like Slack or Trello: they are emails and phone calls.

While those may seem like the most outdated approaches to still be considered as technologies, their value is significant and far-reaching. In addition to a commitment to frequent, relevant, and transparent communication to Alliance stakeholders more broadly, Program Managers must also be successful at one-on-one communication. This is because often the ability to accomplish the Alliance's objectives is directly and positively impacted by having a person or people from member library staff in leadership roles who are committed and engaged.

To build effective leaders in membership, Program Managers need to identify member library staff who have potential and capacity, then actively support them and their colleagues. Given the geographical and institutional barriers Alliance member libraries face, a quick phone call to build support, give encouragement, or provide a time-sensitive update may be building cohesion and engagement one team or WG member at a time, but engaged and cohesive members help encourage other members to be a part of these larger initiatives.

Team and Working Group member support can take many avenues, but perhaps the most effective is combining useful and seamless collaborative technologies with access to the Program Manager as a resource. Program Managers help set reasonable expectations for member participants, including meeting deadlines and setting expectations. PMs also bring historical perspective to inform the team and WG goals, and can be sounding boards for their teams and WGs to explore potential new initiatives.

Even before members interact with PMs on teams or WGs, Program Managers can build their communities by responding quickly to requests for information; by monitoring and encouraging listserv contributions; by recruiting members to share their experiences with each other; and by being a useful conduit of information from the vendor to members.

Because of the large amount of work to be accomplished in any given fiscal year, it can be tempting for PMs to treat member library staff in teams or WGs like direct reports, recruiting for specific expertise and providing job-like assignments. However, that approach makes it harder to build a sustainable leadership capacity, and also makes working at the consortium level less desirable for many member library staff. These staff already have local responsibilities that help keep these shared systems operational as part of their jobs, so a more functional approach is not always seen as useful for developing professionally.

Adding this additional level of responsibility needs to come with opportunities for additional professional growth and development. Even so, Program Managers have responsibilities to their team and WG members to support them as any personnel manager would, by being clear about what effort and commitment is required, and by giving members timely and honest performance feedback. This includes appropriate recognition of members' efforts, both as a part of the ongoing collaboration, and as members end their terms of service on teams or Working Groups. Recognition can come in many forms, but should accurately and enthusiastically reflect the contributions made. Some of the ways the Alliance has formally recognized members' contributions include recognizing team members at consortium-wide annual meetings, and honoring outstanding contributors with awards. These efforts, however, shouldn't take the place of ongoing and regular recognition and encouragement from the Program Managers over the course of the year. Additionally, modeling that behavior on an ongoing basis encourages team and WG members to do the same for their colleagues.

4   USE CASE: ALMA RELEASE TESTING

Setting aside the significant challenges of migrating (at the time) 37 libraries to Primo and Alma, and the extraordinary investment of time and resources brought to bear on that project, effective SILS maintenance continues to require collaborative efforts. While some of the structures put in place over that period are still used today, the consortium continues to evolve to meet current needs effectively. In the pre-SILS era, most Alliance libraries would typically be able to schedule ILS updates when it was most convenient for them. As long as the resource sharing applications worked, library system administrators had a great deal of flexibility in deciding when to upgrade to a newer release. Administrators could upgrade sandbox environments, then take their time to thoroughly test and configure a given release or service pack before applying it in production.

In contrast, Ex Libris' Alma is a product with an Agile development model, with new releases coming out monthly. Releases go first to customers' sandbox environments for review and testing, then are moved to production two weeks later. This review and testing window was previously one week long, but was extended to two weeks in 2017 at the request of the customer base. In addition to the bug fixes typically associated with such a frequent schedule, releases can also contain significant changes to existing functionality, including new functionality. Testing and documenting Alma releases with a smaller core group of dedicated testers, rather than duplicating efforts at every Alliance library, is a significant efficiency for managing this part of the SILS. Still, much of this testing can't be done by central staff. Even with unlimited time for testing and access to every environment, central staff do not operate a library and cannot usefully test workflows with the same accuracy and attention that member library staff bring.

There are complexities to the Alliance's testing environments, as well as the supporting technology and organizational structures, that also make the collaborative testing process challenging. In 2015, two working groups were created with testing as their charge: the cross-functional Sandbox Testing Working Group (STWG), and Discovery and Delivery's Primo Release Testing Working Group (PRTWG). In addition, a Summit working group performed resource sharing testing between members of the working group. The Primo and Summit groups were responsible for reviewing release notes, performing hands-on testing to ensure no functional regressions and to document new functions. Those two groups would then share their results with Alliance member library staff in their functional areas across the consortium.

These testing efforts required coordination and collaboration, and the Summit and Primo WGs had different approaches. The Summit WG was established with additional responsibilities beyond testing, and had regular web-based meetings, a listserv for WG members only, and a Chair who was also a member of the Discovery and Delivery Team. Like other Working Groups in the Discovery and Delivery program area, this group saw their Program Manager leave mid-year, with the position unfilled for six months. Even without that support, the eight-member WG kept collaborative efforts going and regularly shared information back out to Alliance stakeholders about releases and other consortial work. Web meetings were hosted by other Alliance staff, and documentation (including meeting agendas and minutes) was developed and shared in the Alliance's Google Drive. WG members coordinated work outside of meetings on the listserv, by direct email, or by phone for issues with time-sensitivity, such as getting testing goals accomplished in the original one-week window before the move to production. This included reaching out to other Alliance central staff as needed, submitting support issues to the vendor for resolution, and testing end-to-end workflows with resource sharing partners who also had one of the Alliance's six institutional Alma premium sandboxes, as resource sharing can't be usefully tested in Ex Libris' standard sandbox environment [5].

The Primo Release Testing Working Group, in contrast, did all of their work over a group (not listserv) email, with occasional phone calls as necessary between testers. As a part of the Discovery and Delivery program area, they were also without Program Manager support. Like the Summit WG, they also reviewed release notes, distributed information of specific interest to Alliance libraries, performed testing, submitted issues to vendors, shared results, and reached out to Alliance central staff as needed.

These Working Groups and this testing work could not continue to be effective without the support of a Program Manager, whose role is to escalate critical issues with the vendor, to keep the WG members supported and engaged as part of preventing burnout, and to keep the WGs connected to the other work happening across the consortium that may impact them. Still, this persistence and completion of Alliance goals without that PM support is a clear indicator that the essential work of collaboration doesn't reside in either central staff or member library staff alone, and that the core part of that collaborative work is done by member library staff.

5　NEXT STEPS

After reviewing the Alliance's program areas in 2016, the Executive Director and the Program Managers recommended a realignment and an additional full-time position in recognition of the fact that more of the consortium's shared work must have central staff support. Additionally, central staff have recognized deficits in the existing shared technology infrastructure, and have explored using Ryver (a free team communication alternative to the more well-known Slack) as a possible solution. A shared environment used for communication and knowledge management could present fewer barriers to collaboration, including providing easier access for member participants and simpler capturing of the decision-making processes and documentation generated by Teams and WGs.

Additionally, team recruitment in 2017 has started earlier in the calendar year, so that teams can be formed and move on to WG creation and recruitment at the same time across all program areas. This will allow the most flexibility and visibility of opportunities for members considering nominating themselves, as WGs will post their charges and recruit for members at the same time, rather than throughout the fiscal year.

Finally, the Alliance's website, a source for shared documentation, best practices, and policies readily available across the consortium, is also under review, with Atlassian's Confluence product as the initial choice for developing a small-scale pilot. Goals for the proof-of-concept implementation are: improving organization and structure, implementing a better search functionality, and providing additional member access for content creation.

6　CONCLUSIONS

Collaborative technologies, while providing a supportive infrastructure, are not the only (or even the core piece) of successful collaborations at the Alliance. In a geographically distributed environment composed of diverse institutions, providing a good operational infrastructure, paired with an organizational commitment to building leadership capacity, is key to leveraging and multiplying the output from a small central staff. Doing so helps remove barriers to collaboration, and supports the staff and leadership of the consortiums' member libraries to keep achieving great things together.

REFERENCES

[1]　Orbis Cascade Alliance. Retrieved May 20, 2017 from https://www.orbiscascade.org/member/.

[2]　Orbis Cascade Alliance. 2011. Request for Information: Consortial Library Management Service. Retrieved May 20, 2017 from https://www.orbiscascade.org/file_viewer.php?id=683.

[3]　Orbis Cascade Alliance. Strategic Agenda. Retrieved May 20, 2017 from https://www.orbiscascade.org/strategic-agenda

[4]　Orbis Cascade Alliance. Team Overview. Retrieved May 20, 2017 from https://www.orbiscascade.org/team-overview/

[5]　Ex Libris. Alma Sandbox Environments. Retrieved May 20, 2017 from https://knowledge.exlibrisgroup.com/Alma/Product_Documentation/ Alma_Online_Help_(English)/ Getting_Started/040Alma_Sandbox_Environments

A Leadership Framework

Adam Buchwald
Lewis & Clark College
0615 SW Palatine Hill Road
Portland, Oregon 97219
buchwald@lclark.edu

Kelly Wainwright
Lewis & Clark College
0615 SW Palatine Hill Road
Portland, Oregon 97219
kelly@lclark.edu

ABSTRACT

Over the last year, Lewis & Clark's Information Technology has implemented a new leadership framework based on a waterfall of vision, mission, objectives and measureable milestones. The goals, are one of three pillars that constitute the work done by our division—Projects, Objectives and "Keeping the Lights On." By having clear objectives developed by each team, expectations are clearly expressed and negotiated at the beginning of each quarter and graded at the end of each quarter.

Having this framework in place better aligns the mission and objectives of our team with those of the institution. It has also provided each group with focus, and allows the IT leadership team a better understanding of what each group is working on and illustrates where collaborations could be beneficial. When desired, we are now able to produce a list of what IT added as value through measurable, quarterly objectives from each division and how they all are tied to an institutional strategy.

This paper will discuss how our IT Framework provides structure for the work we do in our department and detail the benefits and challenges in adhering to such a framework.

CCS CONCEPTS

CCS ~ Social and professional topics ~ Professional topics ~ Management of computing and information systems ~ Project and people management.

KEYWORDS

Leadership Framework, Mission, Objectives, Professional Development.

1 INTRODUCTION

Lewis & Clark College is a small, liberal arts college located approximately six miles outside of downtown Portland, Oregon. Our student body consists of close to 2000 undergraduates, 800 law students and nearly 1000 graduate students, primarily in education and counseling. Our Information Technology department consists of twenty-six individuals.

In 2013, Information Technology decided the time had come to reorganize to better align our services with the needs of the campus. This include the establishment of a centralized Service Desk and a departmental project management process, .After the reorganization, we ended with six departments: the Service Desk and Educational Technology (both part of Client Engagement), Infrastructure, Academic Operations, Institutional Operations and Web Ops (all under the Infrastructure umbrella), Information Systems, Security and Project Management.

2 The Problem

As the IT department reorganized the end result needed to position us to become true strategic partners with the institution, moving away from a pure service and infrastructure mentality. In order to meet this challenge we saw a need to become more operationally efficient and to be more strategic including a focus on that which is important to the institution. Not only would we need to be able to demonstrate this to others, we needed a way to ensure we continually had a cycle of planning, engagement and execution that would allow this to be repeatable over the years and nimble enough to allow changing priorities.

Issues holding us back included basic things like improving communication within the borders of IT itself. As technologies evolved and became more complex we found multiple areas of expertise were needed to solve problems and yet we were divided up as five distinct and siloed areas within IT - each with their own methods for communication and prioritization. This often broke down, creating frustrations both within and outside IT and it seemed to take a long time for issues to be resolved, if they ever were.

Another issue was the relevance and strategic value of Information Technology. Historically IT operated as a service bureau, offering to fix and install as well as work through designated projects as funds and demand required. Like many other IT shops, we had our own IT Strategic Plan providing our own vision of the next five years. We needed to develop a way to better align the goals and objectives of IT with those of the institution.

SIGUCCS '17, October 1–4, 2017, Seattle, WA, USA
© 2017 Copyright is held by the owner/author(s). Publication rights licensed to ACM.
ACM 978-1-4503-4919-2/17/10...$15.00
https://doi.org/10.1145/3123458.3123482

3   The Solution

Through the reorganization, we altered the model to become advisors to the business units providing direction and input on how to solve problems rather than simply fixing things when broken. To ensure repeatability we abandoned our older planning processes and crafted a new vision and strategy that aligned with the Core Themes, Mission, and Strategic Plan for Lewis & Clark. We thought through our yearly cycles, included budgetary and capital request timelines, decided on the purpose of each meeting we hold and started to document the entire process. In the end, we came up with what we call "the IT Framework" to help us continually iterate through a process with these higher-level goals in mind while tracking and measuring our outcomes along the way.

The primary goal of the IT Framework was to re-align our resources appropriately in an ongoing, continuous manner. Before it could be discussed, we had to have a few fundamental changes within the department to provide the management of various pressures. During the reorganization we introduced a one-stop Service Desk to provide a single point of contact for communication outside of IT. At the same time we created a new Project Management Office to handle outside requests that required a significant portion of IT time or technology. Together, this represents all of the priorities that come from outside of IT and in general represents what our constituents feel is needed. While these two entities handled the 'intake' for all the problems the institution was throwing at IT, we still had a void of all the great ideas within IT to improve the institution and help move us forward. Being in the middle of all the conversations, IT often has insight that can prove invaluable if provided the right opportunity. If implemented effectively, everyone would have a voice for input up, down and throughout the organization, we would all know what projects divisions within IT were working on, and these projects could align directly with the priorities of the institution.

If successful, the framework would also help IT staff understand how to divide their available time across three categories: Support, Projects, and IT-created Objectives. These were the three pillars of our overall concept of supporting the institution. Inside those categories we found places for routine activities, professional development, and working with committees and outside groups. The idea was that in short, if you couldn't fit it into one of the three categories, you shouldn't spend time on it. It also aligned the recurring meetings within IT to support communication, planning and decision-making. By the end, everything a staff member does during the course of any given day, week or month should fit within the framework or it wasn't relevant for them to work on. When combined with our review process, one can easily see how these become powerful tools for both planning and evaluation.

Lastly, as mentioned we included a cycle of yearly and quarterly planning to support our own operational objectives and aligned those directly with the College's Strategic Plan. As the College is about to embark on year one of a new accreditation cycle and re-define some of those higher level strategies for the institution, we are excited to immediately

support and report back on our progress in meeting those goals. Given the complex and diverse roles and duties within IT, we will end up as a model for how other departments can measure their success in supporting that vision.

4   The Framework

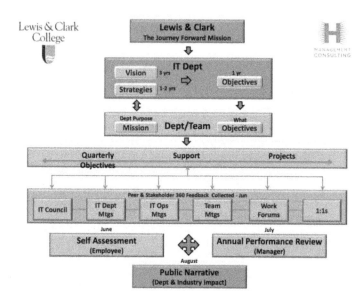

Figure 1: The Framework Diagram ©Lewis & Clark College

4.1 The College's Mission - The Journey Forward

The pinnacle of the framework is the Lewis & Clark strategic plan. The most current form of this was created in 2013 and titled "The Journey Forward." According to L&C's former president Barry Glassner, the plan "lays out the strategic priorities we will pursue for Lewis & Clark today, in 2020, and beyond. It also identifies where we will need to develop our resources going forward and why. And it declares our resolve to take advantage of the changing landscape in higher education to invest in the future, confident that by planning wisely now we will flourish then."

Built by cross-organizational teams across the college, The Journey Forward lays out three priorities for the institution:

- Be an institution to which people across the nation and globe look for distinctive quality in higher education.
- Educate people for life and leadership in an interdependent global and environmental context.
- Make Lewis & Clark known to an ever-growing circle of prospective students and their families and supporters.

In creating the vision for the IT Department, we needed it to align with this mission—we needed to support the direction in which the College was moving.

4.2 IT Department

In creating a vision for IT, we crafted our own subset of language to guide us in the future. IT's vision represents a commitment to support the institution and maintain the core values of Lewis & Clark. Next, we came up with strategies that aligned with the priorities in"The Journey Forward", but also provided some guide rails for IT to follow for the next few years. The point was to select the most important strategies, work through those, and re-evaluate to see if priorities had shifted. Next we identified high level, overarching, operational objectives that allow each area within IT to craft their own supporting objectives and start to measure progress. This was the area where IT was allowed to add our own expertise and help drive the institution forward. It also allowed for better synchronization within IT, enabling us to see where we overlap and how to support each other to allow success. We also used these to better engage the individual IT business units and include their concerns and issues in our planning and resource allocation over the course of a cycle.

Lastly, each department was provided motivation to accomplish objectives on time. Yearly we plan to publish a public narrative of IT department successes and demonstrate to the institution our concrete value. IT Directors are required to incorporate the scoring of quarterly objectives as part of their own annual review process—success or failure to meet our own expectations has now become an important matter!

The IT Departmental vision and objectives developed for our first year included the following:

Vision: To be technology professionals dedicated to enrich the academic experience and support the community of scholars in pursuit of the traditions of the liberal arts.

Objectives:
- Introduce and improve areas for IT governance and engagement while addressing future pressures.
- Identify and address IT processes that should be improved to meet maturity level 2 as identified by the Gartner Maturity Level IT Score Assessment – represented by repeatable, documented processes that are automated where possible and understood by the community.
- Target areas where technology and processes serve as the enabler towards delivering a particular institutional experience in support of those engaged in learning, teaching, research or creative inquiry. If possible, open new pathways for seeking and creating knowledge in an increasingly digital and diverse interdependent world.
- As Information Technology professionals we continually grow within our discipline by developing new abilities and gaining industry insight to maximize our institutional value.

4.3 Individual Departments

Each of the IT departments develops individual purpose and annual objectives to support the IT Vision. These objectives identify areas where that department will dedicate time in order to move the organization forward.

Every departmental objective has a quarterly "as measurable by", or AMB, target. These milestones keep the work progressing. As such, they have become both the motivation to achieve the objectives as we know that they are the piece for which we are each being held accountable. The AMB is the piece each director will use to measure success each quarter.

Over time, we have become much more effective at creating AMBs that are specific and achievable. For example, an early AMB might have stated "Improve customer satisfaction" or "Develop enterprise application SLA pages in the Service Portfolio." These were difficult to quantify. Clearer AMBs would say "Improve level of satisfaction of clients from 93% to 94%" or "Develop a minimum of three enterprise application SLA pages in the Service Portfolio." Making the AMB quantifiable is instrumental in measuring success.

4.4 Types of Work

As mentioned above, with the addition of objectives, each employee's work was classified into the three pillars: Objectives, Support, and Projects.

Objectives consist of the work that Information Technology deems to be important to promote the mission of the college and to promote the maturity of our organization.

The support category is where we keep the IT "lights on". This is where we put out fires, take care of break/fix/repair tickets, consult with faculty and staff, handle system maintenance, and manage all the responsibilities required as an Information Technology department. Many believe that Information Technology has become a utility, and that is no more true than in this category.

Finally, we have the projects which are the items the College community, through the IT Governance Council, has prioritized. The IT Governance Council serves as the ultimate arbiter of resource allocation and departmental prioritization for all institutional technology projects. Projects are defined as a temporary organization of labor to produce one or more deliverables, requiring more than ten hours of planning and implementation, evaluated for strategic alignment, scheduled to occur at a given time, and impacting one or more groups of people.

Depending on the individual and their role in Information Technology, the amount of time spent working in each pillar of work will vary. A Service Desk professional will spend much more time in the Support category and much less time in Projects, while a system administrator may spend much time in Objectives, some time in Projects and little time in Support.

4.5 Meeting Alignment

The next portion of the IT Framework was the layer of communication to allow a clean flow of information both up and down the IT organization. While we established the Framework, we also defined the ongoing meetings that would be needed to support our efforts as well as the purpose of those meetings and who should attend. We needed the Directors to have ongoing fluid conversations about conflicts, obstacles, and successes as we worked through these overlapping objectives. At the manager level, we needed our operations to not only hear about priorities, but to add their first hand experience to the endeavor. Lastly, we needed other meetings to engage with offices outside of IT so we may better understand the issues in each functional area around the institution. Being a smaller school we tend to have the same people in the room for different meetings. Having defined roles assisted in tracking what was at hand to resolve and, more importantly, other forums where an issue could better be addressed.

Meetings retained in the new structure include our individual departmental meetings, IT Department (staff) meetings, and 1:1 meetings between employees and supervisors. Our IT Council (leadership) meeting was also retained, but now includes departmental objective reviews every other week. Added was the IT Core Operations Sync Meeting, where all functional team leaders align operational goals and provide updates.

Guidelines were also provided for meeting lengths, frequency and the structure of a purposeful meeting. This provided for consistency in meetings across the department. While the quality of meetings has improved, this integral mode of communication continues to require fine-tuning.

5 Implementation

To implement this framework we adopted the analogy of being in a fixed position and painting a moving train in front of you. Each time the train goes by you get a chance to put more paint on it, however you don't expect completion until the train has passed by multiple times. In short, we didn't let perfection get in the way of progress, and slowly crafted the language, documentation, and process to support us rolling out our framework. In lieu of this thinking, we broke the framework into sections and followed a similar pattern in addressing each portion. First, we came up with something close to what we envisioned, and used it for a few cycles to ensure it worked as expected. We then explored ways to systematically make modifications over time.

For example, our first set of IT Strategies and IT Objectives were dictated by the CIO. They were based on current trends and information, but were established purely as a place to start and craft individual objectives to support. We used those IT Objectives for a complete cycle and, along the way, crafted a process to seed, evaluate, and determine the following year's IT Objectives. Now we have a yearly process cycle where front-line staff provides input on objectives, which is then evaluated and massaged by IT Directors and culminates in a yearly objective with measurables.

Subsequent years we followed the same process, starting at the top and working our way down. At the top were larger, big picture questions that needed concrete definitions. We scheduled an all-day strategy planning retreat to outline the first year's

vision, strategies and objectives for IT as a whole. Each Director then crafted supporting Objectives under their umbrella and broke them down into quarterly measurables. With the top portion of the Framework defined, we could start to work underneath those priorities.

We continue this iterative process today. We have improved each cycle, making small tweaks to improve. Recently, we discovered the IT Framework was not fully understood by our front-line staff, who often aren't in planning or even operational meetings. In response, we are moving our quarterly presentations on ongoing Objectives to another meeting forum where we can invite more than IT Directors to hear about our plans, pains, and successes. Again and again, we have found a need to be receptive to changes as we utilize this framework, however those changes should always continue to improve.

6 Adjustments

As with any living plan involving many individuals, this is an iterative process. We continue to fine-tune and find areas for improvement within the Framework as we mature as a department.

6.1 Objectives Review

One of the first major tweaks that we made was to adjust the Objectives Review done by each director once a quarter during the IT Council meeting. Originally, this time allowed each director to review what they had identified as their annual objectives and that quarter's AMBs, allowing for further discussion of the AMBs as warranted. This review, however, seemed to be very much rehashing a list of objectives already discussed and didn't achieve the desired goal of identifying obstacles and promoting collaboration between departments. After the first cycle, we implemented a new template for the objectives reviews. With this new template, not only do we identify problems with objectives that may hinder us from achieving an AMB, we also discuss industry trends in our area, share team accomplishments, and provide an opportunity to request help from our colleagues. This allows us the opportunity to learn more about a department both including and beyond objectives.

6.2 Strategic Planning Cycle

With this Framework, it seemed as though deadlines and deliverables were often surprising us. Although based on our fiscal year, with noses to grindstones, it was easy for the quarter ends and beginnings to sneak up on us. Our solution: develop the annual cycle.

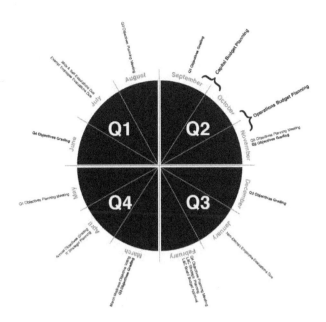

Figure 2: IT Strategic Planning Cycle ©Lewis & Clark College

This illustration allows us to know where we stand at any given moment in the cycle of the plan. It also allowed us to better align our cycle with the academic year and the operations of the College.

We are currently considering the possibility of changing this cycle from quarters to trimesters. Staff have identified that quarters do not fit well with how we look at our work, which aligns to Fall Semester, Spring Semester and Summer. The hope is that by changing to trimesters, we will better align with the natural rhythm of the College and our work.

6.3 March Madness

One criticism we heard from our staff was that they did not feel any ownership or connection with the objectives, which were seen as top down directives. In response, we developed a process "March Madness" due to it happening in March. The goal was to include all IT staff in the objective planning process in the hopes of promoting better understanding and ownership of the process.

The first step was asking all IT staff to contribute ideas to the prompt, "What do you believe Information Technology should be working on in the upcoming year with an eye to the role of technology in Higher Education now and in the future?" Any individual contributing five or more serious ideas was given a small Amazon gift card. Ideas were gathered on a Google Doc and identified by the contributor's initials. The IT Council reviewed all the submissions, consolidated similar ones, and re-wrote others that were considered too specific to be a worthwhile objective.

We then asked the IT staff to help us prioritize the submissions with dots. Each individual was given a number of dots they could spread out over many ideas or use to vote up a few ideas. Because each person had a different color of dots, this allowed us to see which ideas had widespread support and which ideas were supported by a single, passionate individual. The top ideas were then integrated into the IT Council's planning process for the subsequent year's objectives.

We will need to review this process again moving forward because there was some unintentional misunderstanding between the proposed intention and the perceived intention—some IT staff expected there to be a clear winner to be implemented instead of helping leadership identify themes and priorities.

7 Moving Forward/Conclusion

As indicated, this Framework is designed to be an ongoing process that continually helps align our IT resources with the overall Mission of the institution. While not perfect, remember we are still painting boxcars on a moving train. We have found just having a framework as a basis for discussion is helpful. As we go through another cycle of accreditation, our Framework can be used as an example for other departments on how to articulate and measure their support of our core values. It has become a base model for us to now use and refine over time, which hopefully allows us to more efficiently to allocate our IT resources.

Lastly, we feel this framework is important for the long-term survival of our institution. Technology is evolving rapidly and becoming ubiquitous in Higher Education if not the world. As we look into the future, every decision around the institution will involve some digital component. We are not a technical institution, but our expertise will be invaluable as areas are forced to incorporate IT decision-making and evaluation in their strategic planning. If we are to support those pending needs we need to be far more efficient in how we allocate our time and resources. This framework helps us prepare better for that scenario which, in turn, prepares us to succeed.

Taking the Guesswork out of Lab Management

Kenneth Drake-Sargent
Student Technology Specialist
70 Washington Square South
New York, NY 10012
krs4@nyu.edu

Michael Hyde
LabStats
255 B Street Suite 201
Idaho Falls, ID 83402
mike@labstats.com

Dustin Jones
LabStats
255 B Street Suite 201
Idaho Falls, ID 83402
dustin@labstats.com

Brandon Bybee
LabStats
255 B Street Suite 201
Idaho Falls, ID 83402
brandon@labstats.com

ABSTRACT

Managing computer labs and providing effective and efficient computer services to students requires constant decision-making. Lab managers must determine which applications to purchase and include on station images, and where hardware resources should be placed to maximize utilization. The availability of resources must then be effectively communicated to students for resources to be fully utilized. When decisions are based on data, lab managers can be confident that false assumptions are not being made.

CCS CONCEPTS

• **Information Systems → Information Systems Applications → Decision support systems → Data analytics**

KEYWORDS

Computer Lab Usage Tracking; Lab Statistics; Lab Monitoring

1 INTRODUCTION

Computer lab space is expensive and lab managers cannot afford to waste it on underutilized stations. Station images can become unmanageable and lab managers must decide which applications to exclude. Locating available hardware can be difficult for students and faculty, so lab managers need a way to help them quickly and easily identify open computers. Gathering real-time usage data is the most effective way to solve these problems and eliminate the guesswork associated with managing computer labs.

Truly useful statistics provide data that is specific and digestible. Specific, in the sense that it needs to be viewable on an individual computer station, application, and user level. And digestible, so that the data can be used by managers and students to remove the guesswork.

2 DATA COLLECTION

There are different approaches to collecting usage data, but at New York University (NYU), software is used to collect and report on usage data. Accuracy increases and availability is improved when sophisticated software is used instead of tracking usage manually. Taking manual headcounts as students use computers is inefficient and inaccurate. Valuable staff time is consumed during collection and the resulting data is prone to errors and limitations that prevent it from being a true representation of usage. More importantly, it is not feasible to gather certain data manually, like which applications are being used and the duration of their use. Data collection and reporting software also offers easy analysis of the data; it automatically aggregates and segments the data, so it is digestible and meaningful.

Monitoring software needs to answer the questions that lab managers have. Any application used to gather data should be FERPA compliant and only track appropriate user login and application data. The software should work with a variety of operating systems and clients—macOS and Windows; virtual and physical clients.

3 APPLICATION TRACKING

Knowing which applications are being used and how often can be a guessing game, which leads to unnecessary strain on an already limited budget. Tracking the use of every local application or website visited often results in excessive information. Only tracking applications and websites that result in meaningful data helps cultivate digestible insights. For example, tracking many of an operating system's default applications would only clutter the data that is being collected.

Tracking which expensive applications students are using might only show a portion of the full picture. For example, what if a student opens Adobe Photoshop, minimizes the window, and then proceeds to open and use Microsoft Paint? Even though the application was opened, it does not mean that it is being used. It is important to clarify applications that are actively used. Although at first, it might not seem worthwhile to track certain applications, identifying and tracking similar applications can reveal interesting comparisons.

3.1 Application Licenses

Usage data allows identification of software licenses that are being paid for each year but are not being used. This is crucial when imaging stations. Application licenses can be reallocated to different machines or labs where they are more likely to be fully utilized. The data shows which software is used and to what degree and has allowed NYU to negotiate better licensing agreements—more in line with the actual application use. Most schools invest heavily in expensive application packages; application usage data can help when it comes to negotiating renewal prices, and possibly investing money elsewhere. Whether buying licenses on a per-station basis or a campus-wide agreement, this information is key to decision-making. Tracking if each license is being used might give an inaccurate picture of application usage. For example, if at any given time only about 10% of AutoCAD licenses are being used, the number of individual licenses could be drastically lowered or a lower campus-wide price based on the actual usage trends could be negotiated. This problem can be further eliminated by effectively communicating where students can access the application and when the station is available for use.

3.2 Reduce Station Images

Application data can also be beneficial when identifying which users and labs use these applications the most. This data has allowed NYU to reduce its base image and to provide the applications that the students really need. Recently, they also started reviewing monthly metrics on application launches to determine whether software should be removed from the images. NYU images twice a year, so based on the previous usage they can determine if an application should remain available or be removed. It is part of their yearly workflow to improve the software offerings for students in their labs.

Application and login information arranged by station has also helped NYU identify which applications get used versus what they think they need to include on an image. This has allowed them to reduce the base image.

After they image a station or perform a hardware installation they ensure that the stations are handling any changes that were made. This imaging cycle happens twice a year; the rest of the year, they run weekly reports to manage inventory.

Students may be using an online version of a specific software that has been installed. If students are using Microsoft Word Online, for example, then it might make sense to think about removing the Microsoft Word application from the station image.

Tracking Web applications can also add more insight. For example, it might be useful to see how many students prefer to use Google's free G Suite over Microsoft Office. More students might prefer Google's G Suite, in which case it might be best to consider removing Microsoft Office from the station image or limiting the number of licenses purchased.

4 HARDWARE ALLOCATION

Computer lab monitoring shows answers to important questions—which machines are being used and how often, which physical layout is best, and if more or fewer seats are needed in specific labs.

4.1 Station Utilization

NYU often needs to find out the actual usage of stations in a computer lab; this information is useful for driving traffic to underutilized labs or ensuring that stations are operating as expected. They collect individual station usage data to determine when the station is powered on, when there are students actively logged in, and which applications are being used on that station.

There are many reasons why a station might not be used; it might be based on where the machine is physically located, which operating system is installed on it, whether it is a desktop or a laptop, or what the perception of the machine's availability is. When this information is known, the reason for underutilization is understood. NYU collects data on stations and individual computer labs and further subdivides this information into smaller groups based on criteria they are interested in tracking. For example, tracking macOS vs Windows, hardware additions (scanner, more RAM, etc.), and the station's physical location might provide value for different organizations. They segment tracking data to answer many specific questions. This allows them to know with certainty whether stations with Adobe Creative Cloud are used more than stations with Microsoft Office. Stockpiling data helps to curb the uncertainty of the future of computer labs and their impact. Having the flexibility to gather data on anything deemed important helps lab managers prepare to make the correct decisions.

For example, real-time data, when added to the physical layout of a computer lab can help to identify problems in computer utilization due to lab space/setup limitations. This information has helped NYU better understand underutilized machines and gives them ways to help guide more traffic to those machines. Some available options are to provide better software on those machines or put them closer to the windows. Real data tells a story and gives vital information that can help in making important decisions.

4.2 Web Applications

Tracking specific websites that are visited can also add beneficial data. Students may only access computer labs just to surf the web. Nothing is more frustrating than having a lab that is stocked with expensive hardware and software and seeing that students are using it to watch YouTube or browse Facebook. Website visit data can be valuable when learning how to direct students who are looking to just use the internet or closing certain labs during certain hours. Labs that are only used to browse the internet might have applications that can be removed. They may also be put on a slower track for hardware upgrades. All the traditional computers in a lab might be switched out for less expensive Chromebooks or lab usage rules might need to be amended to ensure hardware resources are available to students that can fully utilize them.

4.3 Physical Layout and Applications

Data showcasing station and application usage identifies how frequently stations and applications are being used. This data has helped NYU determine the use of software and machines in labs and has enabled them to reshape the computer labs and software packages for those areas. Application launch and application usage history data has also helped in this regard. This can provide an understanding of what software is used and to what extent the data can be leveraged to negotiate for lower prices during a renewal process. Even just moving a few machines to different locations can impact the usage of specific computers. Some students prefer more privacy while other students need an environment to work on a computer as a group.

5 COMMUNICATING RESOURCES

It is a hassle, and frustrating, for students and faculty to walk from one lab to another just to find out that there are no computers available. Lab spaces are valuable and are always at risk. Thus, providing this information clearly and easily helps students find and use available resources, and further, faculty and IT can see and make decisions on how these labs are being used.

5.1 Real-Time Availability Maps

NYU sees the most value from the real-time computer lab maps. The student tech center web page includes embedded maps so students can see real-time station availability. Additionally, the maps cycle on digital signage in public spaces for all patrons to see.

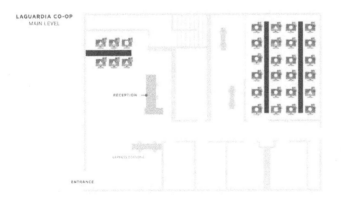

Figure 1: **A website displaying a real-time map that shows the layout of the computer lab and the status of individual computers.**

Real-time computer lab map displays allow students to check which stations are available at their location. The maps can be embedded on a website, can be used in conjunction with a kiosk display, added to a mobile app, or any other way that is beneficial. This information can show students, faculty, and staff where machines and software are available for use at any given moment in a day.

With data from individual labs, determining whether a computer lab's hours meet the needs of students is simple. If data shows that a computer lab is full as soon as it is opened, it may show that opening an hour earlier will be better to allow students to utilize labs. Conversely, a lab might be rarely used and need to have shorter hours or be closed completely. Small adjustments to hours and lab staff can save large amounts of budget. Instead of hiring more employees, there might be lab managers that could be shifted around based on individual lab usage. Trimming or adding open hours can help to more accurately show lab utilization and potentially cut staff costs.

5.2 Public API

The monitoring software also includes a public API which showcases the data in more ways than is natively supported. The API includes status information on a number of stations that are either available, in-use, or offline. It can also be used to display several different labs in a carousel format. This information can be added to an existing school app, website, or anything else that can be imagined.

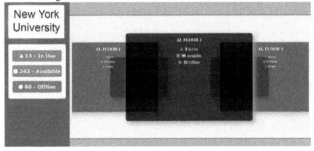

Figure 2: **Information displayed from the API; showing real-time lab usage data for three different computer labs.**

5.3 Computer Lab Peak Usage

Some computer labs appear to be full to students or faculty as they pass by, but is that an accurate picture of the lab's use? Is the lab truly full or could it be that only the computers closest to the door are being used? Gathered data can show when the most computers are in use at the same time. This data may help identify patterns that point to consistent times when many or few computers are in use and might allow for adjusting computer lab hours or making alterations to the number of computer lab staff throughout the day. This can also show whether more computer labs are needed or if students just need to be aware of less-used labs. These problems can be solved with the right information.

5.4 Individual Students

Are the right students able to find computers? School administrators might want to know if differing groups of students have equal access or use computers equally. Tracking individual users and segmenting them into meaningful groupings can clarify. Grouping students by their major, class level, or other characteristics can provide all the answers that administrators need to show that computer labs are being used. This information can bring to light unknown usage situations. For example, English majors using the graphic design lab—that might have different and more expensive applications installed. Other use cases for this type of data can include tracking different student demographic groups to ensure equal access to computer resources. This same information could also be used to prove the demographic diversity needed to receive government grants and other funding.

The usage statistics for each individual user can be used in unique ways, too. For example, login time data could be used to track student lab manager's attendance or classroom attendance in general, to ensure that they were logged in when they were supposed to be; these users can easily be segmented to make them viewable. This data will allow reporting on total campus activity or on a per-lab basis, knowing statistics such as the number of logins per lab or campus-wide logins at all locations.

User data displaying the number of logins for a specific user, the number of stations for that user, the total usage, and average usage for a user are also available. This is used to pinpoint a specific user or figure out a use-case for the average computer lab user.

Individual user tracking can also help to protect hardware and software assets. User data can be used to know which students were last on a school laptop before it was stolen or if students are accessing inappropriate websites or software.

6 CONCLUSIONS

Universities and colleges have always struggled to have enough money available in their budget to cover all their technology needs; technology is a large cost in education. With the cost of always updating and upgrading, do lab managers and administrators really know or understand if they are getting a return on their investment? With useful data, Universities and colleges can make decisions that can save thousands of dollars. Lab managers and administrators can know that they are making the right decisions.

While labs are at risk of being extinct, data on lab statistics can save labs, and in some cases, expand them by taking out the guesswork.

REFERENCES

[1] LabStats Support Center. Accessed April 15, 2017. https://support.labstats.com
[2] LabStats Testimonial. Accessed April 15, 2017. YouTube. https://www.youtube.com/watch?v=ncBrgFtz5c8

Augmented and Virtual Reality: Discovering Their Uses in Natural Science Classrooms and Beyond

Austun Ables

Whitman College

345 Boyer Ave.

Walla Walla, Washington, 99362

ablesaw@whitman.edu

ABSTRACT

Augmented and virtual reality continue to be trending topics in educational technology. The purpose of this paper is to demonstrate a workflow for creating augmented or virtual reality projects on a college campus. It will highlight an augmented reality sandbox project that was a collaboration between the Geology department, a science equipment technician, and Technology Services and provide a roadmap for future work involving these emerging technologies at Whitman College. The sandbox utilizes a gaming PC, short throw projector, Kinect camera, and a virtual reality toolkit developed by Oliver Kreylos at UC Davis to overlay dynamic topographic data onto a sand surface. We will discuss how this technology is currently being used in our Introduction to Geology labs and Science Outreach and how virtual and augmented reality can enhance instruction in the natural sciences.[1]

CCS CONCEPTS

Applied computing~Computer-assisted instruction • *Applied computing~Earth and atmospheric sciences* • *Applied computing~Interactive learning environments* • Hardware~Emerging technologies

KEYWORDS

Augmented reality; virtual reality; immersive learning

1 INTRODUCTION

Augmented and virtual reality features cutting edge, and relatively unexplored, technology that has the potential to provide new tools for educators to increase student engagement and enhance learning. A common difficulty among students is visualizing 3-dimensional concepts in the 2-dimensional medium of books. Augmented and virtual reality offer unprecedented

---

SIGUCCS '17, October 1–4, 2017, Seattle, WA, USA

© 2017 Association for Computing Machinery.

ACM ISBN 978-1-4503-4919-2/17/10...$15.00

https://doi.org/10.1145/3123458.3123464

tools through which students can directly interact with visual models in an intuitive and meaningful way. Adding a tactile interface can greatly aid students' understanding and retention of course materials.

Specifically, the augmented reality sandbox provides students a hands-on learning experience and allows faculty to demonstrate concepts in topographic modeling, elevation, terrain, and hydrology. Users can manipulate the sand surface to create various features like mountains or oceans, while the projected topographic map, contour lines, and elevation colors are updated in real time. The sandbox also has a feature that allows for a virtual rainstorm and provides instant feedback on how water moves over the formed terrain. This type of real-time manipulation and feedback cannot be duplicated in a textbook or video. The sandbox provides students with opportunities to change variables within reality and instantly see the results via augmented reality data visualization. Furthermore, this project has created excitement in how virtual and augmented reality can enhance instruction in the natural sciences.

2 AUGMENTED REALITY SANDBOX PROJECT WORKFLOW

2.1 Initial Request: The Beginning

The idea for this project originated in an email request from a student to a faculty member. The student, a geology major, had seen a video in which an augmented reality sandbox was being used to teach topographic principles. Intrigued by this seemingly new and innovative way to teach geologic concepts, the student thought a similar device would be a great addition to Whitman Geology's pedagogical toolbox. The faculty member proposed the project to an instructional technologist, adding that this tool had the potential to aid instruction. Prior to this request, projects involving augmented or virtual reality did not exist on campus. There was no funding and no plan, just an idea and the enthusiasm that this technology could augment instruction of topographic principles. None of the involved parties knew where to begin, but the excitement and the promise of this project provided the motivation to figure out how to build the sandbox and bring this technology to Whitman College. It is important to point out that this project would not have gained traction without student or faculty sponsorship. In addition, the collaborative nature of the project increased the likelihood of funding approval. It can be difficult to garner faculty support when developing projects that seek to integrate technology into the curriculum. It is necessary to demonstrate that the technology can have a direct impact on learning.

2.2 Project Team and Research

During the Fall 2015 semester, a team began to develop around the proposed idea of building an augmented reality sandbox. However, it became abundantly clear that the project would require additional team members with specialized expertise to assist in various capacities to accomplish the main objective. The team would eventually include Lyman Persico (Geology), Larry North (Science Equipment Technician), Dustin Palmer (Math & Computer Science Technologist), and Austun Ables (Instructional Technologist for Sciences). Because none of the team had any prior experience with this technology, research was needed. Preliminary research included searching the web for example projects, watching sandbox demonstrations on YouTube, and video-conferencing with a colleague at a peer institution who had built an augmented reality sandbox. Throughout the research process, resources were freely shared between team members and communication was clear and frequent. The ability to organize ideas and participate in an open dialogue during the design phase provided a solid foundation for the project. All team members engaged in critical discussions and laid the groundwork for what would become Whitman College's unique augmented reality sandbox build.

Initial research involved obtaining a list of hardware recommendations, operating system requirements, and software to run the simulation. Fortunately, all of the tools necessary to successfully build an augmented reality sandbox had been well documented by Oliver Kreylos and his development team at UC Davis. They created a comprehensive repository of all required hardware and software components, as well as installation instructions on their website [2]. This information proved to be a vital resource for purchasing hardware and installing software. However, the hardware recommendations alone were inadequate for the design of the Whitman College AR Sandbox. The selection of the computer and short throw projector presented a challenge. Multiple options were available for both and needed to be researched. Ultimately, the team decided to purchase hardware that best fit the goal for the project.

2.3 Hardware and Software

The Whitman College AR Sandbox utilizes an Alienware X51 gaming PC with an NVIDIA GeForce GTX 970 graphics card, BenQ short throw projector, first-generation Microsoft Kinect sensor, custom-built sandbox with mounting frame, and quartz sand. An Android tablet was added later and is used to access Google Earth. It is helpful, when sculpting a landform using the AR Sandbox, to be able to reference the location using Google Earth. The original concept for the sandbox required it to be mobile enough to fit through doorways and to be transferred between classrooms. The computer's chassis needed to be lightweight and minimal in design. The Alienware X51 gaming PC offered the preferred balance between compact design and performance. The recommended BenQ short throw projector was no longer available. After consulting with a vendor, the

updated model of the short throw projector was purchased. During this build, the only sensor compatible with the Vrui toolkit was the first-generation Microsoft Kinect sensor. The Vrui toolkit was later updated to allow other versions of the Kinect sensor to be used. The Whitman College AR Sandbox features a custom-welded steel framed cart, wood sandbox, and an aluminum mounting system. Larry North designed the cart, sandbox, and mounting system. Constructing the sandbox using campus resources and materials reduced the overall cost of the project. The Whitman College Geology department provided quartz sand, which also reduced cost. Using quartz sand alleviated the concern that dust would compromise the operation of the projector. The budget for this project totaled $3,000. All necessary hardware was funded by the Whitman College Geology department and an internal equipment funding source.

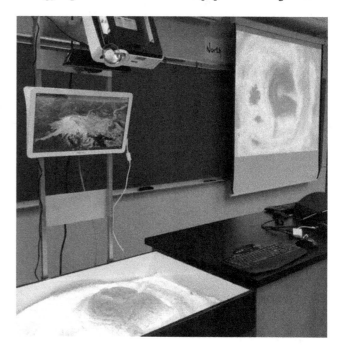

Figure 1: A completed Augmented Reality Sandbox in a classroom, connected to a projection system.

The AR Sandbox runs on an open source virtual reality toolkit (Vrui) and SARndbox software developed by Oliver Kreylos at UC Davis. Both software packages are open source. During the initial calibration, depth and location data of the sand surface was extracted from the Kinect sensor using the Vrui toolkit. The SARndbox software interprets this data and adds a height color map, topographic lines, and a virtual rainstorm to the projected overlay. At the time of this build, the software packages functioned best on Linux Mint. Mint is a distribution of Linux that is considered to be "user friendly." Dustin Palmer was brought on board to help with the introduction to the Linux operating system and to assist with the creation of installation media.

2.4 Installation and Assembly

First, Linux Mint had to be installed on the AlienWare X51 gaming PC to confirm the stability of the operating system. Next, the Vrui toolkit, Kinect sensor software, and SARndbox software was installed via Linux terminal commands. This step required an internet connection to install the prerequisite libraries and appropriate drivers. Installation proceeded without any issues because of the documentation provided by Oliver Kreylos and his team.

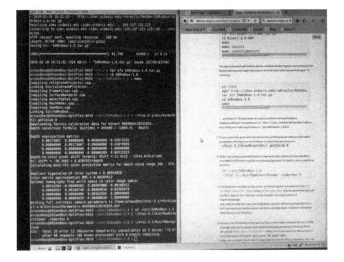

Figure 2: **Screen capture of software installation process.**

Detailed instructions on software installation are available on the AR Sandbox support forum [3]. After the software installation was complete, the Kinect sensor was connected to the computer and powered on. Using a tool located within the Vrui toolkit, the communication between the computer, Kinect sensor, and projector was tested.

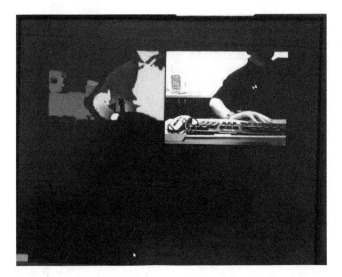

Figure 3: **Calibrating the Kinect sensor using a utility in the virtual reality toolkit.**

A piece of cardboard and the short-throw projector were assembled horizontally on a workbench to accurately measure the distance between the base of the sandbox and the mounting bracket. The cardboard represented the base of the sandbox. This measurement is very important as the projector and Kinect sensor have to be mounted at the same height to ensure proper calibration and correct data visualization while running the SARndbox software. Additionally, the angle of projection was measured to ensure the projected image would be centered over the sandbox. Using this method to test how the projector and Kinect sensor would be mounted over the sandbox, Larry North was able to precisely design the mounting system. Next, the wood sandbox, steel cart, and aluminum mounting frame were constructed.

Figure 4: **An early test of the alignment of the projector and Kinect sensor and representation of the elevation color map.**

The completed sandbox, cart, and mounting frame were moved to a vertical position and the quartz sand was added to the box. A final calibration between the Kinect sensor and the projector was performed. A slight modification to the mounting bracket for the projector was needed. Finally, the completed AR Sandbox was tested to verify that all features were operational. After a year of hard work and dedication, the Whitman AR Sandbox was ready to be deployed.

3 USAGE AND APPLICATION

3.1 Current Usage

Figure 5: **Students experimenting with changing the terrain of the sand.**

In the 2016-2017 academic year, the sandbox was used by Geology faculty in introductory labs to teach concepts in topography and hydrology. Science Outreach staff utilized the sandbox to teach similar topics to younger generations of students enrolled in K-12 schools from surrounding communities. The Outdoor Program recently used the sandbox in a trip-planning meeting to geographically represent an area where students would be hiking. The lead guide demonstrated the type of terrain the trip would cover and pointed out potential hazards along the route. Astronomy faculty are interested in using the sandbox to measure projectiles created from impact craters. A lab exists for this, but the sandbox could enhance the current lab exercise.

It is recommended that faculty or staff schedule a training session before using the AR sandbox. Prior to use, the AR Sandbox must be calibrated. The calibration can take up to an hour. A Google group was created to facilitate requests for scheduling and support. The support group is comprised of Austun Ables (Instructional Technologist for Sciences) and Lyman Persico (Geology). If necessary, additional support can be provided by the Geology technician.

3.2 Future Development

Future development of the AR Sandbox will be a continual process as faculty, staff, and students contribute feedback. The exchange of ideas will advise future iterations of this project. It will be imperative to precisely document evaluations and ask clarifying questions to discern potential functionality. For example, a faculty member observed that an automated startup sequence for the AR Sandbox could improve ease of use and reduce loss of class time. Mounted buttons or a gaming controller could be used to access menus or toggle functions during operation of the AR Sandbox. Additionally, connecting the AR Sandbox to a classroom projection system allows an entire class to view the sandbox demonstration. As interest and usage increase, a request has been submitted for a second AR Sandbox to meet the demand. The purpose for the second sandbox has not been

determined. Early ideas involve a cross-discipline sandbox that can be used by multiple departments or a larger AR Sandbox that would allow more student participation. The specialized nature and size of the current sandbox is a limitation. The inclusion of more disciplines would increase instructional impact.

3.3 Virtual Reality

In contrast to augmented reality, virtual reality is an immersive computer simulation that replicates real or imagined objects and places [1]. The idea for experimenting with virtual reality at Whitman College evolved from early discussions with faculty and students about future development for the AR Sandbox. The potential of the technology excited and inspired both groups to brainstorm preliminary examples of classroom tutorials. That dialogue eventually morphed into the Whitman VR Experience, an attempt to design an immersive virtual reality simulation that can potentially augment teaching and learning at Whitman College. This initiative utilizes a custom-built gaming PC, an HTC VIVE VR headset, and Unity3d software to create educational exercises within a virtual reality environment. A total of three exercises were developed that replicated activities in the natural sciences, social sciences, and humanities. For example, faculty in Geology were interested in using virtual reality to analyze remote geologic outcrops using drone photogrammetry. By capturing georeferenced drone images and processing the images using photogrammetry software, a 3D model of the outcrop can be created. Then, it can be imported into Unity3d and viewed in virtual reality. This process can be useful if physical access to the outcrop is limited. Furthermore, it can save additional time and resources for faculty, students, and the institution. The Whitman VR Experience hopes to explore the educational applications of virtual reality by utilizing existing resources as well as experimenting with original content creation.

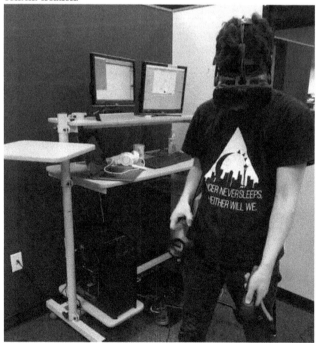

Figure 6: **The Whitman VR Experience development space.**

3.4 Challenges

The Whitman College AR Sandbox project did not have any major disruptions. The demand for a mobile sandbox required specific hardware and materials, but did not produce any delays. The most challenging aspect of the project was understanding the interaction between the individual hardware components and the software.

Implementing functional classroom content presents a major concern for projects involving augmented or virtual reality. Typically, projects involving these technologies require an extensive demonstration period to prove their practical application. Fortunately, the augmented reality sandbox yielded positive results in the classroom. In contrast to most projects of this nature, the Whitman College AR Sandbox emerged from the need for more interactive instruction in the classroom.

Developing augmented and virtual reality projects can be time intensive. Disciplined time management is essential. For example, it has been difficult to find time to add new features to the AR Sandbox. The plan is to hire a development intern and emphasize implementation of feature requests. It can be helpful to create a vision statement for the project to prioritize tasks and inform decisions. This technology offers multiple avenues for research and experimentation. Having a focused vision prevents the accidental misuse of resources.

4 CONCLUSION

Augmented and virtual reality seeks to enhance instruction in the natural sciences and other disciplines by creating an immersive learning environment where students can actively engage with course materials. It offers the ability to transform the classroom into various educational scenarios with relative ease. This paper has demonstrated a workflow for creating an augmented reality sandbox, described how augmented reality is actively being used in the classroom, and summarized current virtual reality development at Whitman College. Providing faculty with tools that allow students to interact with information in an innovative, highly visual way will augment standard lectures and increase student engagement.

ACKNOWLEDGMENTS

I would like to thank David Sprunger for his guidance and leadership. I would also like to thank Lyman Persico, Ian Floyd, and Matt Hill. This work was supported by Whitman College.

REFERENCES

[1] Foundry. 2016. VR? AR? AR? Sorry, I'm Confused. Retrieved from https://www.foundry.com/industries/virtual-reality/vr-mr-ar-confused
[2] Oliver Kreylos. 2017. Augmented Reality Sandbox. (April 2017). Retrieved June 26, 2017 from http://idav.ucdavis.edu/~okreylos/ResDev/SARndbox/index.html
[3] Oliver Kreylos. 2015. Complete Installation Instructions. (March 2015). Retrieved June 26, 2017 from https://arsandbox.ucdavis.edu/forums/topic/complete-installation-instructions/

Jetstream: A Cloud System Enabling Learning in Higher Education Communities

Jeremy Fischer
Indiana University
Pervasive Technology Institute
Bloomington, IN
jeremy@iu.edu

David Y. Hancock
Indiana University
Pervasive Technology Institute
Bloomington, IN
dyhancoc@iu.edu

John Michael Lowe
Indiana University
Pervasive Technology Institute
Bloomington, IN
jomlowe@iu.edu

George Turner
Indiana University
Pervasive Technology Institute
Bloomington, IN
turnerg@iu.edu

Winona Snapp-Childs
Indiana University
Pervasive Technology Institute
Bloomington, IN
wsnappch@iu.edu

Craig A. Stewart
Indiana University
Pervasive Technology Institute
Bloomington, IN
stewart@iu.edu

ABSTRACT

Jetstream is the first production cloud funded by the NSF for conducting general-purpose science and engineering research as well as an easy-to-use platform for education activities. Unlike many high-performance computing systems, Jetstream uses the interactive Atmosphere graphical user interface developed as part of the iPlant (now CyVerse) project and focuses on interactive use on uniprocessor or multiprocessor. This interface provides for a lower barrier of entry for use by educators, students, practicing scientists, and engineers. A key part of Jetstream's mission is to extend the reach of the NSF's eXtreme Digital (XD) program to a community of users who have not previously utilized NSF XD program resources, including those communities and institutions that traditionally lack significant cyberinfrastructure resources. One manner in which Jetstream eases this access is via virtual desktops facilitating use in education and research at small colleges and universities, including Historically Black Colleges and Universities (HBCUs), Minority Serving Institutions (MSIs), Tribal colleges, and higher education institutions in states designated by the NSF as eligible for funding via the Experimental Program to Stimulate Competitive Research (EPSCoR). Jetstream entered into full production in September 2016 and during the first six months it has supported more than a dozen educational efforts across the United States. Here, we discuss how educators at institutions of higher education have been using Jetstream in the classroom and at student-focused workshops. Specifically, we explore success stories, difficulties encountered, and everything in between. We also discuss plans for increasing the use of cloud-based systems in higher education. A primary goal in this paper is to spark discussions between educators and information technologists on how to improve using cloud resources in education.

CCS CONCEPTS

• **Computer systems organization** → **Cloud computing**; • **Applied computing** → *Computer-assisted instruction*; *Interactive learning environments*;

KEYWORDS

cloud; openstack; digital; XSEDE; education; outreach; training; EOT; research; Jetstream; XD; Globus; Atmosphere; cyberinfrastructure

ACM Reference format:
Jeremy Fischer, David Y. Hancock, John Michael Lowe, George Turner, Winona Snapp-Childs, and Craig A. Stewart. 2017. Jetstream: A Cloud System Enabling Learning in Higher Education Communities. In *Proceedings of SIGUCCS '17, Seattle, WA, USA, October 1–4, 2017*, 6 pages.
https://doi.org/10.1145/3123458.3123466

1 INTRODUCTION

Jetstream is a recent addition to the XD (eXtreme Digital) national cyberinfrastructure (CI) funded by the National Science Foundation [20]. Previous awards have been aimed at traditional large-scale high-performance computing (HPC) systems such as Blue Waters, Kraken, and Stampede [15–17] These HPC systems have been utilized by thousands of researchers at almost 400 academic and research institutions in the last five years. [10]

Over time, the focus of the awards has changed somewhat. While the need for HPC resources has not decreased, the desire for different types of computing resources has also been seen as a priority for the national CI. This started with the NSF 13-528 (Track IIf) [18] awards for Comet and Wrangler, showing a diversification into heterogeneous HPC and virtual cluster systems and big data processing respectively.

The next step in these awards was looking at novel approaches to research computing. The solicitation for the NSF 14-536 (Track IIg) proposal asked applicants to "include capabilities suitable for addressing emerging computationally intense scientific and engineering research topics, workflows and communities that are not

Table 1: Survey Instrument Questions

Item	Answer Type
In what context did you use Jetstream?	Course, Workshop, Other
In what context did you use Jetstream? - Other Text	Open-ended Response
What was the course name or workshop/event title?	Open-ended Response
Institution	Open-ended Response
Location	Open-ended Response
Primary target audience of your class/workshop?	K-12 students, undergraduate students, graduate students, researchers, technical staff, faculty, other
How many students/participants did you have?	Open-ended Response
Do you consider the use of Jetstream in your class/workshop a success?	Yes/No
Considering the level of success (or failure) you experienced in using Jetstream in your class/workshop, please elaborate on your experience.	Open-ended Response
In your view, what did Jetstream do especially well in the context of your class/workshop?	Open-ended Response
Considering its educational uses, what aspects of Jetstream could be improved?	Open-ended Response

optimally served by current XD or Blue Waters resources." [19] While not specifically discussing cloud technologies, this was seen as a logical progression for NSF-funded research and education systems. The two winning awards, Jetstream and Bridges, incorporate cloud solutions as part or, in the case of Jetstream, all of their offerings to the US research and education communities.

Though exploring new methods and systems for research was a primary focus, the underlying mandate was to "less traditional computational science communities" [19] where ease of use would be a crucial aspect. In this regard, ease of use could mean both providing a graphical user interface (GUI) as well as creating an application library that would be useful and usable for researchers and educators. Jetstream outlined both of these as primary goals from the start [23] as well as other features and services designed to facilitate the use of Jetstream by educators and researchers who typically did not use the eXtreme Science and Engineering Discovery Environment (XSEDE) resources for their work [9]. Expanding cloud services and creating research-as-a-service will further the goal of creating a programmable cyberinfrastructure that will be flexible in meeting the needs of educators and researchers throughout the United States. Through the course of this paper, we examine what the Jetstream team has attempted to do to enhance educational use of Jetstream and look at use cases where varying degrees of success were achieved.

2 JETSTREAM DESIGN AND FEATURES

Since the mandate was to create a different type of resource for research and education, the Jetstream team took a different approach from the traditional HPC models. Providing on-demand cloud services wasn't enough to differentiate Jetstream from commercial offerings. Jetstream was designed from the start to focus on science, supported and run by staff that are experienced in supporting researchers already. One very important design goal was to make a more user-friendly research and education cloud. Jetstream partnered from the start with iPlant (now CyVerse) to adapt the Atmosphere web-based GUI for creating, managing, and accessing virtual machines (VM) [14]. This removed the need for researchers

and educators to be experts in the methodologies to create and manage VMs. In addition, creating VMs with GUI desktop environments to let people have an environment similar to the desktop environments they are used to already was key for creating a more inviting user experience. Another key feature for making Jetstream use easier was creating a set of curated VMs. The Jetstream team manages a set of "Featured Images" that range from basic Linux operating systems that are routinely updated and patched for security items to images with research software such as Matlab, Galaxy, and R/RStudio. Jetstream users can use these stable and managed VMs to build their own customized workflows and preserve them for future use, creating reproducible, consistent environments for their research or classes and for the Jetstream user community if they choose.

3 USING JETSTREAM FOR EDUCATION

Jetstream's goal is to "provide self-serve academic cloud services, enabling researchers or students to select a virtual machine (VM) image from a published library" or to "customize their own virtual environment." This was the first step to creating a system not only suited for research but also instructional use [23]. Beyond that, the goals for providing for the best electronic learning environment are designing for interactivity, quality content presentation, and appropriate GUI [7]. A key feature of Jetstream is that it allows educators and researchers to create the environment tailored for their needs using command line interface (CLI) or GUI.

One of the best ways to expand the use of new resources beyond the typical researchers and research areas is to use the system to educate other researchers, educators, and students. The Jetstream education, outreach, and training (EOT) team has worked with members of various institutions, including both of Jetstream's physical hosts, Indiana University and University of Texas at Austin, as well as a number of others. Multiple workshops on using Jetstream have taken place at conferences and afternoon seminars to attract researchers and educators to Jetstream by showing its ease of use and discussing how Jetstream would benefit them.

One of the desired side effects of these workshops and seminars is for researchers and educators to create their own XSEDE startup allocations for Jetstream. Though there is no reported metric for defining the number of allocations applied for immediately after a workshop or seminar, anecdotal evidence shows that every workshop does yield a minimum of 2-3 new allocations shortly afterward from attendees. The EOT team, though, is constantly looking for opportunities to expand the reach of Jetstream to new audiences by conducting workshops or partnering with those who teach courses or workshops and helping them move their projects to Jetstream.

3.1 Overview of Education Allocations

Jetstream utilizes the XSEDE Resource Allocation System (XRAS) for awarding allocations. The process for obtaining an Education Allocation is fairly simple, requiring a current curriculum vitae (CV), the course description/syllabus, and a justification of resources [24]. From March 2016 to March 2017, there were twenty-three education allocations awarded on Jetstream totaling over 2.5 million cpu hours [10]. These allocations were awarded for educational program development and limited engagement workshops, as well as for semester-long courses. We will examine some of these varying educational uses as a basis for shaping Jetstream's role as an education resource.

4 MATERIALS AND METHODS

4.1 Participants

Participants for this survey were selected from the list of active Jetstream education allocations; as of March 2017 there were 23 active education allocations on Jetstream. Potential participants were principal investigators (PIs), co-principal investigators (Co-PIs), or key personnel who (as of March 31, 2017) had used or were actively using Jetstream resources to conduct workshops and courses using Jetstream cloud resources for instruction and course assignments. There were fourteen potential participants identified as having used at least a portion of their allocation (more than 0 Service Units, the "currency" of XSEDE, utilized); nine individuals agreed to participate and did so with informed consent. The courses and workshops covered in the survey results that gave permission to disclose are shown in Table 2.

4.2 Survey Instrument

The goal of the survey was to find how Jetstream was used, what went well, what could be improved, and if there were ways that educators felt cloud services in general could be made more attractive for classroom use. This survey was approved by the Human Subjects Office at Indiana University. Survey instrument items and types of responses are in Table 1.

4.3 Survey Administration

After potential participants were identified, they were sent an invitation to participate over email. A follow-up e-mail was sent one week after the initial invitation. A final e-mail was sent out two weeks after the initial request. This survey was unusual in that participants were able to share their identities and all but one did so.

5 RESULTS

Of the 14 active and used or in-use allocations identified, nine individuals (64.29%) agreed to participate. 100% of respondents reported that their use of Jetstream was a success. Several of the allocations had multiple PIs. Of the allocations, two had two respondents each, so results represent six of the allocations. Of these six, one specified that they did not want their results disclosed. One completed the survey but did not include enough information to discuss their workshop in any meaningful fashion. Thus, only four responses are presented below by individual course/workshop.

5.1 Course Review 1

The largest educational use of Jetstream to date was for the course from the Indiana University School of Informatics – "I535 Management, Access, and Use of Big and Complex Data". This course covered topics including "data integration, workflows and pipelines, and distributed noSQL stores" [21]. This course had almost 200 undergraduate and graduate students enrolled and utilized multiple customized images for two projects spanning six weeks of the semester. The instructors installed Hadoop and a modest data lake for doing data retrieval (MapReduce) exercises. They also utilized MongoDB for student exercises using noSQL databases.

This particular use-case started as a discretionary allocation for research awarded by the PI of Jetstream to a faculty partner, Dr. Plale, at Indiana University. The PI expected that the allocation would be used for prototyping Jetstream use for various projects that Dr. Plale was involved with, and not in a classroom setting. The first indication that it was being used for instructional use came when a couple of support requests came in from students in that course; however, it was not until there was a network outage on the IU-based Jetstream cloud that we become aware that there were so many students enrolled in that class.

This course tested Jetstream's limits early in its production. Having several hundred new users pushed on to the system, launching virtual machines (VMs), working with them, and suspending them helped us make Atmosphere more robust for both the users and support. There were several incidents where we had to work with the instructors to quickly solve unexpected issues related to the sudden growth and use of Jetstream. The instructors indicated that they were very pleased with the support provided by Jetstream for their students. They also expressed satisfaction overall with the use of Jetstream in their course. One felt that Jetstream could make tutorials available for students to help make Jetstream easier to learn to use. While the end results were very positive, we learned some valuable lessons about support, expectation management, handling outages, and generally trying to help users with the system.

5.2 Workshop Review 1

By contrast to the longer course by Dr. Plale described above, Dr. C. Titus Brown, Dr. Harriet Alexander, and Dr. Phillip Brooks led a recent two-day course on metagenome analysis at University of California at Santa Cruz [5]. This workshop has been held for

Table 2: Courses and Workshops Covered in Survey

Event Title	Type	Number of Students	Location	Audience
Analysis of large, complex biobehavioral, bioinformatic, and genomic data sets	Workshop	36	Brandeis University	Graduate students
Bioinformatics: Tools for Genome Analysis	Course	9	Online (via Johns Hopkins University)	Graduate students
'Digital Pedagogy' / 'Introduction to Text Analysis'	Course	30	University of Pittsburgh / Carnegie Mellon University	Graduate students
Management, Access, and Uses of Big and Complex Data	Course	200	Indiana University	Undergraduate and graduate students
Data-Driven Neuroimaging	Workshop	30	University of California San Francisco	Researchers and graduate students
2017 Metagenomics Workshop	Workshop	30	University of California Santa Cruz	Researchers, graduate students, and undergraduates

multiple years prior using Amazon Web Services (AWS) for the VM component. For the workshop, they used a base Ubuntu image and added several software packages like trimmomatic and fastqc for working with sequencer data, MEGAHIT assembler for assembling the metagenomes, Prokka for annotating them, and Jupyter Notebooks for doing the workshop exercises [6].

A two-day workshop doesn't allow much room for error on the part of the technology provider. While Dr. Brown was prepared for his part of the workshop, it was up to the Jetstream staff to be ready and able to handle any support issues. Due to staffing and budget constraints, Jetstream currently does not have a 24/7/365 support staff. This means that unless prior arrangements are made, there is a potential for support breakdown for courses or workshops held on the weekend. Fortunately, there were no issues of consequence and Dr. Brown reported that using "Jetstream went more smoothly than AWS in almost every way and seems to perfectly meet our needs for training!" [5]. He reported minor issues with the Jetstream web desktop and a few stalled instance startups, but no major issues.

Overall, this workshop was considered a success. A longer data-intensive workshop is scheduled for this summer using Jetstream. This will have up to 100 users for 30 days using Jetstream for sequencing and data analysis [4]. While this will not be the largest course or workshop to date, it will most likely be the most intense in terms of resources required and simultaneous load. This will be another milestone for Jetstream brought about by an educator well versed in using cloud technologies.

5.3 Workshop Review 2

The Berkeley Institute for Data Science (BIDS) and the University of Washington's eScience Institute teamed up with UCSF researchers to conduct a workshop on data-driven analysis and machine learning for neuroscience imaging data [8]. The demand for this workshop was high, with 60 applicants vying for 30 spots [3]. This workshop required a considerable amount of coordination amongst the three institutions involved, including the technical work before the actual workshop.

In order to utilize as much of the workshop time for actual learning and research techniques, IT staff created the workshop virtual machines in advance in a pre-loaded, customized Docker container that contained Jupyter Notebook, a selection of Python environments, tools, and libraries, as well as a selection of R utilities, based on the Jupyter Notebook Data Science Stack [22]. Additional neuroscience-specific packages such as Dipy [11]. The workshop coordinators then created a VM for each participant and provisioned the customized container on each VM so participants entered the workshop ready to go almost immediately.

This ensured that each person had the most up-to-date environment for the workshop. No installation time was required and no downloading of data or other tools was necessary. The workshop organizers wanted to remove this from their workshop as the process is often error prone [8]. While this could have been done using VM images, the process of using Docker containers worked well for the IT staff supporting the workshop creation. This allowed the the staff to have a consistent working environment for each participant and also saved time by having all data sets needed for the project preloaded into the container rather than being downloaded by each participant.

The workshop was considered a success and plans are being made for future versions. One respondent reported that better resource monitoring and management would help in the overall control of the workshop. With IT staff building and managing the workshop, it was a workable solution, but a goal for their organization is to make instructors more self-sufficient. Better usage and monitoring tools might make that a more achievable goal. Aaron Culich of Berkeley stated that one of Jetstream's strengths is providing "fast and flexible access to computational resources at no cost" and that it was a benefit to researchers to use in workshops because they could apply for their own allocations afterward.

5.4 Workshop Review 3

The last workshop examined was organized by Dr. Francesco Pontiggia, Research Computing specialist at Brandeis University, and taught by Dr. Kene Piasta. This workshop was a week of classroom instruction followed by three months of independent project work. There were thirty-five graduate students enrolled with the purpose of learning methods for conducting statistical analysis of large, complex biobehavioral, bioinformatic, and proteomic data sets.

The VMs for the classroom portion were set up by Dr. Pontiggia in advance. The six shared VMs used R for the statistical analysis and then various other software packages depending on the particular track. The instructors also held a training session on using Jetstream as part of this classroom time to prepare the students for their independent project work. For the project work itself, they created a custom image with all the bioinformatics packages they expected students to need. However, as Dr. Pontiggia noted in the survey, "giving students and instructors the ability to modify, install software on their own and maintain access on demand later on to those images is something of great value, which would not have been easily achieved on our cluster." This flexibility for creating customized, savable, reproducible workflows is part of the design goal of Jetstream.

One issue during this workshop was in the shared VMs used during the classroom portion. In order to control the environment, students used shared VMs; however, individual accounts had to be added (because there was no easy way to use login credentials against the launched VMs inside another account). The workshop organizers reported that having some form of service to facilitate this, whether it's a lightweight directory access protocol (LDAP) server or something other service, it would allow for a shared service inside a specific user account. Nevertheless, overall, the organizers reported that Jetstream provided a comfortable, usable environment for the students. The participants, in general, were not extremely experienced computationally. Dr. Pontiggia in particular felt that having resources available on demand that had a look and feel like a normal workstation made it easier for the students to adapt to using analysis tools.

6 SUGGESTIONS FOR IMPROVEMENT

While the survey respondents all reported that their use of Jetstream was a success, it is important to the evolution and betterment of the system to find out how they felt we could improve the user experience. There were several requests for technical features like allowing persistent internet protocol (IP) addresses in the Atmosphere web interface (this is on the features roadmap but was not implemented at the time of writing). Other suggestions were for things like improved base images for instructional use with specific software. All technical requests are considered, though with budget and staffing being limited, the goal remains to choose those which provide maximum benefit to the most users.

One common thread in regards to improvement was how to better monitor users and usage. In Jetstream's Atmosphere interface, there is no easy way for non-admin users to see what users on their allocation are doing. We have had one successful experiment with using a community account for a two-day workshop. This is something we will explore further in the future. This solution, however, may not be advisable for longer courses where grading is based on coursework done on Jetstream as the potential for academic dishonesty is high. Other solutions may be found for this in the long run.

The last common suggestion was to improve video tutorials for using Jetstream. While we do provide fairly extensive documentation on our wiki [13], it is common practice now to provide more video tutorials for instruction. We plan to continue adding to the videos that we have created [12], looking at a range of areas from using the Atmosphere interface to utilizing more advanced application programming interface (API) techniques for working with Jetstream.

7 ENGAGING EDUCATORS

As with any new technology, the task of getting educators to examine and integrate it into their instructional environment required a concerted and multifaceted effort. Our survey respondents had several things to say about how to best engage educators. While this is a very small group and won't represent all educators, their contributions are valuable. Several of the educators noted that Jetstream simply needed "to get the word out more!" They didn't necessarily offer ideas on how best to do that, though. The Jetstream team has made efforts over the last year to appear at major conferences such as the Plant and Animal Genome (PAG) conference [2] and Super-Computing [1]. We are now targeting domain-specific conferences as well as doing direct outreach and communication, including tutorials, with universities and colleges. However, engaging a larger audience in a survey to find out what broader needs are for technology in education might be prudent. Given the very different needs from classroom to classroom and discipline to discipline, getting the input directly from educators at every level and a variety of institutions might help Jetstream understand how we can best serve the larger audience.

Engaging educators directly is crucial. At the same time, it is also important to engage those who support and train educators to use information technology (IT) components and infrastructure. For example, within the XSEDE framework, Campus Champions act as the liaisons between faculty and staff and XSEDE resources. They provide guidance and training on how to utilize XSEDE resources. This same approach might be worth exploring for Jetstream. If we engage and train the IT staff, they may suggest it as a means of enhancing classroom instruction as well as help their faculty use it. The difficulty again comes in how to best get in contact and train this particular group of people. Looking at EDUCAUSE and SIGUCCS amongst other conferences seems to be a potentially good way to identify and communicate with this group of people.

8 CONCLUSIONS

Initial educational uses of Jetstream have been successful. While there have been minor issues along the way, for the most part, instructors reported that Jetstream met their needs and did so in an easy-to-use, easy-to-implement way for their courses and workshops. In the end, though, the most user friendly system ever created will not be a success without actually having users. We must continue to find ways to increase adoption and usage. Finding new audiences must be a continuing effort. Afterwards, we must follow up to find how we can help individuals use Jetstream effectively in their instruction.

With resources and IT staff being in demand and also constrained at many institutions, utilizing cloud solutions may be of strategic and practical importance. Cloud services like Amazon and Azure are well known and offer introductory usage but often have other strings attached. Jetstream provides a smaller, more limited service but one that is free for US-based researchers and educators. Jetstream also endeavors to be easy to use and responsive to the needs of diverse research and education communities. These qualities give Jetstream the potential to be an extremely valuable tool for the US academic world.

9 ACKNOWLEDGMENTS

Implementation of Jetstream is supported by NSF award #1445604. The Indiana University Pervasive Technology Institute was established with support of funding from the Lilly Endowment, Inc., and partially supported this research. Any opinions expressed here are those of the authors and do not necessarily reflect the views of the National Science Foundation, the Lilly Endowment, or XSEDE leadership as a whole.

REFERENCES

[1] [n. d.]. International Conference for High Performance Computing, Networking, Storage and Analysis. http://dl.acm.org/citation.cfm?id=3014904. ([n. d.]).
[2] [n. d.]. International Plant & Animal Genome Conference. http://www.intlpag.org/. ([n. d.]).
[3] Berkeley Institute for Data Science. 2017. Berkeley and UW Data Scientists Team Up with UCSF Researchers to Deliver Data-Driven Analysis and Machine Learning for Neurosciences. https://bids.berkeley.edu/news/berkeley-and-uw-data-scientists-team-ucsf-researchers-deliver-data-driven-analysis-and-machine. (February 2017).
[4] C. Titus Brown. 2017. Request for Compute Infrastructure to Support the Data Intensive Biology Summer Institute for Sequence Analysis at UC Davis. http://ivory.idyll.org/blog/2017-dibsi-xsede-request.html. (February 2017).
[5] C. Titus Brown. 2017. A (revised and updated) shotgun metagenome workshop at UC Santa Cruz. http://ivory.idyll.org/blog/2017-metagenomics-at-ucsc.html. (2017).
[6] C. Titus Brown. 2017. Short read quality and trimming. https://2017-ucsc-metagenomics.readthedocs.io/en/latest/quality.html. (February 2017).
[7] Alexandru Butoi, Nicolae Tomai, and Loredana Mocean. 2013. Cloud-based mobile learning. *Informatica Economica* 17, 2 (2013), 27.
[8] Aaron Culich. 2017. Jetstream cloud support for multi-institutional data science workshops and research. http://research-it.berkeley.edu/blog/17/02/17/jetstream-cloud-support-multi-institutional-data-science-workshops-and-research. (February 2017).
[9] Jeremy Fischer, Steven Tuecke, Ian Foster, and Craig A. Stewart. 2015. Jetstream: A Distributed Cloud Infrastructure for Underresourced Higher Education Communities. http://doi.acm.org/10.1145/2753524.2753530. In *Proceedings of the 1st Workshop on The Science of Cyberinfrastructure: Research, Experience, Applications and Models (SCREAM '15)*. ACM, New York, NY, USA, 53–61. https://doi.org/10.1145/2753524.2753530
[10] Thomas R. Furlani, Barry L. Schneider, Matthew D. Jones, John Towns, David L. Hart, Steven M. Gallo, Robert L. DeLeon, Charng-Da Lu, Amin Ghadersohi, Ryan J. Gentner, Abani K. Patra, Gregor von Laszewski, Fugang Wang, Jeffrey T. Palmer, and Nikolay Simakov. 2013. Using XDMoD to Facilitate XSEDE Operations, Planning and Analysis. http://doi.acm.org/10.1145/2484762.2484763. In *Proceedings of the Conference on Extreme Science and Engineering Discovery Environment: Gateway to Discovery (XSEDE '13)*. ACM, New York, NY, USA, Article 46, 8 pages. https://doi.org/10.1145/2484762.2484763
[11] Eleftherios Garyfallidis, Matthew Brett, Bagrat Amirbekian, Ariel Rokem, Stefan Van Der Walt, Maxime Descoteaux, and Ian Nimmo-Smith. 2014. Dipy, a library for the analysis of diffusion MRI data. *Frontiers in Neuroinformatics* 8 (2014), 8. https://doi.org/10.3389/fninf.2014.00008
[12] Indiana University. 2017. Jetstream - cloud-based computation videos. https://www.youtube.com/playlist?list=PLqi-7yMgvZy-0Sy94uyOm67MhvN6xgxZ3. (2017).
[13] Jetstream. 2017. Jetstream Help Wiki. https://wiki.jetstream-cloud.org. (2017).
[14] Nirav Merchant, Eric Lyons, Stephen Goff, Matthew Vaughn, Doreen Ware, David Micklos, and Parker Antin. 2016. The iPlant Collaborative: Cyberinfrastructure for Enabling Data to Discovery for the Life Sciences. *PLOS Biology* 14, 1 (01 2016), 1–9. https://doi.org/10.1371/journal.pbio.1002342
[15] National Science Foundation. 2007. Leadership Class Scientific and Engineering Computing: Breaking Through the Limits. https://www.nsf.gov/awardsearch/showAward?AWD_ID=0725070. (2007).
[16] National Science Foundation. 2007. A National Institute for Computational Sciences to Provide Leading-Edge Computational Support for Breakthrough Science and Engineering Research. https://nsf.gov/awardsearch/showAward?AWD_ID=0711134. (2007).
[17] National Science Foundation. 2011. Enabling, Enhancing, and Extending Petascale Computing for Science and Engineering. https://nsf.gov/awardsearch/showAward?AWD_ID=1134872. (2011).
[18] National Science Foundation. 2013. High Performance Computing System Acquisition: Building a More Inclusive Computing Environment for Science and Engineering. https://www.nsf.gov/pubs/2013/nsf13528/nsf13528.htm. (2013).
[19] National Science Foundation. 2014. High Performance Computing System Acquisition: Continuing the Building of a More Inclusive Computing Environment for Science and Engineering. https://www.nsf.gov/pubs/2014/nsf14536/nsf14536.htm. (2014).
[20] National Science Foundation. 2014. High Performance Computing System Acquisition: Jetstream - A Self-Provisioned, Scalable Science and Engineering Cloud Environment. https://www.nsf.gov/awardsearch/showAward?AWD_ID=1445604. (2014).
[21] Beth Plale. 2016. Course Description: I535 Management, Access, and Use of Big and Complex Data. https://www.soic.indiana.edu/graduate/courses/index.html?number=i535&department=INFO. (2016).
[22] Project Jupyter. 2017. Jupyter Notebook Data Science Stack. https://github.com/jupyter/docker-stacks/tree/master/datascience-notebook. (February 2017).
[23] Craig A. Stewart, Timothy M. Cockerill, Ian Foster, David Hancock, Nirav Merchant, Edwin Skidmore, Daniel Stanzione, James Taylor, Steven Tuecke, George Turner, Matthew Vaughn, and Niall I. Gaffney. 2015. Jetstream: A Self-provisioned, Scalable Science and Engineering Cloud Environment. http://doi.acm.org/10.1145/2792745.2792774. In *Proceedings of the 2015 XSEDE Conference: Scientific Advancements Enabled by Enhanced Cyberinfrastructure (XSEDE '15)*. ACM, New York, NY, USA, Article 29, 8 pages. https://doi.org/10.1145/2792745.2792774
[24] XSEDE. 2012. Startup and Education Allocation Proposals. https://portal.xsede.org/allocations-overview#writing-startupeducation. (2012).

Scratching the Surface of Windows Server 2016 and System Center Configuration Manager Current Branch

Muhammed Naazer Ashraf
Lehigh University
19 Memorial Drive West
Dept. of Mechanical Engineering
naazer@lehigh.edu

ABSTRACT

Lehigh University has set a goal to implement System Center Configuration Manager by the end of 2017. This project is being spearheaded by one of our Senior Computing Consultants who has been researching and trained in the Microsoft Virtualization stack. We will discuss our roadmaps, results from our proof-of-concept environments, and discussions in driving this project.

CCS CONCEPTS

• **Computer system implementation** → **Microcomputers**; *personal computers, portable devices, workstations*

KEYWORDS

Virtualization; Microsoft; Windows Server 2016; System Center Configuration Manager; SCCM; ConfigMgr; Data Deduplication; Nano Server; Storage Spaces Direct; Remote Desktop Services; RDS; MDT; Microsoft Deployment Toolkit; Hydration; Virtual Lab

1 INTRODUCTION

1.1 Lehigh University Overview

Lehigh University is a private research institution founded in 1865 and located in Bethlehem, Pennsylvania, USA. It boasts 600 faculty members, 1,100 support staff, and an enrollment of over 5,000 undergraduates and 1,500 graduate students. Library and computer services are combined in one integrated organizational unit known as Library & Technology Services (LTS). LTS owns and maintains over 500 classroom and lab PCs while also supporting nearly 2,300 departmental PCs.

1.2 Path to Prominence

Lehigh University revealed its 10-year plan, the "Path to Prominence," to the Lehigh community at the end of October

SIGUCCS '17, October 1–4, 2017, Seattle, WA, USA
© 2017 Association for Computing Machinery.
ACM ISBN 978-1-4503-4919-2/17/10…$15.00
https://doi.org/10.1145/3123458.3123462

2016. It laid out an ambitious new framework on which Lehigh's future will be built. It is a vision that includes a series of sweeping, decisive steps that will see the university build on historic strengths and evolve into a more dynamic, impactful institution: an increase in student enrollment, renovations to numerous campus buildings, the construction of new academic and residential facilities, the addition of 100 faculty, an expansion in the area of health, and an addition of a new college. This expansion plan will serve as an opportunity to increase the university's visibility, both nationally and internationally, and play a key role in significant areas of education.

1.3 Bigger Problems Will Require Better Tools

Our LTS organization very quickly discovered that there was not going to be a commensurate increase in the support staff, so we formed a committee and launched an investigation into System Center Configuration Manager (SCCM, also known as ConfigMgr) and any other tools and workflows that can help increase our efficiencies. ConfigMgr is a product in the Microsoft System Center suite of management solutions designed to help manage large groups of users and devices. My particular focus was researching Windows Server 2016 and ConfigMgr.

Our preliminary research concluded that Server 2016 and ConfigMgr will play a significant role in our near future. We are currently in proof-of-concept stages with the various Windows Server roles and ConfigMgr Site System roles and they already have the potential to be game-changers. The first part of this paper will discuss some of the highlights from our investigation of Server 2016 and the second part will cover our journey with ConfigMgr.

In October 2016, our President John Simon elaborated on an ambitious framework for the university's future through undergraduate and graduate enrollment growth, faculty hiring, new academic programs and upgraded facilities. The vision foresees an increase in enrollment by 1,500 students over a period of 7 years, the addition of 100 new faculty, and the launching of a new fifth college, focused on health. Our Library & Technology Services team came to the realization that the fleet of desktops, laptops, and mobile devices will also be increasing. The deployment and management techniques we are currently using is just about satisfactory for our current size and already spreading our consultants thin. Trying to scale our existing methodologies seemed impractical and our leadership identified this situation as a high-value project.

Back in 2014, coinciding around the time when our LTS team decided to transition from Ghost to using Windows Images, I started researching options and ConfigMgr came up time and time again as the best-of-breed solution for Windows deployment. I immediately spun up a server and spent the next few weeks sifting through TechNet articles and blog posts about how to set it up, configure it, and get Windows deployed. Looking back from what I know now, I am amazed that it ever worked at all. I did not know any of the best practices or finer nuances of the product and made some unspeakable mistakes along the way. On more than one occasion, I had accidentally "upgraded" a few Windows 7 workstations to Windows 10 without intending to. My ConfigMgr journey over the last 3 years ignited a fire inside and personal zeal to learn as much as I could about the product, and to help educate other administrators who are in the same position as I was. I hope that the reader will have sufficient motivation and guidance when they embark on their own journey to deploy and manage Windows on an enterprise scale.

2 ENTER WINDOWS SERVER 2016

Windows Server 2016 is the latest in a line of Microsoft Server operating systems as of this writing. From Windows Server Containers [1] to Nano Server [2], the latest OS incorporates modern application development principles. It also turns the software-defined datacenter into a reality and it does this without abandoning what you have today. Now virtualization has enabled an enterprise to save money by consolidating server workloads and retiring obsolete hardware. Enterprises can further reduce the cost of doing business, by moving some of their workloads from their on-premises environment into the cloud. Because of these changes, instead of having to deal with a server sprawl in a data center, administrators are now faced with a virtual machine sprawl. In fact, even though it seems like things are much simpler, they can actually become very inconvenient in some situations because it is easier to configure and start up a new virtual machine than it is to procure and provision new server hardware in your environment. And instead of managing only the infrastructure in your datacenter, you now have to deal with managing resources in the cloud as well. And if you are not careful, you might end up with two sets of administrative tools that need twice as much time and staff to manage.

2.1 Licensing Overview

The licensing of Windows Server 2016 is based on physical cores rather than processors, which is different from what it was in the previous licensing model.

Licensing based on cores provides a more consistent licensing metric, regardless of whether the solution is deployed on premise or in the cloud. The Windows Server 2016 licensing model for the Standard and Datacenter editions will be cores plus a client access license (CAL). Now, the Datacenter edition is meant to be used in highly virtualized private and hybrid cloud environments, whereas the Standard edition is targeted toward low-density or non-virtualized environments.

3 SERVER 2016 ENABLING TECHNOLOGIES

We wanted to highlight some of the new technologies and features that we have narrowed down and further investigating. There are numerous enhancements and features that we have not even scratched the surface of yet, but intend on coming back to once we pilot these.

3.1 Squeeze More Out of the Metal

Data is the most valuable resource to an organization, and data growth is a very real problem for an enterprise. There is this constant tension of cost versus retention and an organization has two truths they must reconcile. The first is acknowledging that storage growth is a huge problem. To your layperson this may not look like a significant issue as the cost of storage is always going down. Data growth does not only mean that an organization must buy and install more disks, but must also buy, deploy, operate and monitor more servers. The second truth is that it is difficult to know what data an organization must retain. It is simpler and safer to keep everything, but this is a false trade off. Windows Server 2016 has solved this problem with the Data Deduplication feature.

The technology is best explained with an example. Let us say you have a user, Naazer, that has just delivered a great presentation to his team using PowerPoint. He emails the file to his team and everyone saves the file onto their team file-share for reference. Now we have 4x as much data and are paying 4x as much for the same copy of ones and zeroes. There are several other scenarios in organizations that have duplicated data. For example, VDI deployments and backups. Data deduplication "optimizes" a volume by analyzing files and storing the redundant parts once. This could potentially increase your storage efficiency by upwards of 95% depending on the dataset.

Deduplication is a serious feature worth looking into that will save organizations money. To give you an idea, Fig. 1 shows the folder properties of my VMs folder containing all the virtual machines on one server. Notice that I have over 4TB worth of virtual machines only taking up 315GB of storage on the disk. This translates to about 92% disk savings, which is significant. Always enable deduplication on File Servers, VDI workloads, and backup targets, and evaluate other workloads for potential use with deduplication.

Figure 1: Data deduplication savings of over 92%

3.2 Nano Server

Nano Server is a new Windows Server 2016 installation option with a super small footprint. It can be used as a physical host, as a VM guest, or as a container operating system. Currently, Nano Server supports the following roles: Hyper-V, Scale-Out-File-Server, DNS Server, Failover Clustering, and IIS. Fig. 2 shows how it compares against Server Core and Full Server in terms of boot performance and IO footprint.

Server	Boot Time (s)	Read (MB)	Write (MB)	Total (MB)
2016 Nano Server	9	156	135	290
2016 Server Core	85	2,304	1,170	3,474
2016 Full Server w/ Desktop Experience	135	2,533	2,089	4,622

Figure 2: Comparing Nano Server vs. Server Core vs. Full Server

Nano Server has fewer services running, fewer processes running, and fewer ports open, directly contributing to its superior security and serviceability, which makes it ideal for many scenarios

By default, there are very few modules actually loaded on Nano Server. This helps to keep it lean and small. Other modules can be imported either implicitly or explicitly, as needed.

Nano Server's tiny 400MB footprint is a direct contribution to its superior security, serviceability, resource consumption, and boot performance. While small, it still provides flexible options for management, ranging from PowerShell to the new browser-based server management tools, as well as familiar tools such as Hyper-V Manager, Failover Cluster Manager, Server Manager, and others.

3.3 Storage Spaces Direct

Storage Spaces Direct (S2D) is another new technology in Server 2016. Think of it as software-defined, shared-nothing storage. It allows you to take industry-standard servers with local storage, which are distributed across multiple machines to create highly available and highly scalable storage at a fraction of the cost of traditional SAN or NAS arrays. Essentially, you can create an abstraction from physical storage that can be handled as one large pool and be allocated to virtual machines as volumes.

There are two types of S2D clusters: hyper-converged and disaggregated. See Fig. 3. In the hyper-converged architecture, the compute and storage reside on same system and both scale together as your demand increases. In the disaggregated architecture, the compute and storage are separated and can be scaled independently. For smaller requirements, hyper-converged offers a good value proposition because it is more efficient in terms of cost. If more flexibility is desired, the disaggregated configuration is better because the compute and storage can be scaled independent of each other.

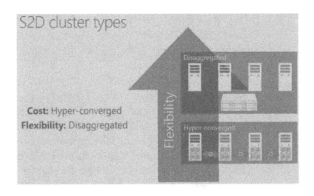

Figure 3: S2D cluster types: disaggregated vs. hyper-converged

3.3 Remote Desktop Services

Remote Desktop Services (RDS) is a collection of role services that is part of Windows Server 2016 and earlier, that provides access to session-based desktops, virtual machine-based desktops, and applications that are running on centralized servers. The idea behind RDS is just what it sounds like: you remotely access a desktop or an application that is truly running on a centralized server. Now, these remote sessions can be accessed either within our internal network or also from outside the network via the internet.

RDS provides a cost-effective way to deliver applications to managed or unmanaged devices. It is the backbone of what solutions like Citrix XenDesktop and VMware Horizon leverage, but it can also be used as a standalone solution. This was an intriguing proposition that we wanted to explore. One of the experiences that we were particularly interested in was being able present remote applications within the Start Menu and Desktop of Windows 10 desktops and laptops. This makes the remote application seem like it is a regular installed application to the end-user, even though behind the scenes it is actually running on the Windows Server 2016 machine in our data center.

4 ENTER CONFIGMGR

We wanted to first focus on the following capabilities of ConfigMgr as these were areas where we could gain the greatest efficiencies.

1. Operating Systems Deployment: our goal was to achieve a Zero-Touch Installation (ZTI) experience in our operating system deployment workflows. Most of our technology teams still employ USB flash drives with batch files and scripts to refresh individual desktops and laptops.

2. Applications Management: this has been a significant pain point to both end-users and system administrators. We had been using a home-grown solution, which was essentially a website where Lehigh students and faculty could browse software titles and download the installation media. It behaved like a Secure File Transfer Protocol (SFTP) site without a way to centrally manage the installations. Coincidentally,

there is another team, our Software Services Committee, that is concurrently investigating secure application delivery with Citrix XenDesktop & XenApp. While the main focus of that project is finding the best solution to deliver applications to our unmanaged student devices, we are confident that the Software Center in ConfigMgr will be a fantastic solution to deliver and manage applications to managed faculty/staff and lab computers. App-V, which is a Microsoft application virtualization technology, is also integrated into ConfigMgr and provides more options to deliver applications. RDS or Remote Desktop Services serves as the foundation of virtualized application delivery that tools like Citrix leverage to deliver a great end-user experience from any device.

4.1 Why ConfigMgr
In my opinion Microsoft System Center Configuration Manager is the best product on the market for deploying and administering Windows in the enterprise. Over 75% of enterprise assets in the world are managed by ConfigMgr. It is designed to deploy and manage desktops, laptops, servers, and mobile devices from the moment they arrive in your environment to the moment they leave, handling operating systems deployment, applications management, patching, compliance, antivirus, and reporting. ConfigMgr has a rich and varied functionality set covering many aspects of system deployment, management, and reporting, and I encourage you to peruse the official list of capabilities online to learn more about it [3].

ConfigMgr interacts with an organization's infrastructure components such as Active Directory Domain Services (AD DS), SQL Server, Windows Server Update Services (WSUS), Windows Deployment Services (WDS), Internet Information Services (IIS), network protocols, and communications. Therefore, it is very important to effectively plan your environment before you install ConfigMgr.

ConfigMgr is by far one of the most complicated and extensive products maintained by Microsoft. It has a vast array of strong and mature capabilities.

4.2 System Center History
To fully appreciate how mature the solution has become, let us step back in time and take a look at the earliest versions of System Center. The first version of System Center was called SMS, or Systems Management Server. This was deployed in the 1990s with Windows NT 4. It was a bit difficult to use, but mainly deployed applications for Microsoft and third-party programs, and controlled and monitored basic computer functions. Microsoft Operations Manager, or MOM, came out in 2000 to incorporate Active Directory to SMS. We could then use group policy and security groups to manage computers and deploy products like applications and operating systems, as well as monitor computers and servers.

In 2007, Microsoft released the very first System Center suite, which was comprised of several different programs. The main program in 2007 System Center Suite was Configuration Manager. Microsoft said it could deploy operating systems, software applications, software updates, and meter software usage. It assessed variation from desired configurations, performed hardware and software inventory, and it also remotely administered computers.

System Center 2012 was then released in April 2012 and improved on the 2007 version by adding additional functionality such as Mobile Management, Orchestrator [4], and better endpoint protection capabilities.

Jumping to 2016, we saw the release of System Center 2016, which is now just referred to as System Center, and it focuses on the management of the software-defined datacenter and assists with cloud transition.

4.3 What Else is in the System Center Suite
There are various products within the System Center Suite. These include the following:

1. System Center Operations Manager: This provides infrastructure monitoring that is flexible and cost-effective, and it also helps to provide predictability of whether programs are going to perform or not. It also works in both private and public cloud environments.
2. System Center Virtual Machine Manager: This product helps to deploy and create virtual machines and services to clouds as well as on premise data centers.
3. Data Protection Manager: This application is an enterprise back-up system. It allows you to back up servers, computers, system states, and allow for bare metal recovery. Bare metal recovery allows you to take a back-up and restore an entire server to a whole new piece of hardware in case you have experienced a catastrophic failure.
4. System Center Orchestrator: This is a workflow management solution that lets you automate the creation, monitoring, and deployment of resources in your environment. It is an excellent tool that lets you standardize best practices and connect different systems from different vendors without requiring knowledge of scripting and programming languages.
5. Service Manager: This application handles incident and problem resolution, change control, and assists with the asset life-cycle management of your PCs and servers. You can think of Service Manager as sort of the help desk program in the System Center suite. This means it can help you communicate issues with other technicians. It could also help you find fixes for problems as well.
6. System Center Endpoint Protection Manager: This allows you to centrally deploy and configure endpoint protection for the clients. This can include anti-malware policies, as well as Windows Firewall settings to groups of computers. It works in conjunction with ConfigMgr.

By understanding the history of System Center, the reader can appreciate the application in its current form and see how Microsoft developed their product over the last two decades.

5 BUILD YOUR OWN LAB

I believe one of the most powerful tools you can provide for yourself is a decent lab. An environment that allows you to test and practice without affecting production, is invaluable to any IT professional.

You do not need a server or fancy hardware on which to run your lab or proof-of-concept environments. Even an old ThinkPad T420 with a Core i5, 16GB of RAM, and a solid-state drive is good enough to run a demo lab environment. You will be able to run all the System Center products, including deployment servers, domain controllers, and file servers on such a machine. Do not be surprised if your lab machine outperforms some of your servers. The key is the solid-state drive. I fondly recall running my first lab on an old ThinkPad T410 with a solid-state drive and it blew me away. The Data Deduplication feature in Windows Server 2016 provides fantastic storage savings and enables you to build any lab environment that you desire.

Several folks in the ConfigMgr community maintain something known as Hydration Kits, which automate the build and configuration of the required virtual machines for a ConfigMgr lab or proof-of-concept environment. The Microsoft Deployment Toolkit (MDT) is a free deployment solution from Microsoft that provides end-to-end guidance, best practices, and tools for planning, building, and deploying Windows operating systems. The details of using MDT and operating system deployment is beyond the scope of this paper, but you can learn more about it in my "Deploying and Managing State-of-the-Art Workstation Labs Like a Boss" paper [5].

Johan Arwidmark's Hydration Kit can automate the complete build of both the current branch and technical preview branch infrastructure of ConfigMgr. You can download it from his blog [6] by searching for the keyword "hydration". I have found Johan's Hydration Kit to be invaluable to my own research and work. It is efficient, easy to use, and works on any virtualization platform. You can also customize it, which is extremely handy.

Windows Server 2016 and ConfigMgr are currently available via the MSDN subscriber portal [7] and the Technet Evaluation Center (a free 180-day trial copy) [8]

Fig. 4 shows the Hydration Kit in the MDT Workbench tool that will generate a large ISO file, which you will use to build the corresponding virtual machines on your favorite virtualization platform. I prefer Hyper-V running on Server 2016 to take advantage of the data deduplication savings it offers. The Hydration Kit is based on MDT and will generate an ISO file disk image (Fig. 5), which will build the virtual infrastructure. The final result is an environment like you see in Fig. 6 that you can use to test and practice. You should also take advantage of snapshots or checkpoints on your virtualization platform to revert your virtual machines to a previous state, if needed.

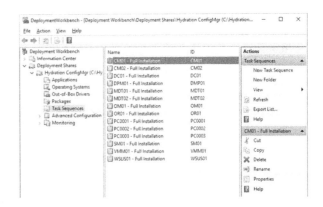

Figure 4: Task Sequences from Hydration Kit on the MDT Deployment Workbench

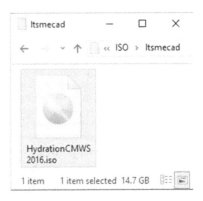

Figure 5: ISO file generated from MDT that builds the virtual machines

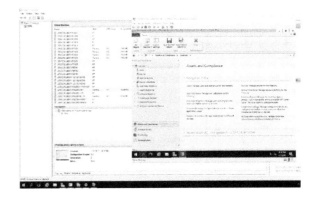

Figure 6: Complete ConfigMgr lab running on Server 2016 Hyper-V

6 TECHNICAL PREVIEW

Microsoft introduced the ConfigMgr current branch model back in December 2015. This transformed the way ConfigMgr was delivered, moving from longer release cycles to regular updates designed to support the faster pace of updates for Windows 10. As of this writing, ConfigMgr shares a similar release cadence to that of Windows 10, where it receives updates about two times a year. Being on the current branch of ConfigMgr ensures that you always have the latest Windows management features available.

Microsoft also maintains a parallel technical preview branch of ConfigMgr that is distinct from the current branch. They also strongly recommended that adopters run and maintain technical preview environment in addition to a current branch production environment. Keep in mind that the technical preview is not for production release, as they are very limited in scope in terms of number of clients, supported operating systems and SQL Server versions. Furthermore, each technical preview build expires after 90 days so it needs to be kept up to date.

The primary advantage of a Technical Preview environment is that you can get a sneak-peek at the new features in ConfigMgr, before they are released to the current branch at some point in the future. This gives you a few different advantages:

1. Early self-learning so that you are ready to take advantage of appropriate new features as they are released into production

2. Make your IT staff aware of new features and even train on them, as appropriate

3. Provide feedback to the ConfigMgr product team at Microsoft

The Microsoft ConfigMgr team does rely on feedback from the product, especially around new features, to know if they are 'ready for primetime'. We should also remember that production releases come out approximately every four months, while Technical Preview releases come out monthly. As a result, there are going to be some features that will be in technical preview for months before they get production ready.

The Hydration Kit and lab environment discussed earlier is a perfect solution to build and maintain a technical preview environment.

7 USEFUL RESOURCES

The ConfigMgr community is fortunate, in that the product has attracted many clever minds who publish what they learn. There are too many to list them all, but here are some core resources to keep a close eye on. First order of business is that if you are not on Twitter, get on Twitter. It is the single best source in this modern age to get up to speed on the latest happenings in your areas of interest. Things are changing faster than ever and we, as an IT Professionals community, need to stay ahead of that. So try to follow these folks on Twitter and also look at the people that they follow.

http://deploymentresearch.com: Johan Arwidmark blogs here, and is the author of the Hydration Kit that we had earlier recommended. There is a lot of good in-depth information on Windows deployment and MDT.

http://www.windows-noob.com: Niall Brady blogs here, and he has authored some of the best how-to guides on ConfigMgr in my opinion. He knows a tremendous amount on Windows Deployment, as well.

http://blog.configmgrftw.com: Jason Sandys blogs here and has a wealth of resources for supercharging your ConfigMgr environment.

http://deploymentbunny.com: Mikael Nystrom blogs here, and it's a great resource for advanced deployment scenarios, as well as some terrific PowerShell tips.

http://blog.coretech.dk: based in Denmark, Coretech employs a lot of Microsoft MVPs and most of them offer great blog content about ConfigMgr and PowerShell. One author in particular, Kent Agerlund, has extensive experience and I recommend his book "System Center 2012 R2 Configuration Manager: Mastering the Fundamentals", to anyone looking to set up a production environment with real-world best practices.

I highly recommend that you reach out to individuals within the ConfigMgr community. Nearly all of them are active on social media and are happy to share their knowledge and give you some ideas.

8 LESSONS LEARNED

We learned several lessons worth sharing in our journey with this project. The first is that if you are not on Twitter, get on Twitter. It boggled our minds how much useful information we could gather from sources like Twitter and Facebook.

The second lesson worth sharing is to not try new things in your Production environment no matter how confident you are about negative consequences. We spent several weekends in the office as a result of the famous last words, "What can possibly go wrong?" It is critical that every IT professional has a decent lab or proof-of-concept environment. This does not just apply to larger projects. With the current prices of SSDs and memory, nobody has an excuse for not having a lab to play and test things in. It is nice to have a spare server or workstation, but any old laptop or desktop with at least a 250GB SSD and 16GB of memory will be fine.

In the ConfigMgr world particularly, it is nearly impossible to understand every concept and moving component. If you wait until you feel you fully understand a topic or workflow, you will drastically slow down your project. Sometimes it is far better to learn enough to be productive, and then come back to the topic in more depth so that you have context as well as a solid, practical foundation upon which to build greater understanding.

The last lesson worth sharing is to steal with pride. This is a metaphor used in the deployment community for not reinventing the wheel, which I find particularly helpful to remind myself every time I encounter a new problem. Do not waste time developing solutions that are already available for free.

ACKNOWLEDGMENTS

I am grateful to my colleagues Timothy J. Foley and Gale D. Fritsche at Lehigh University for their tremendous support of my efforts and training.

Special thanks to my students Shiv Joshi, Jordan Geiger, and Jeevan Jain-Cocks who always made themselves available when I needed their assistance. It has been a privilege and honor to work with these individuals.

The following music was played (often loudly) during the writing of this paper: Dire Straits, Disturbed, Michael Jackson, U2, Taylor Swift, and Celine Dion.

REFERENCES

[1] Windows Containers.
    <https://docs.microsoft.com/en-us/virtualization/windowscontainers/about/>
[2] Install Nano Server
    <https://docs.microsoft.com/en-us/windows-server/get-started/getting-started-with-nano-server>
[3] System Center Configuration Manager features and capabilities.
    <https://www.microsoft.com/en-us/cloud-platform/system-center-configuration-manager-features>
[4] Overview of System Center 2016 – Orchestrator.
    <https://docs.microsoft.com/en-us/system-center/orchestrator/learn-about-orchestrator>
[5] Muhammed Naazer Ashraf. 2015. Deploying and Managing State-of-the-Art Workstation Labs Like a Boss!
    In *Proceedings of the 2015 ACM Annual Conference on SIGUCCS, 43-48*. DOI: http://dx.doi.org/10.1145/2815546.2815570
[6] Johan Arwidmark <http://www.deploymentresearch.com>
[7] MSDN Subscriber portal.
    <https://msdn.microsoft.com/en-us/subscriptions/aa336858.aspx>
[8] TechNet Evaluation Center. <https://www.microsoft.com/en-US/evalcenter/try>

The Student Levels Project

Kelly Wainwright
Lewis & Clark College
0615 SW Palatine Hill Road
Portland, OR, 97202
kelly@lclark.edu

Steve McCurry
Lewis & Clark College
0615 SW Palatine Hill Road
Portland, OR, 97202
smccurry@lclark.edu

ABSTRACT

Employing students is critical to our success in offering service to our campus community. Students comprise the majority of our workforce at our Information Technology Service Desk and we rely on them greatly. However, we were faced with the problem of training our students in a consistent, effective manner with clear expectations and measurable outcomes. Our remedy is the Student Levels Project.

The Student Levels Project guides students to gain knowledge and develop the skills necessary to be successful at the IT Service Desk and to be able to take those same skills with them into the marketplace when they graduate. Through a tiered system, students complete training modules to earn badges. Each level, achieved by earning the associated number of badges, is accompanied by a significant raise and clearly identifiable new skills.

This paper will discuss the development and implementation of the Student Levels Project and review the results a year into using the new system and its effect on our overall service.

CCS CONCEPTS

CCS → Social and professional topics → Professional topics → Computing profession → Testing, certification and licensing

KEYWORDS

Service Desk, Student Employees, Badging, Training

1 INTRODUCTION

Lewis & Clark College is a small, liberal arts college located approximately six miles outside of downtown Portland, Oregon. Our student body consists of close to 2000 undergraduates, 800 law students and nearly 1000 other graduate students, primarily in education and counseling. Our Information Technology department consists of 26 individuals.

In 2013, Information Technology decided that the time had come to reorganize and better align our services with the needs of the campus. One outcome of this reorganization was the clear need to simplify our points of service into a single Service Desk. This would replace the multiple service points that had developed over time: the student staffed help desk, the Information Technology front office, the Instructional Media Services window for equipment checkout, and our high-end computing lab, called the Resource Lab.

The decision was made that we needed to simplify the process of getting help. We needed to have one point of contact for all assistance from Information Technology that could do basic intake and triage of calls, assign them to the appropriate group to fix them, and respond to further inquiries from the clients. However, we realized from the get go that we would need to rely on our student workforce for most of the Service Desk staffing.

2 Service Desk Staffing

2.1 Professional Staffing

In our reorganization plans, there were two professional staff position designated for the Service Desk – one current employee and a newly-created position.

The existing position was our Technology Support Coordinator. This position had been our primary front office point of contact for support. Their duties include triaging incoming issues and requests, management of our lab reservations, daily management of our training resources, and other office administration tasks. In moving them to the Service Desk, they would be gaining extra responsibilities in direct training of the students and managing the pool of checkout equipment.

The new position, which became the Service Desk Manager, was to be responsible for the day-to-day operations of the Service Desk and all aspects of our student staffing – hiring, scheduling, training and managing. We wanted to hire an individual who could also help us be visionary about promoting the Service Desk to the campus community and help us to create the desired Service Desk experience.

With only two professional staff members at the Service Desk, a well-trained student staff was critical to a successful Service Desk.

2.2 Student Staffing

Before our reorganization, we had separately-managed student staffing for the Help Desk, Instructional Media Services (also known as IMS), and our Resource Lab. Our original plans for the Service Desk involved the pooled student workforce to cross-train in all three of these areas, but post-reorganization it was much easier to fit most of the workforce into one of two categories: Service Desk (Help Desk and IMS) and Resource Lab.

The new Service Desk student worker position requires customer service skills both over the phone and in person, the ability to troubleshoot basic software issues, and competency in using our booking software to reserve, issue, and receive equipment. Students are expected to triage problems and enter work orders on a large assortment of topics with the expectation that they can sort out which can be addressed by the student workforce and which must be escalated to staff.

The new Resource Lab position had much the same duties as were assigned before, with the added responsibility of competency in our standard ticketing/work order software so they could document and complete print requests.

2.3   Issues with Student Staffing

Relying on student staffing consistently comes with risk. However they are by far the largest labor pool on any college campus and it is a disservice to not provide them with opportunities in what is often times their first actual job. It was important to identify the issues we had previously encountered in working with students as employees so that we could attempt to address them in the future.

The first issue, of course, is the very nature of their availability -- the fact that they are students paying a large sum of money to study and learn. While working is an important part of helping to pay for their student status, it is by no means a priority, but more of a necessary evil. As many others who rely on student employees, we were constantly dealing with students who had to miss their shifts due to assignment deadlines, study groups, or just becoming overwhelmed by their workload for classes. Less frequently, though also an issue was students who missed for less relevant reasons such as friends coming into town or the snow on the mountain being good. While we had to rely on student employees, some were nothing more than a warm body in a chair.

We understood that we had varying levels of service being offered by our student employees depending on how many hours the student worked and how effective their colleagues were at passing along information. For various reasons, whether it was limitations due to work study maximums or just a concern about work overwhelming their studies, some students would only work a couple hours each week and were therefore just not exposed to as much as those who were working more hours. We tried to have overlap in the schedule but that was difficult due to class schedules. It became difficult to fight the moniker of "the helpless desk" that came with our students consistently giving bad or wrong answers or consistently dropping the ball.

While we were struggling with our student workforce, much of the issue was with the structure of the their positions and how the students were managed. First and foremost was our lack of consistent training for the students. While we had a list of what students needed to know, the actual training of the students was very one-on-one. This took a lot of time on the part of the professional staff and was by no means consistent since training was usually while the student was working and often riddled with interruptions. This meant that different students would receive the same information in different ways and at different times. And when you are training ten new students at the start of the school year, it was sometimes a case where the trainer couldn't remember who they had taught what, even with the lists.

Another issue with our high-touch training was that the rest of Information Technology had no clear understanding of what students had received what training or had special skills. They therefore were not inclined to request student employee assistance with anything beyond the most basic and menial tasks.

It was also difficult because there was no real incentive to learn more or do better. While some students just had an interest in technology support and excelled, some just wanted a place where they could get paid while they did their homework. However, unless something egregious happened, they were all hired back and they all received their minimal raise for working for us another year. There were no clearly defined avenues or rewards for advancing within the organization.

The bottom line was a poorly trained student labor force with no clear expectations or incentive to improve.

4   The Student Levels Project

Our answer for improving training, increasing the level of service we provided, and motivating our student workers to excel was to create what we called our Student Levels Project. We knew going in that this was not going to be an easy task and we ended up spending a substantial amount of time defining, developing and revising the program over the course of many months.

4.1   The Goal

From Day One our goal in formulating this project was twofold. First, we wanted to take the necessary steps to improve the level of service provided at the IT Service Desk. We also wanted the service to be consistent so no matter who assisted the client they could expect to receive the same level of service and the same expertise from each student worker. Basically, we strove to provide a solid customer experience to everyone who took the time to call, email or drop by the IT Service Desk seeking assistance. The effectiveness of this program was also something we could easily monitor through our ongoing customer satisfaction surveys. Since we believed the steps we were taking would increase our overall level of service we could also expect our customer satisfaction rating to increase as a result.

Secondly, we wanted to help our student workers improve their knowledge and develop skills which they could take with them into the marketplace once they graduate from college. Keeping the students' needs in mind, while expressing a genuine desire for them to learn and grow as individuals, we quickly achieved personal buy-in from them for what we were trying to accomplish through this program. This also afforded us the ability to stay focused as a cohesive team committed to excellence.

4.2   The Process

We set out to keep the process as simple as possible for our students. Overcomplicating things never seems to work out as planned and just makes new programs seem more confusing than they ought to be when rolling them out in the department. Therefore, we kept the concept for our program fairly straightforward. In a nutshell, the student workers complete their training and are tested on their understanding of the material. For each course they complete, they earn a "badge". As they earn more badges, they "level up" and as they level up they receive an increase in their hourly salary.

After doing some research on how best to manage the training piece of the program, we settled upon using Moodle. One of the reasons for this was because the student workers were already familiar with the tool since it is used extensively for classes throughout Lewis & Clark College. Using Moodle would also give the IT Service Desk staff more hands on experience to the tool which could help them be more successful when troubleshooting Moodle related issues for our clients. And lastly, Moodle already included the ability to incorporate badging in the training.

Our training consists of a variety of formats. First and foremost, we make good use of our internal knowledge base in Confluence. We also utilize internal and external help sheets, how-to documentation, screencasts, instructional videos, as well as some individual hands on training. We also rely heavily on applicable courses available on lynda.com.

We have three separate levels of training. Both Level 1 and Level 2 each consists of 12 hours worth of training. Level 3, which is more specialized and geared towards the students' personal areas of interest, consists of roughly 16 to 20 hours of training per badge. For Level 1 and Level 2 courses each individual training module is followed up with a quiz that the students much pass to earn their badges. These quizzes help to assess the students understanding of the material presented and tests their knowledge of each subject matter.

Available Badges

Level 1	Level 2	Level 3
Customer Service	Classroom AV	MS Office
Work Order Basics	Video Conferencing	Windows OS
Siso Basics	SiSo Intermediate	Apple OS
Shift Planning	3D Printing	Digital Photography
Service Desk Essentials	Remote Desktop	Photo Editing
Rlab Basics	Colleague Basics	Video Editing
Password Basics	Moodle Basics	Graphic Design
Knowledge Base	Google Apps	Desktop Publishing
Wireless Connectivity		
Workday		
Phone Basics		

Figure 1: Available Badges ©Lewis & Clark College

As the student workers complete their training and pass their quizzes they earn individual and unique badges. There are 27 total badges that may be acquired over the course of the student's career with the IT Service Desk. Level 1 badges focus on the basics needed to successfully carry out the responsibilities of the job. We provide new student workers three months to complete their Level 1 training. If they do not complete their required training in the allotted period of time they are not invited to return to the IT Service Desk the following semester.

Level 2 training constitutes a more advanced skill set beyond the basics needed to do the job. Level 3 consists of eight possible areas of study from which the students would need to select 2 in order to complete the training necessary for achieving the level. What is

unique to the Level 3 badges is that we allow the students some flexibility to choose the areas of study that they are most interested in. These are specialized badges and their training assessment is project-centric rather than quiz-based.

Creating the look for the badges presented a unique challenge all its own. Most of what was available digitally did not meet our vision of having fun creative looking badges that would motivate our students to want to put in the work to earn them. But, as fate had it, one of our student workers possessed superb graphic design skills and through much time and effort they developed a way for creating badges unique to each course. We are very proud of the way these turned out and they have been a huge hit not only within our Information Technology department but with others throughout the college as well.

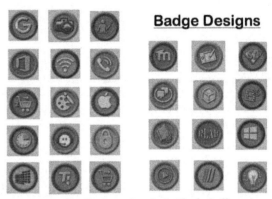

Figure 2: Badge Design ©Lewis & Clark College

Once the student workers have completed the assigned training, passed the skill assessments, and have earned all the specific badges required, they then level up. As mentioned previously, new student workers are required to earn all of their Level 1 badges within the first three months of employment. Since this was a new program we gave our returning students the entire semester to complete their Level 1 training as a stress-free way of easing them into something that was new and different from the previous training methods to which they were accustomed. Besides the pride one receives when they accomplish their goals while maintaining a real sense of purpose, one of the main incentives associated with leveling up is the opportunity to earn more money. As each subsequent level is achieved, the students will typically earn a $1 raise in their hourly wages. Depending upon where our returning students fall within the established pay scale, their increases may be slightly less initially.

In contrast to our previous Service Desk model for training, developing, motivating and compensating our student workers, this new model, based upon ongoing training, earning badges and leveling up, offers some clear-cut advantages. We now have a clear and concrete plan for our student workers so they can continuously learn and advance throughout their time at the IT Service Desk. The training we provide is much more consistent across the board since every new student worker now receives the exact same information during their training. Our student workers now have a greater knowledge and practical understanding of our support tools which, when combined with their new gained experience, helps to provide a more competent and consistent level of service to our client base.

There is no longer any guess work when it comes to salary increases, since compensation is now based upon specific criteria that must first be met rather than just tenure in the department. In addition, the new model also affords us the opportunity to quickly weed out students who are not motivated or interested in learning and who don't desire to put forth the effort needed to be successful in the position. By setting expectations from the onset, based upon firmly establish and measurable criteria, it is much easier to cut students loose who are under performing, which in turns leads to a much stronger and more cohesive team. Finally, the new model helps to ensure that our student workers leave college not only with a degree but also with numerous practical and marketable skills that they can utilize in the real world for the rest of their lives. In short, with the new model the department wins, the student workers win and our clients win.

5   The First Year - Lessons learned

So far, the Student Levels Program has been very well received by both IT Staff and student workers alike. The staff has had to spend less time conducting individual training sessions, which has helped to free up some of their time to focus on other tasks associated with effectively running and managing the department. The students are happy that they now have clear expectations as to what is required of them. They also have easy access to the training they need for learning the job at hand. In addition, they have a much more direct path for advancement which they seem to appreciate.

As far as lesson learned, we were quick to realize that although the new model provided an excellent foundation on which to build, it did not eliminate the need for ongoing coaching and mentoring of the student workers. The time saved by the creation of this program primarily occurs at the start of each semester when the need for training large numbers of new student workers is at its highest.

Another important lesson was learning that students sometimes need to be reminded of the benefits for continuing to learn and earn badges. Many of the students were quick to achieve Level 1 status but then stopped progressing beyond that point. Once reminded that getting to the next level would earn them more money the student workers had the incentive they needed to continue on their journey. As imagined when creating this new model for training, salary increases continues to be the top motivator for active and sustained participation in the program.

We knew going into this that keeping the training materials up-to-date and relevant was going to take a substantial commitment on our part. Software continues to be improved upon and updated. Tools go through various revisions and user interfaces change at a rapid rate. Operating Systems are upgraded regularly resulting in new versions being introduced and released over time. Additional information becomes available as new policies, processes are procedures rolled out on an ongoing basis. Because of all that, materials used in training not only require updates, but new content continually needs to be developed, and new courses will need to be created and added every year. This also means that quizzes need to be modified and updated to reflect new and changing information. All of this will surely take time and effort on our part but it will help ensure that our training stays current and relevant throughout the years.

We want to publicly commend the students for their achievements by highlighting the badges that each student has acquired. This not only celebrates individual successes, but also informs clients who visit the IT Service Desk of the experience levels of the students. Currently, badges are displayed privately in Moodle. We plan on posting the badges that each student has earned under their picture on the IT Service Desk directory, which is accessed by the entire IT department. Furthermore, we want to praise the students' triumphs through our weekly email updates and our display board at the service desk. Finally, we are considering displaying each student's current level on their engraved nametags that they wear while on duty.

We also decided to add a set of badges to reflect life skills that we want to acknowledge. These badges represent valuable skills that are not necessarily technology based. One example is public speaking – e want to be able to reward the student with a badge when they represent Information Technology in a public forum.

6   Conclusion

The process of clearly defining and documenting our expectations has been helpful for all involved. Students can now take ownership of how they want to progress in their position and will come out with badges that we are hoping will be instrumental in their job search beyond their student years. The professional staff can now better understand a student's strengths and weaknesses and help them develop their skills. In all, the student levels project has proved to be a win.

Leveraging the 24x7 Operations Center to Extend Help Desk Service Hours

William Stirling
University of Washington, Seattle
4332 12th Ave. NE
Seattle, WA 98195
wstirlin@uw.edu

Terrie Schrudder
University of Washington, Seattle
4545 15th Ave. NE
Seattle, WA 98195
schrud@uw.edu

ABSTRACT

The University of Washington is a global institution composed of three campuses, several hospitals, affiliate academic units around the world, and a user base of more than 250,000 people. As a result, operations can never suspend regardless of the time or day. In 2013, IT help desk support was limited to standard business hours, Mon-Fri 8:00am to 5:00pm. The University of Washington's central IT department (UW-IT) saw a need for customers to have access to quality IT support whenever they needed it: 24 hours a day, 7 days a week, 365 days a year. 24x7x365 operations are costly and outsourcing was not an option. The Computer Operations team was identified to have both availability and capacity to assist with expanding the hours of the help desk. Opposing schedules, additional unrelated responsibilities, incongruent work cultures, a brand-new ticketing tool, and incorporation of the ITIL framework made merger of these two teams difficult but well worth the effort. By leveraging existing 24x7 operations staff, the University could extend service desk hours to meet the needs of a global institution and an ever-increasing, complex catalogue of services with high-quality, high-availability support.

CCS CONCEPTS

• **Social and professional topics~Computer and information systems training** • *Social and professional topics~Project staffing*

KEYWORDS

24x7; Change Management; Help Desk; ITIL; Service Desk; Service Management; Shared Services

SIGUCCS '17, October 1-4, 2017, Seattle, WA, USA
© 2017 Association for Computing Machinery.
ACM ISBN 978-1-4503-4919-2/17/10. . . $15.00
https://doi.org/10.1145/3123458.3123473

1 INTRODUCTION

The University of Washington's central IT department, usually referred to as "UW-IT", manages the enterprise systems core to the university. Front-line (tier 1 or help desk) support for those systems is provided by the Technology Service Center and had traditionally been limited to rather standard business hours. Around-the-clock access and support of those systems became more critical to a university with hundreds of thousands of active accounts demanding access from time zones all over the globe while handling time-sensitive, urgent issues such as medical emergencies from multiple affiliated hospitals. A call to maximally broaden the contact hours of the central service desk was made. This paper documents the difficulties of UW-IT's situation in accomplishing that goal along with the decisions made and the end results.

2 DRIVERS

It was determined early on that there was no budget for expansion of the existing Technology Service Center to raise staffing to the levels necessary to be able to then cover all the "off-hours", holidays and so on. The task was defined as identifying resources already in place which could step in to cover those extra hours. The volume of work at the service center was already bordering on capacity (weekly incoming requests tend to total several thousand on an average) and since the very large portion of those come in during standard business hours, we could not afford to take personnel away from the normal business hours to have them work night or weekend shifts. This led the search for a solution towards a very limited set of ideas and after consideration, only one looked like it would accomplish our goal.

2.1 Customer Confusion

2.1.1 Single Point of Contact. At the university and within UW-IT there are six separate IT help desks not including all of those for the medical centers, many of the individual academic departments, and even some for other administrative departments. Five of the six central IT help desks handle a specific sub-set of central IT support: telephony, network operations, server operations, learning technologies, and classroom technologies. The sixth central IT help desk is the Technology Service Center and it has been, for decades, the default arrival point for IT questions which either don't apply to one of the other five help desks, or for when the customer (student/staff/faculty/public) doesn't know where to send their question. Not only was this identified as inefficient for the handling of priority incidents our customers were trying to report, but the memorization or notes our customers needed to keep in order to simply understand how to submit a question was deemed unreasonable. The help desk to which "everything else" was routed, the Technology Service Center, was identified as the help desk through which all other queries and reports of incidents should be filed. This concept of how UW-IT should have a "single point of contact (SPOC) brought to light other concerns, most notably the fact that unlike some of the other help desks, the Technology Service Center was only open during normal business hours.

2.2 Availability (24x7x365 Support)

2.2.1 The University Never Sleeps. While the single point of contact concept was ideal in theory, it would require more significant change than simply telling all of UW-IT's customers to go to a single web site, email address, and phone number. To make this concept truly operational, the Technology Service Center needed to find a way to cover every hour of every day including weekends and holidays since other help desks (especially the network and server operations help desks) would rely on this new single point of contact as a conduit for their critical incoming requests and reports of outages. Staffing and the concerns that go into management of staffing (scheduling, training off-hours personnel, providing escalation points for handling unprecedented situations, etc.) would require whole new structures and processes which had to be in place before the personnel fulfilling the new duties could possibly fulfill those roles.

2.3 Consistent Answers & Processes

2.3.1 The ITIL Way. To add further complexity, to the adoption of a 24x7 service desk, UW-IT was amid transforming towards extensive adoption of ITIL. All UW-IT staff had intense ITIL training/testing and received certification. ITIL foundation designed a set of best practices for IT service management, which may be used to fit your organizations goals. The focus on aligning IT services with the needs of the organization rather than simply providing technologies was a clear benefit for our customers (focusing on delivering them end-to-end services), and ITIL certainly calls for coordination amongst help desks and even a single point of contact. The problem with ITIL wasn't one of ideas, but rather timing. This was a significant upheaval in a large IT organization which had two main ideas about why and how most of our work was handled: 1.) "That's the way we've always done it." 2.) Rogue projects/efforts will pull us through. (which was broadly referred to as the "cowboy way" because it was so prevalent).

2.3.2 New Service Management System. Because of our new-found understanding of ITIL, it had become clear to UW-IT that our old service management system did not encompass or allow for many of the processes or ideas set forth in this new framework. We needed a service management system in which we could easily work and collaborate as one central service desk running from different locations. One service management system stood out above the others, and it could be tailored to fit the needs of UW-IT. Our tools development team worked long hours with the external vendor along with other units from UW-IT such as the Technology Service Center, Computer Operations, and the Network Operations center. UW-IT needed to configure a brand-new instance of the software as a service management system which could successfully support the many complexities of an IT department with 850 members. Then it was primarily up to the help desks to provide training on this new tool to all the other UW-IT divisions. Now the service desk needed to fully understand the rest of UW-IT's internal workflows. At the same time, they needed to figure out how to adjust their own to incorporate a previously unrelated team, new service framework, & new service management system.

2.3 Cultural Differences

Of the few teams which already supported 24x7x365 services, none of them were in the same building, had the same types of employees, or even handled similar work. Because we couldn't expand the existing team, we needed to coalesce with another team with a previously unrelated background and business purpose rather quickly. We were about to work very closely every day with a team that did not look at their work in the same light as we did ours. To highlight some of the specific challenges, we should list some of the significant differences we needed to overcome if this change were to work.

2.3.1 Incident Management vs. Request Fulfillment. Incident management involves any unplanned event that causes an interruption or deterioration in service quality. If the service is user/customer impacting, customer requests will be converted to incidents. Requests on the other hand are submitted by user/customers, and involve a single user request or issue. The volume of records for the Technology Service Center is easily 90+% supporting Request Fulfillment and thus forced the unit to be practiced and focused on that process. Computer Operations staff were almost exclusively familiar with managing incidents. To operate as an efficient, integrated general help desk, the service desk would need to transfer their knowledge of Request Fulfillment (and it wouldn't hurt for the service desk to learn from operations how better to handle those occasional user-reported incidents, either).

2.3.2 Internal vs. External Focus. The operations team we needed to incorporate as the after-hours portion of the Technology Service Center had mostly been systems-focused and worked with internal UW-IT staff (as opposed to external customer-focused)—the operations team has never had an external customer drop by for assistance or even needed to write a reply to a request in non-IT terminology.

2.3.3 Place of Business. As if to emphasize our different approaches, and due to space limitations in all UW-IT locations, we did not have the ability to co-locate, further distancing us from cohesion. The operations team is located next to a data center in a secure location and handles e-mail and phone requests only, and the existing service desk would continue to be in a customer-accessible office space.

2.3.4   Troubleshooting vs. Reporting. Another difference that went undiscovered until integration was attempted was the fact that the Technology Service Center had always assumed the (for the most part) undocumented role of performing as much troubleshooting as possible, given normal limitations in resources, access, and authority. Operations mainly dealt with Incident management and support from a completely different point of view: Check the documentation, follow the help text which maybe limited for specific issues, and then, if unable to fix and resolve the problem staff would escalate/report to the proper service/server on-call engineering group for resolution.

2.3.5   Scheduling Conflicts and the Type of Positions. We would not be able to alter any of the existing operations team's schedules to accommodate customer demand. The operations team still had their original duties to consider and monitoring for systems outages comes first—the minimum manpower necessary to support that role could not be reduced. Further these positions were well-established and defined as classified hires, so alteration was restricted beyond just the nature of the work. The service desk contains no classified positions, so initial assumptions that were made regarding potential flexibility turned out to be impossible.

3   Initiatives

Our first two primary initiatives were relatively easy to define, plan, and begin. They were based on the drivers described to us before the project ever began and were under constant consideration throughout. Although complex for some of the previously-mentioned technical issues above, we found the third initiative far more difficult to implement and not merely because consideration of the issue came late in the project.

3.1   Establish a Single Point of Contact

We changed signage on campus so our customers only had one SPOC. We scoured university websites for opportunities to update references to multiple help desks. We redirected literally hundreds of old email addresses so they all routed to our help@u email address. We completely re-designed our phone tree so customers calling to our one phone number had clear options on how to get to the group they needed (when they were certain) and defaulted to the Technology Service Center (when the customer was unsure). We showed the planned changes to small samplings of our customers to make certain what we were doing made sense and was done well from their perspective.

3.2   Consolidate Staff into a Single Help Desk

In the end one team stood out as the best choice for direct collaboration with the existing Technology Service Center to accomplish the 24x7 goal. The Computer Operations unit was already required to cover every hour of every day and had plans in place for a multitude of scenarios including: staff shortages, events preventing support from their standard location, and emergency response. That team was already within the same division as the Technology Service Center (the assistant directors in charge of the two units reported to the same director). Peripheral duties handled by Computer Operations (such as handling major print jobs within the data center) were diminishing in volume. In comparison, the other help desks were limited in hours, highly focused on supporting an extremely limited set of services, and mostly operated out of separate divisions. Computer Operations has the responsibility of monitoring, supporting, and reporting on systems, applications, mainframe, and facilities equipment. This is important as quick assessment and contact are imperative to resolutions of incidents. The first, most obvious means to bring the two teams into alignment was a concentrated effort to train the Computer Operations unit. High-volume and critical services, especially those for which support was most likely to be sought after hours, were identified as foremost for training programs (rather than attempt to train on all 100-200 services supported by the Technology Service Center). Documentation on support for these services was reviewed and then training programs were built to supply the information as efficiently as possible.

3.3   Building a Common Culture

In at least some minds, "Consolidating Staff into a Single Help Desk" was the same task or initiative as "Building a Common Culture". That sort of thinking turned out to be a major problem: Simply telling employees they would cross-train to help another unit does not cause cohesion. We eventually recognized we had two very different cultures and resulting processes. ITIL implementation allowed for a common framework as a starting point, a common service management system further enabled coordination, but these did not cause the integrated unit to suddenly exist.

Previously, the service desk had relied on a new employee to read prepared documentation, ask questions, and then shadow an experienced co-worker to attain a productive level of knowledge. The service center hadn't trained an existing employee to work the phones or request queue before, so the limitations of this method quickly surfaced as the resulting questions and shadowing could not be handled in real time due to the after-hours schedules already in place for these employees.

Because the service desk was so set in its methods and standards, including the operations team in every meeting, email, and announcement was surprisingly difficult to always accomplish. Distribution lists had to be initiated specifically for enabling Computer Operations team members to ask questions and cite concerns. It was found that online, shared forms and documents needed to be formally established to supply channels to encourage information flow between different shifts/teams and between the teams' management. Years before, a subset of the most experienced Technology Service Center team members had been conscripted to populate a rotating on-call group should part of UW-IT suddenly need support from the service center in the middle of the night for a high-priority issue—this group was re-purposed as an escalation point for the new after-hours team to consult if confronted with an urgent issue for which they'd not been trained. We started using campus LMS systems to provide recordings of meetings and training sessions. Finally, exceptions had to be made to personnel schedules: Service desk personnel sometimes needed to come in early and operations personnel occasionally adjusted their schedule for a day to achieve truly collaborative meetings and to accomplish the job shadowing we simply could no longer afford to avoid.

4 CONCLUSIONS

Despite the general agreement that the Technology Service Center needed to operate 24x7x365 and that given our situation there was not a better way forward, this project was very difficult to enact in a fully-functional way. The real effort that caused our collaboration to succeed was a focus on *inclusion*. The cultural differences seemed (for a short time) insurmountable, but fortunately management identified much of the issue to be a failure to address the different groups' perspectives. A new effort at constant communication between the two teams led the way to significant cohesion. Amongst the many specific outcomes of that focus on communication were the following changes, each of which have since been recognized as items of benefit to the Single Point of Contact/24x7 project, gains in efficiency for the teams involved, and improvement in consistency of support for our customers.

It was found that not only was it beneficial to recognize differences between two teams called on to provide the same support, but it was critical to consider *from the initial stages* how each difference might impact the success of such a project. We learned that despite the easily dismissed "soft-skill" nature of team cultures, it could become an impasse if not identified and addressed.

We should also note that we are proud to be able to say that our customer goals were achieved: We are more unified, consistent, and available, let alone the Technology Service Center now has a strong partner in the Computer Operations team for overflow and after-hours support of our UW-IT customers.

5 ACKNOWLEDGMENTS

UW-IT's Customer Service & Support upper management team (especially: Karalee Woody, Assistant Vice President, Damien Koemans, Assistant Director of the Technology Service Center, and Michael Houlihan, Assistant Director of Computer Operations) helped get us started on the project which led to this finished, presentable product.

You Know You Want to Read This – Communicating Effectively in Tech Support

Robert H Guissanie, Jr.
Bucknell University
117 Bertrand Library
Lewisburg, PA 17837
rob.guissanie@bucknell.edu

ABSTRACT

As wonderful as technology can be, it is and will always be a tool that "attempts" to improve the quality of life for the human being. As we support technology we must never lose the perspective that we are, in every way, supporting people. Often, the most important work we do is not about technology at all!

An organization's "technology effectiveness" is largely predicated upon its relationship between the technology support team and its clientele. Successful relationships between people are defined by a number of characteristics, but perhaps there is no characteristic more important than effective, relevant, and meaningful communication.

During my 15 years at Bucknell University we, like all technology support organizations in higher education, have been purveyors of change. Some of our clients embrace it, some resist it. Most clients are in the middle, seeking to understand why the change is necessary and what it means to them.

It's ALL about communication. It's about understanding your audience. It's about using relevant and understandable terminology. It's about understanding people who want to know what they need to know when they need to know it—and how it affects them.

CCS CONCEPTS

• **Social and Professional Topics** → **Professional Topics**; *Computing and Business*

KEYWORDS

Communication; Written Communication; Training; Technical Support; Incident Management; Problem Management; End-User Support; Customer Service; Client Relationship Management

1 INTRODUCTION

The Merriam-Webster dictionary defines communication as "an act or instance of transmitting; information communicated; a verbal or written message; a process by which information is exchanged between individuals through a common system of symbols, signs, or behavior; a personal rapport." [2]

Unfortunately, knowing what communication is does not translate to being able to do it effectively. William H. Whyte, journalist and best-selling author from the 1950's writes, "***The great enemy of communication, we find, is the illusion of it.*** *We have talked enough; but we have not listened. And by not listening we have failed to concede the immense complexity of our society—and thus the great gaps between ourselves and those with whom we seek understanding.*"[3]

Today "communication" is directed at us relentlessly. For some time we have had television, newspapers, magazines, billboards, and radio. However, the evolution of the Internet and mobile technology now expose us to new and more "unrelenting" avenues used to direct information at us—creating the burden of sorting out what we need to know and what we don't.

Ideally, we in higher education technical support are a utility nobody notices unless things go wrong. However, what is different about the "utility" we provide is the need for effective communication. Our clients need to understand how to use it, what to expect when it changes, and how interruptions in these services affect their world.

Amidst all of the "noise" out there, how do we keep our clients informed about the relevancy of our message and—most importantly—earn their trust so they believe what we are telling them?

2 COMMUNICATING WITHIN

There are a variety of areas IT organizations in colleges and universities manage: enterprise systems, telephony, networking, systems administration, digital pedagogy and scholarship,

[2] Merriam-Webster. 2017. Retrieved from https://www.merriam-webster.com/ on August 1, 2017.
[3] 1950 September, Fortune, "Is Anybody Listening?" by William Hollingsworth Whyte, Start Page 77, Quote Page 174, Published by Time, Inc., New York. (Verified on microfilm)
http://quoteinvestigator.com/2014/08/31/illusion/

classroom technology, front-line hardware and software support. There's a lot going on behind the scenes among these varied groups within the organization—all of it interrelated.

Have you ever been in a situation when a technology change "nobody should notice" was implemented and, well, suddenly noticed by a few hundred clients? Not good. It's especially not good when staff within the same organization were also not expecting to notice the changes and are the recipients of an unintentional "blindside."

Of course, I believe we are all good people here at Bucknell and no one intends for these things to happen. After all, if technology were perfect all the time many of us would not have a job! Acknowledging these situations can potentially occur brings us to the first step for effective communication to your campus community—effective communication *within* your internal IT organization. Regular "check in" meetings should be planned among representatives from all IT constituencies to keep a finger on the pulse of activities and projects potentially affecting others. Collaboration is essential!

3 FIGURING OUT WHAT PEOPLE NEED TO KNOW

When you are on the same page internally, your next step is to figure out what information your campus community *needs* to know. For example, if your system administrators are applying security patches to a system that will not cause a noticeable change, service disruption, or bring any perceived value to your clients—why bother telling them? While your staff are demonstrating due diligence and ultimately protecting the interests of critical university systems, clients frankly don't care about the security patches unless it affects their world. We need to view everything we communicate in this way.

4 FIGURING OUT WHO NEEDS TO KNOW

As with any communication, there is the very important question of "Who is your target audience?"

It would be easy to blast the entire campus with every communication about everything. It makes communication simple for us, but puts the burden on the campus community to sort out what information is relevant and what is not. It's like giving someone a book and saying, "I know only a few chapters apply to your situation. Just read through the entire book and pay special attention to the sections that might apply to you." Nobody wants to spend time reading a book where 80% of the information does not apply to them! After a while, they won't bother reading the book at all. Worse, any book you give them in the future probably won't be opened either—even if the entire volume applies to them.

Make every effort to target communications where possible. If there is a certain cohort of individuals nearing a storage limit on a system, do not communicate with *everyone* using the system to more closely monitor their quota. Target just the individuals your message affects whenever possible. Yes, this takes some effort. However, your clients will start to recognize

the communication they receive from you is consistently pertinent and will read it.

5 FIGURING OUT HOW TO SAY IT

At Bucknell there are a number of ways we communicate with our campus community. Email continues to be a primary method, as it can easily be targeted to an audience, referred back to, and followed up on. We also have an online "Message Center" where general information about campus events, academic talks, and even personal classifieds are posted by category. Among these categories is "Technology Alerts and Updates." While this is more of a "communications blast" approach, we do have the ability to specifically target the students by class year, faculty, and staff cohorts within that specific subject area.

In addition to email and the Message Center, we have other ancillary methods of communication we utilize as appropriate including an online blog, web page, Twitter channel, Facebook, and digital signage. We continue to experiment with these methods, but all subsidize our primary communication methods of email and the Message Center. The more significant the message, the more methods used and the more frequent the communication will be.

6 FIGURING OUT THE TIMING

What you say and how you say it is certainly important. However, when you say it is just as relevant to how memorable it will be.

For example, your networking group needs to stage a one-hour wireless networking outage. Let's also assume the internal communication and collaboration in your organization is highly functional and instead of scheduling this outage at 2:00 P.M. on a Wednesday during classes you have agreed to do it at 5:00 A.M. on a Sunday.

The timing of the outage is good, but a critical service such as wireless networking is something that is used 24/7 by a large number constituencies on campus—some you may be able to anticipate, others you may not. Broad communication needs to happen, but when? Communicate too soon and nobody remembers. Communicate too much and it becomes white noise. Communicate too late and you run the risk of creating an unintended inconvenience or a failure to recognize potential "show stopping" circumstances that might have postponed the outage altogether.

In this particular scenario, there's nothing the campus needs to actually "do" to prepare for the outage. If there was, a longer lead time for communication would be required. However, wireless networking is a service affecting pretty much everyone (although at 5:00 A.M. on a Sunday the numbers affected are significantly reduced) so we need to communicate broadly.

In this example, we would most likely communicate three different times. First, we would make an announcement on the preceding Monday to give everyone adequate notice. We would follow with a "reminder" message on Thursday as we draw closer to the outage. Finally, Friday afternoon or even on

Saturday morning we would post a short "imminent" outage reminder. All brief, to the point, and attention grabbing.

7 MAKING YOUR MESSAGE MEMORABLE

Remember elementary school? Sometimes I long for the days when "fun" was integrated with daily learning. Recess in the middle of the day. Engaging games in gym class. Art and music where we had the opportunity to create and perform without judgement. I recall smiles and laughter as a regular occurrence during my "lower education" years.

Now that we have graduated and are actively employed and engaged in "higher education," I think we sometimes take ourselves too seriously. We have "evolved" from creating stories and illustrations on paper without lines to submitting papers for conferences in the highly structured "ACM format."

I don't know about you, but I believe deep down a kid is still alive in all of us somewhere. A smile and a laugh can break down almost any barrier—and very effectively enhance communication.

Most of the material I read is pretty formal and bland. It is understandable, certainly well written, and good information. Every once in a while, though, it's refreshing to change things up.

A few years ago, our network administrator approached me about an issue we were having with wireless networking in the residence halls. Specifically, students had numerous devices "broadcasting" on the network (printers, personal routers, etc.). This was creating interference and negatively affected wireless coverage. We needed to ask the students to "stop it" so the problem would go away. We could have been very "matter of fact" about it, and we were. Below is the text of the message that was sent.

Greetings Bucknell Students!

Want better wireless reception in your residence hall? You can help.

One of the challenges we face with our wireless network at Bucknell is "competition."

From what, you ask?

Well, if you have any wireless device that broadcasts a network name (like personal wireless routers, wireless printers, etc.) it interferes with the wireless signal we are trying to broadcast to you. While the wireless convenience of these devices works great at home, they collectively create some challenges here on campus in close quarters with a few hundred other people.

For example, try connecting to wireless from your room. If you see more than just "bucknell.edu" and "bucknell_guests" as networks available to connect to, there is interference present.

So what can be done? The best solution is to turn off the wireless broadcasting component of these devices. That will help "clear the

air" for everyone and allow our Bucknell wireless network to propagate to you much more effectively.

It could be as easy as a simple conversation:
============================
Chad: (Yelling down the hall) "Hey, I'm seeing a network name called 'Cuddles.' Anyone know anything about that?"

Ivan: "I think that might be my printer. I just read the email from Library and IT. My bad. I'm figuring out how to turn it off right now."

Chad: "Thanks man! You're a gentleman and a scholar."

Ivan: "Love you bro!"
============================

It's a win-win for everyone. ;)

Questions? Please do not hesitate to contact the Tech Desk at techdesk@bucknell.edu or by calling 570-577-7777.

Thank you for your cooperation!

In the end, we communicated what the students needed to know, why it was in their best interests to comply with our request, and had fun creating a disarming message which was very positively received. Here is another example of a message we send to first-year students long before they even arrive on campus. It concerns the importance of safeguarding their Bucknell credentials.

Dear Class of 2020:

Congratulations and Welcome to Bucknell!

It is a busy and exciting time. You've got proms, banquets, graduation to plan for, and now--an "official" Bucknell account complete with your own unique username and password!

Just so you know, your username and password are "the key" to EVERYTHING of online importance at Bucknell. It's pretty hype, and your password should be kept very confidential.

Don't share your password with your best friend, girlfriend, or boyfriend. Don't share it with your brother or sister. You really shouldn't even share it with your parents. No human should know it other than you. If you have a burning desire to share your Bucknell password, you are probably safe confiding in your dog, cat, fish, or perhaps a plant.

Now you're probably thinking, "Wait! My parents need to access my college bills. I don't want to be the one dealing with that stuff!"

No problem. You can create "authorized users" in B-bill who can view your Bucknell financial account and make payments. Just visit: http://www.bucknell.edu/x68164.xml

*One other thing--and this is important. **We will NEVER, EVER ask you for your password in an email or otherwise.** We don't need it to "confirm" anything. No legitimate person or authority here at Bucknell would EVER request it from you, so don't disclose your password under ANY circumstance. There is just too much personal information about you that can potentially be exploited if your password falls into the wrong hands--and that can get MESSY.*

So manage your Bucknell credentials as you would, say, a pair of your underwear. Don't share them with anyone. Change them regularly. Don't leave them laying around. Be mysterious.

I hope you understand my point. ;)

Really and truly, we are excited to have you join our community here at Bucknell. If you have any questions or concerns regarding technology here on campus, please feel free to contact our Tech Support team at techdesk@bucknell.edu or by calling 570-577-7777.

We wish you the best as you wrap up your senior year of high school and hope you enjoy a wonderful summer. See you in August!

Of course, we like to have fun with our faculty and staff too. This excerpt of a message was sent early in July of 2011, when Microsoft Forefront was at the "forefront" of protection from viruses and malware.

"...But when a long train of abuses and usurpations, pursuing invariably the same object evinces a design to reduce them under absolute despotism, it is their right, it is their duty, to throw off such government, and to provide new guards for their future security." ~ Declaration of Independence

Dear Faculty and Staff:

While the United States has enjoyed over 200 years of freedom from repression, we continue to wage a "revolutionary war" against viruses and malware which assault our Windows computers from the Internet.

An updated and improved version of our anti-virus product, Microsoft Forefront, will be released to you to install within the next day or so. When you receive it, we ask you to "take up your arms" and join us in this fight by installing the product on your Windows machine...

8 ESTABLISHING TRUST AND CREDIBILITY

We've discussed several different important aspects of communication: organizational collaboration, relevancy of information, knowing your target audience, various communication methods, timing, and style. These are essential ingredients, but the overall effect of combining them in the proper way is something you cannot command. It is something you must earn—trust and credibility.

At Bucknell, I like to say we have established mutual respect with our campus community. We are purveyors of change, and while our clients are not always happy with that change most respect the fact it needs to happen.

We do the things we say we are going to do. Most times, fortunately, things go the way we said they would go without surprises. When things don't work out as expected, we are quick to accept responsibility and provide explanation. The communication we put out there is always relevant to the individuals who receive it, so our clients pay attention.

In addition, there are very few individuals in our organization who communicate directly with the campus. Primarily, it is handled by one person whose name--after 15 years--is recognizable and has a consistent style and tone. (In hindsight, we should have made up a name, had it trademarked, and passed it down over time.) The messages have a characteristically standard format from beginning to end, creating a differentiation from phishing attempts which have become all too common.

We do all these things to rise above the noise which has become louder than it has ever been from sources varying widely in credibility. In the end, we have learned no matter how rapidly technology change occurs, people tend to gravitate to constants that are credible, can be can relied upon, and have earned their respect over time.

I would like to share one final example with you. As any technology support person will recall, on May 3, 2017, the "Great Phishing Scheme" targeting Google accounts occurred widely across the country. At Bucknell, our finals week had just started and we ended up having over 400 accounts affected. Our campus community was stressed, confused, and communication needed to happen. The following is the message we sent.

Dear Campus Community:

As if finals were not stressful enough...

Bucknell, along with numerous other universities and organizations using Google for email, calendar, docs, etc. fell victim to a massive phishing attack today.

It was disguised as an email notification (probably from a familiar person) stating a Google document was shared with you. You were then directed to a page requesting access to your account.

If you clicked the Allow button, you granted "someone" access to everything in your account and--even worse--it was then used to further propagate the attack.

It appears over 300 Bucknell accounts (and counting) were affected by this security incident. Our systems staff have "cleaned up" the affected accounts reported to us. Some may have noticed this activity, as access was temporarily suspended during the process.

In the meantime, Google took steps to mitigate the attack, preventing it from spreading any further.

We are actively scanning our domain for signs and symptoms of compromised accounts not reported. For now, it appears things are returning to normal--if finals week can ever be defined that way.

Lesson learned: NEVER grant access to your Bmail or Gmail account unless you initiated the process yourself. If you fell for it, don't feel too bad. This was a good one.

As always, please feel free to contact Tech Support with any questions or concerns at techdesk@bucknell.edu or by calling 570-577-7777.

Best of luck the rest of the way.

It was not a time to be clever or funny. It was a time to be clear, calm, and sensitive to the emotions our clients were experiencing. Amid the hundred or so emails I processed that day was this one from a student who was graduating.

Hello Mr. Guissanie,

Just wanted to say thanks for always being so human and cool in your e-mails about cyber security - I was just remarking on this to a fellow student and thought, heck, might as well say it to you.

You write like a human being instead of trying for an official air. For example: your comment- "If you fell for it, don't feel too bad. This was a good one."

Just keep keepin' it real.

-Another human being

I have received positive feedback from messages I have sent before, but few as meaningful as this. Ironically, the sentence meaning the most to this student was not technical at all. It was the human connection that meant as much, if not more, than the information itself.

9 CONCLUSIONS

Communication in higher education technology support organizations is as important now as it has ever been. We are a change-driven environment where new technology is not only infused into our classrooms, but into our daily lives. Rapid adapters of this change arrive on our campuses every fall, becoming "relatively" younger and younger each academic year. Despite the years in age that divide us, guidance and support for the technology they have come to rely upon can unite us. However, no matter how much technology changes, we as human beings will always value people and organizations we can trust and rely upon. There is no better foundation to build this relationship upon than effective communication.

REFERENCES

[1] Merriam-Webster. 2017. Retrieved from https://www.merriam-webster.com/ on August 1, 2017.
[2] 1950 September, Fortune, "Is Anybody Listening?" by William Hollingsworth Whyte, Start Page 77, Quote Page 174, Published by Time, Inc., New York. (Verified on microfilm)
http://quoteinvestigator.com/2014/08/31/illusion/

Beyond Geek Speak: Dedicated Communications Expert is Critical to a Successful Campus IT Shop

Vicki L. Smith
West Virginia University
PO Box 6500 One Waterfront Place
Morgantown, WV 26506-6500
Vicki.Smith@mail.wvu.edu

ABSTRACT

A healthy relationship between an IT shop and the campus it serves is like any other, dependent upon frequent, effective and open communication. With it, you're a partner in critical conversations at the highest levels, establishing credibility, shaping decisions and demonstrating value when resources are dwindling. Without it, you risk becoming an anonymous utility, just one of many bills to be paid. At West Virginia University, communication isn't outsourced to the campus PR shop or delegated to a technical expert as one of 15 duties. It's the primary responsibility of a member of the Information Technology Services senior leadership team, a proactive, practical, professional brand ambassador who helps improve visibility and rapport.

In three years, ITS has developed: formal communication strategies for both planned and unplanned outages, including a DDoS attack; an outage listserv for IT staff and campus VIPs; an emergency texting messaging service with 200+ subscribers; a working partnership with University Relations; comprehensive strategic communication plans for campus on enterprise IT projects; regular IT updates to the campus; an extensive glossary of acronyms to ensure a common language; strong social media engagement; and compelling infographic messaging. But strong external communication requires internal communication, and at WVU, that meant culture change. Learn how a non-traditional team (a journalist, a graphic designer and a web developer) acquired IT expertise organically, and how they helped shape a workplace where frequent, fearless questioning is valued and where outreach is engaging, personal and producing tangible results.

SIGUCCS '17, October 1–4, 2017, Seattle, WA, USA
© 2017 Association for Computing Machinery.
ACM ISBN 978-1-4503-4919-2/17/10...$15.00
https://doi.org/10.1145/3123458.3123483

CCS CONCEPTS

• *Social and professional topics~Project staffing*
• *Social and professional topics~Employment issues*

KEYWORDS

Strategic communication; Leadership; Collaboration; Culture Change

1 INTRODUCTION

A healthy, constructive relationship between an IT shop and the campus it serves is like any marriage: It's a partnership whose success depends upon effective, frequent and bilateral communication. For a CIO or an executive leadership team in higher education, that means building and sustaining relationships with the faculty, staff and students you support. At West Virginia University, those relationships are so important to both our short- and long-term success of Information Technology Services that we believe they deserve the constant attention that only a full-time communications expert can provide. Done right, communications can help ensure that these relationships are productive, positive and mutually beneficial.

With effective communication, IT can become a partner in critical conversations at the highest levels, establishing credibility, shaping decisions and demonstrating value when resources are dwindling. Without the soft skills to balance the analytical, you risk becoming an anonymous utility, just one of many bills to be paid. At WVU, IT communication isn't outsourced to the campus PR shop or delegated to a technical expert as one of 15 other duties. It's the primary responsibility of a member of the senior leadership team. This proactive brand ambassador oversees a small but full-service creative shop whose primary role is to help improve visibility. Simply put, we tell IT's story – and we make IT interesting.

Increasingly, CIOs in the corporate world are recognizing [1] that a dedicated communications professional is an essential component of a thriving, relevant and valued IT leadership team. Universities are no different. In an EDUCAUSE "Viewpoints" piece [2], Marquette University CIO Kathy Lang espoused the value of communication clearly and explained how she takes the lead on her campus. But when a typical 40-hour work week may include 50 hours of meetings for an in-demand CIO, that's not sustainable. The CIO may be the most visible, engaged IT representative on campus, but he or she cannot be everywhere. The CIO's values, therefore, must be consistently and widely articulated. They must be emulated and repeated, and enshrined in every message that comes out of the department. At WVU, our mission is to support, empower and advance [3]. Put more simply, "We're here to help."

WVU's experience from 2013 to 2017 has taught us to let the CIO and technologists focus on the areas where they excel, while dedicating responsibility for messaging and public relations to the communicators. We recommend you devote the time, money and patience it takes to find the right person to do it well. In IT, your most effective communicator probably isn't a technologist; what you really need is a translator, a facilitator, a marketer and a relationship builder. A professional communicator is your image maker and your Storyteller-in-Chief, this person can help demonstrate your value when things are working well and help move IT beyond being a nameless, faceless voice on the phone when something breaks. If faculty, staff and students feel a connection to IT when things are working well, they may have more patience when they aren't.

2 Execution

2.1 Where do you start?

Our success so far began in 2013 with a single building block: The CIO had to promote his vision for what communication could be like, then convince those holding the purse strings why it was essential to hire an expert from outside. He had to push back when others argued, "You're an IT shop; we can do that for you." They would have tried, to be sure. But they weren't going to be able to deal with the daily outages, security issues and product updates, let alone a never-ending list of projects, services, tools and initiatives.

Although IT appreciated the offer of support, we understood the reality: To convey information quickly, you need to be able to understand the lingo and the issues at hand without hours to brush up. You also need to have relationships with critical IT personnel so you can get information you need quickly; that's how you communicate early and often with your customers. That wasn't going to happen with an offsite public relations person who has five other areas of responsibility. Minutes matter when the LMS crashes or the networks drop. Hours of silence would be unacceptable.

The CIO also argued that we must be responsive and transparent when the news is bad, and proactive and positive when it's good. The old way of thinking was essentially, "We don't talk about what we do." There was, in some quarters, either a reluctance to acknowledge problems and/or a tendency to look for where to lay the blame for them. The CIO wanted to move beyond that, to

instill an appreciation for transparency in the staff and, to some extent, push them beyond their previous comfort level. Should you try to create this position in your university, be mindful that institutionally, there is likely no frame of reference for your vision. You may have to sell it. And outside your unit, you'll have to explain why an IT communicator is NOT the same as the communicator for an academic college. The duties are much broader, more urgent, often sensitive and frequently system-wide.

Next, you must clearly identify the necessary skills and abilities. An effective communicator:

- understands how to match the message to the audience;
- displays an inherent but appropriate sense of urgency;
- is proactive, not just responsive;
- can process complex concepts and translate them concisely and accurately, avoiding jargon, acronyms and technical terms;
- must deliver the "news" from IT and make it relevant;
- must reinforce the idea that communicating, not hiding, is the best approach;
- can teach a new way of thinking, respectfully working with people who were hired for very specific technical skills and not necessarily for their ability to communicate with each other or our customers;
- must be willing to learn a whole new language, culture and expanding set of issues;
- must have the courage to take risks and make mistakes, and learn from them;
- needs to bring a broader, outsider's perspective to discussions that by nature tend to focus on technology, not the people using it.

So where do you find someone like that? Turns out there are many kinds of communicators. When the Director of Communication and Marketing position was posted, WVU got about 80 applicants. Recent graduates looking to use their degrees. Technical writers. Traditional corporate PR officers. Newspaper writers looking to flee a shrinking industry. As the search committee sifted through the diverse resumes, two rose to the top – a traditionalist from the corporate world and a wire-service journalist whose experience covering crises and crisis mismanagement had taught her how they should be handled. WVU hired the journalist.

2.2 The 5Ws and the H: Who, What, Where, When, Why and How

Journalists tend to be effective communicators because they are taught to answer basic questions every time they report the news. To be solid, each story must, at a minimum, address "the five Ws and the H" -- Who, What, Where, When, Why and How. At WVU, we apply that to all IT messaging: We clearly, succinctly articulate what is happening and WHO will be affected (students, faculty, staff, parents, visitors, vendors, etc.) as that will determine what channels we to use to communicate. We explain HOW people will be affected, WHEN it will happen and, whenever possible, WHY. Even the WHERE is relevant, as situations may apply only to a particular building or campus, while other locations may be unaffected.

In creating the team, the same questions apply:

WHO: Find someone who can become an "instant expert," a person who can quickly digest complex information and concepts, ask the right questions to determine the practical impact for customers, then translate the jargon for a lay audience. This person must be unafraid to ask "dumb" questions and masterful at anticipating variations of "What does this mean to me?" Support that person with a balance of technologists and creative talent.

WHAT: The chief communicator must be able to not only manage a crisis, but also carve out time every day to think strategically about how to communicate the work IT does and what it means to faculty, students and staff. The communicator must explain when, where and why change is coming, and how it will affect the ability of the individual to succeed in work, study or research. This person must understand technologists but resist the temptation to regurgitate acronyms and "geek speak." Instead, the communicator must zealously convey the essential information and relatable examples in plain English.

WHY: IT people already know that faculty, staff, administrators and students can't succeed in their own work without robust technology tools and reliable infrastructure. Customers need to appreciate that, too. To be a partner in the important conversations and changes occurring on campus, IT must talk about what it does, why it matters and how it can help solve problems or improve efficiency. These conversations are also vital to ensuring that IT has the financial and human resources it needs to grow and flourish at a time when state educational funding is dwindling [4].

HOW: Effective communication is consistent, clear, concise and conversational. These are the words that drive WVU's approach to engagement. We ask questions of each other fearlessly and frequently. We design colorful, creative infographics to convey data that might otherwise appear dull. We occasionally seek out news coverage from campus and outside media. We converse regularly with students and employees, virtually and in person. We seek to defuse anger by being proactive, and we aim to respond constructively when people are frustrated. We are credible, accessible and accountable. We are not perfect, but we are constantly trying to engage and improve.

At WVU, the communications team has:
- created formal communication strategies for both planned and unplanned outages, including a DDos attack;
- created an outage listserv for both central and distributed IT staff, and campus VIPs;
- created an emergency text messaging service as a backup to email, with hundreds of subscribers;
- consolidated website control, resulting in more cohesive, consistent and clear content from IT teams;
- built a partnership and improved coordination with University Relations;
- developed comprehensive strategic communication plans for enterprise IT projects such as a new online hiring and purchasing systems, and, in the second half of 2017, the campus-wide rollout of two-factor authentication [5];
- developed how-to documentation for the Communications team and generated regular IT updates to campus stakeholders;
- developed an extensive glossary of acronyms [6] to ensure that within IT, there is a common language;
- embraced social media engagement;
- developed visually compelling forms of messaging.

But strong external communication requires good internal communication, and at WVU, that meant culture change. Here's where the "how" defies a simple, tweetable explanation, and where culture change is still occurring. Over four years, our team has included a journalist, a graphic designer, two web developers, a student worker majoring in strategic marketing and most recently, a former systems administrator with a background in English and journalism. Together, we have pooled our unique talents and perspectives to acquire IT expertise organically, then share our knowledge thoughtfully, strategically and plainly.

2.2 We're here. Now what do we do?
Our team quickly learned that you can't communicate effectively with your customers if you aren't communicating effectively in-house. Add a merger to the equation, and things get even more complicated. In 2014, the Office of Information Technology merged with four other units (Student Systems Management, Administrative Technology Solutions, Research Office IT and Printing Services) to form Information Technology Services. Since then, Student Life IT and the Mountaineer ID Card Services group have joined the fold, more than doubling our numbers to about 230 employees.

Not only did we have different cultures, but different ideas about how and what to communicate, let alone to whom and when. So, we first developed a shared set of expectations, then began working on a common language that includes an ever-evolving glossary of acronyms and phrases. The same acronym can have different meanings, depending on the context of the discussion and the IT unit involved. We created standardized templates to announce both planned maintenance and unplanned outages, giving everyone the same information about every outage in the central IT unit every time. We began explaining WHY we make changes rather than just announcing that they're coming. We began to encourage and embrace feedback.

As we continue to improve and refine our processes, we are expanding the lead time that we provide, giving our faculty, students and staff more time to plan for the down time. Today, all planned maintenance must be entered into a standard template in our service management tool, TeamDynamix [7], the same day the work is approved by the Change Approval Board (CAB). This helps Communications determine whether there will be an interruption of service, and when and how to convey the information to customers. As of December 2016, all non-emergency CAB requests must be submitted 15 days in advance.

Mass messages are delivered through social media platforms (Twitter and Facebook) as well as targeted LISTSERV lists and system wide eNews (a daily email newsletter from University Relations). We also dedicate significant time to in-person interaction: We attend new student orientation (NSO) every weekday in June and special, smaller NSO events throughout the year. We attend new employee orientation to talk about ITS every Monday year-round. We attend faculty training events, prospective students' visitation days and many other campus events. When new freshmen move into residence halls for the first time every August, more than 100 IT staff are on hand to get them hooked up to our networks and services through an initiative called Team Connect.

Now and then, all that face time pays off. When we had a serious, three-day outage of eCampus, our mission-critical Learning Management System (LMS), we told people what the problem was, updated them every few hours, and eventually explained how we fixed it and how we hoped to prevent a recurrence. We emerged from that crisis with virtually no residual customer resentment; instead, we received compliments on how well-informed we kept our customers as we struggled to solve the problem.

2.3 "A goal without a plan is just a wish." - *Antoine de Saint-Exupéry*

To act and react consistently, you need a plan. When we started in the fall of 2013, there was none. We started by identifying both challenges and opportunities. To draft a plan, you must first anticipate the types of things you'll need to communicate and understand that the plan will be a living document, growing more specific and nuanced all the time. That plan should include a comprehensive toolbox that outlines the mechanisms through which you will convey your message and backup tools when those are down. There is no silver bullet. Reaching a fractured audience requires many tools, including social media. You have to reach your customers where they live, physically and virtually. The strategy must also consider how you will collaborate with external IT groups on campus, your campus PR shop and the university administration.

When WVU IT leaders feared that we could be targeted by a DDoS (Distributed Denial of Service) attack, ITS took the lead in crafting what we would say, when, how and to whom, then worked with University Relations to fine-tune the plan. Our text messages and social media messages are already scripted for those first few hours. This paid off in October 2016, when DDoS attack disrupted

social media and other services our students use and enjoy [8]. On a rainy Friday afternoon when the ITS communicator was out of town and students were headed back to their dorms to watch Netflix, the University Relations team was able to use the boilerplate language that had been prepared a year earlier to proactively warn students what was going on.

There will be challenges. At WVU, the central IT staff had gone through many leadership changes, and many employees had long embraced a culture of silence. They were reluctant to talk about their work and often felt under attack. Some units came from a rigid hierarchical structure where employees could not go directly to supervisors/directors in other units with ideas, questions or concerns. Open-door policies were not common.

Social media is where our customers live today. Yet we had a Facebook account that went unused. The Twitter account was locked, requiring would-be followers to provide their name to a third-party authentication service. It was unnecessary and counter-productive for a social media tool designed to create an audience, and we lost most potential followers as a result. The communications director unlocked the account on her second day on the job, began using it aggressively, and grew the audience from about 800 to 2,600 in about 18 months.

There were other challenges, too. We had to get people to buy in to the value of what we were doing. That process takes time. But when people started to see positive feedback rather than just complaints, the value of communication became apparent. Today, there's virtually no resistance to sending out announcements, acknowledging problems and getting in front of potential problems. Typically, unit leaders now come to communications with suggestions. The team works with those subject matter experts to refine the message, then vets it with the larger ITS leadership group. Whenever possible, we "tell family first" in IT, sharing with our academic and external IT groups across campus before we make our messaging public. That courtesy and involvement has created good will and helped support a strong and growing spirit of cooperation between central IT and the decentralized units.

Another challenge was the director's lack of familiarity and experience with IT. Though she had a general appreciation for technical people, she didn't understand the language or how things worked. She had to tackle a huge learning curve, and did so the way any good reporter tackles a new subject: Learn everything you can from anyone who will talk to you, and get others to start talking. Knowledge, credibility and trust are earned gradually. Today, nearly everyone in ITS has come to see the value of communication. The staff know more than ever about what other groups in the department are doing because information is shared both informally and formally, through a weekly IT Update that is distributed to all staff. The individuals who make ITS collectively successful are coming to understand that the value of knowledge and information comes from sharing it, not hoarding it.

If your university creates a dedicated communications group, you'll want to keep it lean and efficient. IT shops properly spend their limited dollars on high-value, high-dollar technical positions. But we recommend you carve out a budget to make communications a priority, too. One person is a great start, but be sure to consider the preparedness mantra, "Two is one and one is none." It means everyone and everything needs a backup. Like your CIO, the chief communicator can't always be available either. However, if you develop a plan, assemble a team, then create and reinforce the expectations from the top down and the bottom up, a small team is enough.

ACKNOWLEDGMENTS

The ITS Communications team and its work would not exist without the vision and support of former CIO and current West Virginia University Vice Provost John Campbell, as well as the support he received from the central administration. Nor would ITS have realized the possibilities of visual communication without the creativity and imagination of web developer/graphic designer Lisa Bridges, who has been critical to the team's success. Finally, the ITS Communications team is grateful to all the technologists who have accepted, embraced and recognized the value of their non-traditional peers.

REFERENCES

[1] B. Stackpole. Budding role of IT communications director helps IT deliver its message. ComputerWorld. July 2015. http://www.computerworld.com/article/2936179/it-management/budding-role-of-it-communications-director-helps-it-deliver-its-message.html

[2] K. Lang. Effective Communication: Not as easy as it seems. Educause Review. September/October 2015. https://er.educause.edu/~/media/files/articles/2015/8/erm1559.pdf

[3] WVU Information Technology Services. http://it.wvu.edu/governance

[4] M. Mitchell, M. Leachman, K. Masterson. Funding down, tuition up. Center on Budget and Policy Priorities. August 2016. http://www.cbpp.org/research/state-budget-and-tax/funding-down-tuition-up.

[5] Two-Factor Authentication (Duo) articles. WVU Information Technology Services. https://wvu.teamdynamix.com/TDClient/KB/Default?CategoryID=3626

[6] Glossary of ITS Acronyms. WVU Information Technology Services. https://wvu.teamdynamix.com/TDClient/KB/ArticleDet?ID=12913.

[7] How Can We Help? WVU Information Technology Services. https://wvu.teamdynamix.com/TDClient/Home/

[8] N. Woolf. DDoS attack that disrupted internet was largest of its kind in history, experts say. The Guardian – US Edition. Oct 26 2016. https://www.theguardian.com/technology/2016/oct/26/ddos-attack-dyn-mirai-botnet

Intentional Transparency - How to Develop One Service Catalog for All IT Services

Elizabeth Rugg
UNC Charlotte
9201 University City Blvd
Charlotte, NC 28033
erugg@uncc.edu

ABSTRACT

UNC Charlotte recently embarked on a journey to develop a Unified Service Catalog representing the IT services provided by over 50 IT service providers from across campus. The goal was to increase transparency internally and externally, enabling the institution to identify redundant services.

Using the ECAR Service Catalog as a starting point, the team developed a common vocabulary and framework to identify and categorize services; defined a methodology for data collection, designed the user interface, conducted usability studies and developed a roadmap to maintain the service catalog for years to come. The vision and strategic mandate, the general strategy and methodology as well as lessons learned will be discussed so that this process can be adopted by other institutions.

CCS CONCEPTS

Human-centered computing > Interaction design > Interaction design process and methods > User centered design

KEYWORDS

Service Management; Centralized; Decentralized; Transparency; Unified

1 BACKGROUND

UNC Charlotte is a public research university with 29,000 students and 4000 faculty and staff. UNC Charlotte offers 21 doctoral, 64 master's, and 90 bachelor's degree programs through nine colleges: the College of Arts + Architecture, the College of Liberal Arts & Sciences, the Belk College of Business, the College of Computing and Informatics, the Cato College of Education, the William States Lee College of Engineering, the College of Health and Human Services, the Honors College, and the

SIGUCCS '17, October 1–4, 2017, Seattle, WA, USA
© 2017 Association for Computing Machinery.
ACM ISBN 978-1-4503-4919-2/17/10...$15.00
https://doi.org/10.1145/3123458.3123471

University College. UNC Charlotte is part of the 17 member UNC system.

UNC Charlotte's has approximately 300 staff in centralized and distributed IT. Central IT has approximately 120 staff, and supports the infrastructure and enterprise (or common good) services for the institution. Within Central IT, the Client Engagement (CE) team is responsible for many service management functions including change, incident and problem management. In 2016, Central IT migrated to Cherwell Service Management system for incident, problem and change management; the existing system was no longer supported.

Distributed IT staff provide a variety of services for their colleges or units. These services vary depending on organizational need; most distributed IT teams provide support; while, others provide customized programming and application development. The independent nature of these units makes it difficult to develop a comprehensive understanding of the overall infrastructure, services and costs associated with IT across the institution. It also difficult to coordinate projects and evaluate impact of initiatives.

IT governance exists but is not effective and is currently undergoing a review process. The new process will be designed to increase transparency around IT projects and services. Currently, Central IT is often not involved in projects until late in the selection process, and it has been difficult to coordinate and prioritize changes related to projects and their impact on the campus community. In recent years, many enterprise changes were put into effect in a short period of time causing "change fatigue." For example, in 2015, the email and calendaring, HR, Early Alert, Advising and LMS systems all changed.

2 IT MASTER PLAN

Because of this complex environment and siloed approach, university leadership commissioned a strategic analysis in 2013-2014, that resulted in a new IT Master Plan. Over 300 faculty, staff and students had input into this five-year, University-wide IT Master Plan. This plan identified 16 IT priorities and reflects the "One University" concept developed by University Chancellor Philip Dubois. The master plan set the direction for all IT service providers at the University--not just Central IT--and identified issues related to transparency, service management and communication.

3 UNIFIED SERVICE CATALOG

Initiative 4.3 of the IT Master Plan charged IT staff with the development of *"a customer centric Service Catalog that improves visibility of IT services across the University....the University needs to take steps to improve the completeness, convenience, and usefulness of the IT service catalog."* This unified catalog should contain all services provided by all IT service providers across the institution. The development of this catalog required a clear executive mandate (provided by the IT Master Plan), strong leadership, transparency, robust collaboration and a good data collection and implementation plan.

The Unified Service Catalog would improve customer experience (people would know what was offered and how to request the service) and visibility into redundant services. It would also be easier to quantify the total cost of IT and evaluate the impact of projects and initiatives on the service portfolio.

Central IT staff began working on the Unified Service Catalog in the summer of 2016. The team decided to follow the service catalog framework recommended by EDUCAUSE Center for Analysis and Research (ECAR) in *The Higher Education IT Service Catalog: A Working Model for Comparison and Collaboration.*

3.1 Service Catalog Committee

Although the project was initiated by the CIO and managed by Central IT, it was important for this to be a collaborative, university-wide effort, so a steering committee was formed. The committee met over the summer, reviewed the ECAR paper, discussed the framework and created an RFP to enlist the help of a consultant for the actual data collection and implementation.

After some research, it appeared that few organizations had tackled a unified service catalog compiling all IT services together in one place. Finding a consultant with that experience was a key differentiator when RFP responses were reviewed.

The committee approach worked well; committee members understood the value and importance of this project and were transparent about services and issues. Committee members developed a common understanding about the project and the service catalog language and identified questions and areas of concern before the consultant was brought on-site.

Prior to the formation of this group, executive leadership feared that individual units would not disclose their services. So far, this has not been an issue. The committee has been very cohesive enabling the project to move forward at a rapid pace.

3.2 RFP

An RFP was authorized in fall 2016. The RFP said

> The scope of work for implementing a Unified IT Service Catalog should include the following elements:
>
> - Analyze and review the scope and functionality of the existing Central ITS IT Service Catalog for inclusion in Unified Service Catalog effort and recommend changes

> as needed; meet with ITS subject matter experts and service owners
>
> - Collect and analyze data related to services offered by sample Distributed IT units
>
> - Based on general guidelines of ECAR framework, develop recommendation for Unified IT Service Catalog from analysis and review of Central ITS and Distributed IT units offerings
>
> - Present and review initial recommendation and initial Unified Service Catalog with stakeholders
>
> - Assist, configure, create initial Unified IT Service Catalog in Cherwell Service Management solution
>
> - Gather customer feedback on initial Unified Service Catalog and revise accordingly
>
> - Develop strategy for completion and maintenance of Unified IT Service Catalog
>
> - Present and review final recommendation with stakeholders

The effort had three phases: 1) initial information gathering, 2) draft proposal with initial Unified Service Catalog and 3) the final roadmap/strategy for continued development and maintenance.

The committee selected the company with prior experience developing this type of catalog, had staff who had worked in higher education and were affordable. Having identified funding in advance was important since fees varied dramatically and was a factor in awarding the contract.

3.3 Data Collection

Prior to the consultant coming on-site, the Steering Committee created a draft unified service catalog. This effort helped identify questions and concerns and allowed the team to develop a cohesive focus and common vocabulary.

The formal engagement with the consultant began with a one day workshop; all committee members and a few other key representatives attended. In this workshop, the team identified the lines of service and appropriate services. Modifications to the ECAR guidelines were identified. After the workshop, the data collection started in earnest. Over three days, the consultant and a business analyst met with 11 key areas and identified over 50 services.

IT staff were asked to go through the lines of service and identify whether or not they offered services in a specific category. If yes, they identified the service owner, the functional owner and who would be able to see/use/request the service with choices being all faculty, staff and students, or only faculty, staff and students associated with a certain college or department.

Early on, the Steering Committee decided that a consultant would be engaged to do some, but not all, of the data collection since someone at UNC Charlotte would have to maintain the catalog. The Client Engagement Business Analyst was tasked with knowing the data collection process and procedures; he worked in tandem with the consultant doing the initial assessment and completed the data collection. By participating in the early sessions (11), he learned the interviewing and data collection process and helped ensure consistency as information was gathered from an additional 40 departments. Developing in-house expertise is paramount to being able to successfully maintain the service catalog. The "train-the-implementer" process worked well.

After the initial engagement, 8 lines of service were identified which contained 56 services. The 8 lines of service are:

- Business & Administrative

- Communication & Collaboration

- Device Computing

- Infrastructure

- IT Professional Services

- Research, Security

- Teaching & Learning.

When developing a service catalog:

- Keep in mind that some services may be a good fit for more than one line of service; but it is important to identify the most appropriate final landing place.

- Keep the conversations at a high level; it is very easy to get bogged down in too many details.

- Don't worry about the interface and the presentation layer during the initial data collection phase. You want to collect a comprehensive list of services and not restrict your collection based on how you anticipate how the services will be displayed.

Identifying the service and functional owners was difficult especially for shared services and services that did not have clear escalation points. Our preference was to identify an individual, preferably a manager rather than an executive or front-line staff; however, for some services (e.g. Device Support), a group (Client-Facing Technology Committee) seemed more appropriate.

Over 50 departments were interviewed, and the initial Unified Service Catalog was 1400 lines long!

3.4   Focus Groups

After the initial data collection, mock-ups of the Unified Service Catalog were shown to faculty, staff and student focus groups. We didn't want to get too far into the new design without factoring in their input to ensure we were on target.

Each group had its own perspective and feedback. We had to explain what we were doing and the value of this work. Both faculty and staff were concerned that we were not going to provide them with the option to call in and talk to someone. Faculty wanted the tool to know their role and only present services that were available to them. Everyone wanted an easy search option. All of the groups were concerned about the number of clicks to get to a service. The groups were also confused by the "device computing" category, but no one was able to come up with better terminology.

The feedback was valuable and helped inform the final design.

3.5   Implementation Plan

Phase two involved finalizing the service catalog, collecting focus group feedback and configuring the unified service catalog in Cherwell. These were the priorities:

- Have a clean, visually appealing design with ample white space (not a link farm) and icons that graphically depict services.

- Allow customers to self-identify their role as faculty, staff, or student instead of trying to pull in this information from another source. Many community members have dual roles, and it would be difficult to get this information from the ERP system

- Provide easy search options for the Service Catalog and our FAQs. We didn't want customers to have to navigate a web page hierarchy.

- Use out of the box functionality and not do customer coding. We don't have a dedicated Cherwell application administrator, so we want to leverage out of the box functionality as much as possible.

As of May 2016, the technical implementation is underway and should be completed over the summer. The plan is for the Unified Service Catalog to have a "soft" roll-out in July so that issues can be identified prior to the start of fall semester.

3.6   Cherwell Configuration

Once the data was gathered, the initial design developed and feedback processed, it was time to develop the actual Unified Service Catalog in Cherwell.

After the initial work was done and 1400 services were identified, our Business Analyst reviewed the data, entered missing information and reviewed the logic. We worked with individuals and departments and made changes as needed. If you undertake a similar effort, make sure you have someone tasked with doing this detail work.

The project plan allotted 15 days for the Cherwell redesign and Unified Service Catalog implementation. This work is just starting but will be completed by mid-June 2017 and available to the campus community by early July. We expect unforeseen challenges, and we will report on those at the SIGUCCS conference in November 2017.

4.0 CONCLUSION

To summarize, UNC Charlotte has developed a Unified Service Catalog for all IT service providers. We have learned to:

- Make sure there is a clear mandate (such as our UNC Charlotte IT Master Plan) and clear executive support (we had the Chancellor's One University initiative and the CIO's charge).

- Put together a steering committee that represents Central and distributed IT interests, and keep the steering committee to 12-15 people.

- Identify funding in advance.

- Define a process. We broke the project into three phases: initial data collection, focus group feedback and implementation and roadmap for the future.

- Decide whether you need the expertise/mediation of an outside consultant.

- Decide whether you are going to start from scratch or adopt an existing framework (like the ECAR framework).

- Identify who will be the guardian of the Unified Service Catalog and how it will be maintained.

- Devote resources to the project.

- Define a reasonable timeline for the work. Our entire project took one year: six months for development of Steering Committee and RFP and six months for comprehensive data collection and implementation.

- Allow some flexibility for defining the service and functional owners. In some cases we were able to identify individuals, but in other cases--like device support--a group was identified as the service owner.

This Unified Service Catalog will benefit our customers, all IT staff and university leadership.

- Customers will have an easier time requesting services and help.

- The Unified Service Catalog will be the "one-stop shop" for IT requests and information, helping to alleviate customer confusion and speed up time to resolution.

- IT staff and leadership will have a comprehensive understanding of IT services offered by central and distributed IT allowing for better reporting, analysis and identification of redundant services.

- The new governance model will have committees dedicated to maintaining the Unified Service Catalog (Technology Portfolio Committees – TPCs). These committees will advise on projects and IT change efforts.

Since these committees will be made up of representative from the campus community, this clear alignment of the Unified Service Catalog to IT governance committees and IT projects will enable us to effectively manage IT services in a collaborative and transparent way. Our constituents want to know what and why change is being implemented, and we, as IT leaders, need to understand the overall impact of projects, initiatives and operational change. We believe this model will allow us to achieve these goals.

We are being intentionally transparent. The Unified Service Catalog will enable university leadership to better understand all of the services available to our campus community and the challenges and costs of offering these services.

ACKNOWLEDGMENTS

Many thanks to the UNC Charlotte Unified Service Catalog Committee, Jeff Wetherbee, Business Analyst, Change Manager and Cherwell Administrator, Brent Smith, Service Desk Manager, Cherwell Developer and Programmer and Andy Rivers, a knowledgeable, calm, level-headed partner. I can't imagine doing this without you!

New Educational ICT Environment with Cloud in Kyushu University

Naomi Fujimura
Information Infrastructure Initiative
Kyushu University
Japan
fujimura.naomi.274@m.kyushu-u.ac.jp

Satoshi Hashikura
Information Infrastructure Initiative
Kyushu University
Japan
hashikura.satoshi.057@m.kyushu-u.ac.jp

ABSTRACT

We reported the status of the educational ICT (Information and Communication Technology) environment in Kyushu University in SIGUCCS 2009. At that time, we provided the host computer and many iMacs as terminals for students. We have been using BYOD in our university since April 2013 as we reported in SIGUCCS 2013. At last, we almost completed the BYOD (Bring Your Own Device) project in Kyushu University

As our next step, we are going to move all servers such as Moodle, Mahara, application server, LDAP, and AD (Active Directory) from "on the premises" to the cloud. The cloud provides many advantages for us, namely physical space, power, budget, performance, and so on. It is now desirable for us to use cloud aggressively. However, many important people remain concerned about potential security issues. We have provided detailed measures against the problems in order to persuade the old guard.

In addition, it is important for us to provide a common ICT environment for students including Windows PCs and Macs. We are planning to introduce the VDI (Virtual Desktop Infrastructure) interface to make every student use a common Windows environment in classes without any limit in September 2017. Students can also use a Linux instance if they require it. For that purpose, we are going to develop the budget management system to control the usage of individual students under the specified budget level.

We are realizing the next generation educational ICT environment under BYOD with AWS cloud. It should be the model case for new higher education in the world.

CCS CONCEPTS

• **Applied computing ~ Learning management systems** • *Information systems ~ Enterprise resource planning*

KEYWORDS

Education; BYOD; Cloud; AWS; Servers; Moodle; VDI

1 INTRODUCTION

Kyushu University established the Educational Center for Information Processing in April 1979. The center introduced the host computer and 40 proper terminals for the first time [1]. Teachers taught students programing languages such as FORTRAN in this facility. It was the beginning of our struggle to improve our ICT environment for education. The number of leased terminals/host computers and PCs have been changing as shown in Table 1.

Table 1: The number of leased terminals/hosts and PCs

Year	Host Computer	Type	Numbers
1978	NEAC ACOS-7/600	Proper	40
1980	NEAC ACOS-7/700	Proper	**60**
1983	FACOM M-360	Proper	**160**
1985	FACOM M-380Q	Proper	**188**
1992	FACOM M-770/6	FMR-60HE	245
1996	FUJITSU S-4	FMV-575D	369
2000	FUJITSU GP7000F	FMV-6500	398
2005	FUJITSU PRIMEPOWER	FMV-C330	**598**
2009	None	iMac	**1087**
2014	None	iMac	**581**
2017	None	iMac	**0**

We changed the terminal type from proper one to Windows PC in 1992. We also changed from Windows PC to iMac machines to reduce cost in 2009. All free printers were also eliminated at that time. We confirmed that the number of terminals was never enough for students as expected.

Since each department has different computing needs, the same machines in each PC room didn't make sense. The department of Literature might require iPad, the department of Engineering requires high performance PCs, and the department of Design prefers Macs for their design purpose.

This difference in computing needs for each department was the most important reason for us to imagine BYOD (Bring Your Own Device). Consequently, we proposed the BYOD project and started it in 2013 [2]. The new incoming students buy their own

PCs and bring them to university to use them in classes. Full four years has passed since April 2013. All students have their own PCs except those of Medical, Dentistry, and Pharmacy which consist of 6 school years. We need one more year to perfectly complete our BYOD Project.

2 NECESSITY OF THE CLOUD

2.1 Lack and New Requirement in Class

We have almost finished the BYOD project in Kyushu University as mentioned. All students have their own PCs now which is very useful for students to use in class and home. However, students have some difficulty due to the variation of the computers that they bring.

It is necessary to provide the same ICT environment for students to make excise easy to practice with some kind of VDI (Virtual Desktop Infrastructure). In addition, students want to use Linux in some classes especially in graduate school when it is difficult for students to install Linux on their own PCs.

While it is impossible to expect students to infect their own PCs with viruses and worms, we are creating a disposable Windows PC environment for students who need special environments. We are planning to make a sandbox where students can experience the symptoms of a virus and worm infection to learn firsthand about cyber security. Students can then throw the infected Windows instance away after they experienced the case.

2.2 Another Reason for Cloud

Our administration feels it is now necessary to explore using the cloud aggressively. While we have concerns about usability, load, and manageability, administration is concerned with cost, physical space, flexible performance, especially when it comes to dynamic load balancing. The most promising solution is to adopt IaaS cloud resources as soon as possible. Our specific needs include:

- Reducing amount of electric power needed to operate servers from our campus.
- Saving space in our earthquake-proof server room.
- Shifting the hardware cost to the vendor
- Flexible load-balancing.

We adopted AWS (Amazon Web Service) to operate the servers for our Web learning system, application servers, CALL servers, and authentication servers, and they will start operating in June 2017. We are also going to introduce our VDI (Virtual Desktop Infrastructure) in September 2017. After an aggressive bidding-war in May 2017, we chose AWS instead of Azure to host our VDI solution.

3 SYSTEM CONFIGURATION

We have been operating several servers on the premises for the Moodle and Mahara Web Learning Systems, application server, CALL (Computer Assisted Language Learning) server, and authentication server for LDAP and AD (Active Directory). We are going to move these servers to AWS (Amazon Web Service) cloud as IaaS.

3.1 Moodle and Mahara Server

We designed our system to ensure the stable operation of servers in spite of the load. We adopted multiple servers that vary the number of active servers from 2 to 8 to adjust the total performance according to the user activity with the load balancer. However, we encountered a problem with our Moodle server.

It seems that Moodle is not designed for multiple servers. Moodle saves the important information for a session in the local temporary files. As a result, a server cannot get the information in the temporary file if the session is switched to another server by the load balancer. We changed the location of the working temporary files from the local disk to a shared location to make access possible to the necessary information among all servers.

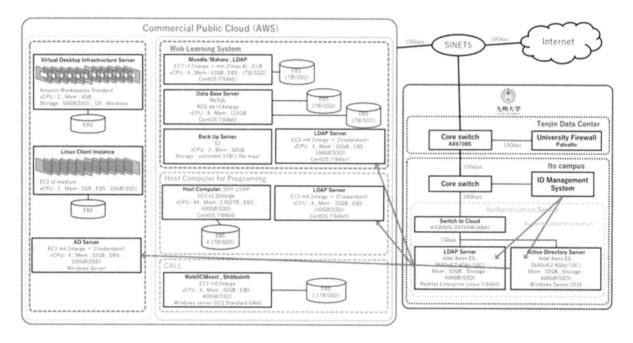

Figure 1: System Configuration

We still had a similar problem with the cache. Each server uses the cache to improve the performance of sharing files. The cache affected the performance of Moodle because each server had the long cache lifetime of 1 minute. When the value is changed in the shared files by the current server, the values contained in the cache on other servers don't change to the latest values. We were forced to change the lifetime of the cache from one minute to 100 milliseconds to make the value of cache void as soon as possible.

3.2 Application Server

The application server provides services such as GNU compiler (C and FORTRAN) and X window facility to the students. Students log into the application server with "ssh" protocol (Xterm of Cygwin on Windows or ssh in Mac). To accommodate this, we planned to make X windows facility available to the BYOD PCs. The server has the main memory of 1.5TB.

3.3 CALL Server

The lectures for English are not assigned as part of a lecture series. Students are expected to learn English with CALL system by themselves at anytime and anywhere during the semester.

The CALL system is developed by the staff members of Osaka University. It is called WebOCMnext[3]. We are going to update the OS from Windows server 2012 standard to Windows server 2012 R2 standard during the overarching system upgrade.

Kyushu University has been hosting the CALL server locally and are planning to move them to the AWS cloud. Our concern is the volume for traffic because the pricing depends on the volume of downloaded data in AWS. We estimated the traffic for CALL will be about 1TB in a year. If that is right, it will cost several hundred US dollars each year.

3.4 Authentication Server

The authentication working group of III (Information Infrastructure Initiative) operates the IDMS (IDentification Management System) for other information services. Our authentication servers receive the necessary data for LDAP and AD as the top of educational information services from IDMS. They are currently on the premises in the earthquake-proof server room in Ito campus. LDAP servers for Moodle, Mahara, and our application server are all prepared to move to the cloud. CALL uses Shibboleth for authentication and the AD server is arranged to use the VDI facility in cloud when we transition everything else.

3.5 Network

AWS is connected to SINET5 which is operated by NII (National Institute of Informatics, which is supported by the Ministry of Education) for the academic purpose of connecting higher education organizations. The speed between our university and NII is 10Gbps so far. We can set up a VPN with direct connect between our university and AWS cloud. This connects part of the AWS cloud to our university network and shares the same global IP address group. This allows us to maintain security requirements described in CIA below.

Table 1: Confidentiality

No.	Problem	Measure
1-1	Information leak through general service such as Web	Security measure similar to "on the premise"
1-2	Information leak through the usage of stolen administrator ID and password	To make it impossible to login as an administrator with multi-factor authentication even if administrative ID and password were stolen.
1-3	Leak of image such as AMI (Amazon Machine Image), snapshot, EBS volume, and so on.	To encrypt the EBS volume supported by AWS when we prepare the new instance in AWS. As a result, the exported image is also encrypted and make it impossible to decipher it without the key. The key is also encrypted by the AWS KMS master key (Measure 1-4).
1-4	Leak of the secret key for EBS volume.	Secret key is encrypted by the AWS KMS Master key. It is decoded by the AWS KMS and used only when the timing of mounting the volume on only memory. The master key for AWS KMS is designed so that anyone cannot retrieve it even if the staff members and administrators want to get it.The administration authority is required to decode the secret key by AWS KMS (Measure 1-2).All operations are recorded and can be used for inspection for who did and what was done.
1-5	Information leak by accessing virtual machine by administrator account.	The secret key corresponding to key pair is required in order to login and set up the virtual machine as a administrator for the first time. We direct the vendor to keep it safely and not to leak the secret key because we have the risk that outsider can login as an administrator with the secret key if it is leaked. As the operation after the first set up is similar to that of general remote management, we manage account security protection same to "on the premise".
1-6	Information leak by tapping communication lines.	Use the VLAN connection (Direct Connect) supported by AWS to prevent the tapping. Use the encryption facility such as http and "ssh" to manage the system.
1-7	Information leak through the abandoned volume.	Outsider cannot access the volume because of Measure 1-4. Formal white paper guaranteed the security action against abandoning the volume. https://d0.awsstatic.com/International/ja_JP/Whitepapers/AWS%20Security%20Whitepaper.pdf

4 CIA (CONFIDENTIALITY, INTEGRITY, AVAILABILITY)

The most serious problem with computing in the cloud is security and many leaders in our organization are concerned. Security has made it extremely difficult for us to use cloud computing in Japan for a long time. However, the common opinion has shifted enough that it appears the right time has come.

We have analyzed the problems and found the way to clear enough security issues to persuade the old guard to use the cloud. We call our solution CIA (Confidentiality, Integrity, and Availability). As a result, our CISO (Chief Information Security Officer) agreed to use cloud even for the information that requires higher security such as authentication data and personal information like student personal learning records to analyze.

4.1 Confidentiality

Table 1 shows a part of our discussion about the problems and the corresponding measure around confidentiality.

4.2 Integrity

Table 2 shows a part of our discussion about the problems and the corresponding measure around integrity.

4.3 Availability

Table 3 shows a part of our discussion about the problems and the corresponding measure around availability.

Table 2: Integrity

	Problem	Measure
2-1	Data falsification through Web service etc.	Security measure similar to "on the premise"
2-2	Illegal operation of virtual machine image by AWS administrator account.	Same to Measure 1-2 and 1-3 in Table 1
2-3	Falsification and/or illegal operation against virtual machine by administrator account.	Same to measure 1-5

5 VDI (Virtual Desktop Infrastructure)

It is important for us to provide the common ICT (Information and Communication Technology) environment for students in spite of various PCs including PCs and Macs. We are introducing the VDI (Virtual Desktop Infrastructure) interface to make every student use a common Windows environment in classes beginning September 2017. Students can also use a Linux instance if they require it.

The cost for a VDI license is usually expensive. Therefore, the number of VDI licenses is too few to provide a VDI instance to all the students on the premise. It makes it difficult for students to use their own VDI instance by themselves at anytime and anywhere. We intended to provide a VDI instance to all students whenever they want to use their own VDI instance as requested.

VDI is still expensive, even in the cloud. Therefore, we are planning to manage and reduce the cost for VDI as much as possible. For that purpose, we are going to develop the budget management system to control the usage and cost of individual student under the specified budget level. We were considering Azure and AWS, but in May of 2017, AWS won the contract.

Table 3: Availability

	Problem	Measure
3-1	Attack by DOS (Denial of Service)	Similar to "on the premise", use load balancer if needed.
3-2	Service interruption by losing electric power	Power sources are prepared redundantly in AWS.
3-3	Service interruption by disconnect of network	Difficult to solve this problem because it depends on SINET5, we accept the risk.
3-4	Service interruption or data lost by the trouble of hardware	Save snapshot and backup periodically on S3. The information is encrypted automatically (Measure 1-3).
3-5	Service obstruction by intruding with administrator account.	Same to Measure 1-2

6 CONCLUSION

We moved the servers for the Web learning system, application, and CALL to take full advantage of the cloud. We reduced TCO (Total Cost of Operation), physical space for servers, provided dynamically adjustable performance of servers, and maintained security in the cloud.

All students have their own Windows environment via VDI that provides a completely common ICT environment for learning. The usage of Android tablets and iPads instead of PCs is coming into our view with VDI. We are realizing a next generation educational ICT environment under BYOD with cloud. It should be the model case for new higher education around the world.

ACKNOWLEDGMENTS

We appreciate all of the students, teachers, and administrative staff members who supported our BYOD activity and the innovative change our ICT environment from "on the premise" to Cloud.

REFERENCES

[1] Naomi Fujimura, Hitoshi Inoue, and Satoshi Hashikura : Experience with the Educational ICT Environment in Kyushu University, Proc. of SIGUCCS 2009 (Technical Session), pp.167-171, Oct. 2009.
[2] Naomi Fujimura, Bring your own computers project in Kyushu university, Proc. of ACM SIGUCCS 2013, ACM, pp.43-50, Nov.7, 2013. http://dl.acm.org/citation.cfm?id=2504789
[3] http://www.mle.cmc.osaka-u.ac.jp/WebOCMnext/index.html

Our Experience with Introducing Microsoft Office 365 in Kyushu University

Yoshiaki Kasahara
Kyushu University
744 Motooka Nishi-ku
Fukuoka 819-0395, Japan
kasahara.yoshiaki.820@m.kyushu-u.ac.jp

Takao Shimayoshi
Kyushu University
744 Motooka Nishi-ku
Fukuoka 819-0395, Japan
simayosi@cc.kyushu-u.ac.jp

Masahiro Obana
Kyushu University
744 Motooka Nishi-ku
Fukuoka 819-0395, Japan
obana.masahiro.049@m.kyushu-u.ac.jp

Naomi Fujimura
Kyushu University
744 Motooka Nishi-ku
Fukuoka 819-0395, Japan
fujimura.naomi.274@m.kyushu-u.ac.jp

ABSTRACT

Information Infrastructure Initiative of Kyushu University started serving Office 365 Education for all students and staff members at Kyushu University in November 2016. Since 2007, the university had signed Microsoft EES (Enrollment for Education Solutions) including licenses for the latest Microsoft Windows and Office suite. The EES agreement includes an advantage to provide Office 365 Education to the university members with minimum investments, and there was a demand for Skype for Business which is included in Office 365. To deploy Office 365 for our users, we first needed to configure our on-premises user authentication infrastructure to coordinate with Office 365. During trials, we had a couple of difficulties attributed to some disagreements between Microsoft's and our policy on whether the user identifier, namely the user principal name in Active Directory, was open or private. Additionally, we had to consider which services should be applied to the users, because we have been operating an on-premises email service which is competing with Microsoft Exchange mail service. In this presentation, we share our experiences in Office 365 deployment.

SIGUCCS '17, October 1–4, 2017, Seattle, WA, USA
© 2017 Copyright is held by the owner/author(s). Publication rights licensed to ACM. ACM 978-1-4503-4919-2/17/10...$15.00
https://doi.org/10.1145/3123458.3123491

CCS CONCEPTS

• **Social and professional topics** → **Software selection and adaptation;** • *Security and privacy* → *Authentication;* • Information systems → Enterprise applications

KEYWORDS

Microsoft Office 365; User Account Management; Public Cloud Service

1 INTRODUCTION

For research, education, and office procedure activities, university staff members and students use productivity software known as "Office suite" every day, for tasks such as writing a document with a word processor, analyzing various data in a spreadsheet, and making a presentation. There are a few alternatives for such software including open-source LibreOffice, but Microsoft's Office suite dominates the enterprise world because of compatibility and interoperability. When most members in a university needs to purchase and use the same commercial software, it is not cost-effective to purchase the software (licenses) individually because usually there is a "volume discount" available.

To reduce the cost to purchase such software and prevent software piracy, Kyushu University decided to sign a contract with Microsoft called "Campus Agreement" in 2007. The agreement allowed all the staff members to install unlimited number of copies of the latest Microsoft Office suite to PC's owned by our university, and staff members and students to install one copy per person to their private PC. Information Infrastructure Initiative of Kyushu University handled the actual deployment. The agreement also included upgrade licenses of Windows OS, so we could upgrade our PCs to the latest Windows OS. Later the name of the agreement was changed to

"Enrollment for Education Solutions (EES)." The agreement was the foundation for our BYOD project for students [1].

In late 2014, we negotiated with Microsoft for our EES contract to include "Student Advantage" and "Teacher Advantage" options which allowed us to use "Office 365 ProPlus" for all the eligible members without additional cost. Office 365 seemed attractive because it allowed each user to install Microsoft Office on up to 5 PCs, 5 phones, and 5 tablets, and "Office 365 Education" (free) also included Skype for Business, OneDrive for Business (up to 1TB of storage), SharePoint Online, and so on. At that time, Office 365 supported synchronizing user credentials with on-premises Active Directory (AD), so it seemed feasible to deploy Office 365 in our university with minimum cost.

In this paper, we describe how we tested and deployed Office 365 in Kyushu University, issues discovered during tests and deployment, current status, and future plans.

2 DESIGN AND IMPLEMENTATION

In this section, we describe our requirements/policies for handling user credentials, how we designed and tested our Office 365 deployment scenario, and the result and current status.

2.1 Identity Management System

In Kyushu University, Information Infrastructure Initiative is operating an identity management system (IDM) for staff members and students [2]. The total number of IDs is about 30,000. The current system was introduced in the end of the 2013 fiscal year. Each user was assigned a unique 10-digit pseudorandom number as a user ID called "SSO-KID." [3] The IDM provides users' personal information including their credentials, names, email addresses, etc. to various information services in Kyushu University through LDAP, AD, Shibboleth Identity Provider (IdP), and CSV files.

SSO-KID was designed in a way to protect users from dictionary and ID generation attacks [3], so there is a policy not to disclose SSO-KID in public (treated somewhat like a social security number in US). The policy prohibits providing a search facility which can disclose SSO-KID directly. Also, there is another policy not to transfer passwords associated with each SSO-KID outside our campus network (even hashed or encrypted). So, we need to build and deploy an Office 365 environment while maintaining these policies.

2.2 First Test

In 2015, we started to test and evaluate Office 365 deployment. First, we designed our test environment as shown in Figure 1. The IDM system can export user information to AD. To synchronize user information with Office 365, we needed an AD Federation Services (ADFS) and DirSync server. Also, to process user authentication requests without providing password information to Office 365, we needed an ADFS Proxy server to receive and redirect requests from Office 365 to our AD Domain Services server. We decided to use "SSO-KID@ms.kyushu-u.ac.jp" as a User Principal Name (UPN) to log on to Office 365 because it

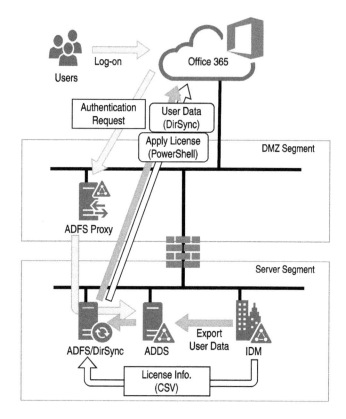

Figure 1: System Overview of the First Test Environment.

seemed natural to use SSO-KID as a part of the login ID. Also, we needed to prepare PowerShell scripts to apply Office 365 licenses to each user (which couldn't be done through AD).

After the whole AD environment was built and tested with a small dataset, we synchronized all the members of Kyushu University with Office 365. The synchronization itself was almost successful, but we realized that some functionality of Office 365 violated our ID policy.

First, we found that Lync (now called Skype for Business) allowed users to search other users using a prefix of UPN. That meant that if a user searched "0", all the users whose SSO-KID started from "0" would be listed. Also, the search result showed both email addresses and UPN. Microsoft answered that it was a "feature" and we couldn't control the output of the search result. Microsoft treated UPN as a public information, and this didn't fit well with our policy. Because there were many other services in Office 365 which provided search function, it seemed difficult to control and make sure SSO-KID was not disclosed, and we had to abandon the tested environment and design another.

2.3 Current Implementation

To prevent SSO-KID from being disclosed in Office 365, we needed to use another string as UPN. We didn't have many candidates, and ended up using email addresses of Kyushu University Primary Mail Service [4] and changed the domain part to "ms.kyushu-u.ac.jp." In that case, there was little point to sharing the same password from SSO-KID with this new UPN, so

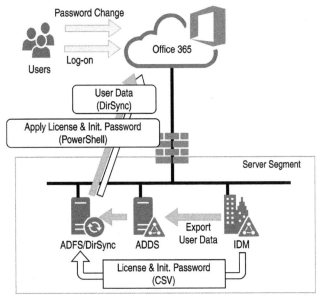

we decided to let Office 365 handle its own password internally.

Figure 2: System Overview of the Current Environment.

Still, we needed to ensure that only valid users could sign up with a UPN, so we modified our IDM to generate a random string as an "initial" password for each UPN and exported this to Office 365. A user needed to access our IDM's web UI to retrieve the initial password for Office 365 from their profile page. The first login to Office 365 using this password would start the initial sign-up process including choosing a new password and selecting account recovery options (such as registering a mobile phone number). Figure 2 shows the overview of new environment. There was some strong demand to deploy Office 365 as early as possible, so we decided to go for this design after some tests. We officially announced the availability of Office 365 to the members of Kyushu University in April 2016.

3 REMAINING ISSUES AND FUTURE PLANS

We had been providing Office 365 to our users for more than one year, but we still have several issues which need to be resolved.

3.1 Multi-Factor Authentication

To protect our users' accounts from unauthorized access, we want to encourage users to use multi-factor authentication (MFA) implemented in Office 365. For personal Microsoft accounts, users can enable/disable MFA by themselves, but Office 365 doesn't allow users to do this for some reason. Only an administrator can change users' setting via Admin Center or using PowerShell script.

We modified our IDM to include a switch in a user's profile page to enable/disable MFA. Due to technical difficulty, we had to synchronize the MFA states to Office 365 once a day with a batch process. Later we realized that there were three MFA states: *disabled*, *enabled*, and *enforced*. After an *enabled* user

completed the initial MFA registration process, the state would change to *enforced*. The problem was that overwriting the MFA state from *enforced* to *enabled* (by our batch) was not supported by Office 365 and might cause a login problem. We need a bit more complicated procedure to properly update users' MFA states, but it is not yet implemented. Temporarily we disabled the MFA switch in user's profile page.

3.2 Changing UPN

The email address assigned for our Primary Mail Service is based on a user's real name (for staff members) or Student ID (for students). A user's name may change by some life events, and Student IDs always change when the student proceeds from undergraduate to graduate or changes his/her department [5]. The same thing happens for UPNs in Office 365. The mail system automatically processes such an event and notifies users with an email message, but our Office 365 environment doesn't. Currently we process the UPN change manually, but we should decide how to treat the events automatically and implement it. Also, changing the UPN has some ill effects such as broken file sharing URL and online meeting URL. We wanted to use SSO-KID because it was much more stable, so we are still investigating the possibility to use SSO-KID for Office 365 without disclosing it in public.

3.3 Shibboleth/SAML

One such possibility to allow users to log in using SSO-KID is to utilize Shibboleth IdP. Office 365 partially supports Shibboleth IdP. During the initial stage, we discussed the feasibility of using Shibboleth IdP, but Skype for Business didn't support authentication via Shibboleth, so we abandoned the idea.

Recently we were informed that Kyoto University was using Shibboleth with Office 365, but they mainly used email service of Office 365 (Exchange Online). Also, more applications for Office 365 support SAML 2.0. We will continue to collect information about Shibboleth/SAML with Office 365.

3.4 Our mail system versus Exchange Online

Kyushu University is operating an in-house email service called Primary Mail Service [4]. The operation of the current system started at the end of the 2013 fiscal year. Exchange Online bundled with Office 365 offered a 50GB mail box which was much larger than our current email system (8GB). Because we didn't want to discourage users using our email service, we didn't assign Exchange Online license to our Office 365 users in initial deployment.

Later, we realized that Exchange Online was much more tightly integrated with other Office 365 services than we expected. For example, reservation of an online meeting with Skype for Business was much harder and restricted without using Microsoft Outlook with an Exchange account. Notification messages from various Office 365 services were also delivered to the Exchange mail box. As a compromise, we decided to assign Exchange Online license to each user, but forced the Exchange address to forward received messages to Primary Mail Service and disable changing forwarding address by users. Also, we are discussing whether it is feasible to migrate our Primary Mail to Office 365, because we must replace the current system before the end of the 2018 fiscal year.

3.5 Rights Management Services

Recently Kyushu University formulated a rule for document classification. A problem is how to implement a real-world procedure to classify and protect documents based on the classification rule. We are evaluating Microsoft Rights Management Services (RMS) to classify, protect, and track digital documents. Our Office 365 contract doesn't include RMS licenses, and we cannot afford the license fee to cover all the staff members (~9000). Our current plan is to purchase a small number of licenses and assign them to the people who need RMS.

In late 2016, Microsoft introduced "Azure Information Protection", and included some basic functionality in Office 365. Additional licenses are still required to use advanced functionality such as automatic classification and tracking. We don't fully understand the whole picture of Azure Information Protection, and we need to study more.

3.6 OneDrive for Business

For users, OneDrive for Business is also an attractive service because it offers 1TB storage. A major issue is how to handle confidential documents. Currently our security policy prohibits users from exporting confidential information outside our campus network, but it is difficult to use a cloud storage service if we enforce such a rule strictly. RMS might solve the problem if we can enforce a policy to encrypt every document uploaded to OneDrive.

3.7 DirSync to Azure AD Connect

As described in Section 2.2 and 2.3, we used DirSync to synchronize our AD and Office 365. But the official support of DirSync ended on April 13, 2017. Office 365 will stop accepting connection from DirSync on December 31, 2017, so we must upgrade DirSync to Azure AD Connect as soon as possible.

Also, we built the current environment quickly by reusing some parts of the first test environment. Due to this, the system is overly complicated and sometimes unstable. Another concern is that currently we use PowerShell scripts heavily to assign licenses to each user or to change some setting (such as MFA states described in Section 3.1). We need to consult a company with more knowledge about Office 365 and other Microsoft products to improve and stabilize our system.

4 SUMMARY

In this paper, we described the background and motivation to introduce Microsoft Office 365 to the members of Kyushu University, how we designed to coordinate our existing IDM and Office 365, current issues, and some future plans.

Office 365 consists of many services and seems to have a lot of potential to improve our information service, but we don't fully understand the whole picture yet. We will continue to research about Office 365 functionality and encourage our users to use them.

ACKNOWLEDGMENTS

Our thanks to all the users using our IT services, and staff members of the Office 365 task force and the authentication infrastructure working group to develop and maintain these systems in Information Infrastructure Initiative of Kyushu University.

REFERENCES

[1] Fujimura, N. 2013. Bring your own computers project in Kyushu University. In *Proceedings of the SIGUCCS 2013* (Chicago, IL, November 3 – 8, 2013). ACM, New York, NY, 43-50. DOI: http://dx.doi.org/10.1145/2504776.2504789

[2] Ito, E., Kasahara, Y., and Fujimura, N. 2013. Implementation and operation of the Kyushu university authentication system. In *Proceedings of the SIGUCCS 2013* (Chicago, IL, November 3 - 8, 2013). ACM, New York, NY, 137-142. DOI: http://dx.doi.org/10.1145/2504776.2504788.

[3] Nogita, M., Kasahara, Y., Ito. E., and Suzuki, T. 2006. A Study of Identifier Naming Conventions Suitable for User Authentication. *Technical report of IEICE.* ISEC Vol.106, No. 411 (20061206), 67-72.

[4] Kasahara, Y., Ito, E., and Fujimura, N. 2014. Introduction of New Kyushu University Primary Mail Service for Staff Members and Students. In *Proceedings of the SIGUCCS 2014* (Salt Lake City, UT, November 2 - 7, 2014). ACM, New York, NY, 103-106. DOI: http://dx.doi.org/10.1145/2661172.2662965.

[5] Fujimura, N., Togawa, T., Kasahara, Y., and Ito, E. 2012. Introduction and experience with the Primary Mail Service based on their names for students. In *Proceedings of the SIGUCCS 2012* (Memphis, TN, October 17 - 19, 2012). ACM, New York, NY, 11-14. DOI: http://dx.doi.org/10.1145/2382456.2382460.

Calling Up IT Prospects

Angel C. Williams
Tulane University
1555 Poydras Street
New Orleans, LA 70112
angel@tulane.edu

ABSTRACT

The Network Operations Center (NOC) at Tulane University has been coined as the "farm team". The NOC staff members are in a very unique position; they have to be educated on how to troubleshoot all Tulane applications as well being familiar with Tulane processes. Staff members, students, affiliates, faculty, parents and external candidates contact the NOC team for technology related support. As the staff member gains tremendous experience over the years, these positions unfortunately have a shelf-life and many begin to look for other opportunities. When positions in other teams have become open, NOC staff members have applied, and in the majority of the cases, ventured into other Tulane technology positions. The key role as a manager requires hiring quality applicants, adding to their skill set and seeing them move on to further their IT career within Tulane instead of letting them walk away. Some may say that I have a revolving door, but I strongly believe that it is adding to the future of Tulane technology.

CCS CONCEPTS

• **Social and professional topics** → Employment issues

KEYWORDS

Farm team; employment; career opportunities

1 RECRUITMENT

In 2013 Tulane University decided to make some improvements to their technology department and created the Emergency

SIGUCCS '17, October 1–4, 2017, Seattle, WA, USA
© 2017 Association for Computing Machinery.
ACM ISBN 978-1-4503-4919-2/17/10...$15.00
https://doi.org/10.1145/3123458.3123492

Command Center (ECC). The ECC is a highly-controlled environment with Activu monitors on the walls that display real time network usage/outages, enterprise servers, and applications (http://activu.net/). One of the first steps in establishing the ECC is to bring the university's first line of technical support back in house. This service had been outsourced to Blackboard Student Service in late 2006 (https://www.parature.com/). The new team was named the Technical Support and Network Operations Center (TSNOC) which we hoped would differentiate from a call center or helpdesk environment.

The TSNOC staff shares a common space with the Tulane University Police Dispatchers. On the opposite side of the room the Tulane University Police Department (TUPD) Activu wall monitors provide real time data of crimes, news, live video footage, and hot zone areas across all campuses. The TSNOC staff consists of one director and six highly experience technical support specialists. For accessibility, there are several ways users can contact the TSNOC for support. They can request assistance by phone, chat, email, or on-line ticket submissions. In addition to providing remote desktop support, TSNOC staff also are responsible for troubleshooting all software applications and reporting and/or identifying any unusual activity.

2 TRAINING

On July 1st, 2013 the TSNOC went live and was ready to assist the entire Tulane community. An announcement was sent out via email and was meet with great feedback and high expectations. The six staff members developed a training and plan worked diligently to ensure they would be ready to restore the community's confidence in remote technical support.

For approximately six weeks before the go live date staff reviewed and updated all knowledge base articles and met with some of the other internal technology teams. This review allow the newly hired staff to not only introduce themselves but to also gain an in-depth knowledge of the other team's responsibilities, specific systems, and/or applications. The TSNOC staff worked closely with onsite, networking, advanced applications, enterprise Microsoft exchange and Unix systems groups to understand how to properly troubleshoot and offer assistance to users. During this process the TSNOC staff developed a great relationship with the other technical support groups. This relationship and the resulting understanding and appreciation of one another's work ethic allows for easy communication between groups and the TSNOC to this day.

3 CAREER DEVELOPMENT

Being a part of the TSNOC staff has many benefits. These particular staff members are able to gain a wealth of knowledge regarding every department within the university not just technology related. Unfortunately, the TSNOC itself does not allow for career advancement opportunities. For career advancement these staff members will start to look at other teams for opportunities within the university. At times if an opening becomes available in other technical support teams they will let the TSNOC staff members aware of new career opportunities. A majority of the hiring managers know TSNOC staff have not only technical experience but exceptional customer service skills, and an in-depth knowledge of how other Tulane IT teams operate. Many TSNOC staff members have made themselves more marketable for advancement by working towards an advanced degree, adding certifications to their resume, or taking specialized courses.

4 ADVANCEMENT

When the TSNOC began operations in May 2013 there were six staff members and a Director. A majority of the original members have progressed in their careers. Below is a breakdown of where their careers have taken them:

- The director moved into a position with Google as a Hardware Operations Manager
- One staff member moved into the Advanced Applications group as a Developer
- Three staff members moved into the Unix group as Systems Administrators
- I have advanced to become the Manager of the TSNOC

5 FUTURE

The TSNOC has been nicknamed "The Farm Team" because so many individuals start their technical career at Tulane University in the TSNOC and then advance to more senior positions within the department. As the manager of the "Farm Team," I will continue to have staff members who gain knowledge and obtain new skills leave in order to advance on their career path. I will also continue to develop new talent for the other TS teams to look to for excellent candidates when they need to fill open positions. The process then starts all over as I hire new TSNOC staff members to fill the positions of those who have moved on.

When one of my most recent staff members moved to another team he stated he was nervous to tell me that he received the job opportunity. I told him that "I was very happy for him, and that the opportunity is a good step in the right direction on his career path. Also, I was glad he decided to look within Tulane University to further his career. One of the most satisfying parts of my position as being the TSNOC manager is my unique position of hiring quality applications for my team, developing their skill set, and then watching them move on to advance their careers within the university.

First Year's Efforts and Operational Results of BYOD Action in TUAT with New Style Virtual Computer Classroom

Kazuhiro Mishima
Information Media Center, Tokyo University of
Agriculture and Technology
2-24-16 Naka-cho
Koganei-city, Tokyo 184-8588
three@cc.tuat.ac.jp

Yoshikazu Kawamura
Information Media Center, Tokyo University of
Agriculture and Technology
2-24-16 Naka-cho
Koganei-city, Tokyo 184-8588
k-y81496@cc.tuat.ac.jp

Takeshi Sakurada
Information Media Center, Tokyo University of
Agriculture and Technology
2-24-16 Naka-cho
Koganei-city, Tokyo 184-8588
take-s@cc.tuat.ac.jp

Yoichi Hagiwara
Information Media Center, Tokyo University of
Agriculture and Technology
2-24-16 Naka-cho
Koganei-city, Tokyo 184-8588
hagi@cc.tuat.ac.jp

ABSTRACT

In April of 2016, Tokyo University of Agriculture and Technology (TUAT) transitioned from an educational computer system to Bring Your Own Device (BYOD). In response, a brand-new computer system for the classroom, called TUAT Virtual Computer Classroom (TUAT-VCCR), replaced the old computer rooms and terminals. TUAT-VCCR is based in virtual desktop technology and users can access the tools with any HTML5-compliant web browser (e.g. Chrome, Firefox), removing the differences for various operating systems (e.g. Windows, macOS).

In this article, we would like to share our efforts and operational reports for our first year. The project itself included redesigning lecture halls, creation of user guides and other ways to support users to efficiently use new system. We would also like to share the first year adoption experience and the reality of BYOD in the university of science and technology. In this article, we provide valuable information to other organizations planning a similar BYOD initiative.

CCS CONCEPTS

• **Information systems** → *Computing platforms*; • **Networks** → *Cloud computing*; • **Applied computing** → *Computer-assisted instruction*; • **Computer systems organization** → *Cloud computing*;

KEYWORDS

BYOD; Educational Computer System; Virtual Computer Room; Orientation Lecture Redesign; Evaluation of Actual Operation

ACM Reference format:
Kazuhiro Mishima, Takeshi Sakurada, Yoshikazu Kawamura, and Yoichi Hagiwara. 2017. First Year's Efforts and Operational Results of BYOD Action in TUAT with New Style Virtual Computer Classroom. In *Proceedings of SIGUCCS'17, October 1–4, 2017, Seattle, WA, USA.*, 4 pages.
https://doi.org/10.1145/3123458.3123493

1 INTRODUCTION

Along with the changes in the computing environment, user demand for easy access is higher than ever. The BYOD (Bring Your Own Device) [1, 2, 4] trend is progressing and institutions of higher education are no exception. To address this need, there is growing momentum for BYOD in some Japanese Universities, e.g. Kyushu University [3], Kanazawa University, Tokyo Gakugei University and Tokyo University of Agriculture and Technology (as TUAT) implemented BYOD in 2016. The new educational computer system, called edu@2016, was implemented the same year. It is designed as a BYOD concept and brought an end to all old-style computer rooms on campus.

2 ADVANTAGE AND DISADVANTAGE OF BYOD

There are several advantages of BYOD. First of all, improved utilization capacity of the information devices is expected. Hand-held devices are portable, allowing them to be used not only in the computer lecture available classroom, but also in other areas like general classrooms, the cafeteria, and outside campus.

Next, since the students own the property, they take better care of the equipment and there are fewer failures with which to contend. In addition, the cost reduction for owning and managing a large number of terminals by university can be significant. In particular, the cost of maintaining a dedicated computer room is very high (e.g. managing the application software, system update, equipment failure, cleaning). BYOD can not only reduce the cost to manage the terminal, it also be more convenient for the users. Previously, a student would need to go to a computer room in order to complete exercises on a terminal. Now, students can complete their work anywhere on the campus network.

One issue we have seen with BYOD is in dealing with the different models of computers (e.g. computer model, OS type) the students and faculty use. This could be avoided if we limited what machines people were allowed to use, but because we are at a university, we did not want to place strict limits on the equipment. What we did to mitigate the differences was encourage the faculty to help each student make sure they have a computer that will work correctly. If they check each machine, they can ensure their students will have access. This presents a big burden to the faculty though and we needed to find another way to solve this issue.

3 OVERVIEW OF VIRTUAL COMPUTER CLASSROOM (TUAT-VCCR)

In order to enjoy the benefits of BYOD, we needed to find a way to minimize the effect of people having many different kinds of computers. In the edu@2016 environment, we implemented a brand-new system using virtual desktops that provide access to the BYOD environment. It is called "Virtual Computer Room (TUAT-VCCR)" [5]. TUAT-VCCR can virtually group multiple virtual desktop environments, a virtual classroom, in the cloud. It is as if there is a classroom equipped with multiple terminals in virtual space, like a conventional computer lab. By using the Virtual Computer Classroom and BYOD user terminal, a general classroom (with no computers) can be transformed into a computer lab. This system, using HTML5-compliant Web Browsers to launch virtual desktop, allows users to remotely access the desktop environment. As a result, in any classroom, a lecturer and students can utilize a unified desktop environment, as if they were in a computer lab. Our system can be used in Windows, macOS, Linux and Chrome OS as source terminal's OS, and IE, Edge, Safari, Firefox, Chrome as Browser.

3.1 Use of TUAT-VCCR

Users can access the TUAT-VCCR through the dedicated Web Portal. A Usage Flow of TUAT-VCCR is shown in Figure 1. Once the user is logged into the portal, the list of the virtual desktop environments (virtual classroom for each class) is shown. The list includes only virtual classrooms that can be accessed during that time. By selecting the target virtual classroom, each user can use the appropriate environment. When each user connects to the virtual classroom from the portal, a virtual desktop server will be selected automatically, and the desktop screen is displayed on the user's browser window or tab, like Figure 2.

3.2 Reservation of TUAT-VCCR

Usage of TUAT-VCCR for lectures requires advanced reservation. With the information included in each reservation, it is possible to make the virtual computer room for each class.

A lecturer reserves the virtual classroom on the registration web portal, shown in Figure 3. The lecturer can assign the number of terminals required for class from a dedicated reservation page. The

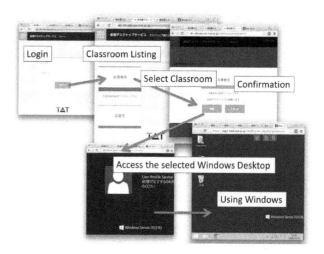

Figure 1: Usage Flow of TUAT-VCCR.

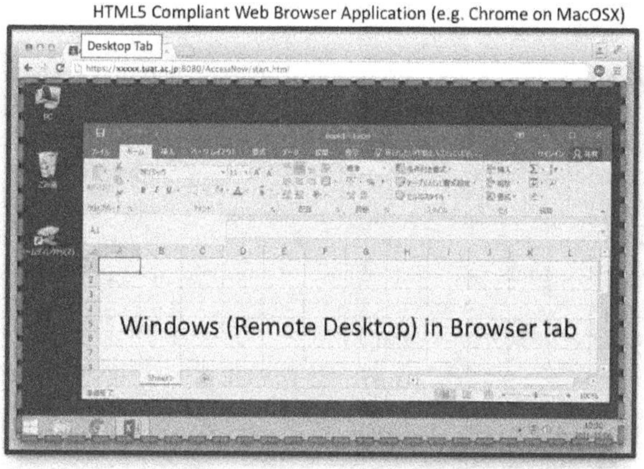

Figure 2: Using Virtual Desktop with Web Browser.

terminals that are not reserved will be automatically used as a terminal for self-study users.

4 CORRESPONDENCE FOR STARTING THE OPERATION OF TUAT-VCCR

4.1 Enhancing the Wi-Fi System and Classroom Classification

Before starting the BYOD action, we enhanced the Wi-Fi system in our university. Our Wi-Fi system is based on Cisco Systems' central-controlled Wireless LAN System. Instead of focusing on increasing the number of areas where there were wired connections, we chose to increase coverage of our wireless network (especially to general classrooms) so more people could take advantage of the new system and we could decrease the failure of the LAN terminal (Ethernet/LAN jack).

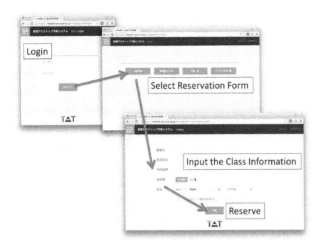

Figure 3: Usage Flow of TUAT VCCR Reservation.

Having better wireless coverage helped promote the use of TUAT-VCCR in general classroom. Based on our advance survey of utilization trends, we decided which classrooms would be used for TUAT-VCCR and which ones would not. The classrooms used for TUAT-VCCR had more access points installed than usual assuming higher capacity during exams. This classification is provided to the academic affairs department, and used for classroom assignment.

4.2 Creating User Startup Manual and Taking User Briefing Session

For the users, we created and distributed a brief "Getting Started Guide" which gives an overview and guidelines of our new computer system. This guide is an A3-sized two-fold brochure, consisting of four double-sided pages. This guide is like Figure 4. This summarized the usage of the new system easily and comprehensively for students and faculty. Furthermore, we created a briefing session about our new computer system. This was presented to faculty staff and teaching assistant staff. This session was recorded, and the content of this session was published to our university's LMS. In addition, for freshmen, we provided information about the system during orientation.

5 OPERATION STATUS OF THE NEW SYSTEM

The new computer system, including TUAT-VCCR, is based on virtualization technology and is run in the cloud (almost all servers are in a remote network data center, and the only Wi-Fi controller system is housed on our campus). After the installation of the new computer system, we decreased the number of server racks from 6 to 0, drastically reducing our space cost. System operation can be outsourced, reducing human resource needs as well. Also, as a service provider, ordinary maintenance is needed to bring the service person to university, because all equipment is located in university facility. But, on our new system, since equipments are located on provider's side, it is not necessary to consider the university's possible maintenance schedule for dispatching a university employee, and it is easy to perform maintenance on holidays and at night. It is a great advantage for both our university and provider.

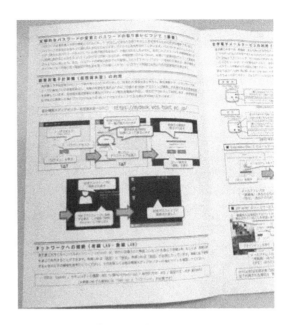

Figure 4: TUAT Educational Computer System Startup Guide.

Figure 5: Practice Lecture on Classroom After BYOD Action.

5.1 Utilization of TUAT-VCCR

TUAT-VCCR began operation in February 2016, and full-fledged use began in April. The actual situation of classroom use with BYOD is shown as Figure 5. The number of virtual desktops is about 400 units, which was the same number of terminals already installed in our conventional computer lab. Since then we have removed all of the terminals in our computer labs and campus kiosks. Regarding the actual usage, between April 1, 2016 to February 7, 2017, we show 36 lectures using TUAT-VCCR in the spring semester and 19 in the fall semester, and these numbers have not changed significantly from the previous computer room usage. We have decreased the amount of overlap and ease of use during class.

5.2 User's Terminal Trend on TUAT

We analyzed the our university user's trend in OS and Web Browser from the usage of TUAT-VCCR's Web Portal Site. This is shown in Figure 6. While we recommend using Firefox or Chorme, other browsers are also widely used. In addition, users, especially students, tend to use terminals in university libraries or co-op buildings (mainly cafeterias) rather than in classrooms.

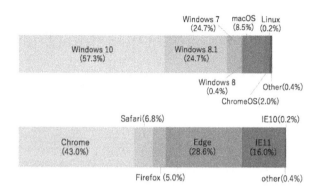

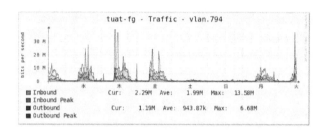

Figure 6: First Year's User Trend on TUAT.

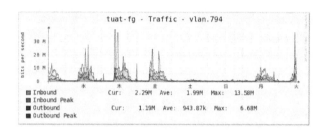

Figure 7: Bandwidth Usage of TUAT VCCR.

5.3 Traffic of TUAT-VCCR Usage

Traffic data at the time of using the TUAT-VCCR is shown in Figure 7. The data is from April 12, 2016 to April 19, 2016 on network equipment in our service provider's network data center. Max bandwidth usage is about 30Mbps on the Inbound side (from data center to our university) with approximately 500 simultaneous users connected. Because of the data compression function, each user's bandwidth usage is relatively low. For this reason, even through a Wi-Fi network, the screen data loss or screen delay is little or none. Therefore, we have not encountered serious troubles, and these systems are currently running steadily.

6 IMPROVEMENT OF FIRST-TIME INFORMATION CLASS FOR FRESHMAN (INFORMATION ORIENTATION)

Faculty staff members in the Information Media Center teach a class called "Information Orientation" to freshman every April. This class includes the basics of the information technology, and useful information for life in our university. We needed to redesign the course material for this Information Orientation class to include the new BYOD computing environment.

During the new design, we emphasized the following elements:

- Assuming that the user brings own device (BYOD)
- Strengthen the system introduction in our university
- Lead to the utilization of information system by orientation
- Contents to be completed within class hour (90min)

Based on this design, we created content for the class. The details of content are as below:

- Use of campus Wi-Fi network by BYOD terminal

- ID, Password, The handing of own Password
- Use of TUAT-VCCR's virtual terminal
- Use of Campus E-mail System (Gmail, O365)
- Introduction of other convenient services (printing, storage, software license, LMS)

7 CONCLUSION

In this article, we presented a brief summary of our brand-new virtual computer system, called TUAT-VCCR, which uses virtual desktop technology. It can be used with HTML5-compliant web browsers and helps eliminate the impact of different operating systems and device models. We provided the implementation steps for BYOD in first year. We introduce the result of redesigning the lecture curriculum, and actual situations of the conducted class, along with new computer systems. We also introduce the effort to create a service usage guide and other support programs in order to help users use the new system more efficiently. In addition, we discussed operation results from the new system's first year. In the future, we will share insights from the implementation. Based on these insights, we plan to eventually design an even better virtual computer classroom, and want to share our lessons learned.

ACKNOWLEDGMENTS

Our thanks to Hokkaido Telecommunication Network Co., Inc. and Bitstar Inc. for preparing this presentation.

REFERENCES

[1] Rahat Afreen. 2014. Bring Your Own Device (BYOD) in Higher Education: Opportunities and Challenges. *International Journal of Emerging Trends & Technology in Computer Science (IJETTCS)* 3, 1 (January-February 2014), 233–236.
[2] Hilary Berger and James Symonds. 2016. Adoption of Bring Your Own Device in HE & FE Institutions. In *Proceedings of the The 11th International Knowledge Management in Organizations Conference on The Changing Face of Knowledge Management Impacting Society (KMO '16)*. ACM, New York, NY, USA, Article 43, 6 pages. https://doi.org/10.1145/2925995.2926027
[3] Naomi Fujimura. 2013. Bring Your Own Computers Project in Kyushu University. In *Proceedings of the 41st Annual ACM SIGUCCS Conference on User Services (SIGUCCS '13)*. ACM, New York, NY, USA, 43–50. https://doi.org/10.1145/2504776.2504789
[4] Cisco Systems Inc. 2017. Bring your own device (BYOD). http://www.cisco.com/c/en/us/solutions/byod-smart-solution/overview.html. (2017). [Online; Accessed April-2017].
[5] Kazuhiro Mishima, Takeshi Sakurada, and Yoichi Hagiwara. 2016. Brand New Designed Virtual Computer Classroom in BYOD Era. In *Proceedings of the 2016 ACM on SIGUCCS Annual Conference (SIGUCCS '16)*. ACM, New York, NY, USA, 99–102. https://doi.org/10.1145/2974927.2974931

Conquering Student Printing

Brian Yulke
40 Washington Sq South
New York, NY 10012
brian.yulke@nyu.edu

ABSTRACT

After many years of operating informal free student printing services, Law ITS identified the needs for a higher level of service, reduced waste, and lower cost to the department. Over the course of several years, Law ITS collaborated with the university IT group and the student government to implement new systems and improved service. These efforts resulted in significantly reduced waste, more convenient and centralized printing services, the addition of color printing, improved service response time and reliability, and a dramatic decrease in cost, all without any elimination or reduction of service and without the introduction of a printing charge.

CCS CONCEPTS

• **Applied computing~Business-IT alignment**

KEYWORDS

Service; Printing; Cost reduction; Efficiency; Collaboration

1 INTRODUCTION

Over the course of several years, student printing at NYU School of Law went through a major transformation. Once a veritable free-for-all, printing services now run like a well-oiled machine. This transformation took considerable effort and was not without mishaps along the way. However, persistence paid off, and the Law ITS group won-over the student body and conquered student printing.

The approach to student printing will vary based on each campus. In some schools it may be a critical, daily activity for students, while elsewhere it may be only an occasional occurrence. No two printing operations will be alike, but the underlying ideas and considerations should be similar. The IT group managing printing must have an understanding of the students' needs based on evidence and engagement with the

SIGUCCS '17, October 1–4, 2017, Seattle, WA, USA
© 2017 Association for Computing Machinery.
ACM ISBN 978-1-4503-4919-2/17/10...$15.00
https://doi.org/10.1145/3123458.3123498

student body, be willing to adapt to those needs especially as they change, and insightful enough to know where to compromise.

In collaboration with various groups, Law ITS identified key areas that needed improvement and sought both traditional and less conventional solutions to the challenge of student printing. First off, there was a university-wide green initiative that led to efforts to reduce waste, including reducing redundant and unnecessary print jobs. Law student feedback to the IT department sparked a project to improve service quality and to seek out continued feedback. Finally, the IT department recognized that it could not meet all these new needs without changing the printing operations and its support system.

Although the student printing services provided by NYU School of Law are not perfect, the students' needs are now met, and whenever these needs change, so will the services and operations supporting them.

2 THE BEGINNING OF TIME

2.1 The Way Things Were

Once upon a time, student printing was little more than a collection of printers on a network scattered throughout the academic buildings and dorms. Although the school maintains nearly 100 lab computers throughout the Law School buildings, each with nearby printers pre-installed. However, students prefer to print from their own laptops, requiring them to install drivers for each of the nearly three dozen school-wide printers they wished to use. This direct printing system meant that students had the ability to print an unlimited number pages at no cost.

Students typically used the most popular printers in the busiest areas the most, while lesser-known printers sat underutilized. Knowing they would have to wait in line for their job to print, many students would send the same job to multiple printers and take the one that finished first, abandoning the other jobs that were discarded by other students or our lab technicians. The resulting bottlenecks from the majority of print jobs being sent to a few select printers led to wasteful behavior by the students, which in turn worsened the problem. And, based on observation, this behavior most frequently occurred with the largest print jobs – often law cases or court proceedings that were more than 100 pages long.

Without a central print management system, toner levels, printer jams, and other problems were difficult to track. Maintenance was purely reactive. Our lab technicians checked printers periodically during their rounds and students occasionally reported issues to the systems group who were, at the time, in charge of printing. The lab technicians, all student workers, had varying work schedules and little training which led to inconsistent coverage, especially outside of regular business hours when no full-time employees were available.

Supply management was also difficult without a reporting mechanism or historical data. Toner cartridges were stock piled, yet we would not know when to replenish the supply until it was exhausted. Unfortunately, this resulted in days' worth of downtime for some printers. Confounding this problem, students were not restricted from tweaking the printers on their own. For instance, they misunderstood printer status messages such as "low toner," and the occasionally attempted to fix an otherwise unrelated issue like a paper jam or broken paper tray with sometimes tragic or comic outcomes.

2.2 Some Insight

The printing needs of a law school are admittedly different from those of a typical institution. Law is a profession rooted in the printed page. As part of the admissions requirements, every NYU School of Law student must have a modern laptop that meets the school's minimum requirements. As such, law students print voluminous materials for class and for study. The very culture encouraged students to print nearly everything. Without any limits, quotas, or costs to the students, there was no disincentive to print as much as they could.

3 EVOLUTION

3.1 Looking Inward

With a directive from our CIO, we knew we had to improve the printing services and cut costs. It became clear that in order to make any progress, the first step was to implement a print management system. It was not possible for Law ITS to make a unilateral decision on such a sweeping change. However, with the existing buy-in from our CIO, he presented the idea to the dean with the promise that it would not limit students' ability to print as much as they needed, but simply enable us to get a handle on printing and eventually improve our services to the community. In other words, we would institute print management, but we would continue not charging students for printing.

After evaluating several print management systems, we settled on Pharos, the same system already in use by other schools in the university. Although the system offered similar features to other solutions, Pharos has the distinct advantage of the lowest barrier of entry and the promise of leveraging existing institutional knowledge. With the system in place, we were able to begin collecting data. We analyzed the data over time to identify potential improvement possibilities in our printing services.

Communicating this change to the student body was key to our success, so we reached out to the Student Bar Association, the law school's student government. In a similar fashion to our CIO's pitch to the dean, we sold the idea to the SBA and gained their support. From there we planned the implementation to take place over the summer giving us time to work through any issues during summer classes before the fall semester began. The SBA enthusiastically shared this plan with the student body, touting the many benefits such as shorter wait times and better availability, and offered reassurance that while the university's instance of Pharos incorporated quotas and printing costs, we had no plans to do so.

3.2 Looking Outward

After a couple years of running the printing service with a print management system, we began to consider what else we could do to improve the service. A few main areas of concern remained. With the usage reporting from Pharos, we were able to better predict how much toner we would need throughout the semester, but we still stock piled it and occasionally ran out. Our response times for toner replacement and printer errors were still less than consistent and thus, not satisfactory to the students.

Our printer repair vendor reached out to us with an offer to supply toner, printer repair, and preventative maintenance for a set per page fee. We determined that with this agreement, our annual toner cost would be lower, plus we would have additional savings from not spending any additional money on maintenance and repair. Beyond that, the same vendor offered competitive pricing on new printers, which included installation and disposal of the old equipment. The vendor implemented their own monitoring system. The printing trend data allowed them to ship toner cartridges to us in one or two business days before it was needed. The benefits of this of outsourcing this work were many. We no longer needed to stock pile toner and the supply never ran out. Printer maintenance was automatically scheduled and completed without any effort on our part. Repairs were submitted through their ticketing system as before and were resolved within a business day. Even when not considering the cost savings, this agreement solved the problems of toner management and preventative maintenance.

Although the student worker lab technicians provided an invaluable service, supporting the printers most evenings and weekends, their class schedules rarely enabled them to work during regular business hours. After considering options such as hiring graduate students at a higher rate or employing temporary workers or consultants we decided to incorporate printer rounds into the daily routine of our Helpdesk while maintaining our existing student worker staff. The cost of one to two hours of work for one full time Helpdesk technician provided us with the right amount of coverage to ensure that toner was changed, paper was stocked at each printer location, and repairs were reported all in a reasonable amount of time. Leveraging our existing monitoring system, we were able to keep an eye on the printers between rounds and further reduce response time.

The final, and arguably the most impactful, step we took was to reach out to our Student Bar Association leadership to establish a relationship of open communication and semi-regular meetings. This collaboration allowed us to stay in touch with the community we were serving so we could respond to their needs. By meeting with the SBA we were able to help them understand our operation, the limitations we faced, and the efforts we were taking to improve the service we provided. In turn, they were able to help us understand the needs and the viewpoint of the students. Through this collaboration, we identified new locations where students wanted additional printing stations, and existing locations where they wanted more printing capacity. Based on the results of a student survey, the SBA presented to us the need for color printing, a service we would have never known to offer. Because of our ongoing conversations, the SBA were able to appropriately express to the students that such a service could not be offered for free, which would be a big change as presently there is not charge for the black and white printing.

Law ITS also created a separate e-mail queue for printing support inquiries, thus allowing Helpdesk to better prioritize and respond to printing support requests. The SBA was able to sell the benefits of this support by email service to the students in a way we likely could not have.

4 CONCLUSIONS

The Law ITS group know that we have made great progress with the student printing service. We know the journey is not over. We will continue to look for new and better ways of providing printing services, and we will revisit old decisions to determine whether those choices made are still the right ones. As the technology changes and the needs of the students evolve, so will our operations and services.

Although we do not know all the changes we will make going forward, we do have a few ideas and projects on the horizon. Over the course of the next academic year, we will deploy new signage to offer more information on the printing services at each printing station to provide better information on how to get help, and maps to show where other printing stations are located. System maintenance and the occasional network blips sometimes throw the printers or the Pharos terminals off the network, usually in the evenings and over the weekend when full time staff are not on site. We will soon begin connecting all terminals and printers to network-controlled outlets to allow us to remotely power-cycle any equipment which has lost its connection in order to more quickly restore service.

Although, largely for political reasons, we have never charged for black and white printing. We are in discussions with the law school leadership to implement the same printing quota and costs as the rest of the university. If we move forward with charging for black and white printing, we expect to reduce overall printing volume, recover costs to support current and future needs, and better align with the university's renewed focus on affordability and sustainability. We also look forward to discovering and investigating other ideas which promise similar benefits to ITS and to the community in the future.

ACKNOWLEDGMENTS

Thanks go to Lisa Barnett and Tolga Ergunay for providing the leadership, support, and data crunching to make these changes possible. The SBA representatives, past and present, provided a crucial link to the student body, and offered us the reassurance we needed to know we were on the right track.

From eLearning to eScience: Building a Service Oriented Architecture to Support Research

Marius Politze
RWTH Aachen University
Templergraben 55
52062 Aachen, Germany
politze@itc.rwth-aachen.de

Thomas Eifert
RWTH Aachen University
Templergraben 55
52062 Aachen, Germany
eifert@itc.rwth-aachen.de

ABSTRACT

By supporting a wide range of eLearning scenarios with an integrated software suite and API, RWTH Aachen University was able to achieve a high standardization, high rate of adoption of technology and seamless integration into various learning processes by teachers and students in the past years. As students emerge to researchers, they are often missing this kind of integrated support. To close this gap the experiences gained from setting up an eLearning infrastructure are being used to design and implement a service-oriented architecture to support a wide range of eScience scenarios.

KEYWORDS

software architecture; service oriented architecture; process support; eLearning; eScience

ACM Reference format:
Marius Politze and Thomas Eifert. 2017. From eLearning to eScience: Building a Service Oriented Architecture to Support Research. In *Proceedings of SIGUCCS'17, Seattle, WA, USA, October 1–4, 2017,* 3 pages.
https://dx.doi.org/10.1145/3123458.3123495

1 INTRODUCTION

Teaching and research are two core university processes. Many initiatives focus on eLearning to develop, streamline and standardize technology-enhanced teaching and learning. Even though used by the same user group and at the same organizations, supporting technology for scientific research still lack significant investments to build a foundation for eScience services.

On the one hand, researchers have rising demands for existing IT systems and infrastructure to deliver business value in the short term. On the other hand, many organizational issues must be addressed, such as defining when and how Research Data Management (RDM) systems are used within the research process. The challenge for central IT service providers is to implement services that researchers want to use today that are also flexible to support tomorrow's processes.

In contrast to the research processes, the learning processes at universities have been supported by central IT services for almost a decade. While the processes may be very different, to meet the posed high demands, an IT infrastructure supporting the research processes needs to learn from pre-established infrastructures for eLearning.

A project group at university level focuses on consulting, training and development of technical solutions for RDM. Since managing data requires extra effort from researchers, usability and seamless integration into existing workflows are key: Solutions need to cover the whole research process: private and collaborative domain, in which researchers actively work with the data, as well as the archive and publication domain, in which data access is less frequently [5].

2 RELATED WORK

Mobility and ubiquity of information technology and therefore global accessibility and reachability have become part of our daily life and processes [6]. Over more than a decade, initiatives in eLearning and, more generally, student lifecycle management (SLM) standardized supporting IT infrastructures. Barkhuus and Dourish have discussed different needs of students related to ubiquitous services offered by their university [3]. While the technological basis has changed since the study in 2004, social roles, relationships and responsibilities of students remain comparable. Lucke and Tavangarian introduced a model for the pervasive university that takes the heterogeneous existing systems into account [8]. Mincer-Daszkiewicz and Barata et al. show practical examples of SOA in the field of SLM [2, 9].

In the RADAR (Research Data Repository) project Kraft et al. established a software as a service (SaaS) model scientists may use to preserve and publish their research data, providing long-term storage, persistent object identifiers and metadata [7]. Other approaches such as ProjektRepository [10] or TR32DB [4] additionally introduce the researchers' need for collaboration within a research repository.

3 CONCEPTUAL MODEL FROM EXISTING ELEARNING APPLICATIONS

Today's researchers often are former students that have witnessed the dawn of the eLearning landscape as it exists at universities today. Naturally, they expect university IT to support their research activities in the same way it supports learning. This model originates from the experience of building an infrastructure that supports a variety of eLearning scenarios. Digital literacy increases among researchers and changes the way IT services are used [1]. While a

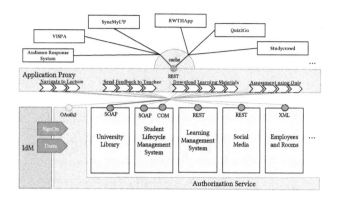

Figure 1: Overview of the architecture supporting individualized eLearning processes

set of base services are required, individualization and adoption of the processes is becoming more important to heavy users: a core concept behind the presented architecture.

The conceptual architecture for supporting eLearning services adds an application proxy, cache and a uniform API [13]. Figure 1 shows the service organizing access to backend systems using vendor-specific or legacy APIs. Basing the API on the processes rather than underlying backend systems reduces the impact of vendor lock-in enabling the additon of new systems or scattering of requests between multiple systems. This decouples the systems into smaller functional units, increasing long-term sustainability.

Appropriate and consistent use of names matching the definition and wording within defined processes is crucial. This allows users to transfer their knowledge about processes to applications. Consider the following (simplified) example of an LMS: For every lecture, an LMS stores files of three categories: lecture slides, exercises and video recordings. Internally, it stores them in a folder matching the category. Thus, naming of these folders is only by convention. The generic API of the LMS offers methods to access files in arbitrary folders. This, however, does not model conventions used for storing files as slides, exercises or video recordings. An application could use different folder names, which leads to errors in other applications. A process specific API should therefore enforce this convention by either restricting access to allowed folders or supplying separate methods for each category therefore making the implicit convention explicit in the API.

If the API is not specific to processes, it may invite users to use it for other than the intended workflows. This can be beneficial for the short-term interests of the user but service providers usually desire usage only within the specified parameters to meet technical bounding conditions such as CPU load, disk sizes and the like. Enforcing such boundaries within the API is crucial for failure-free operation of services but also limits the spectrum of individualization.

Programmatic access to services potentially exposes personal and/or confidential data. As such, security is another design principle of a process supporting API. Applications work on behalf of or within the context of a user. Often a user supplies credentials such as a username and a password to authenticate. By giving user credentials to an application it gains full power to perform every

possible action within the context of the user, which may be undesirable in many cases. Distinguishing applications and their needs as well as securely identifying the user is therefore crucial.

Users of the services: Users in eLearning applications consist of students and teachers, all associated with the university. Typical lectures have 20-100 participants, though sometimes number up to 1500 due to increased cooperation and new styles of teaching such as, Massive Open Online Courses (MOOCs) which require invitation of externals.

Kind of data: Files that eLearning systems deal with are commonly small and standardized, like slides, scripts or homework. In addition, 1-2 GB video recordings have become common in recent years. Commodity software and hardware handle them quite well.

Kind of services and applications: Services like distribution of learning materials and contacting students are a key success factor of integrated eLearning systems. A LMS should allow teachers to communicate with the right audience: students participating in a lecture. Individualized services and applications like online programming environments or audience response systems reuse these groups. Most of the services are web applications or mobile apps.

Maturity of the processes: Teaching styles and didactic methods can vary, while student lifecycle and eLearning processes are well understood. Most faculties and institutes have coordinators to develop teaching methodologies. Existing IT services enhance already existing processes.

4   ADOPTION OF THE CONCEPTUAL MODEL TO ESCIENCE

eScience processes are supported by IT services as well. A comparison points out the difference and the common core before applying the findings from the reference model to eScience.

Users of the services: National and international collaboration is mandatory for many research projects. While there are research groups with as few as ten members, regional, national and international collaborations may have far more than 100 researchers from various universities and research facilities. Number and diversity of users thus are equivalent to previous scenarios.

Kind of data: File formats and software used by researchers is very heterogeneous and mostly specialized on the scientific disciplines. Research data varies greatly in file sizes and count. Nevertheless, research also involves documents like papers, grant applications, and dissertations that are well-standardized.

Kind of services and applications: Centralized services for researchers mostly focus on the archival of research data and publishing of results. Instead of the researchers themselves, technical personnel often use these services. There exist a lot of decentralized discipline-specific applications, services and implementations not connected to centralized systems. Offering APIs would allow the integration of discipline-specific tools into generic services.

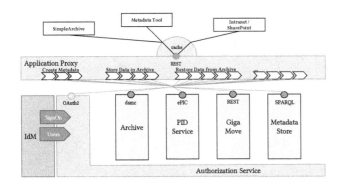

Figure 2: Overview of the architecture supporting eScience processes

Maturity of the processes: Research groups essentially follow their own research processes. Connections to university administration are rare and mostly related to funding. Developments of the research process remain within the research group, and few coordinate with other research groups. IT service providers should thus promote communities developing eScience methodology.

When put side-by-side, it becomes evident that even though the reference model emerges from eLearning applications, it provides a general structure for process-specific APIs in university context. Implementation of first APIs supporting eScience processes are based on this conceptual model. A proof-of-concept implemented two workflows within the research data management processes: metadata assignment [11] and long term archival [12]. Figure 2 shows a concept of the API that now publishes process-centric methods such as *Archive File* or *Create Metadata for File*, hiding implementation details of underlying systems or storage technologies from the user.

Both workflows are independent. This allows individualization and short-term benefits for the users by picking those parts that solve their current problems. Furthermore, it allows the implementation of more complex applications as the more concrete definition of research process in general and especially the RDM processes yield further results. The goal is to learn from more complex individual solutions, then build new generation of central IT services for all users within the university.

Keeping in mind the conceptual model also helps in defining desired functionalities of future IT systems as well as integrating already existing infrastructures used by research process at the universities.

5 CONCLUSION

The presented strategy is a work-in-progress, bottom-up approach from a technical perspective. Additionally, from an organizational point of view, there are still open questions. Actually defining a framework for the research process with roles and duties is a challenge that the university as a whole has to meet.

Two current projects allowed for the independent application of the conceptual model to eScience scenarios. This allows individualizations and short-term benefits for the users by picking those

parts that solve their current problems. Furthermore, it allows the implementation of more complex applications as a more precise definition of research processes in general – especially the RDM processes – yields further results. The goal is to learn from more complex individual solutions, then build a new generation of central IT services for all users within the university.

While it was possible to transfer technical knowledge, this methodology bears the risk that researchers most certainly will not use APIs directly. The implementation of user interfaces that lead the user through supported processes is mandatory. Again working out the existing processes is key for successful implementation of an RDM landscape at universities. Key technologies like centralized layers for authorization, communication and caching, as well as continuously adding process centric APIs to off-the-shelf IT components is an emerging competence for IT service providers.

REFERENCES

[1] Lerzan Aksoy, Ruth N. Bolton, A. Parasuraman, Ankie Hoefnagels, Nanne Migchels, Sertan Kabadayi, Thorsten Gruber, Yuliya Komarova Loureiro, and David Solnet. 2013. Understanding Generation Y and their use of social media: A review and research agenda. *Journal of Service Management* 24, 3 (2013), 245–267. https://doi.org/10.1108/09564231311326987

[2] Ricardo Barata, Sérgio Silva, David Martinho, Luís Cruz, and Luís Guerra e Silva. 2014. Open APIs in Information Systems for Higher Education. In *20th EUNIS Congress*, Johan Bergström (Ed.). Umeå, Sweden.

[3] Louise Barkhuus and Paul Dourish. 2004. Everyday Encounters with Context-Aware Computing in a Campus Environment. In *UbiComp 2004: Ubiquitous Computing*, David Hutchison, Takeo Kanade, Josef Kittler, Jon M. Kleinberg, Friedemann Mattern, John C. Mitchell, Moni Naor, Oscar Nierstrasz, C. Pandu Rangan, Bernhard Steffen, Madhu Sudan, Demetri Terzopoulos, Dough Tygar, Moshe Y. Vardi, Gerhard Weikum, Nigel Davies, Elizabeth D. Mynatt, and Itiro Siio (Eds.). Lecture Notes in Computer Science, Vol. 3205. Springer Berlin Heidelberg, Berlin, Heidelberg, 232–249. https://doi.org/10.1007/978-3-540-30119-6_14

[4] Constanze Curdt. 2014. *Design and Implementation of a Research Data Management System: The CRC/TR32 Project Database (TR32DB)*. Dissertation. Universität zu Köln, Cologne. http://kups.ub.uni-koeln.de/5882/

[5] Thomas Eifert, Stephan Muckel, and Dominik Schmitz. 2016. Introducing Research Data Management as a Service Suite at RWTH Aachen University. In *9. DFN-Forum Kommunikationstechnologien*, Paul Müller, Bernhard Neumair, Helmut Reiser, and Gabi Dreo Rodosek (Eds.). GI Edition Lecture Notes in Informatics Proceedings (LNI), Vol. 257. Köllen, Bonn, 55–66.

[6] Wilfried Juling. 2009. Vom Rechnernetz zu e-Science. *PIK - Praxis der Informationsverarbeitung und Kommunikation* 32, 1 (2009), 33–36. https://doi.org/10.1515/piko.2009.007

[7] Angelina Kraft, Matthias Razum, Jan Potthoff, Andrea Porzel, Thomas Engel, Frank Lange, Karina van den Broek, and Filipe Furtado. 2016. The RADAR Project - A Service for Research Data Archival and Publication. *ISPRS International Journal of Geo-Information* 5, 3 (2016), 28. https://doi.org/10.3390/ijgi5030028

[8] Ulrike Lucke and Djamshid Tavangarian. 2009. Eine Service- und Kontext-basierte Infrastruktur für die Pervasive University. In *INFORMATIK 2009: Im Focus das Leben*, Stefan Fischer, Erik Maehle, and Rüdiger Reischuk (Eds.). GI Edition Lecture Notes in Informatics Proceedings (LNI), Vol. 154. Köllen, Bonn, 1935–1949.

[9] Janina Mincer-Daszkiewicz. 2014. We Publish, You Subscribe — Hubbub as a Natural Habitat for Students and Academic Teachers. In *20th EUNIS Congress*, Johan Bergström (Ed.). Umeå, Sweden.

[10] Marius Politze and Bernd Decker. 2016. Ontology Based Semantic Data Management for Pandisciplinary Research Projects. In *Proceedings of the 2nd Data Management Workshop*, Constanze Curdt and Christian Wilmes (Eds.). Kölner Geographische Arbeiten, Vol. 96. Cologne, Germany. https://doi.org/10.5880/TR32DB.KGA96.10

[11] Marius Politze and Florian Krämer. 2016. Towards a distributed research data management system. In *22nd EUNIS Congress*, Yiannis Salmatzidis (Ed.). Thessaloniki, Greece, 184–186.

[12] Marius Politze and Florian Krämer. 2017. simpleArchive – Making an Archive Accessible to the User. In *23rd EUNIS Congress*, Raimund Vogl (Ed.). Münster, Germany, 121–123.

[13] Marius Politze, Steffen Schaffert, and Bernd Decker. 2016. A secure infrastructure for mobile blended learning applications. In *European Journal of Higher Education IT 2016-1*, Johan Bergström (Ed.). Umeå.

Games: Facilitating Communications Training (and Fun)

Eric Handler
1600 Grand Ave.
Saint Paul, MN 55105
ehandler@macalester.edu

ABSTRACT

Communication is an important aspect to providing technical support. Specialized training towards communication skills can dramatically help apprentice support staff grow comfortable fielding questions and provide excellent support even as their technical knowledge expands. Tabletop and video games can be used, with or without modification, to facilitate communication training for students and team building for full time staff. This poster will explore key aspects of communication like facilitating an understanding of the terminology of constituents, facilitating translation into technical terms. Additional topics include avoiding terms that have multiple meanings, especially to non-technical users, pattern recognition. The games used in this poster Include Taboo, Codenames, and Keep Talking and Nobody Explodes. These games, as well as many other, will be used to showcase the variety of tools that can be used to facilitate training and team building. The goal of this poster is to explain a few of these tools and include an interactive element where attendees can participate in at least one of the games.

CCS CONCEPTS

• **Social and professional topics** → Computer and information systems training; **Software and its engineering** → Virtual worlds training simulations; **Applied computing** → Computer games;

KEYWORDS

ACM proceedings; gamification; communication; training

1 INTRODUCTION

Acknowledging the nuanced nature of communication is a key aspect to providing technical support. Specialized

communication training can dramatically help apprentice support staff grow comfortable fielding questions and provide excellent support even as their technical knowledge expands. There are areas of skillful communication that can be highlighted through fun training exercises using selected board and video games as well as by creating new modules of games. Additionally, developing training modules and advanced training exercises creates team-building experiences robust enough for ongoing training and relationship management between professional staff. Gamification of training also creates opportunities to develop skills in communication areas vital to technical support.

2 TRANSLATION

2.1 What is translation?

The first area is translation. The ability to translate the language of a technology novice—often obscured by frustration—is a key skill for a successful support representative. This is a key skill for both new student staff as well as professional staff. It is particularly important for staff who work closely with students, as some student workers may not develop a sophisticated technology vocabulary over a short period of employment.

2.2 Translation training with games

Macalester College IT staff collaborated to create Taboo cards for common issues encountered at our support desks. Taboo is a game for two two-person teams where one player prompts another to guess a word or phrase within a fixed time limit while avoiding using a list of prohibited key words. This particular exercise is useful for both the clue giver and the guesser for very different reasons. As the guesser, one quickly learns how hard it is to communicate when someone isn't using the same vocabulary, and must ask questions in a helpful and calm manor that doesn't agitate one's partner (client). As the clue giver or the client, a participant gains first-hand experience and sympathy towards our constituents, learning how frustrating it can be when the person who is supposed to be able to help can't understand. Understanding this feeling is key to providing comfort and developing empathy. As the guesser, a trainee gains insight into how to use knowledge they bring to situation and the information provided by a client to synthesize helpful replies in the midst of stress that may arise from working with certain members of the institution's staff and faculty.

3 CLARITY

3.1 Defining and Developing Clarity

The second area is clarity. Information technology is riddled with phrases that sound similar even to the most technically savvy. Helping people sort through these overloaded phrases requires a keen understanding of technology. Macalester IT staff have started playing "Keep Talking and Nobody Explodes" together during lunches as a team building and communication development tool. Keep Talking and Nobody Explodes is a VR game where one player has a digital bomb on screen and controls to interact with modules that need to be disarmed. The other players are unable to see the screen, the countdown clock, and the way the individual modules look. The person in VR must communicate all kinds of information about the bomb and the game designers have taken great steps to take advantage of common conversational shortcuts. The module shown in Fig. 1 requires the players to press a different number or position depending on the number displayed. If the players don't communicate clearly the need to press a position or a label, their attempt to disarm the bomb will end.

Figure 1: A module from Keep Talking and Nobody Explodes that requires different numerals or positions on the keypad to be pressed depending on the number displayed.

Fig. 2 highlights how difficult it can be to get someone to do something as simple as press a button when the manual reading players may say words like "press", "wait", and "no" (perhaps with some sense of urgency).

Figure 2: A module from Keep Talking and Nobody Explodes that uses phrases someone may use to describe how to complete the module.

Spending time working through modules like this and establishing how important it is to provide clear instructions helps student employees and staff understand the importance of the clarity when communicating with constituents.

4 FUTURE DIRECTIONS

4.1 New games and new lessons

Future directions for the use of games in training are numerous. Staff, students, or mixed teams could visit escape rooms[2], which would be excellent training because of the timed nature of the experience. Additionally, like many of the major challenges that face a support team, the answer requires novel thinking and pattern recognition. The solution to the escape room isn't going to be found in a departmental wiki (unless the first team building exercise incudes the documentation specialists). In addition to taking the team off site for enhanced challenges, there are additional board games that can be adapted into training tools. The first game that we intend to pursue is the game Concept where one player must explain a popular idiom, movie title, or famous figure using a board of infographics. Customizing the board and cards to encompass information technology topics could be useful for helping develop nonverbal and unwritten communication skills in a fun setting, as well help evaluate the effectiveness of departmental. The last game under consideration for adaptation into a training module is Codenames. Codenames is a team game where players must successfully identify a single word and a number, for example "computer, 3" which indicates a set of words to select from a 5 x 5 grid of words on the table corresponding to the team's goals. Creating a set of words for distribution into the grid could be an excellent evolution of the experience provided by Taboo.

5 CONCLUSIONS

Using gamification to improve training highlights the opportunities to teach student workers new skills as well as empathy for the clients served by IT staff. The methods used at Macalester as well as those implemented in the future, provide a foundation for interested teams to build upon to improve communication with constituents.

ACKNOWLEDGMENTS

I'd like to thank my colleagues Alison Sommer, Absalon Prieto and Gabe Stizel for their work playing these games with me and developing our training program. I'd also like to thank Steel Crate Games the developers of Keep Talking and Nobody Explodes for their approval to include images from their game.

---

[2] Escapes rooms are a large team based puzzle experience where participants need to solve a series of puzzles in a specified period of time in order to win.

Producing Video Clips for Information Ethics and Security in Higher Education

Tomohito Wada
National Institute of Fitness and Sports
1 Shiromizu
Kanoya, Kagoshima, Japan
wada@nifs-k.ac.jp

Izumi Fuse
Hokkaido University
Kita 8, Nishi 5
Kita-ku, Sapporo, Hokkaido, Japan
ifuse@iic.hokudai.ac.jp

Shigeto Okabe
Hokkaido University
Kita 8, Nishi 5
Kita-ku, Sapporo, Hokkaido, Japan
okabe@iic.hokudai.ac.jp

Takeo Tatsumi
The Open University of Japan
2-11 Wakaba
Mihama-ku, Chiba, Japan
ttmtko@ouj.ac.jp

Hiroshi Ueda
Kyoto University
Yoshida-honmachi
Sakyo-ku, Kyoto, Japan
ueda.hiroshi.4n@kyoto-u.ac.jp

Tetsutaro Uehara
Ritsumeikan University
1-1-1 Noji-higashi
Kusatsu, Shiga, Japan
t-uehara@fc.ritsumei.ac.jp

Michio Nakanishi
Osaka Institute of Technology
1-79-1 Kitayama
Hirakata, Osaka, Japan
naka@is.oit.ac.jp

Takahiro Tagawa
Kyushu University
744 Motooka
Nishi-ku, Fukuoka, Japan
tagawa@cc.kyushu-u.ac.jp

Ikuya Murata
University of Teacher Education Fukuoka
1-1 Akamabunkyo-machi
Munakata, Fukuoka, Japan
ikuyam@fukuoka-edu.ac.jp

ABSTRACT

A consortium of IT professionals across various universities in Japan has been producing educational video clips regarding information ethics and cyber security issues for university students. The clips were revised and supplemented several times, with the most recent version released in late 2016. This video collection consists of twenty-two short stories involving three university students who were involved in IT issues or incidents. The video topics and original scripts were discussed and written by various university faculty members. Professionals at a production company then refined the scripts and made the videos. The video clips have been widely used by many Japanese universities and have been well received by students. Most importantly, the videos raise important issues about information ethics and help students understand their role in computer security.

CCS CONCEPTS

• *Security and privacy* → *Social aspects of security and privacy* • *Social and professional topics* → *Computing education*

KEYWORDS

Information ethics, computer security, educational material, inter-university collaboration

1 INTRODUCTION

Working in information technology carries ethical issues along with technical issues. Each time a new technology evolves, new social and security implications arise as well. To maintain information security at the university, it is imperative for educators to grasp the ever-changing context of information technology and its ethical and social impact, identify educational opportunities, devise teaching methods, and develop teaching materials. None of this, however, is easy to do.

In an effort to address these issues, the Association of National University's Education Center for Information Processing in Japan, in cooperation with the National Institute of Multimedia Education, has developed short videos on the subject of information ethics and computer security for university students based on changes in information technology and its impact on society since 2002[1]. This ongoing effort aims to provide up-to-date educational materials to university educators to share rather than as a curriculum or a course. The project's first release was in 2003 and included eight videos. After the third edition, responsibility for the project shifted to AXIES, an EDUCAUSE-like organization in Japan. A number of clips in 3rd and 4th edition are now released [2] under the Creative Commons license (BY-NC-ND 4.0) [3]. The videos have been revised and supplemented over time and the latest, the sixth edition, was released in late 2016. In this paper, we will address the most recent versions of the videos and their practical use in a Japanese university.

2 THE SIXTH EDITION

The sixth edition of "Video Clips for Information Ethics and Security" was released in 2016. This collection consists of twenty-two short topics about three university students who were involved in IT issues or incidents. The titles and duration of the clips are listed in Table 1. The clip numbers with an asterisk indicate that they were newly added to the collection, and clips without asterisk were republished from previous editions. The eleven new stories were selected from current issues affecting university students. Malware on smartphones (#4), ransomware (#10), digital signatures (#7), attacking by email (#9), losing devices or media (#6) and software update (#8) are topics related to IT security. Personalized search (#11), flaming (#13), anonymous defamation (#14), online friends (#12) and web accessibility (#16) are topics related to ethics in the IT community.

Most of the topics consist of two short movies: a "story clip" and a "commentary clip." Story clips are short dramas involving university students, while commentary clips respond to the story clip and contain commentary by a narrator. The topics with only story clips (#5, #12, #17 and #18) are issues it might be more important for students to consider themselves rather than receiving commentary. The product provides guidelines for educators to use. Fig. 1 shows a sample of the guidelines such as outline of the clip, points for study, related clips and links to related web sites.

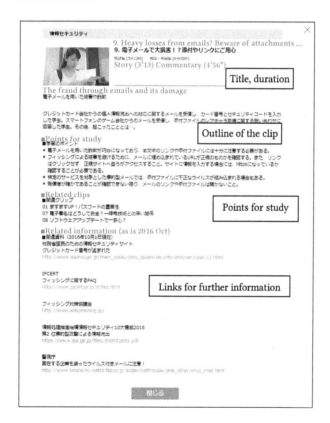

Figure 1: A sample of a guideline for the clip #9 included into the product.

Table 1: **Title and durations of the clips**

No.	Title	Duration	
		Story clip	Commentary clip
1	More than ever! The importance of passwords	5'59"	5'39"
2	Where is that data?	2'03"	2'46"
3	Is personal information leaked when saving up points?	1'51"	3'50"
4*	Is that App OK? Malware in your smartphone?	3'20"	3'01"
5	Texting while walking	1'23"	---
6*	Lost PC! Lost smartphone! Lost flash drive! What should we do?	3'10"	3'24"
7*	Why are digital signatures safe? -The close relation to encryption technology	2'35"	a:4'33" b:8'45"
8*	Software update - Safe for the time being?	2'28"	4'56"
9*	Heavy losses from emails!? Beware of attachments and links	3'13"	6'42"
10*	Ransomware - I shouldn't pay money?	3'52"	6'03"
11*	Majority in the Internet, is it really the majority?	3'00"	4'22"
12*	Online friends, is it OK to trust them?	5'32"	---
13*	Misunderstanding or going up in flame! Be careful with spreading information	3'56"	5'07"
14*	Community website, a casual posting caused uproar!	2'44"	4'57"
15	Posting on the Internet is difficult to cancel	2'29"	6'15"
16*	Web accessibility	1'20"	3'52"
17	GPS and privacy	2'31"	---
18	Photograph without permission, upload without permission	2'29"	---
19	Smartphones know everything	2'58"	7'20"
20	Proper quotation	2'38"	5'58"
21	Plagiarism and forgery are criminal	3'47"	1'52"
22	Copyright of an unpublished work	3'25"	2'28"

3 PRODUCTION AND MARKETING

The project team for the 6th edition had nine core members and four advisers from various universities. All members are academic with a background in computer science. Many of them are responsible for fundamental IT-related courses and/or belong to the IT service organization at their universities. The timeline used for the 6th edition is listed in Table 2. Discussion began in February, 2016 and took place in a public groupware system.

The original version of the stories and scripts were developed by members of the project team and were then polished by a production company. Project members remained involved in casting auditions, location shooting, and narration recording to offer advice and make it possible for prompt decisions when questions arose. Fig. 2 shows a snapshot of a location shooting.

While it is more difficult for project members to be involved during the whole process, our group believes it keeps the product's quality high.

The video clips were completed in October and released as a package on December 14th, 2016.

The product licenses are available individually or as a campus subscription by a distributer. The video clips have been used in many Japanese universities. In 2016, twenty-five universities subscribed to the campus license and more than 2200 individual licenses were sold. In addition, many university co-op stores pre-install our product on their PCs. Approximately 50,000 licenses were sold for co-op PCs in 2016.

Table 2: **Timeline of the project**

date	event
Feb. 4, 2016	Started discussion
Mar. 14 - 15	Meeting (in-person)
May 19	AXIES approved the budget
Jun. 21	Started to write scenarios
Aug. 8	Revised scenarios by production company
Aug. 11	An audition for casting
Aug. 31 - Sep.3	Location shooting
Sep. 13	The first preview Finalized guidelines for a clip
Sep. 30	The second preview
Oct. 17	Recorded narrations
Oct. 25	Completed the video clips
Dec. 14	Released the product

Figure 2: **A snapshot of a location shooting.**

4 UTILIZATION IN A CLASS

The videos were modularized to be more usable in university lectures and have been well-received by students. Fig. 3 shows the results of student surveys about the videos. Even though not all students found the videos interesting, they did learn from them. Many students showed they underestimated the way information technology can impact them personally with comments like, "It was surprising that people are cheated like this." These comments helped teachers know where to lead students who needed further information, like the rankings of security threats.

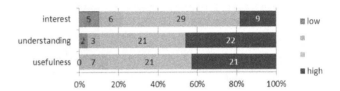

Figure 3: **Impressions after watching the clip #9 "Heavy Losses from Emails!?" (n=49)**

5 CONCLUSIONS

The video clips about information ethics and security were produced in collaboration with members from various universities and a production company. Eleven topics including ransomware, personalized search, digital signature, etc. were newly added to the collection. Groupware was used as a key tool for remote collaboration. The videos were modularized into short clips to be used for university lectures. The video provided good starting points to consider the matter and have made easier to lead students to further related information.

ACKNOWLEDGMENTS

We would like to thank Performa Co. Ltd for producing the video clips. The continuing effort is managed and supported by AXIES in Japan and is supported by Information Initiative Center, Hokkaido University.

REFERENCES

[1] T. Yamanoue, et al. 2014. Computer Ethics Video Clips for University Students in Japan from 2003 until 2013. COMPSACW '14 Proceedings of the 2014 IEEE 38th International Computer Software and Applications Conference Workshops, (Jul. 2014), 96–101. DOI: 10.1109/COMPSACW.2014.21
[2] https://axies.jp/ja/video/8hc6fl as is June 21th, 2017.
[3] https://creativecommons.org/licenses/by-nc-nd/4.0/ as is June 21th, 2017.

Management of Carrying PC Terminals and Initialization of User Directory by Shifts for Students

Masayuki Mori
Kyoto Institute of Technology
Matsugasaki, Sakyo
Kyoto, JAPAN 606-8585
+81 75 724 7957
morim@kit.ac.jp

Hideo Masuda
Kyoto Institute of Technology
Matsugasaki, Sakyo
Kyoto, JAPAN 606-8585
h-masuda@kit.ac.jp

Takayuki Nagai
Kyoto Institute of Technology
Matsugasaki, Sakyo
Kyoto, JAPAN 606-8585
nagai@kit.ac.jp

ABSTRACT

In Center for Information Science, Kyoto Institute of Technology, 90 laptop computers used in laboratory courses are managed by an image of Windows 7. As a requirement of a laptop, in order to carry these, it is necessary to use it offline without connecting the wired LAN while in class. Further, classes of different themes in three classrooms are continued at the same time. After that, classes are continued again by shifts for students. Therefore, Laptop users were created for each theme, and at the end of the theme the user directory was required to be initialized. These tasks are labor intensive because it is necessary to collect laptops and connect to the wired LAN. Moreover, since regular security updates are necessary, the maintenance schedule becomes very tight. Therefore, it is necessary to consider not only the image management system, but also the method of collecting laptops and timing of maintenance. In this paper, we describe the customization and management method of PC terminals management system implemented to satisfy these requirements. In addition, we describe verification of management method by Windows 10 assumed after replacement

CCS CONCEPTS

• **Social and professional topics** ~ Computing equipment management

KEYWORDS

Image Management, User Directory, Windows10, System Center Configuration Manager

1 INTRODUCTION

The computer infrastructure system called System 9 is managed and operated in the Center for Information Science, Kyoto Institute of Technology. System 9 is composed of hardware and software that assume the information infrastructure of university such as PC Terminals, Virtualization Infrastructure, Storage, Authentication, E-mail, Web services [1]. Especially, PC Terminals of Windows 7 is one of the systems with many inquiries because teachers and students often use these in class.

PC Terminals for the whole university adopt a thin client terminal by a desktop PC of constant network connection. These are arranged in classrooms for exercises and self-study. In PC Terminals for laboratory of information science, laptop computers are adopted for convenience of connection to equipment and group handling. Also, laptop computers are used outside of the classrooms. Therefore, the system is managed by image distribution so that the computers can be used offline. Moreover, setting and software configuration according to multiple laboratory themes are necessary.

In this paper, we will demonstrate how the management and operation of laptops meets the requirements of laboratory courses. Also, we will describe the operational experiment with Windows 10 assuming the next computer infrastructure system.

2 LABORATORY COURSES OF DEPARTMENT OF INFORMATION SCIENCE

Kyoto Institute of Technology Department of Information Science is conducting courses using PC Terminals for laboratory in three courses related to information science: "Laboratory in Basic Information Science", "Laboratory in Information Science 1", and "Laboratory in Information Science 2". Table 1 shows the content of laboratory courses in 2016. Students in the classes use PC Terminals for laboratory by connecting equipment and programming. Although laboratories are group work, students can use one PC Terminal for laboratory per person. Students are divided into 3 classrooms, where each classroom laboratory has a different theme. One laboratory takes five weeks to finish, which is one set. After one set, students change classrooms.

One theme is assigned to one or two Teachers and two Teaching Assistant. Because three classrooms will proceed simultaneously, only one theme can't be canceled. Therefore,

SIGUCCS '17, October 1–4, 2017, Seattle, WA, USA
© 2017 Association for Computing Machinery.
ACM ISBN 978-1-4503-4919-2/17/10...$15.00
https://doi.org/10.1145/3123458.3123478

Table 1: Class in 2016.

Year / Semester	Day	Period	Course Title	theme	classroom	Instructor	TA
2nd / Second term	Mon	3-5	Laboratory in Basic Information Science	Human interface (a)	A, C	1	2
				Embedded system (b)	A, C	1	2
				Electronics (c)	A, C	2	2
3rd / First term	Fri	3-5	Laboratory in Information Science 1	Signal processing (a)	C	2	2
				System control (b)	A	1	2
				CPU (c)	B	1	2
3rd / Second term	Wed	3-5	Laboratory in Information Science 2	Pattern Recognition (a)	C	1	2
				Artificial intelligence (b)	A	1	2
				Logical design (c)	B	1	2

Table 2: Software list of PC terminals.

Software	Description
Microsoft Office 2013 Pro	Office software
Adobe Reader	PDF viewer
Mozilla Firefox	Web browser
Eclipse	Development environment
Scilab	Software for numerical computation
SIVP	Scilab Image and Video Processing Toolbox
SWT	Scilab Wavelet Toolbox
OpenCV	Computer vision library
Processing	Processing development environment
Microsoft Visual Studio	Microsoft development environment
Altera Quartus	FPGA/CPLD/HardCopy ASIC development environment
TI Code Composer Studio	TI development environment
Arduino	Arduino development environment
Keil MDK-Lite	ARM development environment

Table 3: PC terminals details.

Part	Description
Model number	NEC PC-VK30HDZNG
CPU	Core i7-3540M 3.00GHz
Memory	8.00GB
HDD	120GB （C:97.6GB D:21.4GB）
OS	Windows 7 Professional SP1 64bit
Keyboard	key pitch 19mm
monitor	15.6 type full HD LCD monitor
Wired LAN	1port
Quantity	Classroom A 38 Classroom B 26 Classroom C 26 (Total 90)

department of Information Science makes teams ((a) to (c) of Table 1) with teachers between different courses. If teachers are absent, the team gives support. These class compositions are discussed at the examination committee of Department of Information Science. A Center for information Science attends as the person in charge of management and operation of PC Terminals in the laboratory.

In laboratory courses, followings [R-a] to [R-f] are required for PC terminal.

[R-a] Normal operation of the software using laboratory courses.

Equipment to be connected and Software for programming must operate normally. Table 2 shows the list of software installed in PC terminals for laboratory courses.

[R-b] Students cannot see other set of information.

At the end of the set, data created by students remain in HDD, so those must be deleted before the next set begins.

[R-c] Portable.

Sharing within the group and move to equipment, so PC terminals is necessary to assume to portable.

[R-d] Used Offline.

Because students carry a PC terminal, stable high-speed network connection by wired LAN is not available in class.

[R-e] Environment construction completed before term of classes begins.

Settings and installs for changing class contents and software update completed before term of classes begins. Also, in term of classes, since it is necessary to prioritize stable operation, don't setting and install.

[R-f] Applying security updates

Periodic installation is necessary for important security of Microsoft update.

Table 4: Schedule for class.

Man	Tue	Wed	Thu	Fri
9/19 (Holiday)	9/20	9/21	9/22 (Holiday)	9/23
9/26	9/27	09/28 LIS2(1-1/4)	9/29	9/30
10/03 LB(1-1/5)	10/4	10/05 LIS2 (1-2/4)	10/6	10/7
10/10 (Holiday)	10/11	10/12 LIS2 (1-3/4) Security	10/13	10/14
10/17 LB (1-2/5)	10/18	10/19 LIS2 (1-4/4)	10/20	10/21
10/24 LB (1-3/5)	10/25	10/26 LIS2 (2-1/4)	10/27	10/28
10/31 LB (1-4/5)	11/1	11/02 LIS2 (2-2/4)	11/03 (Holiday)	11/4
11/07 LB (1-5/5)	11/8	11/09 LIS2 (2-3/4) Security, LB-User Reset	11/10	11/11
11/14 LB (2-1/5)	11/15	11/16 LIS2 (2-4/4) LIS2- UserReset	11/17	11/18 (Festival)
11/21 LB (2-2/5)	11/22	11/23 (Holiday)	11/24	11/25
11/28 LB (2-3/5)	11/29	11/30 LIS2 (3-1/4)	12/1	12/2
12/05 LB (2-4/5)	12/6	12/07 LIS2 (3-2/4)	12/8	12/9
12/12 LB (2-5/5)	12/13	12/14 LIS2 (3-3/4) Security, LB- User Reset	12/15	12/16
12/19 LB (3-1/5)	12/20	12/21 LIS2 (3-4/4) LIS2- User Reset	12/22 (Year End)	12/23 (Holiday)
12/26	12/27	12/28	12/29	12/30
1/2	1/3	1/4	1/5	1/06 (Year Start)
1/09 (Holiday)	1/10 LB (3-2/5)	1/11 Security	1/12	1/13
1/16 LB (3-3/5)	1/17	1/18	1/19	1/20
1/23 LB (3-4/5)	1/24	1/25	1/26	1/27
1/30 LB (3-5/5)	1/31	2/01 LB- User Reset (Last Day of Class)	2/02	2/03

3 PC TERMINALS FOR LABORATORY CPURSES

Management of PC terminals for laboratory courses started in March 2014 as part of Information Science Education System in System 9. Table 3 shows the specifications of PC terminals for laboratory courses. Management and operation to match the necessary requirements in "laboratory courses" which are described as follows.

Figure 1: PC Terminals shelf of classroom B.

Figure 2: PC Terminals arrangement of classroom A.

3.1 Adoption of Laptop Computer

We adopted the laptop from portability [R-c]. Also, the following items are required for student programing work [R-a].

Keyboard key pitch is 19 mm.

15.6 type full HD LCD monitor.

3.2 Management of PC Terminals Environment by Image Distribution

Because PC terminals can't connect network all the time, we can't adopt thin client environment [R-d] [R-e]. Therefore, we adopted image distribution by connecting PC terminals to the wired LAN outside class hours. Symantec Deployment Solution 7.5 (DS 7.5) was adopted for image distribution. DS 7.5 can distribute images of Windows 7 client terminal with dedicated agent installed from Windows Server 2012 server. A client terminal that has completed all setup and installation is used to capture of image. The captured image is distributed all at once to the terminal restarted with Windows PE. As a result, we can build the same environment as the capture source terminal. Also, because the captured image is generalized by Sysprep so that PC-specific information is reset, unique information will never be the same on all distributed terminals [2].

Each of three subjects of laboratory courses is in different classrooms. Therefore, a unique terminal image is created for each classroom. Of the three classrooms, in the classroom B, there is a shelf to store all laptops connected by power and wired LAN. Figure 1 shows the laptops storage shelf. If a teacher instructs students to return to the shelf at the end of class, terminal management via the network is possible. On the other hand, the classroom A and C are only lockers, and there is no place to connect the power supply and wired LAN. Thus, AC taps and switching hubs were installed in each desk in the classroom A and C so that 4 laptops could be connected. Consequently, if a teacher instructs students to connect laptops at the end of class, terminal management via the network is possible. Figure 2 shows how to connect terminals in classroom A.

3.3 Reset User Area

We considered to reset the user area in personal files were saved [R-b]. Because laptops can't manage users in a centralized manner via Active Directory, students login to local users created for each theme [R-d]. Therefore, students continue to use the same local user of the same laptop each time during one theme. Hence, at the end of one theme, it is necessary to reset the corresponding local user from all laptops.

DS 7.5 has the function called Personality that can capture and distribute user information. However, Personality function can't distribute local user's registry files, and laptops didn't operate properly after use the function. So, before term of classes begins, we proposed to copy and store the user area(C:\Users\[user name]) on D drive of laptops. At the end of the set, the user area is replaced with the copy stored in D drive. As a result, this process means that all files created by students have been deleted. In this method, we used the function to execute scripts simultaneously from DS 7.5 server to client terminals.

4 OPERATION DURING TERM OF CLASSES

Table 4 shows the operational schedule during term of classes of the latter half of 2016. Because laboratory courses of "Laboratory in Basic Information Science"(table 4:"LB") on Monday and "Laboratory in Information Science 2"(table 4:"LIS2") on Wednesday are conducted, resetting user area and maintaining is conducted after the class on Wednesday. Especially, a time-consuming security update ("Security" from Table 4) leaves the terminal connected from Wednesday night to Thursday. After that, on Thursday or Friday, classroom A and C were stored from desk to locker. For these tasks, students connect laptops after class on Wednesday. In addition, one to two staff members of Center for Information Science are responsible for storage after completion.

5 OPERATION PROBLEMS

There was a case that the laptop was offline because the wired LAN was not inserted properly. In this case, we were able to deal with connecting to the classroom again because we can check to see which laptops are offline on the server. However, in case of trouble due to contact failure, in many cases it is not noticed during work. For example, in the case of a wired LAN, there was a terminal that fails in image distribution. In the case of the AC adapter, the battery may be shut down due to a decrease in the remaining amount of the battery. The laptop can't be started if it fails in image distribution. In this case, we had to run the image distribution on each laptop individually after booting with the Windows PE boot CD-ROM.

As a cause of the connection error, deterioration of the terminal due to frequent insertion / removal and operator's confirmation error may be considered. Therefore, measures such as thorough checking of cable connection after work are necessary.

6 WINDOWS 10 CLIENT

Currently, nearly three years have passed since System 9 was introduced in March 2014. Since the lease term is four years, we are considering options for the next computer infrastructure system (System 10). PC terminals for laboratory courses are candidates for the latest Windows 10 terminals.

Therefore, we conducted an operation test using Microsoft Surface Pro 4 with Windows 10 Build 1511 in one theme of "Laboratory in Basic Information Science" in the latter half of fiscal 2016. When I captured the image of Surface Pro 4 at DS 7.5, Sysprep processing failed. It is thought that this is the effect of the function (Microsoft Consumer Experience) that the store application is automatically installed by connecting to the Internet added from Windows 10 Build 1511. Because the installed store application is not included in the provisioning package which is Windows configuration information, Sysprep to reset them can't run [3].

Therefore, we configured a terminal without any store applications or user profile, and captured images generalized by Sysprep. In addition, Symantec Altiris Deployment Solution used version 8.0 HotFix 3 (DS 8.0 HF 3) compatible with Windows 10.

As a result, Windows 10 image distribution is possible, but user setting can't be done. We should set software and user profile settings for each terminal. Also, because the store applications can't be used, the teachers may not use them in classes.

7 OPERATION WITH MICROSOFT SYSTEM CENTER CONFIGURATION MANAGER (SCCM)

We examined Microsoft SCCM and Windows ADK (Assessment and Deployment Kit) from the problem of management by image distribution using DS 8.0 HF 3 of Windows 10 [4] [5]. SCCM is a tool to manage the configuration of client terminals. In addition, Windows ADK is a collection of tools to support Windows image distribution. In the examination in the first half of fiscal year 2017 we conducted an operation test using Surface Pro 4 with Windows 10 Build 1607 installed as one theme of " Laboratory in Information Science 2".

7.1 Environment Construction of Windows 10

The environment construction of the client terminal by SCCM is performed not by copying the image, but by deploying an installer which installs and sets the OS and application as an automatic task. Since installation of the OS is executed, generalization is performed in all client terminals before store applications and user profiles are constructed.

In this method, applications must be capable of silent installation in order to automate environment construction. In the operation test, all client terminals were manually installed for applications not compatible with silent installation. Even for applications that support silent installations, there are more requirements that can't be automated enough to meet the needs of users, such as plug-ins and detailed settings. As a result, the operation time has increased considerably compared with the conventional image distribution method. Also, as the number of manual settings increases, the possibility of mistakes increases, making it difficult to provide a unified environment for all client terminals.

7.2 User Reset

The Windows ADK contains tools to help manage users. The USMT (User State Migration Tool) can migrate a user to another client terminal for each user area. A migrated user also reflects settings recorded in registry files.

In the operational experiment, we copy the information of the target user by USMT before the start of 1 set. We considered using UMST to reset the user area by migrating to the client terminal at the end of 1 set. SCCM had the function of executing UMST on all client terminals managed only for Active Directory users. However, since the client terminal used the local user, this function can't be used. Therefore, we used the function to execute scripts by command prompt all at once to managed clients. The following is the processing of executed scripts.

Before the start of set
  (1) Get the information of the target user from the model terminal in USMT and save it in the shared folder.

After the end of set
  (2) Delete a target user from all client terminals.
  (3) Delete user area (c:\Users\[user name]) of target user of all client terminals.
  (4) Migration to all client terminals by referring to user information from shared folder.
  (5) Set indefinite password for the target user created on all client terminals.

In this method, we were able to reset the user environment each time set changes. Also, unlike the conventional method, since there is only one model of user information, risk at the time of copying is considered to be small.

8 CONCLUSIONS

In this paper, we report the operation method based on the requirements such as offline use and reset user at the end of set about PC terminals for laboratory equipped with Windows 7 and examined problems. Especially since troubles caused by inserting and removing power supply and wired LAN are burdens of support staff, it is necessary to consider exclusive storage shelf installation and measures to reduce cable connection abnormality.

We also tested the operation of the Windows 10 terminal assuming the next computer infrastructure system. SCCM proved that it is possible to create a dedicated Windows 10 installer. However, since part of application installation and setting are manual work, it turned out to be more time consuming than the conventional method.

In the future, we will investigate solutions related to conventional image distribution such as offline booting.

REFERENCES

[1] Hideo, M., Kazuyoshi, M., Yu, S., Kouichiro, W. and Yasuaki, K.:Distributed Campus Computer Infrastructure - Integrate Education, Research, Library and Office Activities, In Proceedings of the 42nd annual ACM SIGUCCS conference on User services, 93-96 (2014).
DOI= http://dx.doi.org/10.1145/2661172.2668055 .
[2] Microsoft Windows IT Center: What is Sysprep?, https://technet.microsoft.com/library/cc721940(v=ws.10).aspx.
[3] Ask CORE Microsoft Japan Windows Technology Support: Notes on running Sysprep in Windows 10 (version 1511), https://blogs.technet.microsoft.com/askcorejp/2015/12/20/windows-10-1511-sysprep/.
[4] Microsoft Docs: Introduction to System Center Configuration Manager, https://docs.microsoft.com/en-us/sccm/core/understand/introduction.
[5] Microsoft Developer Network: Windows Assessment and Deployment Kit (Windows ADK), https://msdn.microsoft.com/ja-jp/library/hh825420.aspx.

Developing a Help Desk Board Game

Casey Babcock
SUNY Geneseo
1 College Circle
Geneseo, NY, 14454
babcock@geneseo.edu

ABSTRACT

The terms "educational games" and "gamification" are used with increasing frequency as tools used to make learning engaging, but if you've played any recent educational games chances are good that you weren't having fun being educated meaningfully, or effectively. In addition to making a successful game, which is challenging enough on its own, you must integrate learning into the project from the outset and ensure the core aspects of your game reinforce your learning outcomes.

When properly integrated, educational games can make a world of difference in the level of engagement and comprehension in players. In this paper, I'll explain core game design principles and provide a template spanning ideation to implementation for creating a game for training your student employees. I'll also show how focusing on the mechanics of my game reinforces troubleshooting skills, communication, and teamwork with my student employees.

CCS CONCEPTS

• Theory of computation~Models of learning   • Theory of computation~Active learning   • Theory of computation~Convergence and learning in games   • Applied computing~Interactive learning environments   • Applied computing~Collaborative learning

KEYWORDS

Design; Help; Desk; Game; Board; Learning; Play; Education; Training

1   INTRODUCTION

I've been a gamer ever since I could hold a controller. There's something about the engrossing nature of games that allows us

SIGUCCS '17, October 1–4, 2017, Seattle, WA, USA
© 2017 Association for Computing Machinery.
ACM ISBN 978-1-4503-4919-2/17/10...$15.00
https://doi.org/10.1145/3123458.3123487

to escape from the normal burdens of reality and takes us to different worlds with boundless possibilities. Freely entering this space can teach us wonderful things about life, cooperation, strategy, and other innumerable skills. But when designed to focus on teaching specific and complicated sets of interconnected skills games can take education into a realm seldom accomplished in a traditional classroom setting. It was with this idea of broad and deep education that we set out to create a board game that could teach student help desk staff about troubleshooting skills, interpersonal communication, task management, and understanding their importance as the frontline of Computing and Information Technology at SUNY Geneseo.

Throughout this paper, I will explain gamification and how it differs from games, the benefits of teaching with games, a model for making your own board games, and our journey through making a help desk board game.

2   PROCESS AND METHOD FOR BOARD GAME DEVELOPMENT

2.1   Gamification vs Games – Pros and Cons

A lot of talk goes on about using gamification to make work and learning more engaging and fun, but what exactly is gamification? For our purposes, we will be using Gatautis'[1] definition: "Gamification is the use of mechanics, dynamics, and components of games in everyday situations that are not directly related to games and appear in non-game context." Gamfication has proven itself to be beneficial in a number of ways, summarized by Oravec[2] and Chang & Wei[3]: gamification of tasks can be an effective way to relieve stress and improve focus in chaotic work environments, decrease the monotony of routine mental and physical tasks, simultaneously impart training and education, and improve learning in peer groups.

While these are all great benefits, there can be some substantial issues when gamification is used improperly. Oravec[2] goes into some of the potential drawbacks to gamification such as: undercutting the processes associated with emotionally involving and playful gaming, enforcing an idea of mandatory fun in the workplace, a risk of ignoring the participants' context and psychological needs, and increased stress if used to evaluate job performance on a competitive basis. These negative side effects of gamification show us that gamification can be a very useful tool to engage workers at a help desk, but without sufficient planning and considerations to the specific workforce and environment an effort to make mundane tasks more engaging and exciting can fall flat or have serious and unintended consequences which damage morale and motivation.

2.2 Why Use Games for Training?

This brings us to the cross roads of gamification and actual games where we stop borrowing the mechanics, dynamics, and aesthetics from games and start using games themselves to make learning and work more engaging. Before we delve into the strengths of using games for learning we will define what a game is via Salen and Zimmerman's[4] definition, "A game is a system in which players engage in an artificial conflict defined by rules, that results in a quantifiable outcome." Taking that definition, we can start to think about what the essential pieces are to take a simple game and turn it into something educational and useful for training people to perform complex tasks. This is accomplished by focusing on how we construct the internal game systems, the nature of our conflict, what rules we give our self-contained universe, and what our desired outcome will be from playing the game into a unified and cohesive experience which trains specific and quantifiable skills in our players.

Drilling down further into why games are so effective for training and learning, Ballance[5] gives an excellent and concise explanation of the merits of using games for training, "With game-based learning, we work toward a goal, take action, experience consequences of our actions and make mistakes in a risk-free setting. We actively learn and practice the right way to do something. This keeps us highly engaged in practicing behaviors and thought processes that we can easily transfer from the simulated environment to real-life." Games allow players to explore options without having to fear repercussions that can have a serious impact on their lives and the lives of others. In terms of interactivity and experience, learning games are far more advanced than traditional methods of teaching such as: lecture style training, reading and review of procedures, and simple repetition of a specific task. Arslan[6] showcases these advantages when describing the benefits they observed from a serious game they built to train network admin students:

> Simulations help overcome the major obstacle to effectiveness of classroom-based training in which the context is different from day-to-day work context. Based on the experience of people on different areas simulations serve to compress and speed up the learning experience at a fraction of cost and risk. Moreover, simulations serve as a more enjoyable learning activity in comparison to reading a textbook, listening to a lecture, or being part of a team work."

2.3 Hide the Learning–Tangential Learning

One of the other and often overlooked potentials of learning through games is the idea of tangential learning. Borrowing an explanation from Extra Credit's [7] YouTube series,

> Tangential learning is not what you learn by being taught, rather it's what you learn by being exposed to things in a context which are already engaged in. For example, consider the movie 300. Clearly not a film

intended to educate, right? Yet just about everyone you know now knows who Leonidas is... This is what tangential learning is all about. It's the idea that some portion of your audience will self-educate if you can introduce them to topics in the context they already find exciting and engaging.

Now let's apply that explanation to the idea of using games for training by focusing in on some related information to a help desk that doesn't directly deal with customer service. For example, our campus help desk student staff don't go much deeper into networking issues than updating drivers. If we did want to find students with interest in networking however, we could drop some details into a game about the TCP/IP stack or configuring firewalls without that being a primary focus of the game. If afterwards one of the players took us aside and asked some meaningful questions about networking based on their experience in the game, we may have found a student that would be a good candidate to promote to into being one of our networking assistants. Without that game experience, we may have never known they were interested in networking and that opportunity would have been lost. If the core of your game is already engaging, using tangential learning will only serve to enhance the experience far beyond simple information dumps and practicing routine scenarios over and over.

2.4 Aim Low - Minimum Viable Product

The last thing I'd like to bring up before we proceed into how to actually construct a board game is the idea of only making a minimum viable product. Most of the time when you start thinking about games it's easy to jump right into the aesthetics or designing complex multilayered systems of rules and you'll want to start working on those ideas right away, but it is extremely important when starting the development cycle to focus on creating the bare minimum needed to playtest your game. Making sure that the mechanics are pure and simplified will increase your game's playability, ease of use, and give you clear indications of where to make changes as you playtest. If you start spending a lot of time developing systems that you end up never using a lot of time will be wasted in your development cycles. This time could be better spent fine tuning things before trying to make them visually appealing or mechanically complex.

2.5 The Development Process – The Iterative Model

Now that we've covered the background and important elements of creating an educational game it's time to start working on one. If you have an idea in mind for a game it can be pretty daunting to figure out where to get started and what process to follow. Our solution to this problem is to use the iterative game design model. There are several models for game design but the iterative model is one of the fastest, easiest, and most effective for board games. The core of the iterative model runs through the following cycle in the listed order: design, implement, playtest, evaluate, and then either release or repeat the cycle. Theoretically the more times that you can make it through this cycle the better your game will be.

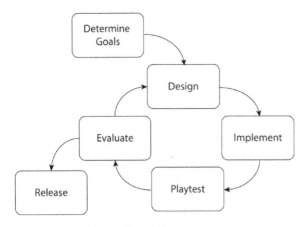

Figure 1: Iterative Design Model

2.6 Determine Your Goals

The first step in the iterative model happens before you start working on the design of any game mechanics or pieces and it is collecting your ideas and determining your goals. Even though this step only has to occur once and is outside of the main cycle of development it is arguably the most important step. Without carefully compiling your ideas ahead of time you may rush into development without a clear picture of what you're trying to accomplish and end up spending time and energy on ideas that don't help you achieve your initial objectives. This can be especially true of educational games because if you don't hit your learning objectives your game may end up being a diversion from training and not helpful for your students. If you get lost during development come back to your objectives and refocus your efforts.

2.7 Design – The Nuts and Bolts

Once you've fleshed out what ideas and concepts you're going to be designing towards it's time to start focusing on the specific mechanics and strategies you're going to employ. You'll want to try to align your design goals with mechanics that have meaning to the actions your players are performing. All mechanics have some kind of inherent meaning in them and if you ignore this you lose any potential enhancements to your game and may overlook some things that will detract from the experience. For example, using dice rolls to handle client interactions in a help desk game could make players feel that all client interactions are based off chance when the reality is that student workers always have some level of control in every interaction with a client. By introducing a randomized mechanic we're taking the power away from the player and influencing how our players perceive client interactions both inside and outside of the game. Instead of dice rolling, using role playing for this type of interaction would be much more meaningful and realistic. When deciding on what mechanics to employ always be mindful of your choices and refine your ideas with playtesting.

Some of the mechanics that you can choose to employ in a board game are: role playing, dice rolling, memory, trading, deck building, simulation, as well as dozens of others. A full list of board game mechanics can be found on BoardGameGeek.com [8].

2.8 Implementation – Time to Make Something

Implementation is the time when you actually sit down to construct your designs and the physical objects used to play your game. Coming back to the idea of the minimum viable product, when you're going through the first few cycles of iteration you really want to focus on keeping it simple and not putting a ton of time into the look and feel of each individual item. As you make changes to your work and your game develops, you will need to be able to shed old ideas and move onto better ones. If you've spent dozens of hours designing a card layout that simply doesn't work for your game you'll be much less willing to throw away that idea simply because so much time has been spent on it even if it's not helpful to your game anymore.

If you have students with any design experience or interest in design this may be a good place to have them help you. You also want to stay away from using design software like Photoshop and Illustrator for brand new ideas. Pencil and paper make for fast designs that are easily changed or re-done and if you need some kind of token or game piece, stones or coins work well to get your ideas out of your head and into the game without the need for extra work in Adobe Creative Cloud.

2.9 Playtesting – Is it Any Good?

Playtesting is the time when you have people sit down to actually play your game and it is the bread and butter of every game designer. Playtesting is so valuable because it's the only way to definitively tell if what you've made is any good and if it matches up with your design goals. The best way to get good results from your playtesters is to sit back and observe them without jumping in to give instructions right away when your players run into questions or issues with the game. When people are confused it means there's some flaw in your designs that will need to be addressed. When that happens take explicit notes about the situation and your players feedback and carry it on into the last phase of iteration.

The best kind of playtester you can have is one who doesn't know you and has no investment in your game at all. The closer someone is to you the more likely they are to try to spare your feelings if the game is bad. That kind of protection may be good for your ego, but it's bad for your game. Don't take it personally if your players are direct about a bad experience. Negative feedback on your game merely means that you need to make changes to the design in the next iteration.

2.10 Evaluate – Changing Based on Observations

The evaluation phase is when you sit down with your playtesting notes and consider how you need to improve your game. Are there issues with the mechanics that were confusing to the players and need to be revised or explained more clearly in the rules? Is one of the mechanics way out of balance and was easily exploited by some players which led to the game being too one-sided? The easiest way to focus in on these issues is to start looking at your mechanics for problems and then look at balancing them. When balancing, your best bet is to at least double the change you're making to see how it affects your systems and then dial back the changes as needed. Making smaller changes to start with usually won't show you a noticeable effect and will lead to eating up a lot of time.

2.11 Release or Repeat – Are we there yet?

This is the final step in the cycle of iteration and it is deciding if your game is ready to release or if it needs another trip through the cycle of iteration. If your game it is ready to be played and enjoyed then congratulations on a successful project! If it's not then simply start back over at the design phase and make the necessary adjustments to your game based on the last evaluation phase you completed. The more times you cycle through this the faster it will go and the better you will become at tightening up your game and fixing its issues.

3 HELP DESK MANIA DESIGN

3.1 Help Desk Mania – Goal Setting

The concept for our game was originally a single player video game with mechanics similar to Diner Dash[9] where clients would come up to a help desk and the player needing to troubleshoot their way through the different problems and make correct decisions to advance in the game. After some deliberation, it was determined that any single player digital experience wouldn't be very representational of the actual experience of working at a real college help desk which is by its nature a collaborative and interpersonal experience. So, after a brief discussion, we switched gears and moved to a more analog medium for this game that would bring people together to sit down and play it. Next, we determined it would be most valuable to focus on building the following skills in our players: troubleshooting problems in person and remotely, dealing with clients of different personality types, understanding that individual interactions with clients impact our larger IT organization, problem solving, communication skills, and teamwork among the players.

3.2 Design – First Iteration

At the beginning of our first design phase, we decided on trying to simulate an actual help desk experience within the game itself for new students to get some practice working before they would ever even step behind the desk and for returning students to refine their skills before returning to work each semester. We drew out some plans on a white board trying to design a game board that tokens would move across to represent clients and a desk that players would keep between their player tokens and the client tokens. As we continued trying to figure

out how that would work we discovered that a lot of the components we were originally thinking about using were unnecessary to represent a customer service interaction at its core. Stripping down a technician and client interaction left us with only the client, the technician, the problem, and how the client felt after the interaction. This revelation moved our project away from a board game and on the path to making a card game.

3.3 Implementation – First Iteration

Now that we had decided that we would be making a card game we began again focusing on our initial goals. We created a system that used only three major components: client cards, problem cards, and a satisfaction score. We prototyped the cards using index cards. On one card we put the information needed to troubleshoot a particular problem. On the other card we put basic biography information about the client including an image, any special modifiers that card would have, and a satisfaction gauge. As we tried to position the cards around each other we came up with the idea of using the client card to hide some of the information on the problem card and then taking guesses at the solution. The client card would overlay directly on top of the problem card and slide down the problem, revealing a clue about the root of the problem every round. The faster the player could solve the problem and determine the cause the more reputation points that interaction would give them. If they couldn't solve a problem fast enough the client card would slide off the problem card, revealing the answer and giving a negative reputation score to the player. After making a few test cards for this system we moved onto our playtesting phase.

Figure 2: Game Cards Version 1

3.4 Playtesting – First Iteration

When our development team played through the game we were able to make it through a couple of rounds with some difficulty but overall the system seemed to be playable. We knew that it didn't feel great to play, but we couldn't see exactly where the problems were so we turned to a student worker to test it out. Immediately we saw issues with the rigid nature of the clues on the problem cards where the player would try to guess something, but the card did not reflect their guess and they would only get partial information in a way that didn't process well. The gameplay was clumsy and lacked the kind of or back and forth that a real help desk interaction has. The player walked away confused and our design just wasn't working so we knew changes had to be made.

3.5 Evaluation – First Iteration

We took our first playtest feedback as a sign that our system was too convoluted and the ideas we were trying to get across were too complicated to be put down on a single card. It was at this point we started to move away from a self-contained game that could be played with only minor facilitator involvement and moved into making full use of the training environment. If we could strip down the cards to only the absolute bare essential information that a person would get when someone walks up we could put the rest of the onus on the facilitator to give each interaction meaning. Doing so would mean needing to spend extra time training facilitators for the game, but the game and our students would benefit immensely. We moved forward with this idea into our next iteration.

3.6 Design – Latest Iteration

We started our next iteration with developing a guide for our facilitators to use when coaching players through each interaction. To this end we had one of our senior students develop a list of every common problem our help desk saw and some of the most likely reasons for those issues to happen. The result was a problem and solution set from which we could base our problem cards and give to our facilitators with instructions about how they should respond to the various things a student could try to solve a problem. This guide provided background and root cause information for facilitators to answer questions like: "When was the last time your laptop was working?". With the development of this question and answer mechanic our players would be able to really practice role-playing in their job in the safe environment of the game before they ever stepped foot behind the desk to help real clients.

It was at this point that we also developed a formal set of options that players would be able to use on their turn to try to solve an issue. These options were: asking the client a question, performing a troubleshooting task on the client's device, looking up information online until their next turn, asking another player for help, escalating the problem to a professional staff member, and solving the issue by explaining the cause and solution for the issue. These gameplay options all mimicked the real-life actions that a student could take in the course of their job and both reinforced the team-based gameplay and the skills we wanted to develop. For each action that a player took the facilitator would give the client's or the devices response to the player.

3.7 Implementation – Latest Iteration

We moved on to re-designing our two cards and stripping them down to their bare essentials. After several hours of trying to re-design the client card into all sorts of different combinations we started looking at how big the cards needed to be and my co-developer Joe Dolce had the brilliant idea to model our client cards after a SUNY Geneseo ID card. This was a fantastic idea because it was something which players would have instant recognition of and know right where information would be located. The layout of our campus ID cards also had all of the information we wanted to include with enough room to fit an icon for the number of troubleshooting rounds players would be allowed to take for each problem.

This left us with our last client card design challenge; finding a replacement mechanic to keep score for each interaction. With the cards no longer using the clue-hiding mechanic we needed to find a new way to keep track of the score without adding any sort of extra counter to the game. To do this we placed the satisfaction gauge at the bottom of our now horizontally oriented client cards and broke it up into 3 sections: a green section for the most points and fastest resolution, a yellow section for an acceptable rate of resolution, and a red section for a penalty for taking too long to solve the client's issue. Now that the problem cards were much simpler and only contained the problem name, a code to reference the card in the facilitator's manual, and a brief description of the problem we could drastically reduce their size down from index cards into a "micro-card". The micro-card is about an inch wide and two inches long. The problem card would now slide across the bottom of the card as the player took turns to showcase where they were in the problem and how many chances they had remaining for each guess. Confident that this new mechanic would make sense and teach the skills we set out to teach we moved forward onto our next playtest.

Figure 3: Game Cards Version 2

3.8 Playtesting – Latest Iteration

We sat down with one of our student employees and a basic overview of the rules was explained to her. She drew a client and problem card and began trying to troubleshoot the problem at a rapid pace, almost immediately reaching the two-action limit we had imposed for her turn. She gave some immediate feedback that stopping mid-way through the problem felt really awkward and she wanted to keep going without interruption so we adjusted the design and let her continue with no limit on the actions she could take.

Eventually our student employee came to a point where she could no longer think of any options to troubleshoot the issue, but had not found the cause and resolution. Even though our student wasn't able to complete the card on her own we knew were onto something by allowing her to try until she was out of ideas. If our playtester were allowed to ask a fellow player for assistance, much like she would do with a co-worker, she would have been able to come to a resolution. This moment was a turning point in our playtest. We had found a process that felt more natural and translated to an authentic representation of actually working at our help desk. With this new revelation, we moved onto our evaluation phase.

3.9 Evaluation – Latest Iteration

Upon evaluating the feedback and player experience from our playtest we recognized that it was possible to emulate the help desk experience in an even more mechanically stripped-down than we previously thought possible. Based on the suggestions from our student we modified the dynamic of the game to use a cooperative round robin approach to issues instead of individual focused turn-based gameplay. Under this new system each player would have the ability to attempt as many troubleshooting tasks and ask as many questions as they wanted with no impediment. If they came to the point where they were out of ideas and still hadn't found the root cause and appropriate solution to the issue it would fall to the next player to pick-up where they left off; continuing down the line until the last player had a chance to try. If no players could solve the issue then it would count against all players as a strike and if too many strikes accrue, the game is over for all players.

We had originally steered away from this kind of design in our early design phases because this model runs the risk of inherently low player engagement due to the potential downtime for the non-active players. We plan on combating this in future versions through mechanics that could keep players engaged such as: having non-active players lookup potential fixes on the internet to assist the active player, mechanics that reward players for not repeating troubleshooting steps performed by a previous player, and equivalent actions for passing issues to professional staff members or submitting tickets for an issue. We may also incentivize our game with rewards for the highest performing students in the game with prizes to keep players engaged even when it's not their turn.

4 CONCLUSION

As we continue development on our game we plan on focusing most of our efforts on driving engagement and interactions between players and less on fine tuning and balancing the mechanics now that we have a clear and working set of mechanics to build on. It is my hope that having a glimpse into the development of a game will inspire you to start designing your own games for training your student workers.

ACKNOWLEDGMENTS

This paper was made possible by the extensive efforts of Joseph Dolce instructional designer at SUNY Geneseo. Special thanks also goes to student employees Meredith Condren and Spozhmai Qaidiri for feedback and playtesting during development and my supervisor Nik Varrone for allowing me creative freedom in training my student employees.

REFERENCES

[1] Rimantas Gatautis, Elena Vitkauskaite, Agne Gadeikiene, and Zaneta Piligrimiene. 2016. Gamification as a Mean of Driving Online Consumer Behavior: SOR Model Perspective. *Inzinerine Ekonomika-Engineering Economics* 27, 1 (2016), 90–97. DOI: http://dx.doi.org/10.5755/j01.ee.27.1.13198
[2] Jo Ann Oravec. 2015. Gamification and multigamification in the workplace: Expanding the ludic dimensions of work and challenging the work/play dichotomy. *Cyberpsychology: Journal of Psychosocial Research on Cyberspace* 9, 3 (2015). DOI:http://dx.doi.org/10.5817/cp2015-3-6
[3] Jen-Wei Chang and Hung-Yu Wei. 2016. Exploring Engaging Gamification Mechanics in Massive Online Open Courses. *Educational Technology & Society* 19, 2 (2016), 177–203.
[4] Katie Salen and Eric Zimmerman. 2010. *Rules of play: game design fundamentals*, Cambridge, Mass.: The MIT Press.
[5] Chanin Ballance. 2013. Use of games in training: interactive experiences that engage us to learn. *Industrial and Commercial Training* 45, 4 (July 2013), 218–221. DOI:http://dx.doi.org/10.1108/00197851311323501
[6] Engin Arslan, Murat Yuksel, and Mehmet Hadi Gunes. 2015. Training network administrators in a game-like environment. *Journal of Network and Computer Applications* 53 (2015), 14–23. DOI:http://dx.doi.org/10.1016/j.jnca.2015.03.005
[7] Extra Credits. 2012. Tangential Learning - How Games Can Teach Us While We Play. *Youtube.* https://youtu.be/rlQrTHrwyxQ
[8] Anon. Board Game Mechanics. Retrieved June 22, 2017 from https://boardgamegeek.com/browse/boardgamemechanic

Increasing Security by Focusing on Endpoints

Beth Rugg
UNC Charlotte
9201 University City Blvd
Charlotte, NC 28223
erugg@uncc.edu

Brandon DeLeeuw
UNC Charlotte
9201 University City Blvd
Charlotte, NC 28223
bdeleeuw@uncc.edu

ABSTRACT

End user devices are among the most vulnerable parts of an IT infrastructure. To help mitigate the vulnerabilities associated with these devices, the University of North Carolina at Charlotte has focused on leveraging built-in tools that secure these endpoints and reduce costs by leveraging tools that already exist. We have changed our anti-virus software, deployed security software (i.e., FileVault and BitLocker) to encrypt laptop hard drives, locked down printers, reviewed and changed our PCI compliance methods, changed the way we deploy updates for Windows and Mac devices, and have begun pushing Mac OS updates. This paper will discuss the organizational and technical changes we made to accomplish these goals along the tips and tricks we learned along the way.

CCS CONCEPTS

Security and privacy → Systems security → Operating systems security → Trusted computing

Security and privacy → Security in hardware → Hardware security implementation

KEYWORDS

Hardware; Encryption; Anti-Virus; Endpoints; SCCM; Casper

1 INTRODUCTION

UNC Charlotte is a public, research university with 29,000 students and 4000 faculty and staff. UNC Charlotte offers 21 doctoral, 64 masters, and 90 bachelor's degree programs through 9 colleges: the College of Arts & Architecture, the College of Liberal Arts & Sciences, the Belk College of Business, the College of Computing and Informatics, the Cato College of Education, the William States Lee College of Engineering, the College of Health and Human Services, the Honors College, and the University College.

SIGUCCS '17, October 1–4, 2017, Seattle, WA, USA
© 2017 Association for Computing Machinery.
ACM ISBN 978-1-4503-4919-2/17/10...$15.00
https://doi.org/10.1145/3123458.3123475

UNC Charlotte's IT organization is comprised of a centralized and distributed staff. Central IT staff (ITS) support IT infrastructure and enterprise services for the institution. Approximately 120 staff work for ITS. Within ITS, the Client Engagement team is responsible for many of the front-line services including the service desk, desktop support and endpoint management. The work of the Desktop Support team was reorganized in 2015 to better align with leadership's vision and goals. This realignment has allowed the team to focus on securing the endpoints.

The functions of the distributed IT staff vary depending on the college or department needs. Distributed IT staff often provide primary support for their department and escalate issues to ITS staff, as needed. Distributed IT staff may also provide specialized support, custom programming and application development, as needed. Approximately 150 employees are classified as "Distributed IT" staff.

ITS and distributed IT work together to manage approximately 11,000 endpoints. Approximately 75% of these endpoints are Windows based machines, while 25% are Mac machines. ITS staff use Microsoft's System Center Configuration Manager (SCCM) JAMF Casper and provide access to the distributed IT staff to allow them to manage their own groups and collection of devices. ITS sets standards and collaborates with distributed IT staff. This partnership approach requires open and ongoing communication and training.

2 Securing the Endpoints

To be successful, it is important to identify the standards that matter and to allow flexibility for the individual units. If all endpoints were managed centrally in the same way, the environment would be simpler and the collaboration easier. However, historically, colleges and business units have been able to function somewhat independently from ITS. The independence is related to the specific needs of individual colleges. For example, there are 3 Casper instances, the College of Engineering uses its own Active Directory (AD) structure that supports roaming profiles, other colleges customize software images and the Student Union and Activities group do not provide administrative privileges to users.

2.1 Organizational Changes

Some of these deviations developed because ITS was the "land of no." Recently, ITS has worked tirelessly to change this image and behavior. Specifically, the Desktop Support team was split into two functions: Support and Solutions. Team members on the Solutions team were tasked with being innovators and fully developing solutions to meet campus needs. This led the Solutions team to take on the management of some of the software as a service (SaaS) solutions including Dropbox, WebEX and Adobe Creative Cloud. The team is also the service owner for SCCM, Casper, LabStats, Payment Card Industry (PCI) desktops, Citrix and the antivirus application solutions.

The Solutions team does not provide 2nd tier support enabling them up to fully build out endpoint management solutions. They have a standard roll-out and testing methodology. Testing begins with the Solutions team, then the Client Engagement team, then ITS, then distributed IT partners and early adopters and finally the campus community. This approach allows them to identify problems and engage distributed IT staff much earlier in the deployment. As a result, most implementations are very successful resulting in few unidentified problems and less calls into the Service Desk.

As the solutions became more robust, distributed IT teams have started to partner and engage with ITS and are more willing to leverage ITS solutions for their areas. An example is the College of Art & Architecture may join the centralized Casper solution instead of managing their own.

2.2 Anti-virus

UNC Charlotte used Trend Micro anti-virus (AV) software for many years. Trend AV software is highly regarded by Gartner and is considered the "Cadillac" of AV software because of its many options. Anti-virus software was managed by the Security team and deployed on both Windows and Macs. Trend AV software worked well on Windows computers but not Macs.

In 2016, service ownership was transferred to the newly created Solutions team. The Solutions team looked at compliance and found that 90% of the Windows computers were compliant (had Trend AV software installed and running) but less than 10% of the Macs. The team made configuration changes to see if that would help improve performance; they changed the max CPU usage configuration, created folder and file exclusions, delayed startup scans, and disabled new Windows 10 features like Cortana and indexing on lab machines. Performance was still a problem so they investigated other options.

They reviewed Windows Defender and Sophos. Windows Defender part of the Microsoft campus agreement and free of charge but it wasn't the best option for Macs. Sophos would work on both platforms; on the Macs, it looks for Mac viruses, malware, ransomware and email scams, and is free for home use. Since we got Defender for free, we decided to deploy Defender for Windows and Sophos for Macs. We saved approximately $50,000 annually when we moved away from Trend.

Defender was piloted in the Library to help solve slow login issues at the beginning of the fall semester. The team changed scanning options from running a quick scan on Saturday at 4:00 AM to running a quick scan daily and a full scan on Saturday at 4:00 AM. The pilot was very successful and login times dropped from 7 to 15 minutes per login to 1 minute per login. The pilot

then extended to Library staff using Windows machines and within 3 months, the Defender product was deployed throughout the entire campus community.

Sophos (SaaS) was piloted and then deployed on new Macs purchased as part of the annual Academic Affairs renewal process. Sophos was deployed to the campus community over the summer of 2017.

2.3 New Active Directory Scheme

We decided to redesign Active Directory (AD). The existing AD structure contained nested groups with conflicting policies making it difficult to troubleshoot. Distributed IT could not manage their groups and machines as part of their day-to-day operations. An AD redesign project was initiated with the goal of a simpler, logical, design that enabled ITS to distribute management and target group policy to the appropriate objects.

The Storage and Server team partnered with the Solutions team to implement this new AD structure. The AD structure is being phased in to each college/business unit over time and will take over a year to implement.

With this new structure, it will be much easier to apply specific group policies at the appropriate group level. It has also provided ITS the ability to partner with Distributed IT on implementing these changes. The challenge is to better secure the endpoints while allowing for some flexibility. Additional training and monthly distributed user groups take place so that all groups are aware of how to best manage their endpoints.

2.4 Operating System Updates

Windows 10 was released in 2015. UNC Charlotte IT teams have typically waited until end of life to move to new Windows operating systems. The team was challenged to release Windows 10 within 1 year of general release. The project team developed plan that relied on scheduled upgrades and would get the majority of machines to Windows 10 within 2 years.

ITS developed the Windows 10 image, updating group policy and identifying key questions and risks that needed to be answered before the OS could be deployed. The questions and risks included how we would handle the Microsoft Store, what customizations we would make, what peripherals would/would not work with Windows 10 and what software constraints and dependencies (primarily with the Enterprise systems) had to be accommodated. One of the primary changes that had to be communicated to the campus community was that the **"My Documents"** feature of Windows would no longer redirect to network storage. This change was made because Google Drive and Dropbox are also file storage options.

Once the initial work was completed, we followed our standard testing and deployment procedure. For the campus roll out, the team worked with individual departments to schedule upgrade. At the peak of the upgrades, 10 upgrades were scheduled daily. Labs were upgraded to Windows 10 during summer 2016 and the classroom podiums will be upgraded in the summer of 2017.

There are many challenges to being an early adopter; however, the overall campus culture is changing. We have proven that we can implement these changes in a non-disruptive way which will allow us to maintain a more current, up to date posture moving forward.

The Solutions team is currently focused on deploying Windows 10 1607 version. The plan is to push this update just as we would for monthly patches however, at a 2 GB size, the update is much larger and does pose some risk to performance. This "push" will start in the summer of 2017. If this methodology is successful, then the Windows OS updates should be much less disruptive moving forward.

The Solutions team is also working to do something similar with Macs. Historically, the latest Mac OS is released to existing machines for voluntary update approximately 6 months after Apple releases it. Central IT has never "pushed" the Mac OS update. Starting in the summer of 2017, this will change; the latest Mac OS upgrade will be released through Casper. Since this change will begin during the summer months, we can still plan for a phased approach, voluntary upgrade and then a "forced" upgrade.

In general, the Solution team is working towards a cohesive end point management philosophy that is similar for Mac and Windows devices. The team has also configured the operating systems to follow the Center for Internet Security (CIS) benchmark recommendations and leveraging Software Center and Self Service (Casper) to distribute institutional software to machines.

2.5 Monthly Patching

The team has developed a standard methodology for patching the operating system and applications.

Windows patches are immediately deployed to the Solutions team, they are then deployed to the various groups following the standard format. Monthly patches become available to the campus community within three weeks of their release from Microsoft. Users are given 48 hours to update or the machines restart on their own. Recently, the methodology was changed to align with Microsoft's recommendation; 20% of campus machines received the patching after the initial internal testing and then the rest of the community receive it in the following week. So far, this procedure has worked well.

We have 1200 Macs enrolled in Casper and recently started patching the Microsoft Office applications. This is an important change for us because we are starting to manage the Macs much like we manage the Windows workstations.

2.6 Encryption

Up until recently, there was no centralized encryption option for the campus community. Different colleges and departments were performing standalone encryption for workstations used in sensitive research areas. Distributed IT would store encryption keys on printed paper in cabinets.

ITS tasked the Solutions team with identifying a laptop encryption option for Windows and Mac machines which would include having the keys stored in Active Directory and Casper. The new AD structure allows us to provide granular access to encryption keys.

The team recommended using the built in hard drive encryption tools for Windows and Macs: BitLocker and FileVault, respectively. Although these tools could be used on workstations and laptops, laptops were identified as the most "at risk" type of device and a university standard was that requires encryption for laptops. Workstations could be encrypted as requested. We identified the solution, tested and piloted it, and the standard was developed and then campus wide deployment. This project is a good example of technology and policy working hand-in-hand to minimize risk. Some Distributed IT teams were hesitant to encrypt drives until the standard was developed; the standard is now used to help educate end users regarding the new "requirement."

The team decided on a hands-on approach to encrypting the drives. In order for the encryption to work, the Windows laptop must have a TPM chip, this chip is manually enabled and then a script is run. It generally requires approximately 1 hour to encrypt a drive depending on operating system and local storage needs. The technician also verifies that the key is stored in AD. A similar process is used on the Mac machines. It is expected that it will take several years to get all laptops encrypted. New laptops are being encrypted before they are given to the end users. This roll out has been very successful with few tickets generated for the Service Desk and no performance issues reported.

2.7 Printers

Printing and printers are also a security risk. Printers and printing at UNC Charlotte is like the Wild West; every department purchases and deploys their own printer. There is no printer standard for manufacturer or initial setup and configuration. There is a print-service run by the Auxiliary Services team, but less than 100 printers are part of that "fleet". It is not clear how many local and networked printers are owned by the University. Additionally, many printers use direct Internet Protocol (IP) printing. However, in recent years a print-server was created that new printers for certain departments are being added to.

To help the ITS Solutions team understand the risk, the ITS Security department runs a vulnerability scan on ITS printers. Based on this assessment, the team documents and addresses common issues such as default or no passwords on websites, enabled protocols that are not being used, default SNMP settings, etc. Printers are then reconfigured, tested and rescanned by the Security department.

We received a clean report except for SNMP settings. If we change this, end users no longer receive feedback on print jobs. We decided to leverage Web Services for Devices (WSD) for compatible printers. For all others, we have accepted the risk and used standard SNMP settings.

Web Services for Devices (WSD) allows network-connected IP-based devices to advertise their functionality and offer these services to clients by using the Web Services protocol. WSD-based devices and clients communicate over the network using a series of SOAP (Simple Object Access Protocol) messages over UDP (User Datagram Protocol) and HTTP(S) (Hyper Text Transfer Protocol (Secure)). WSD provides a network plug-and-play experience that is similar to installing a USB device and also defines a security profile that may be extended to provide additional protection and authentication using device-based certificates.

Next steps will be to share the new "standards" and collaborate with IT partners to put together a project to reconfigure printer settings and add existing printers to the print server.

2.8 PCI

The Payment Card Industry Data Security Standard (PCI-DSS or simply referred to as PCI) is a set of security standards designed to ensure that all companies that accept, process, store or transmit credit card information maintain a secure environment. When departments collect credit card information, this information must be collected, stored and transmitted using a PCI compliant device.

A PCI desktop must meet the PCI as well as the performance and usability needs of the end user. At UNC Charlotte, there are over 100 PCI desktops that are maintained and supported by Central IT. At UNC Charlotte, we have seen several iterations of the PCI desktop, each one improving on the previous.

The Security team was responsible for PCI compliance prior to 2016 but that responsibility transferred to the Solutions team when the Solutions team was formed and the Security team refocused.

When the Solutions team became the service owner of PCI compliance, they identified some area for improvement and implemented the Hyper-V virtual operating system as an alternative to the free Virtualbox virtual operating system previously used by the Security team; Hyper-V is included in our Microsoft campus agreement. This change significantly improved the customer experience, providing a more stable and better performing environment. We leveraged the standard campus image and used Group Policy to lock down the machines. We also installed SCCM to manage updates and deployments.

Although this was a huge step forward, the technicians still found it very time consuming and difficult to set up since there were additional firewall tools that needed to be installed. The overall process was more than 20 steps long!

The Solutions team then began to consider Citrix as a way to move the PCI machines into a centralized and more controlled system. Working with the Security team we built out two Citrix servers based on industry best practices for PCI. They ran some PCI vulnerability scans prior to a third-party contractor validating the new environment. We now deploy the Citrix receiver to PCI machines; minimizing a several hour time intensive process to a matter of minutes. In Citrix the user is presented with a PCI Browser (an Internet Explorer browser that runs on the PCI Citrix servers). Clients use the browser to access the campus banking systems. The old PCI image used the standard faculty/staff campus image with no extra precautions.

2.9 Nexpose Vulnerability Scans

In the spring of 2017, the Security team started performing regular network scans identifying vulnerabilities on servers and workstations. The Security team created logins for IT Security Liaisons (ISLs) to view and correct vulnerabilities. The team had to create views that were easily understood by the ISLs. Initially,

the goal was to create awareness but the long term goal is for the ITS and distributed IT staff to take corrective action, as well.

Most vulnerabilities are with third party applications such as Java or Adobe Reader. However, currently, the Solutions team is not patching third party applications. The Solutions team is, however, starting to investigate Microsoft's System Center Updates Publisher (SCUP), a stand-alone tool used in conjunction with Microsoft's System Center Configuration Manager (SCCM) which allows administrators to install and update software. The Solutions team is starting to test the capabilities of these tools and will be working to leverage other vendors for additional application patches. The Solutions team will also be looking into third party patching solutions for Mac devices.

2.10 DUO

ITS deployed DUO for two factor authentication. The team has identified and targeted departments that work with sensitive data to adopt DUO. The deployment of DUO followed standard methodology: Over 1200 faculty and staff are using DUO, approximately 25% of the population. There have been some discussions about deploying DUO to everyone but that idea has not gained momentum.

3.0 CONCLUSION

Over the last two years, ITS made significant strides in securing the endpoints. We have accomplished these changes by using a variety of engagement strategies, standard testing, and deployment methodologies.

ITS and Distributed IT teams collaborated and continue to collaborate to proactively identify problems, risks and solutions. Each change has been a discrete project with clearly defined goals. Despite all of these changes, service requests into the Service Desk team have declined.

The organizational team realignments are directly responsible for this success. It is critical that staff managing devices have the skills, technical knowledge and the time to develop effective solutions. It is also important that strategic goals be set and communicated to help drive change.

We have more work to do but the pace with which we are able to implement these changes has improved and the general resistance has declined. In fact, more Distributed IT teams are partnering with ITS to accomplish new goals; some areas relate to assuming an increasing role in device support. Working together across silos, departments and colleges will enable us to become more efficient and realign resources (human and financial) in strategic ways that benefit the entire university system.

Ready, Set, GOOGLE!

Phedra Henninger
Muhlenberg College
2400 Chew Street
Allentown, PA, 18104
phedrahenninger@muhlenberg.edu

ABSTRACT

This is the true story, of two teams, picked to launch a new communication & collaboration platform, work together, and have their lives taped (a few select moments, anyway). Find out what happens, when people stop using GroupWise, and start getting G Suite... The Real Google!

While members of the Muhlenberg College Infrastructure & Networking team toiled away migrating GroupWise to Google in mere months, Client Support Services and Instructional Technology & Digital Learning joined forces to educate and support the community during this large scale change.

This presentation walks through the highlights of developing a communication and training plan in record time with good old-fashioned teamwork, dedication, creativity and fun.

Highlights include:

- Create a complete training schedule in one hour using 5 brains and whiteboard painted walls.
- How to exploit the creativity of select team members (make that one) and BRAND, BRAND, BRAND!
- Scripts? Overrated. You want authenticity? Plan, schedule and shoot promos in 30 minutes or less.
- How do we get them to listen? Ways to engage your community. Buttons and badges and prizes, oh my!
- Retaining your audience post launch. The support never ends.

We do not recommend trying this at home without a sense of humor and a solid team.

CCS CONCEPTS

Social and professional topics → Professional topics → Computing education → Computing education programs

KEYWORDS

Collaboration; communication; Google; G Suite; training.

SIGUCCS '17, October 1–4, 2017, Seattle, WA, USA
© 2017 Association for Computing Machinery.
ACM ISBN 978-1-4503-4919-2/17/10...$15.00
https://doi.org/10.1145/3123458.3123489

1 INTRODUCTION

Founded in 1848, Muhlenberg is a highly selective, private, four-year residential, liberal arts college located in Allentown, Pa., approximately 90 miles west of New York City. With an undergraduate enrollment of approximately 2200 students. A member of the Centennial Conference, Muhlenberg competes in 22 varsity sports. Muhlenberg is affiliated with the Evangelical Lutheran Church in America. [1]

Muhlenberg launched G Suite (formerly known as Google Apps for Education) at the end of winter break 2016. This paper will discuss the communication and training plans developed and implemented to transition faculty and staff to this new collaboration and communication tool, including lessons learned and next steps.

2 PROJECT BACKGROUND

2.1 Communication and Collaboration Committee

Muhlenberg had been using GroupWise for email and calendar since 2005. While GroupWise offered a number of features, it lagged behind in many other areas critical to the communication and collaboration needs of the campus community. In light of the desire for change, a new committee was formed to examine communication and collaboration suites to replace GroupWise. The committee made its recommendation to the Office of Information Technology after evaluating and testing Google Apps for Education and Microsoft Office 365. Their process included product research, survey feedback solicited from the entire community, as well as input from a select group of faculty, staff and student testers. In May 2016, an announcement was made to the College community that Google Apps for Education had been officially selected by The Communication & Collaboration committee.

2.2 Call to Action

Google Apps for Education (now G Suite) was selected in May 2016, with sights set to transition students to Google Apps prior to orientation for fall 2016. Many factors led to a delay and the migration was pushed to winter break for students, faculty and staff. The post about the delay was the first communication to the community at large, since the original announcement. [2] This was followed by another post explaining about the delay and new timeline. It was not long before we received feedback from faculty and staff asking questions about the transition from one system to another. They were looking for answers and we needed to provide them.

Given the daunting task of migrating twenty million plus emails into nine hundred faculty and staff accounts, the focus was on the job at hand. Communication with the community was limited which led to faculty and staff feeling apprehensive about the transition. Faculty and staff needed to feel prepared for the move from GroupWise to Google and thus a plan was hatched.

2.3 Internal Testing

In order to prepare the community for the migration from GroupWise to Google, we needed to get a real glimpse at what that transition would look like. What better testers than the Office of Information Technology? The following is an excerpt from an email sent to the entire OIT department from the Director of Client Support Services.:

> In an effort to smoothly transition the campus to Google Apps for Education, our department will be testing Google accounts in two phases. OIT Google accounts Phase 1 migration is complete and now available for testing. Content prior to September 1, 2016 will be present in your account.
>
> Attached you will find details on what testing needs to be completed. It's crucial that our department test our accounts thoroughly, providing feedback on missing content and/or usability matters. We will rely on this internal testing to help shape training materials and prepare for the campus wide rollout.

While each director in the department was tasked with strongly encouraging their team members to test and provide feedback, participation was voluntary and unfortunately limited. It was still extremely helpful for those creating documentation and training materials for end users in preparation for the launch to be working with real accounts, but it was only a glimpse at what was to come. We couldn't accurately predict all the issues that would arise when one email & calendaring system is traded for another. When the final cut-over happened, the real world issues instantly came to light. While we felt moderately prepared, there wasn't enough time to solve all the potential problems. There were however issues that became evident during testing and while we could not fix them, we were relatively prepared for what would need to be done after the launch.

One example of a known issue involved the functionality of the mailto protocol for the operating system on an end user's device as well as administrative systems. The mailto protocol "is a Uniform Resource Identifier (URI) scheme for email addresses. It is used to produce hyperlinks on websites that allow users to send an email to a specific address without first having to copy it and enter it into an email client." [3] In layman's terms, any time an end user clicks on an email address, either in a web browser or an application, the mailto protocol is evoked and the default email client (if one is set) is launched. We knew changing the mailto

protocol would be a manual effort after the initial launch. End users were still using GroupWise (legacy email client) to crosscheck email and therefore, it was the default until the end user made the manual change. The process was documented and instructions were released, as soon as possible. During testing there were administrative systems that were not working with Gmail set as their default for this functionality. We narrowed it down to only a few systems and after vigorous testing, decided that a select group of users would require Outlook in order to take full advantage of the email functionality in certain systems. Internal testing allowed us to prepare.

On the other hand, the limited testing did not uncover other concerns that arose almost immediately after launch. Below is just a small sampling of this issues.

- Messaging Application Programming Interface (MAPI), the function that allows you to email a Microsoft Office document directly from the MS Office program does not work with Gmail, at least not without a third party product.
- In GroupWise, Delegate access is known as Proxy access. Proxy lets you perform various actions, such as reading, accepting, and declining items on behalf of another user, within the restrictions the other user sets. [4] This may include access to the calendar, as well. In the G Suite apps, delegation was the closest equivalent, but that addresses email. The calendar sharing needing to be handled separately and while the shared rights were migrated, there was a learning curve for trainers and trainees.
- Shared address books, widely used by our community within GroupWise, a little known fact until we launched, is not an available feature in Google Contacts.

3 COMMUNICATION AND TRAINING

3.1 Training Plan

While members of the Muhlenberg College Infrastructure & Networking team were actively migrating GroupWise accounts to Google (in mere months), Client Support Services (CSS) and Instructional Technology & Digital Learning (ITDL) joined forces to educate and support the community during this large scale change.

Our initial training plan was broken down into two phases. The Phase One objective was to transition faculty and staff from GroupWise to Google with a concentration on Gmail, Calendar and Contacts. This phase would kick off with info sessions in November leading up to and including G day (January 2), and then continue into the Spring semester until the community was transitioned smoothly and ready to embark on Phase Two. Phase Two would include Drive, Docs, Sheets and Slides, along with integration of Canvas, our learning management system, with Drive.

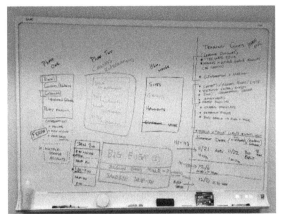

Figure 1: Whiteboard from "G Suite Training Game Plan" Nov 3, 2016.

3.2 Building a Campaign

The campaign needed a goal. That goal was G Day.

Figure 2: Image from G Day Campaign poster. ©Muhlenberg College

We gathered members of the CSS and ITDL teams in a room to hammer out the details. Some of the questions we asked include:

- What events will lead up to G Day?

- How much information can we provide? How much information SHOULD we provide?

- What happens ON G Day?

- What support is offered after G Day passes and the real work begins?

3.3 Branding the Campaign

Image is everything. Well, not everything, but it counts. It was recognized from the start that a visual brand for G Suite training and G Day was critical to the promotion of our training and support plans.

In addition, the team needed to call themselves something. It was a mix of OIT staff, forming a team to support the community during the transition to this new software.

Who did they call? Our resident marketing guru and Digital Cultures Media Assistant. This one-man branding and marketing show is a member of the OIT staff and he always delivers with creativity and enthusiasm, even under the pressure of a tight

deadline. The kickoff meeting was November 6 and on November 8, they had the following badges and buttons designs to choose from. The only question being "What took you so long?!"

Figure 3: Draft logos for G Suite and GWhiz by Anthony Dalton. Nov. 9, 2016. ©Muhlenberg College

Without further ado, the NASA inspired training badge was ready for circulation, as the GWhiz Crew began to craft communications for their info sessions and G Day programming.

3.4 Let the Communication Begin!

"Get ready, set, mark your calendars!
GSuite Info Sessions are scheduled!" [5]

On November 23, 2016, Client Support Services published a blog post to announce G Suite Info Sessions. And so began the ongoing communications leading up to the cut-over to G Suite and post launch.

The IT blog [6], email and muhlenberg.edu/gsuite website were used in tandem to disseminate information to faculty and staff about the migration, training and support.

3.5 Info Sessions: Get Prepared

How do you prepare users for a major system changes without allowing them a sneak peek? You accentuate the positive and reinforce that theme that MOST people have some experience with Google, more specifically Gmail and Google Calendar, so they already know more than they think. Or do they?

We needed to focus on the transition from GroupWise to Google, with a concentration on the applications that were being replaced, so that faculty and staff felt they were transitioned as seamlessly as possible to a new system, without losing the ability to perform their day to day functions.

We stuck to the script (so to speak) and delivered the pre-launch information session "Getting Ready for G Suite" with the following goals and objectives. [7]

- **Get users to login to the application portal BEFORE cut-over and launch**. Our Network Team was very adamant that our users needed to demonstrate success logging into the portal prior to launch. Troubleshooting the SSO and user authentication issues on the first few days of the cut-over to G Suite would be less than optimal. We promoted the portal at every turn, including providing documentation and one-on-one login sessions for first timers.

- **Project Background 101**. We needed to provide more background information about the project and the migration process. It was currently a black box for most individuals outside (and some inside) OIT. The Network Team of 2 working on this project was too busy migrating data and getting all the moving parts to come together to explain it to the masses. That's where the GWhiz team stepped in. The community needed to feel confident about the migration and understand the enormity of the project. We knew there would be some issues after the cut-over and we wanted to provide realistic expectations. Our CIO reinforced the sheer magnitude of work being done in a blog post titled "Getting to Google in 20 Million Short Steps" [8] as well as another plug for the steps we were asking users to take before the cut-over.

- **Clear expectations**. Training and support after the cut-over needed to be done in a phased approach, as previously mentioned. This needed to be clear to the end users for two reasons. One, let faculty and staff know that the GWhiz Crew and OIT Support Team would be available to answer their questions pertaining to the migration from GroupWise to G Suite to ensure they would be able to perform the functions in the new system they had come to rely on (if possible). Two, we needed to set boundaries, given the time and resources available. We were new to the system ourselves and could not commit to supporting the entire G Suite core. We needed to be able to say "That will be supported in Phase 2. Right now, our focus is on successfully transitioning users from GroupWise to G Suite. We will begin supporting additional Google apps after phase one is complete."

- **Relax, it's Google!** Everyone knows Google, right? Most users have a personal Gmail account (we hoped). It was important to make the users feel in control of their own future. This included embracing familiarity with a product they were either already using in their personal life or, at least, knew existed. They could, quite literally, "Google it!" if they had a question. We made sure that was never our stock answer. In our pre-launch info sessions, we asked for a show of hands of those who had used Gmail, Google Contacts and /or Google Calendar. Reassuring those users that they were already ahead of the game. In most cases, this was true. However, we quickly came to realize that using G Suite apps for personal use can be vastly different than professional usage.

- **Compare and Contrast – GroupWise vs G Suite**. In an effort to explain the migration of over 20+ million emails and over 900 calendars, we needed to explain what was being migrated to G Suite and how (or better yet, what). At the same time, we did not want to overwhelm the end users with too many details, knowing it would all be rather abstract until they could login and explore. The major takeaway being that the migration is being done for you. All your email, contacts and calendar events will be migrated and there is nothing for the end user to do. In fact, any clean up on the GroupWise side will be in vain, as the migration was phased and much of the mail was already in the Gmail test environment. Some key concepts included:
  - No thick client – web-based interface
  - Folders are Labels
  - Rules are Filters
  - Personal Address Books equate to Contact Groups (and cannot be shared)
  - Robust search capabilities
  - Busy Search is Find a Time
  - Sharing your calendar
  - Tasks and Reminders (when to use what)
  - Appointment Slots

- **Where can they learn more?** From the onset, we knew it was not possible (nor practical) to create our own documentation for every feature and functionality. Google provides good documentation themselves. We wanted to provide custom documentation for GroupWise to Google specific tasks, as well as, areas that were of particular use to our community. For everything else, we wanted to direct our users to the G Suite Learning Center, Google Support and Lynda.com training available to all faculty, staff and students.

4 PROMOTING G DAY

4.1 Create a Buzz

It was imperative that we generated enough excitement about the event to get people to show up on the first day back from winter break. We didn't have the budget for food, which is usually the best way to ensure a crowd, and while we had a few raffle prizes, what we were really selling was hands-on support all day long.

We knew the Support Team would be inundated with calls on the first day back to campus. It was critical that we provided a place for faculty and staff to get the help they needed without bogging down our two-person support team. The G Day Launch event need to be a success...and it was.

4.2 Say It With Video

On December 20 at 8:30am, we held a meeting titled "G Day Promo Video Brainstorm". At approximately 11am, the camera was locked and loaded, ready to capture our video promos for G Day [9]. Some may think that timeline seems a wee bit rushed, but sometimes spontaneity is just what the occasion ordered. With full confidence that January 2 would indeed come to pass, we filmed our "G Day is Here" video at the same time.

Figure 4: Still from "G Day is Here" [10] promotional video. ©Muhlenberg College

4.3 Get the Word Out!

Blog it, tweet it, post it, email it...whatever it takes. Let everyone know that this January starts with a "G".

Blog post: Coming Soon: G Suite & Google Day [11]

4.4 Did We Mention Prizes?

It never hurts to offer some incentives. The Office of Information Technology acquired giveaways (through purchase or donation) which included meal tickets, six $25 Amazon Gift Cards, and two Grand Prizes – an Amazon Kindle and an Acer 11″ Chromebook. Attendees were eligible for most prizes by simply submitting a raffle ticket at check-in, however, a fully stamped card, indicating they had visited all four drop-in stations (Gmail, Calendar, Mobile and Beyond the Basics) was the only way to win the Kindle or Chromebook.

5 THE INTERIM

5.1 Waiting by Our Inboxes

We officially cut-over to G Suite between Dec 27-29, 2016. Our CIO sent out an email on Dec. 29 with the subject "G Suite Live" reiterating the need to log in through the application portal and using our legacy email system as a reference only. Approximately thirty people reached out via email between December 29 and January 1 to the Support Team. Other individuals in OIT received communications from varied end users, but the volume was not unmanageable. We addressed what we could prior to G Day and advised end users to participate in the event, if possible.

5.2 Checklist! Why Thank You

Everyone loves a list. Well, maybe not loves, but certainly appreciates one. We compiled a G Suite checklist of action items to complete after the cut-over. We wanted users to have tasks that they could work on before G Day.

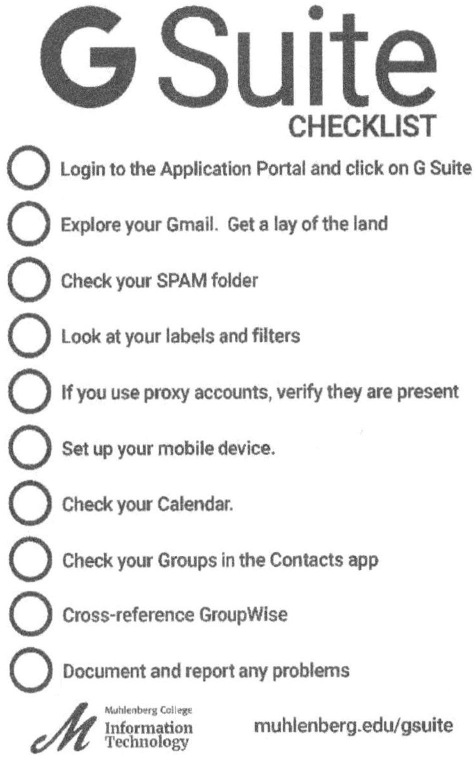

G Suite CHECKLIST

○ Login to the Application Portal and click on G Suite

○ Explore your Gmail. Get a lay of the land

○ Check your SPAM folder

○ Look at your labels and filters

○ If you use proxy accounts, verify they are present

○ Set up your mobile device.

○ Check your Calendar.

○ Check your Groups in the Contacts app

○ Cross-reference GroupWise

○ Document and report any problems

Muhlenberg College Information Technology   muhlenberg.edu/gsuite

Figure 5: G Suite Checklist. Dec. 23, 2016. ©Muhlenberg College

6 G DAY LAUNCH EVENT – THIS JANUARY STARTS WITH A "G"

6.1 G Day Is Here!

The location was secured. The schedule was set. The flyers and training materials were ready and the blog post was published.

Figure 6: G Day Flyer by Anthony Dalton. Dec. 22, 2016. ©Muhlenberg College

The promotional materials lined the hallways of the student union.

The stations were properly staffed with IT professionals, armed with raffle stamps borrowed from our CIO's one-and-a-half-year-old daughter.

The CIO took the stage to kick-off the G Day Launch event at 8:30am. There was a modest crowd to start, but the pace quickly picked up with approximately twenty guests sat in for the first info session, while other participants engaged with IT staff at the drop-in stations.

6.2 Drop-In Stations

By far, the most successful element of G Day was the drop-in stations. Members of the OIT staff were scheduled to work the stations throughout the course of the day. The stations were as follows: Gmail, Mobile, Calendar, Beyond the Basics. We wanted to focus on the Phase One objectives of transitioning from one system to the other. We knew that some people would require handholding, particularly when it came to setting up mobile devices. We had one station dedicated to doing just that and it had non-stop traffic most of the day.

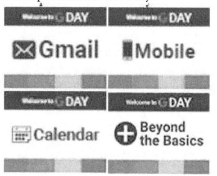

Figure 7: G Day signage drop-in stations by Anthony Dalton. Dec. 22, 2016. ©Muhlenberg College

6.3 Gathering Information from the Users

There was no way to efficiently generate support tickets on the fly during this event. We decided that a shared document in Google Drive was the best way to keep a running log of issues and questions, that we would address in a recap meeting the next day. We needed to record our interactions, but couldn't spend time organizing during the event. In addition, we had a slack channel set up specifically for G Day, where technicians could communicate with one another and get quick answers to end user questions. In many cases, we were learning with the end user. We needed to be agile, responsive, and honest. We may have been the in-house experts, but time had not allowed for Google certification. The GWhiz team and other members of the OIT staff were early adopters with varying technical expertise brought together with one central purpose–get the end-user through the launch, feeling supported and reasonably comfortable in their new communication tool.

6.4 END USER TAKEAWAYS

We had the Google Checklist on hand, so that people could walk away with their "to dos", as well as, documentation on some of the focal areas identified in the information sessions. In addition, we made sure that every end user knew that the support did not end on January 3. We had a full training schedule mapped out for January and provided the attendees with a training flyer identifying the upcoming opportunities.

Figure 8: G Suite training schedule by Anthony Dalton. Dec. 22, 2016. ©Muhlenberg College

7 AFTER THE LAUNCH

7.1 G Day Wrap Up

Key members of the GWhiz crew met with the CIO and the members of Network Team on January 4th to talk about new and outstanding issues, to process the G Day log, review support tickets and calls, and formulate next steps.

7.2 The Stats

- Number of info session (4) attendees (estimation) = 135 (In 2016, Muhlenberg employed 536 Full time employees and 247 part-time employees.
- Number of views of online info sessions = 263
- Number of attendees on G Day = over 150
- Number of support tickets on G Day = 8
- Number of support tickets related to G Suite during the first 30 days = 83

7.3 January G Suite Training

The first week of January, including G Day, was dedicated to providing a hands-on support system for faculty and staff as they transitioned from GroupWise to G Suite. We used various approaches to connect with the end users.

- **Work Sessions** – These sessions were conducted in computer labs so that users could log in and get hands-on assistance with their issues and inquiries. They were broken down into two topics–Mail & Contacts and Calendar & Contacts. The first session, scheduled on January 3, was pretty quiet. Only a handful of users filtered in throughout the block of time. Many individuals had not yet officially returned from winter break and those that had, were either too busy to attend or had not yet spent enough time using G Suite to be comfortable asking questions. This was learned of anecdotally, through conversations at later sessions.

  The three remaining sessions were well attended, inviting lively conversation and opportunities to demonstrate some of the basic functions in G Suite, like turning off Conversation mode or setting your vacation message.
- **Online Sessions** – Using the Zoom web conferencing solution, two online sessions were held, allowing users to participate from any location. Questions were fielded over chat and the sessions were recorded for on-demand viewing.
- **Brown Bag Sessions** - The user community intentionally lead the way in planning for G Suite brown bag sessions, basing topics on support calls and general inquiries/interest. The January brown bags started with a Q&A session, followed by Beyond the Basics, Gmail, Beyond the Basics, Calendar, Contacts & Groups, Labels & Filters and Calendar, and Tips & Tricks. It was still the first month and our end users were still in need of learning the basics to perform their daily business needs.

All of the early sessions, provided a forum for users to communicate their experiences in G Suite–good, bad and indifferent. A lot of information was gathered about what users were encountering informing documentation and support around these experiences. Each session provided the trainers with a hands on opportunity to learn about the products. The team quickly became invested in continuing with these training methods as a high impact part of our general approach to training users on new technologies.

7.4 Spring Training

January had come and gone. The Google dust had settled, for the most part. We felt ready to plan for Phase Two training and support, and so released the schedule for the rest of the semester. Some sessions had as few as two attendees, while others garnered over twenty guests. No matter the size of the session, they have all been valuable experiences for the trainers and trainees. Due to the success of January's programming, it was decided that the varying formats were useful and would be continued to until the end of the semester. The G Suite training programs for the spring semester consisted of the following events:

Spring Brown Bag & Online Sessions

- G Suite - Google Calendar
- G Suite App Overview
- Google Drive
- Google Docs, Sheets and Slides
- Yet Another Mail Merge (live Zoom Session)
- Maximizing your productivity

Common Hour (designated time when no classes or campus wide events are scheduled)

- G Suite-Beyond the Basics: This common hour touched on the next phase of training for G Suite as it related to G Suite apps beyond Gmail, Calendar and Contacts. Topics included: Drive, Sheets, Docs, Slides and more.

Two Open Work Sessions (took place at the close of the Spring semester)

7.5 Community Feedback

The training and support provided for G Suite was the first of its kind and the community responded. From large scale events to one-on-one training sessions, we knew that we had an opportunity to provide the type of support our department strives to provide on a daily basis. The difference is doing so in a coordinated and intentional way, consistently and continually.

The response from the user community was overwhelmingly positive. They were thirsting for this type of interaction and engagement. Technology can be intimating, even to the seasoned end-user. The varied training opportunities and multiple mediums provided just the right mix of instruction and collaboration. We are still learning from one another, discovering better ways to work and opportunities for enhancements.

8 LESSONS LEARNED

8.1 Personal Versus Professional Accounts

Other than a familiarity with the interface, personal and professional use of Google apps is vastly different. How often do you need to track emails, invoke mailto functionality, schedule emails, share contact lists and so many more examples in your personal life? While users rarely need this type of functionality with personal communications, they frequently require these tools on the job.

G Suite apps are great for collaboration, search functionality and ease of use, not to mention the convenience of the web based interface and cloud storage. As a business communication tool, it takes some getting used to. G Suite being a web based suite of applications, will never take the place of a thick email client. For a small group of users that meet the criteria, Outlook using Google Apps Sync is the prescribed alternative.

8.2 Anything Email Related Must be Tested

When it comes to administrative systems, discoveries were made post launch for months. Many systems use SMTP (Simple Mail Transfer Protocol) for email transmission. While not a directly caused by the migration to Google, it was a missed byproduct. In the course of the migration, the SMTP server changed, affecting multiple systems. This was discovered when emails failed to reach Gmail, but still got through to GroupWise. Thankfully the legacy system was still receiving mail. GroupWise was critical in the early stages of the transition. When it showed up in GroupWise and not Gmail, it was often SMTP related or some other idiosyncrasy that needed to be researched. Unless, the users were emailing each from within the legacy system, which did not flow to Gmail, intentionally.

8.3 Garbage In/Garbage Out

Had communications gone out earlier end users could have been instructed to clean-up of their current environment. Due to the enormity of the migration effort (remember twenty million plus emails), it had to be done in phases. By the time communication started with end users regarding timelines and training, it was too late for them to clean out old mail or reorganize folder structures in preparation for label creation, as part of the migration work had already been completed.

8.4 Sometimes Support Is Just Understanding

Not everyone is a fan of change. In some cases, the product is just different and some functionality is either vastly different or lost entirely. You can offer alternatives, but very often, it just helps to understand and listen. Be the understanding ear, willing to collaborate to overcome the challenges, even when the answer is finding an alternate to a functionality that no longer exists for the end user due to differences in the legacy application versus the new product.

8.5 Tracking and Surveying

The biggest part of the process missed was measurement. The majority of feedback solicited and received was anecdotal. While the team was able to put together a solid communication and training plan at an accelerated pace, the process by which to measure and track success was not a priority. As the team and department embark on future initiatives and projects, measuring success and failure will be a top priority.

REFERENCES

[1] Muhlenberg College. 2017. Retrieved from http://muhlenberg.edu/main/aboutus.
[2] Allan Chen. 2016. Google Apps for Education – Our Next Collaboration Platform (May 11 2016). Retrieved June 12, 2017 from http://it.blogs.muhlenberg.edu/2016/05/11/google-apps-for-education-our-next-collaboration-platform/.
[3] Wikipedia 29 April 2016. Retrieved from https://en.wikipedia.org/wiki/Mailto
[4] Novell 20 December 2016. Retrieved from https://www.novell.com/documentation/
[5] Phedra Henninger. 2016. GSuite Info Sessions Announced (Nov 23, 2016) Retrieved June 12, 2017 from http://it.blogs.muhlenberg.edu/2016/11/23/gsuite-info-sessions-announced/.
[6] IT blog 6 June 2017. http://it.blogs.muhlenberg.edu/
[7] Phedra Henninger, Thomas Sciarrino and Timothy Clarke. 2016. Getting Ready for G Suite (Nov 2016). Retrieved June 12, 2017 from https://docs.google.com/presentation/d/1Ag5zSl5XOemEmlrxohm5VBWd2UiodAvCKMxyV2pA-PA/edit?usp=sharing.
[8] Allan Chen, 2016. Getting to Google in 20 million short steps (Nov 30 2016). Retrieved June 12, 2017 from http://it.blogs.muhlenberg.edu/2016/11/30/getting-to-google-in-20-million-short-steps/
[9] Anthony Dalton. 2016. G Day is Coming. Video. (22 December 2016). Retrieved June 12 2017 from https://video.muhlenberg.edu/media/G Day+is+Coming/1_3al5jtlt
[10] Anthony Dalton. 2016. G Day is Here. Video. (22 December 2016). Retrieved June 12 2017 from https://video.muhlenberg.edu/media/G Day+is+Here/1_y25iphh1
[11] Allan Chen, 2016. Coming Soon: G Suite & Google Day! (Dec 23 2016). Retrieved June 12, 2017 from http://it.blogs.muhlenberg.edu/2016/12/23/coming-soon-g-suite-google-day/

Understaffed? A Case Study in Empowering a User Community to Get a Large Project Done

Amanda Johnson
University of Minnesota Duluth
1208 Kirby Plaza
Duluth, MN, 55812
aljohnso@d.umn.edu

Brennan Atchison
University of Minnesota Duluth
1208 Kirby Plaza
Duluth, MN, 55812
batchiso@d.umn.edu

ABSTRACT

The University of Minnesota Duluth made the decision to transition the majority of its websites into Drupal, a content management system (CMS). Additionally, during the process the university's website underwent a complete redesign as well as a content overhaul. Prior to the move to Drupal, there were few technical, design, or brand standards being enforced; each department or unit took its own unique approach to web design, development, and maintenance. Tight budgets meant that there were no staff available to commit full time to the project. The historical approach of letting units manage their websites however they wished also meant a huge cultural shift for members of the campus community. In this paper, we will address how through the formation of user and technical groups, we built trust, harnessed technical expertise, addressed bugs and feature requests, created training opportunities, developed documentation, provided viable channels for feedback, and successfully united a previously fragmented campus community to successfully get the job done.

CCS CONCEPTS

• **Social and professional topics**   • **Social and professional topics~Professional topics**   • **Social and professional topics~Computing education**   • *Social and professional topics~Computing literacy*

KEYWORDS

accidental techie; cms, community; content management systems; culture; documentation, drupal; group feedback; low staffing; project help; project management; self-help; tech groups; train the trainer; training; trust, user groups; websites.

SIGUCCS '17, October 1–4, 2017, Seattle, WA, USA
© 2017 Association for Computing Machinery.
ACM ISBN 978-1-4503-4919-2/17/10...$15.00
https://doi.org/10.1145/3123458.3123488

1 INTRODUCTION

The University of Minnesota Duluth (UMD) made the decision to transition the majority of its websites into Drupal, a content management system (CMS). Additionally, during the process, the university's website underwent a complete redesign as well as a content overhaul. Prior to the move to Drupal, there were few technical, design, or brand standards being enforced; each department or unit took its own unique approach to web design, development, and maintenance.

Tight budgets meant that there were no staff available to commit full time to the project. The historical approach of letting units manage their websites however they wished also meant a huge cultural shift for members of the campus community.

In this paper, we will address how through the formation of user and technical groups, we built trust, harnessed technical expertise, addressed bugs and feature requests, created training opportunities, developed documentation, provided viable channels for feedback, and successfully united a previously siloed campus community to get the content overhauled and migrated to Drupal. It is our hope that similar approaches can be successfully applied to many different types of technical projects at institutions of higher education.

2 BACKGROUND AND MAJOR CHALLENGES

The major challenges we faced in moving our campus to Drupal included:

- Tight budgets
- Low staffing levels
- No consistent historical approach to web development
- Lack of transparency regarding planning and decision making
- Siloed or fragmented work culture
- General lack of trust between IT Professionals in different units, as well as between IT and the marketing and public relations department

The mandate to move our entire website of approximately half a million pages into Drupal meant our campus was faced with a huge project, the likes of which had never been previously attempted. Although standardized Dreamweaver HTML templates had been available for several years, not every unit or department used them. Some sites had been developed and hosted by outside vendors. Some sites had been created by student workers. Some colleges had dedicated web development professionals who historically had the freedom to create sites however they wished. Other units used Google Sites or WordPress or paid UMD's central IT department (Information Technology Systems & Services - ITSS) to develop and maintain their websites. In short, website development and maintenance was all over the map. Many people felt that the move to a Content Management System (CMS) and the consistency it offered was long overdue, but many people also highly valued the freedom of doing things their own way.

Money can go a long way towards soothing the pains that accompany any large change, however our requests to administration for funding to dedicate staff to this major project were denied. Like many colleges and universities, the University of Minnesota Duluth has been struggling through years of tight budgets and staffing retrenchments, and so early on we realized that any solution we developed could not be dependent on large amounts of money: we were going to have to work with the staff and resources that already existed.

The main push for this change in approach to website management came from our newly revitalized University Marketing and Public Relations (UMPR) department. After years of stability, waves of retirements brought significant changes to upper administration at UMD. The push for this project began with a new UMPR director who wanted to assert central control over website content for the very first time. (Previously, UMPR had been called External Affairs and had little to do with websites or other internal decisions.) Unfortunately, leadership in that unit experienced rapid turnover, meaning that the project was subsequently inherited by various new employees with little understanding of UMD culture and minimal background knowledge regarding the true scope of the project. This contributed heavily to a lack of transparency and feelings of distrust surrounding the project.

Although decisions made by UMPR were the impetus for the move to Drupal, UMD's central IT department (ITSS) was ultimately tasked with technically implementing the new website design and assisting with the bulk of the migration. Initially, challenges did arise from feelings associated with being assigned what was essentially an unfunded mandate, and not a project that ITSS would have likely pursued given the choice. Asking other independent units to begin migrating into a standardized system also contributed to "Big Brother" type concerns across campus. Although there was plenty of work to be done, certainly some employees were worried about losing their jobs or at the very least, losing the ability to exercise their own professional judgment and make good use of their many years of experience.

3   SOLUTIONS

The solutions to our challenges were many fold and required significant patience, persistence, and a willingness to try new things. We had to break down barriers, build trust, share knowledge, and teach the campus community to use and enjoy Drupal. Ultimately, the following were key to our success:

- An agile development method, using regularly scheduled sprints

- Formation of a technical group for Drupal administrators across campus
- Formation of a user group focused on everyday users of Drupal
- Drupal cohorts for building out sites
- Creation of easy to use Google forms as a means of providing feedback, with a process that included regular, timely responses to bug reports and feature requests
- The development of a documentation website that is easy to browse and search and is consistently kept up-to-date
- Regularly hosted drop-in sessions for hands-on Drupal help

3.1   Development Method

To make things even more interesting, UMD's version of Drupal is not the standard version of Drupal 7 offered the world over. Instead, our version is a variation on the implementation of Drupal being used at the University of Minnesota Twin Cities campus, which is a variation of a version customized for another university, that the University of Minnesota licensed and then paid an external developer to further customize.

UMD administration chose Drupal 7 as its CMS only because the larger Twin Cities campus selected it as their platform of choice. On the Twin Cities campus however, Drupal is just one of many tools offered to develop websites - at UMD it was mandated that all websites move into Drupal. Because of this mandate, and to meet the wildly varying demands on websites at UMD, as well as technical limitations of the greater UMD staff, we needed to customize our version of Drupal even further, so that it could meet our technical needs while actually being somewhat user friendly.

Lacking the ability to hire a dedicated Drupal developer and administrator, we instead asked one of the software developers whom we already had on staff to begin dedicating a portion of his time to working with Drupal. At first, the going was tough. Work on Drupal was constantly being interrupted by work on other enterprise system projects. It was exceedingly difficult to predict when work would actually get done, and therefore keeping the project on track proved problematic. Not being able to consistently deliver on promises made it hard to build trust or interest in the project amongst the campus community. It also made it challenging for users to test for bugs or provide valuable feedback - they had no way of knowing when issues had supposedly been addressed or if improvements had simply been put on the backburner.

The solution to this dilemma was to begin working on Drupal in dedicated sprints. Generally, one week each month was reserved for our developer to focus primarily on Drupal programming and administration. The sprint schedule was planned a semester at a time, allowing us to predict when work would be done. This allowed us to better prioritize our development goals, plan testing and feedback, communicate more accurately with our users, as well as provide training on new features in a timely manner.

3.2   Drupal Technical Group

Another major challenge to Drupal development was the fact that our developer was not a major user of Drupal. It is exceedingly difficult to know what features and fixes are most needed and whether or not the software is working properly without having people who are actually using the tool actively providing feedback. To help address this issue we formed the Drupal Technical Group.

The Drupal Technical Group was made up primarily of the IT, website, and marketing professionals from across campus, who were handling the bulk of the website migration work for their individual units. However, in order to help build trust and establish transparency, anyone interested in Drupal development was invited to join the group. We would much rather have people opt themselves out after deciding that the group was not for them, rather than feel excluded and imagine that they were intentionally being kept out of the loop.

The one exception to this was management: due to a highly politicized campus environment and the controversial nature of the decision to migrate all websites to a standardized platform and template, we asked that management recuse themselves from the group. This was key to establishing trust amongst group members. It allowed staff to feel more comfortable and gave them the opportunity to speak freely amongst their peers. At the start, there was a lot of distrust and resentment of university management, which many group members had to work through before any real progress could be made.

Management was initially not too keen on the idea of staff meeting regularly on such a big project without direct oversight. Some feared that decisions would be made without management having a say. To assuage those worries, it was agreed that all major decisions would be run through a separate team that had representatives from both ITSS and UMPR management.

Establishing the Drupal Technical Group was slow going at first. Professionals from different units had not traditionally worked together very closely. There was a lot of uncertainty regarding roles, whether or not expertise and experience would be valued, and it was unclear what work actually needed to be done. There were many rather awkward and somewhat quiet meetings at first. To really get the group going, it took a few dedicated and respected folks from across the campus community who truly believed that it was in all of our best interests to stay involved. These staff persisted in attending meetings and encouraged others to do the same. In time, staff began building relationships and a rapport, and we began to see the results of what we could accomplish when we worked together.

Work for the Drupal Technical Group became easier after the sprint development model was adopted. We began scheduling two meetings per month. One, the week prior to the sprint, where the group could review bug reports, discuss feature requests, and work together to prioritize development goals. The second meeting was scheduled for the week after the sprint, where we could discuss what development work had actually been finished and talk about what specifically needed testing. Eventually, the group also began holding "deep dive" sessions, where we would spend about an hour covering a single technical topic in depth.

The Technical Group was essential for providing Drupal testing and feedback. There was no way we could have known what work really needed to be done without input from this group of professionals who were actively building websites using UMD Drupal. But what made attending Drupal Technical Group meetings worth the time of its members was the transparency the group provided to the development process. It allowed the members to really see the scope of the development demands and come to a consensus on priorities. Instead of feeling like their requests were being ignored, individuals could readily see why their requests may have been delayed. By regularly interacting with other professionals on campus who were doing similar work, they could more easily identify common needs and challenges and brainstorm universal solutions, rather than requesting custom development projects. The Technical Group truly allowed members to have a voice in the process, with regular, predictable, and transparent results.

3.3   Drupal Users Group

While the Drupal Technical Group was aimed primarily at staff who were involved in some aspect of website development as a major part of their professional jobs, many of the people who had been maintaining websites at UMD did not have it included as a part of their job descriptions. Nevertheless, website updates were their responsibility, and major changes to both the look and feel of their websites, combined with the migration to the Drupal CMS, was the source of significant amounts of stress. By creating the Drupal Users Group, we hoped to offer both assurance and support to users. Our goals included establishing a similar level of transparency into the migration process for the wider campus community, as well as finding ways to train the hundreds of faculty, staff, and student employees who would be updating websites in Drupal. Once again, we had to accomplish this with no additional funding or staff time allocated for the project.

The most important thing about the Drupal Users Group was its openness. Just as with the Technical Group, we would much rather have people opt themselves out of the group after deciding it wasn't for them, rather than engage in conspiratorial thinking, and in the process potentially convince themselves or others that they were being kept out of the loop for some nefarious reason or another.

Additionally, demonstrating responsiveness was key for building trust and ensuring active engagement by group members. We did this by regularly showing when and how their feedback was used and proving that complaints and ideas did not simply disappear into a void. We showed them where their feedback ended up, when it was reviewed, and actively communicated what improvements were being made to the system and why. We went out of our way to thank people when they provided feedback and to assure them that there is truly no dumb question or suggestion; if they were wondering about it, certainly someone else was too. By participating, they were not only helping themselves, but they were helping their coworkers as well.

We used the feedback we received to help determine meeting topics. Whenever we would see a certain question or idea begin to trend, we would quickly host a session covering that topic from an end user perspective. Meetings were casual - there was generally no need to RSVP, and users could come and go as they pleased. Popular sessions would be hosted more than once, and meeting times were varied so that employees with scheduling conflicts would not always be out of luck when it came time to attend. Group members were encouraged to bring friends. Examples of session topics include: posting news stories, writing for the web, file management best practices, image editing basics, etc.

In order to train content contributors on how to use Drupal, the Users Group also offers regular Drupal 101 training sessions, approximately once every two weeks. This allows us to consolidate new users into groups, as opposed to having to offer training on an individual basis. When a new staff or faculty member comes on board, they can quickly get the personalized training they need by attending one of these sessions.

3.4 Drupal Cohorts

The colleges and other major units at UMD all had professional staff members who could dedicate significant amounts of time towards migrating their websites to Drupal. This was not the case for many of the non-academic departments at UMD. These units had important websites that needed to be migrated, but no one with the time or the expertise to do the work. Our initial solution to this dilemma was to establish Drupal Cohorts.

When a unit was ready to migrate their site to Drupal, we asked them to select one or two staff members to participate in a Drupal cohort. We would then team these staff up with others who also had sites ready to move. We would limit cohorts to three or four sites at a time.

IT Professionals would then meet with the cohort and walk them through the process of building out their sites in Drupal and transferring their content in. This allowed us to get several sites built and launched at once, while at the same time, providing training for the new Drupal users. Working alongside other, non-IT Professionals also allowed cohort members to feel more comfortable and less intimidated by the process. They were able to form relationships with others on campus who were in similar situations. When they had future questions, they now knew other people who might know the answer, or at the very least, they felt better assured that they were not alone.

3.5 Feedback

As mentioned several times, a transparent and responsive feedback process was necessary for making our Drupal Migration a success. The University of Minnesota is a Google Apps customer, and so an easy solution for us was to create Google Forms as a means to submit feedback. We created forms for bug reports, feature questions, and documentation requests.

Users can view and comment on existing feedback and requests, adding to the transparency of the process. We encourage users to submit feedback even if someone else has already requested something similar, as this helps us to gauge demand and prioritize the development work we do. We actively comment on the feedback received so that users know we are reading their feedback and working hard to implement their ideas when possible.

It took a lot of encouragement to convince users to submit feedback regularly. But by directly connecting their feedback with results, we have demonstrated to them that it is worth their time to do so.

3.6 Documentation

Documentation is incredibly valuable when it is accessible, robust, and accurate. But who has time to create and maintain documentation? We were pleased to discover that we could successfully delegate this responsibility to a student worker.

We partnered with our Writing Studies Department to create a paid internship within ITSS - a first for our department. In the end, our first student hire ended up being a Computer Science major who did not actually take advantage of the internship credit, but by working with the Writing Studies Department we were better able to determine and articulate our needs for the documentation position.

Our student worker did an amazing job at capturing questions and identifying documentation needs while attending Drupal User Group and Technical Group meetings. She quickly learned how to use UMD's version of Drupal and created easy to use instructions complete with screenshots for all levels of Drupal users, from content contributors to administrators. Because the sprint method made updates predictable, she was able to keep documentation up-to-date, which ensured its usefulness to those accessing it.

Being a Google Apps campus, we created our documentation using Google Docs, with a Google Sites front end that allows users to either navigate by subject or to search directly for their topics. This means that users can actually find the documentation they are looking for. We developed this approach based on general document management research conducted by University of Minnesota Libraries. (For more information, see: z.umn.edu/docmanagement)

Having quality documentation available to users has been an essential part of our support model. When responding to questions, we make sure to link back to associated documentation, which teaches our users to try to help themselves as a first step. It cuts way back on the amount of questions we need to spend time fielding. We use the feedback we receive to continue to develop and improve our documentation.

Since our documentation is now mostly established, we have a single student worker who maintains and creates new documentation as just one part of her job duties. We have had great success in continuing to find talented and responsible student workers.

3.7 Drupal Drop-in Sessions

Sometimes, it's better simply to help people face-to-face. It can be easier to determine what the problem is, and many users prefer a more personalized approach. But meeting with users one-on-one is just not something we're staffed to do.

Our solution was to begin hosting Drupal Drop-in sessions. Sessions are held at least once a week in an active learning classroom. Laptops are available for staff members who may only have use of a desktop computer back in their office. Generally, at least two IT Professionals and one UMPR representative staff the drop-ins, waiting to help users on demand when they pop-in with questions ranging from simple to complicated.

We vary the times and days of the sessions, so that no user is stuck with a regularly conflicting meeting. The sessions are incredibly popular, with up to a dozen users dropping in at a time. No one is ever annoyed at having to wait a short amount of time for help, because they are generally busy establishing relationships with co-workers from around campus that they might rarely see otherwise. By encountering others with similar questions, they grow assured that they are not alone when struggles arise with their websites.

Some users will provide feedback in person for which they would never bother submitting a form. The in-person assistance also gives the IT Professionals a chance to see how people are *actually* using Drupal. When we can't provide an immediate solution for an issue, users can observe us documenting the problem, and they have a name and face to put with the promise of a resolution. This goes a long way towards building trust.

Drupal Drop-ins have become such a success, that we have several users who come even when they don't have questions. They attend because they enjoy the community and appreciate having dedicated working time and space. Some users are so overjoyed by the fact that they found an actual person to help them, that they burst into rounds of applause. The positive attitudes displayed at Drupal Drop-in sessions are the result of years of persistent hard work towards building trust, creating transparency, and delivering results. These are the things that have made our major website migration project possible. Amazingly enough, it was all accomplished without a dedicated budget or the hiring of additional professional staff.

4 CONTINUING CHALLENGES

Although UMD's migration to Drupal has been successful, it would be disingenuous to give the impression that's it's all gone perfectly well. Although we eventually earned great buy-in from the majority of the campus community, there are still some holdouts who would rather try to work completely independently. These users, some of whom are IT Professionals, continue to complicate the project as a whole. Still, we haven't given up on the idea of breaking down the remaining silos and partnering closely with everyone involved with website work on campus.

Additionally, although we've been able to produce amazing results with a limited budget and resources, we do worry about staff burn-out. Single points of failure and not always being able to take breaks when needed can be both stressful and exhausting. More staff and higher pay would help retention rates, morale, and improve work quality and speed. This is undoubtedly true at all Universities and on all major projects.

5 CONCLUSION

As of the summer of 2017, the vast majority of University of Minnesota Duluth websites have been successfully migrated to Drupal. Overall, the response from the end users has been extremely positive–instead of dread, users are actually feeling excited to work on their websites.

Despite the fact that most of the initial migration work is now complete, the Drupal User and Technical groups, as well as the Drupal Drop-in sessions, remain quite active. Users are now focusing on improving the content of their websites. Basic lessons continue to be offered for new hires and also act as refresher courses for those who appreciate additional training. As users become increasingly confident with their web management skills, new, more advanced sessions are routinely requested and offered. This has led to a significant increase in the quality of websites across our campus.

IT Professionals are now focused on developing new feature requests and improving the overall Drupal user experience. Of course, we are wrapping up our migration to Drupal 7 just in time to begin our move to Drupal 8, which will likely be another major undertaking. However, having established a manageable development process and supported by a new culture of transparency and trust, we now truly look forward to the challenges ahead.

ACKNOWLEDGMENTS
We would like to thank the University of Minnesota Duluth staff, faculty, and students who made our successes possible. Special acknowledgements to Logan West and his work on the School of Fine Arts pilot site, Alexa Chiu, for her amazing documentation skills, and our highest regards to Aaron Richner, our lead Drupal developer.

Giving More Effective Feedback

Ella Tschopik
UW Madison School of Education
225 N Mills St
Madison, WI 53706
ella.tschopik@wisc.edu

ABSTRACT

Have you ever wondered what exactly was "good" about the "good job" you received from your supervisor? Have you ever debated the best way to constructively critique an employee? Have you ever considered how to accurately evaluate your own work? Effective feedback is a must for creating team growth, personal development (in both ourselves and others) and furthering the mission of our organizations. Today let's take the time to discuss and try best practices in both giving and receiving feedback. In this facilitated discussion, you'll have the opportunity to learn and practice feedback techniques as well as learn the organizational value of feedback and reasoning behind what makes effective feedback. We will also take time to discuss and practice self-assessment including how to give ourselves open and honest feedback. Giving and receiving effective feedback are valuable skills for relationships both personal and professional; come work on honing your feedback skills to better those around you.

CCS CONCEPTS

• **Social and professional topics~Project and people management** • **Social and professional topics~Adult education** • *Social and professional topics~Informal education*

KEYWORDS

Feedback; mindfulness; interpersonal

1 INTRODUCTION

Feedback is all around us. We are constantly bombarded by environmental feedback that has helped us understand the physical world since we were born. If we drink a cup of hot coffee, we get burned so we learn to let it cool. If we run too fast and trip, we learn how to be more aware of our surroundings.

SIGUCCS 2017, October 2017, Seattle, Washington USA
© 2017 Association for Computing Machinery.
ACM ISBN 978-1-4503-4919-2/17/10...$15.00
https://doi.org/10.1145/3123458.3123481

Our bodies take in physical feedback without much focus on our part, but when it comes to interpersonal feedback, our educational systems and workplaces need some assistance bringing this valuable tool into practice.

2 Overview of Workshop

2.1 Opening Activity

The workshop will open with a brief guided mindfulness meditation. The purpose is twofold, in both bringing participants out of the conference and into their bodies and the space, and giving us an introduction to listening to feedback within our bodies which we will reflect on. Participants will then be asked to fill out a set of questions about how they felt during the mindfulness activity and if they started to notice cues from their bodies they have blocked out.

When we block out cues from our environment, whether physical as in our own bodies or interpersonal as in the workplace, we lose important information on how to best accept and maneuver within any given situation. Learning how to listen to these cues as well as act on them and share them with others can enhance our work, our relationships and our lives. The workshop will then move into the three main parts of feedback: giving, receiving and self-assessment.

2.2 Praise: helpful or harmful?

When a child brings home a drawing from school, a parent will often say "good job" or "nice work." Research into this has shown that when children are praised for an attribute rather than the effort or act of creation that they are more likely to connect future successes or failures to the attribute rather than the effort[1]. Brining this concept into the work place, what this means is that if we hear "good work" on a project, we have two reactions, one being that our work is based on our attributions and the other being that in the future we will succeed or fail based on our fixed attributions leading to a fixed mindset. Learning how to give and receive interpersonal feedback can lead to a growth mindset, where we and those we work with see our effort as the focus of our work rather than our fixed attributes.

2.3 Giving Feedback

The first aspect of giving good interpersonal feedback is that it needs to be specific[4], and as mentioned above, focus on effort over attributes. For this part of the workshop participants will read written scenarios; the first of which will have multiple choices what the best feedback in a given situation would be, the second will encourage participants to write their own feedback for the scenario. We will then work in pairs to discuss why choices were made by each and a share out to the broader group on best feedback as chosen by the pairs, including group discussion over any discrepancies.

I will then lead the group on a broader discussion of what else is important for giving effective feedback which includes the receivers willingness to listen, the time and place and the overall goals of the giver and the receiver[3]. Having this discussion as a group will keep participants engaged and bring out the wisdom of the crowd rather than have participants be passive learners in this workshop.

2.4 Receiving Feedback

Giving feedback, once you understand how and have practiced the skill, is easy; receiving feedback is much harder. When we hear feedback, especially negative feedback, our brains want to shut out uncomfortable information. We may reject outright the feedback we receive, we may act defensively instead of respectfully. Receiving feedback can, however, get better with practice and we can learn some tactful phrases to deflect in the moment and allow us to process at a later time.

Participants will be asked to reflect on a time that they received feedback and did not respond well in the moment. I will share a story of my own as well. We will then use our negative experiences to discuss what we can do as receivers of feedback to best respond and use the incoming information.

2.5 Mindfulness and Self-Assessment

Lastly the workshop will focus on self-assessment both physical and mental. We will return to the mindfulness answers from the first activity. Mindfulness is a skill used for recognizing and accepting one's current state that can lead to myriad benefits from job satisfaction to stress reduction to emotional regulation[2]. While no direct research has yet been done between mindfulness and self-assessment, it follows that the best first step to self-assessment is understanding the current state of one's self.

We will discuss in small groups the mindfulness experience at the opening of the workshop and the answers we wrote down after. As a big group, we will talk about different types of mindfulness such as walking mindfulness or reading mindfully and how to create a mindfulness practice that works for each of us.

Participants will then be given a course evaluation form and be asked to give effective feedback on the presenter, the content and their own participation and engagement.

2.6 Conclusions

Feedback is how we learn about the world around us. Without clear, concise, frequent feedback we cannot become our best selves. In this workshop we have practiced skills for giving feedback, receiving feedback and started to look at our own work in a mindful way. As with all skills we wish to improve, giving and receiving feedback will need sustained practice. These skills can be used with those we supervise and those who supervise us. They can help create a culture of support, trust and growth. Feedback is all around us but to bring feedback into the workplace, we need to practice and be more mindful our own behaviors.

ACKNOWLEDGMENTS

Support and encouragement for this work was provided by UW Madison School of Education Media, Educational Resources and IT.

REFERENCES

[1]Grusec, J.E. and Redler, E. 1980. Attribution, Reinforcement, and Altruism: A Developmental Analysis. *Developmental Psychology*. 16, 5 (1980), 252–534.
[2]Hülsheger, H. et al. 2013. Benefits of Mindfulness at Work: The Role of Mindfulness in Emotion Regulation, Emotional Exhaustion, and Job Satisfaction. *Journal of Applied Psychology*. 98, 2 (2013), 310–325.
[3]Sachdeva MD, A.K. 1996. Use of Effective Feedback to Facilitate Adult Learning. *Journal of Cancer Education*. 11, 2 (Summer 1996), 106–118.
[4]Westberg, J. and Jason, H. 2001. *Providing Feedback Effectively*. Springer Publishing Company.

Fostering Independence

Project Work for Student Technicians

Kendra Strode
Carleton College
1 N. College St
Northfield, Minnesota 55057
kstrode@carleton.edu

ABSTRACT

Helpdesk student training and management at Carleton has focused largely on providing topical training to develop competency in customer support and Carleton's technical infrastructure so that our student techs (CarlTechs) are prepared to answer calls and support clients. However, there is always "bigger-picture" project work that can be done beyond basic ticketing and phone support. In recent years, leveraging student hours to help complete larger-scale projects at the helpdesk has become a useful tool for increasing CarlTechs' competence and engagement in all aspects of helpdesk work. This paper outlines the structures used at Carleton to support our student technicians in this work and how those structures developed, using a few past projects as examples.

1 SUPPORT OVERVIEW

The structure of technical support at Carleton is based on our centralized helpdesk. Three full-time staff members (Primaries) work with approximately ten other IT staff (Secondaries) who have a weekly two-hour shift at the desk. Primaries and Secondaries field phone calls from staff and facfulty members. Student calls and walk-up issues are addressed first by our team of approximately 60 student technicians (CarlTechs), which they then document in tickets that receive further support if needed.

1.1 Background

The "staff-talk-to-staff" model described above was developed after the advent of a call-routing VoIP system at the helpdesk, and was in response to campus frustration at the lack of preparation student technicians had when answering calls[1]. The under-preparation of students was not a surprise; several factors had contributed to the situation over the years.

The once-separate student and staff/faculty helpdesks combined in 2011. At that time, training was designed to bridge the knowledge

---

[1]This feedback came through qualitative, anecdotal feedback sought by the new CTO at Carleton.

gap of already-trained students at each desk and address new processes. After the initial implementation, training was never fully reviewed to provide a complete start-to-finish program. Experienced students mentored their peers, but as they graduated that on-the-job teaching shifted back to the busy full-time staff. Everything came to a head when, during the summer and fall term of 2014, the helpdesk was down a staff member, and the department was facing a variety of campus-wide issues that generated a high volume of calls and support requests.

In that situation, the helpdesk could not keep up with competing and changing high-volume needs while also providing holistic training to the students. As a result, students at the helpdesk learned enough to answer a call and transfer it to a supervisor, and ended the fall term of 2014 inexperienced and disengaged.

In December 2014, Carleton hired a new staff member to balance workloads, reduce outstanding tickets, and design a training program for student technicians. In the pursuit of these objectives, independent student project work surfaced as a means of using the abundance of student time to help solve these problems. The resulting project structure was based on student-led projects that emerged during the helpdesk combination and modified to address the short-term stresses on the helpdesk. It is now formalized into a reusable template which has since been utilized for approximately a dozen projects over two years.

2 CONSTRAINTS

The need for independent student project work was not the obvious conclusion to address the ticket backlog and training needs. However, the problems presented by those issues, combined with the constraints within which they needed to be solved set up the perfect opportunity to incorporate independent work for our CarlTechs. In this way, identifying limitations helped clarify the central issues and questions the helpdesk faced and paved the way for effective solutions.

2.1 Imbalanced Workload

A large majority of Carleton support calls come from staff and faculty. By comparison, a small portion of the overall helpdesk staff fielded those calls. In addition to answering the phones, primaries performed in-depth troubleshooting and issue resolution, especially as experienced students graduated. In this structure, 4-5% of available helpdesk personnel were responsible for the majority of the requests.

The initial problem voiced by Carleton's staff and faculty was alleviated - they found their initial experiences at the helpdesk to be more satisfying[2], but the overall structure was unsustainable, with overtaxed staff and under-engaged students.

The issue came to a head when the open ticket count spiked in Fall of 2014, which prompted the initial question: how can we better prepare and utilize students to avoid the workload imbalance and prevent renewed frustrations with slow or delayed support at the helpdesk?

2.2 Project Time Allocation

The skewed daily workload compounded another problem the helpdesk faced. Major projects, whether known recurring projects such as the annual hardware and software maintenance and upgrades, or one-time projects like migrating the campus to a new email and calendar system, involve helpdesk primaries as project managers or team members. The time and energy invested in executing these extensive projects meant that smaller side projects fell by the wayside year after year, even if those projects would ultimately improve the functionality of the helpdesk.

As a result, another question evolved: if these side projects will alleviate pressures at the helpdesk, how can we invest enough time in them for them to be successful, without derailing daily operations or major projects?

2.3 Underprepared Student Techs

In the aforementioned constraints, better utilizing our CarlTech population seemed the logical response. However, the techs were unprepared, and adequately training them and finding ways to engage them meaningfully required lots of time. The feedback loop these circumstances seemingly create is one of the biggest obstacles to overcome. Students must be properly trained and engaged in order to manage daily operations and project work, but until they are, it is hard to get enough time to develop the very projects and training that would allow the students to provide meaningful help. The early stages of developing project structures for our student techs were driven by these constraints as a means of escaping this feedback loop.

3 EARLY PROJECT STRUCTURES

Two main situations served as catalysts for developing project infrastructures for independent student work. Though each case led to slightly different project environments at the time, both were significant enough to justify taking time out of daily operations and have since informed the current model of project work at the Carleton helpdesk.

3.1 Combination of Helpdesks

One of the major impacts of the helpdesk combination in 2011 was the reduction of staffing, from three staff who had overseen the two separate locations, to two supervising the joint location. This decrease was concurrent with bringing a new technologically-rich building and remote support location online. The high volume of routine work, along with defining a new combined helpdesk

structure was simply too much for the staff members to take on alone.

Our students at the time were highly trained, but before we could offload some of that work to our student techs, they needed clear expectations and enough information to move their projects forward independently. We identified all the critical tasks to accomplish before the combined helpdesk came online, and then roughly arranged into cohesive groups which we assigned to individual students as their primary project.

Each student tech received a brief writeup of their grouped tasks, summarized in Table 1, along with a verbal description of expectations for leading their own projects and supporting their coworkers. Each student was designated as the lead for one particular project. They were tasked with developing an overall timeline and making sure they were prepared to get past roadblocks. They were also designated as a co-lead on another project and were expected to collaborate with that project lead. Other than that generalized structure, the project was left up to the students to execute. At the end of the break they wrote a project summary of the work they completed and where that work was located.

Though informal, this simple structure met the immediate needs of the combined helpdesk. Table 1 also includes a brief note of the final status of the project for reference. In many cases, the students completed the most critical elements of a project, but even if they outlined follow-up work for their project, it did not happen.

One of the greatest lessons learned was that in an urgent situation such as the imminent helpdesk combination, the simple project plan was streamlined enough that we could implement it quickly, but to ensure a functional transition between project work and ongoing maintenance, or from one student project manager to another, a more detailed plan was necessary.

3.2 Helpdesk Ticket Backlog

The accidental "alpha" version of student projects from the helpdesk consolidation informed the response to the next "situationally motivated" project structure for our CarlTechs. As described in the background section of this paper, summer and fall of 2014 saw an unusually high level of service requests and a backlog of requests accrued due to understaffing. When the new hire was brought on, fully staffing the helpdesk, the charge of addressing tickets was the first project assigned.

With the imbalanced staff-to-student workload ratio, it was clear that investing time to utilize the CarlTechs would be one of the best ways to distribute ticket processing across available resources. However, training was outdated or did not exist, so any ticket review structure had to minimize decisions on the part of the CarlTechs that would rely on training. After analyzing over 400 open tickets, a few categories emerged that lent themselves to a flow-chart style set of questions and actions. With this chart and a set of scripts and templates, both veteran and novice CarlTechs could analyze and process tickets quickly and consistently.

An example of one of the question flows is shown in Figure 1. Once a tech identified the state of a ticket, they referenced a related template or phone script, reached out to the client, and moved the issue forward. In addition to the documentation provided, techs were encouraged to collaborate and brainstorming when analyzing

---

[2] As measured by a drop in documented feedback, and a trend which has continued to improve marginally as measured by our 2016 and 2014 participation in the MISO survey, http://www.misosurvey.org/

Project Name	Description	Outcome Notes
Helpdesk Combination Management	- Identify shared and new processes - Define communication plan - Find and update posted information	Wide array of combination changes identified, vital changes made, plans for further changes after project stalled.
Documentation Update	- Review all documentation - Flag for deletion or update - Complete Documentation Updates	The cataloging of information was successful, and updates ended up being about 80% complete at the end of the project. Continued updates stagnated.
Training Development	- Review existing separate training - Reuse shared training - Write new training plan	The project successfully identified overlap for re-use, and developed cross-training materials. Planning for maintenance did not occur and there was not enough time to write generalized combined training.
Network Consultant (NetCon)	- Learn from existing NetCon - Install new WiFi Access Points (APs) - Update NetCon Documentation	Installation of WiFi APs was complete and successful. Documentation did not get revised and NetCon program dissolved in first term of combined helpdesk.
Drop-Off Consultants (DOCs)	- Learn from existing DOCs and staff - Repair all student drop-off computers - Update DOC Documentation	Students were able to drop-off personal computers for repair which were returned in a timely manner. New DOCs learned proper procedures and techniques and basic training and on-boarding was developed for additional DOCs going forward.
Summer Lab Management	- Clean all public lab computers - Carry out lab updates and replacements - Update lab status documentation	Summer lab maintenance was completed successfully and on-time using existing practices.

Table 1: List of projects assigned during helpdesk combinations, with brief outline of major tasks and a summary of overall outcome.

a ticket state. The flow-chart and scripts allowed all CarlTechs to independently advance client issues and support from peers reduced the need for significant staff oversight.

This approach proved tremendously successful as it allowed more tickets to be reviewed in a much shorter time span. The CarlTechs quickly identified and consolidated duplicate tickets and culled tickets from the queue that were already done but had not yet been closed. In just over five months, we reduced our open ticket backlog by 92% to 34 open tickets. Offloading ticket analysis to our techs accomplished two related goals: staff time was freed up, allowing them to focus on solving more complex issues; and CarlTechs received exposure to a wide range of troubleshooting scenarios which provided hands-on training. The ticket project immediately increased student engagement at work and laid the foundation for the development of more detailed and complex project work.

4 REQUIRED FOUNDATIONAL ELEMENTS

These previous project iterations provided valuable insights when implementing more project-based work for our student CarlTechs. In reviewing these structures, a few key elements surfaced as being important for long-term project success.

4.1 Training

A basic level of training allows student techs to feel comfortable working independently on projects. However, training can be incorporated into the structure of a project if that foundation does not already exist.

For the projects that emerged from the helpdesk combination, the students from each desk had training and experience at the separate desk locations. They were able to bring that information to the table and share it with each other to bridge gaps in their knowledge. This background provided experience in making informed decisions on support topics they might address in the joint environment and confidence in using shared resources to figure out how to solve novel problems that arose.

As a direct contrast, in the ticket review project, the students explicitly did not have training on the technical content of ticket resolution. They had basic customer service information and knew how to use the ticketing system. The project correspondingly used those existing skills as a tool for rapid assessment and categorization of ticket states. Doing so removed the uncertainty and pressure of trying to solve problems without training and instead focused student effort on an approachable but essential task.

An important takeaway is that student techs do not need to be experts in an environment, or have comprehensive training before beginning a project. However, they do need to be confident in their ability to contribute meaningfully to the project. If they do not have extensive training or experience as a foundation for that confidence, then the project must be much more precisely articulated, with clear and limited tasks and options. In this way, the project structure provides the decision-making ability that experience eventually teaches.

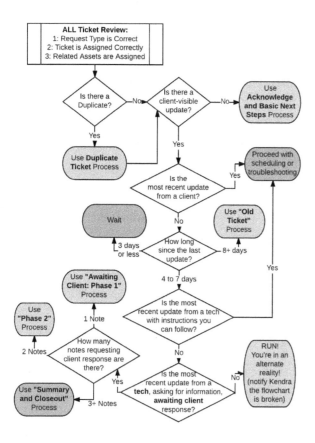

Figure 1: This is a condensed and simplified version of the flowchart given to CarlTechs to assist with ticket analysis. The goal was to have very clearly defined cases that untrained techs could identify. It was partnered with external documentation which included specific action details and scripts for the specified processes. ©Kendra Strode

4.2 Preparation Time

Regardless of specific details for a particular project, it is necessary to take the time to develop a clear framework for project management with student techs in mind. Some student staff at Carleton are working at the helpdesk as their first job, few have extensive experience in tech support, and fewer still have had the opportunity to manage a work project. However, most of them can draw on project experience from coursework. Taking enough time to provide a clear framework, set expectations and develop a support structure before initiating a project enables the students to transfer their coursework experience into professional project management techniques.

In addition to facilitating the work by the student techs, a predictable structure yields consistent project results. Some projects are large and complex, requiring work and review over time. In these situations, a student may take on a project previously managed by another tech who has graduated. When documentation

and project management practices are consistent, anybody can efficiently pick up a project where a predecessor left off, reducing the time needed to get up to speed or re-create solutions to problems.

The early independent projects at Carleton were minimally structured and reactionary in nature, so the end results were highly varied and did not transfer well to continued work. It was necessary to invest more time to define a generalized template for preparing projects for students.

4.3 Support and Trust

This final element is the least concrete but arguably the most crucial to student success. For students to work independently, you have to support them in their efforts while trusting them to find the best solution to the problem they have been assigned.

Establishing this trust has become so central to our current project structure that it is explicitly discussed with students as they take on their assignments. Their scope document emphasizes that they are responsible for their project, and outlines the impact of their work on the helpdesk and department. The framework details project documentation and communication requirements, but beyond that, CarlTechs are allowed to use any tools available to them to document, update, and complete their projects. Students are trusted to make decisions that are best for them and their project, with the support of the project structure to guide those choices.

This trust requires supervisors to respect the diversity of choices their techs might make, and serve in a mentoring role. Problems with the project will undoubtedly arise, and it is important that supervisors refrain from stepping in and solving things directly, except in urgent situations. Instead, with regular communication and feedback, supervisors can help identify issues, and suggest resources and potential courses of action for the student to pursue. They should also ask students to reflect on and develop strategies to avoid similar issues in the future. By doing this, students continue to hone their project management skills and the delegation of the work is maintained.

5 MODERN PROJECT STRUCTURE

After initial trials of project work for students, we have refined the overall implementation and are going into our third cycle of students managing their independent projects.

The current structure consists of a general project management document which defines roles and required project elements, and accompanies an individualized project definition document for the designated lead of each project. The components in each document are described below[3].

5.1 General Documentation: Roles

The project lead is expected to run the project throughout the designated time period, typically a summer or winter break. They break the project down into smaller milestones and tasks to establish a timeline, regularly review and update those tasks and any project documentation, and coordinate conversation with their peers and the helpdesk staff. During a given period a student will typically be the lead for one project.

---

[3]Full sample documents can be found in the zipped file at https://tinyurl.com/SIGUCCS17-FosterIndependence

The project secondary is expected to know the general status of the project and help review and assess the timeline against the project scope. They should be available to touch base and brainstorm with the project lead and to help make sure all documentation is clear and understandable. Project secondaries also need to be ready to complete project tasks temporarily when the lead is out sick or on vacation.

The project backup has minimal ongoing responsibility for the project, but if the lead or secondary has a scheduled vacation, then in the time leading up to that departure, the backup is brought up-to-speed on the project and should be available to assist with any defined tasks during the project member's absence.

5.2 General Documentation: Project Elements

While the documentation does not go into specific details regarding how projects should be carried out, it does outline elements the CarlTechs must incorporate when structuring their project.

A project timeline is required, and the lead is expected to review the project definition to identify milestones and set anticipated deadlines. However, they are encouraged to think proactively about how they would adjust the schedule to handle external delays or accommodate new information learned in the course of pursuing the project. While they must define this timeline somewhere, there is no restriction on how they accomplish this and can use calendaring, note taking or available project management tools.

Project leads must also determine how they will provide updates to their staff mentor. They need to keep written records of project progress and must meet in-person at least every other week to discuss progress and problems. Meeting often allows students to raise and resolve roadblocks quickly, avoiding delays that could hinder project completion.

The final element required of each lead is a resource guide. Because they are allowed to use tools that work best for them, leads must document the location of all components of their project. Though some projects may have more extensive materials, the following elements must be identified: timeline, task list, files and folders, and the closing summary - a document they produce at the end of the project that outlines the state of all goals of the project.

5.3 Project-specific Definition Documentation

In addition to the general project management information, students receive a document specifically tailored to their project. Using a template significantly speeds up the development of these materials.

The project definition includes primary goals to complete for the project to be considered successful at the end of the break. When identifying these, it is helpful to use some evaluation structure, such as the S.M.A.R.T.[4] technique or a rubric. Most projects end up having two to four primary goals.

There are secondary goals for each project as well. A secondary goal may complement or coincide with primary goals but does not need to be completed for the project to be considered successful. These are included to help address the natural ebb and flow of work

pacing during breaks; for example, it is possible that a major project element requires input from a staff member who is on vacation, so having secondary goals helps preemptively answer questions about what else is available to do. The list of secondary goals tends to be only one or two items if the project is weighted toward primary goals, but can include up to five or six objectives.

After goals, there is a section identifying account access and permissions the techs may need. Known existing documentation is listed, along with additional possible materials, so the student can explore and aggregate all relevant information. This section was added to make these proactive tasks to complete, rather than reactive issues to resolve. This has allowed projects to be up and running smoothly within days, rather stalling off and on for up to a week or two.

Finally, each project definition includes a brief list of relevant dates and deadlines. Many important dates, such as the first day of classes, are the same across concurrent projects. However, some individualized dates may be incorporated to account for inter-dependencies of projects or campus events, such as reunion or a trustee meeting, that only affect a particular project.

6 BENEFITS

Incorporating students in projects has greatly improved the functionality and work culture of the helpdesk and the department. Short-term issues have faster resolution, long-term issues do not stagnate as often, and the CarlTechs proactively address issues they notice without needing prompting. There are further benefits as well, in line with the mission of the College and the Strategic Plan goal to better prepare students practically for life after Carleton[1].

Jonathan Ahn graduated in 2014 as a Studio Art and Computer Science double major, and was in the first cohort to do independent project work. As such he is the only graduate, and offered this reflection on the real-world impact of these projects:

> One might feel the types of project work you're assigned at ITS do not closely resemble the types of projects and assignments one gets to do in an academic setting, especially because the scope and direction of projects at ITS were mostly self-initiated and negotiated with full-time ITS staff versus the regular school assignments where you're often assigned the clear scope, goal and team members of the project.
>
> I didn't fully realize the value of self-initiated project management and development works I did at ITS until I got my first real job after Carleton—the facts that I had prior project management and client-interaction experiences definitely gave me a leg up over other new graduates when I first started. Now I am working as a transportation planner and consultant at an engineering consulting firm, managing and developing similar types of projects I dealt with at Carleton ITS. The only difference is that I manage about four projects simultaneously instead of one.

---

[4]"S.M.A.R.T." is a goal-setting technique that stands for "Specific, Measurable, Assignable, Realistic, and Time-related" as concepts to keep in mind when creating objectives for oneself or for employees.[2]

JordiKai Watanabe-Inouye, a 2017 Computer Science major, describes her project and how it helped not only future CarlTechs, but also improved her own expertise as well:

> Over winter break, I revamped the content of the Networking training for our CarlTechs. This training series acts as a reference and supplement to the visits from ITS's Network Admin. This training provides a basic understanding of networking terminology and demystifies many rumors and preconceived notions of wireless. I went into this project knowing who to contact and what questions to ask, but not what any of the answers were. This role allowed me to walk away knowing much more than I ever would about Carleton's network infrastructure- wishing this training was available for me when I first started 4 years ago.

Martin Hoffman, a 2019 Computer Science major, was assigned the project of reviewing our ticketing system to evaluate how well it was working at the helpdesk and propose potential changes. He shares how the project structure helped make a large task more manageable:

> This was certainly a large project for a freshman to take on, but Kendra made it clear that I wasn't expected to actually solve many problems directly. Rather, my goal was simply to diagnose our current system and make the first step towards understanding what a new or updated ticketing solution would require. By keeping the goals manageable and providing a whole lot of support, I felt pretty successful by the end of the summer.

Sacha Greenfield is a 2019 physics major and was assigned to work on a document review project as we migrated from Zimbra to Gmail as our email provider. Her feedback highlights how the project helped her improve both her work at the helpdesk and also has informed how she addresses project-based work in academic and research settings:

> This project gave me a greater sense of focus in all of my other work that winter and provided many learning opportunities. Sifting through documentation exposed me to the wide array of troubleshooting we do at the Helpdesk, prompting many interesting conversations with fellow Helpdesk workers that expanded my knowledge of the technology we support. Rewriting sentences and sections of wiki pages made me think about what makes good, clear documentation, and reaching out to people throughout ITS to get guidance for updating wiki pages helped me get to know the department.
>
> Outside of my work at ITS, the project work helped me think about time management as a balancing of more "urgent" tasks with slower-moving, but more rewarding, long-term projects. It has also served as a constant reminder that

seeking support is the best way to move any project forward, be it a difficult assignment, studying for a test, or even research. Finally, it has taught me that first-hand exposure is the best (and perhaps only) way to learn, which has made me more proactive in seeking the answers to my questions.

7 CONCLUSION

Given the high demand and cyclical nature of work in higher-ed helpdesks, it can be difficult to prioritize time to work on project infrastructure rather than working on projects directly. However the long-term benefits that come with student project management quickly justify the efforts.

The student responses, in particular, highlight how these projects directly change the feedback loop from a detrimental one that reinforces student isolation, to an enriching cycle that benefits all parties. Students who have worked independently continue to be more engaged in general helpdesk work. They informally serve as mentors to less experienced techs so the new techs receive more one-on-one support than the primary staff members can provide. As a result, the new students are more engaged and have more experience than peers who previously completed the same exact training sequence. Finally, techs often benefit directly from the results of their project work that would otherwise go uncompleted, and the helpdesk makes improvements more dynamically by utilizing the capabilities of the student techs we employ.

A PROJECT SUMMARIES

Below is a short summary of all student managed projects not detailed elsewhere in the project.

Training Development

2016 Summer, 2016 Winter, 2017 Summer
The most significant ongoing project, each break focuses on developing or finishing training modules on a wide range of content from network infrastructure, to software systems, to departmental staff roles and introductions. The project work to date has generated two online training modules, two in-person workshops and the foundation for two additional modules. The projects also include review of already-existing training and documentation.

Ticketing Review

2016 Summer, 2016 Winter
This project spanned two project periods, and involved continual review and updating of tickets as described in the paper. However this project also involved an in-depth assessment of the current structure of our ticketing system and proposed changes that would improve ticket management within the helpdesk. Additionally the ticket processing flow-chart originally developed to handle the high backlog of old tickets was updated to a modern process to address incoming and current tickets.

Documentation Review

2016 Winter, 2016 Spring, 2017 Summer
After campus migrations to Gmail, Google Calendar, Drive and

Dropbox, a lot of documentation was out-of-date, referencing old systems and no-longer-advised best practices. This ongoing project identified and catalogued all references to these obsolete systems and categorized the necessary work to update the page or article. This work included simple changes such as updating the names of systems and finding external help resources to link to, as well as more in-depth work creating new documentation for Carleton-specific processes.

Helpdesk Operations

2017 Summer

There are two central goals for this project: first, creating a quick-access printed reference book for vital helpdesk tasks that we need access to even if our online knowledge base is unavailable, and second, developing an Emergency Plan for responding to a variety of natural, campus, or departmental emergencies.

Small Independent Project Development

2017 Summer

This is a partner project to the 2017 Documentation Review project. There are often small tasks to be completed that crop up during the year, such as creating a poster for student outreach, or self-service information for a common question. These are small enough they do not get prioritized in projects, but because they are small they provide a good opportunity for newer techs to do more advanced, short-term work at the helpdesk. This project will create an infrastructure to support submission, claiming, and documentation of these Small Independent Projects, or "SIPs" and will populate it with initial ideas.

Checkout Center Overhaul

2017 Summer

Our checkout center, Web Checkout, needs a full inventory and policy update. Additionally quick-reference materials for checking out and returning equipment needs to be created. This project will review and re-structure all the checkout center policies and permissions for equipment and techs and create the training.

Video and Media Outreach

2017 Summer

The student computing helpdesk had an introductory video that served as outreach to the student population, and an introduction to the helpdesk for the technicians. No similar introduction video has been created for the combined helpdesk. This project will create that video, in addition to other short training videos for select tasks such as printer maintenance or copying. They will also produce videos introducing the teams within ITS and describe how they work for both internal and external use.

ACKNOWLEDGMENTS

The author would like to thank her offical reader, Rachel Weaver, from Macalester College, as well as her other editors, Austin Robinson-Coolidge from Carleton, and her mother Lisa Strode, for the valuable feedback. For their unending daily support she cannot thank her colleagues at the Carleton ITS helpdesk enough: R. Kevin Chapman and Travis Freudenberg.

REFERENCES

[1] Carleton College 2012. *Carleton's Future: A Strategic Plan for the College 2012.* Carleton College. Retrieved from https://apps.carleton.edu/strategic/assets/ FINAL___Strategic_Planning_Synthesis.pdf on 16 June 2017.

[2] G.T. Doran. 1981. There's a S.M.A.R.T. Way to Write Management's Goals and Objectives. *Management Review* 70 (November 1981), 35–36.

Monitoring Servers, With a Little Help from my Bots

Takashi Yamanoue
Fukuyama University
Sanzo, 1, Gakuen-cho
Fukuyama, Hiroshima, 729-0292
yamanoue@fukuyama-u.ac.jp

ABSTRACT

This paper discusses a method of employing bots instead of people to monitor servers or server rooms. A bot is a remote controlled computer or a remote controlled program. A bot is usually a malicious program which is an element of a botnet. A botnet is used for doing malicious things such as spreading spam mails or doing DDoS Attacks. We have made bots and we are using bots for doing beneficial things such as monitoring a server instead of doing malicious things. We are monitoring a web server in our campus using a bot. This bot is tweeting whether the server is running or not periodically on the twitter. We are also monitoring a server room in our campus using another bot. This bot shows managers transition of the room temperature and others.

CCS CONCEPTS

• **Social and professional topics → Professional topics → Management of computing and information systems → System management** → *Centralization / decentralization, Network operations*

KEYWORDS

Bot, Monitoring, Management, Twitter, Wiki, Raspberry Pi.g

1 INTRODUCTION

Information and Communication Technology (ICT) infrastructure managers of universities are always monitoring many servers and server rooms in their campus[2][3]. Monitoring a server or a server room seems easy work for people who have never worked at an ICT administration department. However, we know, it is hard work. If we failed to identify potential trouble with a server or server room, or if we could not cope with the trouble, users can't do their business. It could also cause a serious trouble such as a fire in a building.

SIGUCCS 2017, October 1-4, 2017, Seattle, WA, USA
© 2017 Association for Computing Machinery.
ACM ISBN 978-1-4503-4919-2/17/10. . . $15.00
https://doi.org/DOI: 10.1145/3123458.3123461

No one is perfect, so an ICT infrastructure manager could potentially fail to identify trouble with a server or the server room. So managers are using various ways to identify trouble in advance.

As a way of monitoring servers or server rooms, we show a way of employing bots instead of employing people to monitor servers or server rooms. A bot is a remote-controlled computer or a remote-controlled program. A bot is usually a malicious program which is an element of a botnet[1]. We use the bot for beneficial things[4][5][6][7].

We are monitoring a Web server in our campus using a bot. This bot is tweeting whether the server is running or not periodically on Twitter. We are also monitoring a server room in our campus using another bot. This bot shows managers changes in the room temperature and the room brightness. These bots are doing a good job.

Our monitoring way is an Internet of Things (IoT) because bots of the way are not operated by a person directly and they are connected to the Internet.

Figure 1: A scene of the computer ethics video clips.

2 TROUBLES WITHOUT MY BOTS

2.1 A Server Trouble

We are using computer ethics video clips for enhancing cyber security of our campus (Figure 1)[8][9]. The video clips were installed in a Web server of our campus and we can't access the Web server from the outside of our campus because of the license of the video clips.

The video clips are used in the classes of the author and other faculties in out campus. The Web server is maintained by the author.

When the author went to overseas business trip, the author received a mail from a faculty member of our university, which told the author that the Web server was down and asked the author to cope with the situation.

At that time, the author forgot to confirm that the Web server is working or not. Even if the author remembers that the author should confirm that the server is working or not, every day, the author could not confirm the Web server because the author was not in the campus.

After all, the author asked his students to cope with the situation.

2.2 A Server Room Trouble

There was air conditioner problem in a server room in our campus. The air conditioner malfunctioned during the weekend and no one could notice this trouble until a Monday class, which uses PCs in a computer laboratory. Servers in the server room also malfunctioned because of the high temperature in the room. There could be a fire in the room if there had been a longer delay in noticing the problem.

As a result of the server malfunctions, we could not use the computer laboratories at that time, because PCs use the Active Directory servers and file servers in the server room.

A server room usually has no window and no one in the server room except when someone maintains servers. So, it is hard to know server room conditions from the outside without using appropriate tools.

There are commercial services for monitoring a server from outside. These services usually require installing a monitoring program in the server. However, it is hard to install such programs in a server which is not a property of our university.

We have called the maintenance company of the air conditioner and another maintenance company of the servers at that time. Fortunately, they fixed the trouble in a few days.

3 WHAT ARE MY BOTS

We are using bots for doing beneficial things such as to cope with such troubles in the section two instead of doing malicious things. Some bots are Raspberry PIs with the bot software. Others are android smart phones with sensors and the bot software. These bots are controlled by commands and programs in Wiki pages of web servers. Managers can control bots in a LAN, which is protected from the outside by NAT routers, from the outside of the LAN, by writing commands and programs in Wiki pages of web servers which is located at the outside of the LAN or which can be accessed from the outside of the LAN.

When a server was connected to a campus LAN, which cannot be accessed from the Internet directly, it is impossible to monitor the server from the outside of the campus directly. However, the ability to monitor the server from outside of campus would be convenient for times the manager is not on campus. A bot can help the manager to monitor the server in such cases. A server room is usually isolated from outside and there is no one in the server room. A bot also can help the manager to monitor the server room. There may be a server which is maintained by a third party company and the manager cannot install monitoring software into the server. A bot can help the manager to monitor the server in such cases.

Figure. 2 shows the behavior of our bot. The bot repeats the following.

1) Wait for a moment.

2) Read commands and a program from the Wiki page from the specific Wiki site which is assigned to the bot.

3) Execute these commands and the program. The program can read other Wiki pages and Web pages. The program can read tweets from Twitter and can tweet on Twitter. If the bot has sensors, it also can read data from the sensors. If the bot has actuators, it can send data to the actuators.

4) Write results of the execution to the send buffer. Data in the send buffer are written back to the Wiki page which contains the commands and the program.

The series of commands on the wiki page is read and interpreted when the page has it. If a program is embedded in the series of commands, then the program is transferred to the language processor of the bot. The program is translated into its internal representation. The internal representation of the program is evaluated by the interpreter.

Figure 3 shows an example of a program which is embedded in a series of commands. In this example, lines which start with "command:" are the commands. The first line,

command: set readInterval=3600000

shows that the mobile terminal reads the page of the given URL every one hour after that. The right hand side of the equation shows the interval time in milliseconds. Lines which start with "program:" are lines of the program. A program is enclosed by the following two command lines. In this example, the program is named "ex" by these lines.

command: program ex

command: end ex

The last command line,

command: run ex

shows that the program "ex" is translated into its internal representation and executed after that when this command line is interpreted. Figure 4 shows the output of the program.

A Wiki page for the bot also can contain the "set pageName" command and the "include" command. When the "set pageName" command is interpreted in the bot, the bot will use the Wiki page which is designated by the set pageName command, as the main Wiki page, next time. The page name of the designated Wiki page can include the current time or the current date. For example, when the following command was interpreted at the time of eight o'clock, the bot use the page of "pir-1-8", in the same Wiki server of the current Wiki page, as the main Wiki page, next time.

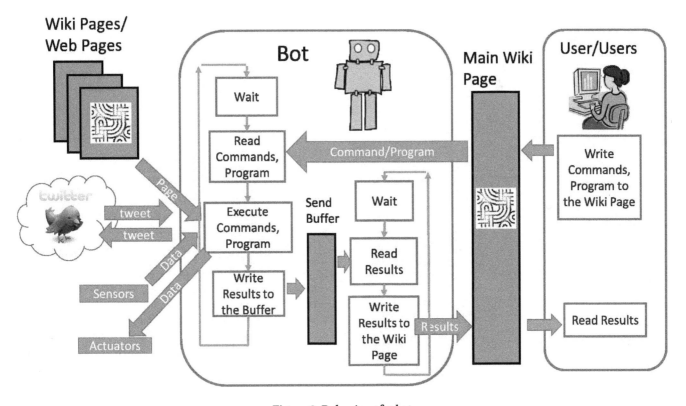

Figure 2: Behavior of a bot.

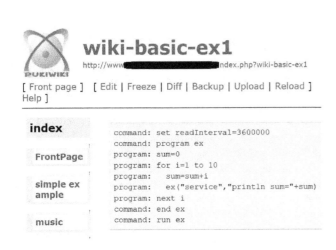

Figure 3: Example of a program which is embedded in a series of commands.

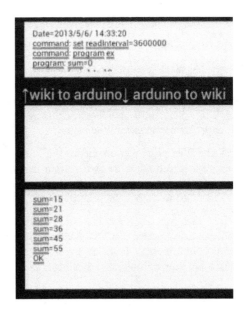

Figure 4: The output of the program of Figure 6.

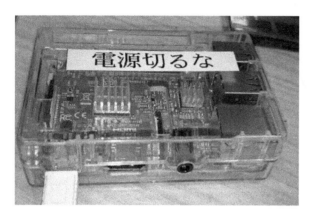

Figure 5: RPi-Bot, Raspberry Pi with the bot program.

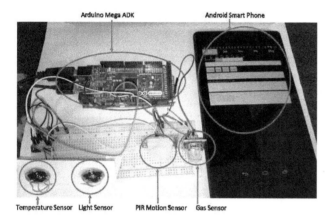

Figure 6: ADK-Bot, Android smartphone with the bot program which is equipped with an Arduino board with sensors.

set pageName="pir-1-<hour>"

When the "include" command is interpreted in the bot, the bot insert the Wiki page, which is designated by the include command, into the place at the include command of the original Wiki page. This command is useful when there are identical commands or program in many of Wiki pages.

We call the Wiki page, which contains the commands, the program, and data which are write backed from the bot, as the main Wiki page. Commands and the program of the main Wiki page can be modified to change the behavior of the bot without stopping the bot.

The bot can be connected to a LAN which is protected by a router with the NAT or NAPT function. The manager of the bot can control the bot from the outside of the LAN.

We have developed two kinds of bots. One kind of them is *RPi-Bot*, a Raspberry Pi with the bot program for the Raspberry Pi (Figure 5), and another kind of them is *ADK-Bot*, an android smartphone with the bot program for the android, which is equipped with an Arduino board with sensors (Figure 6). ADK-Bot has a temperature sensor, a light sensor, a PIR motion sensor

and a Gas sensor. The PIR motion sensor detects whether a person is near the sensor or not. The Gas sensor detects the air pollution level.

4 EMPLOYMENT OF MY BOTS

We have made two kinds of monitoring system by employing two kinds of bots. One kind of the monitoring system is the Web server monitoring system which monitors whether the Web server is running or not. Another kind of the monitoring system is the server room monitoring system which monitors the transition of temperature and other environmental factors in a server room.

4.1 Web Server Monitoring System

The Web server monitoring system consists of a RPi-Bot, A Wiki page of PukiWiki software and Twitter (Figure 7). The system monitors our Web server which contains the computer ethics video clips. The bot is located in the campus LAN in order to see the status of the Web server which can not seen from the outside of the LAN. The bot repeats to read the Wiki page which contains the program for monitoring the Web server, and to execute the program. The bot monitors whether the Web server is running or not, and reports the status of the Web server to managers by tweeting on Twitter directed by the program.

Figure 8 shows the main Wiki page for the RPi-Bot of the Web server monitoring system. This page includes the program for the RPi-Bot. The program do the followings

1. Tries to read the Web page of the Web server.
2. If the Bot could not read the page, tweet the following.

   "rinri down <hour:min>"
3. If the Bot could read the page, tweet the following.

   "rinri up <hour:min>"

4.2 Server Room Monitoring System

The server room monitoring system consists of a ADK-Bot, a RPi-Bot, 24 Wiki pages for for each hour in a day (H-WIKIs), 31 Wiki pages for each day in a month (D-WIKIs), and the class page. The ADK-Bot is placed in the server room for monitoring the environmental factors of the room. The ADK-Bot reads the H-WIKI which is corresponding to the current time, interprets the commands in the page, and writes back the current data of temperature and others to the H-WIKI. The class page is inserted into the D-WIKI of the current day. The class page contains the program which computes the average of data of every H-WIKI and writes back the results to the D-WIKI of the current day (Figure 9).

H-WIKIs and D-WIKIs have the link to a page which displays graphs of data in H-WIKIs and D-WIKIs. The manager can see the transitions of each item of data, such as the transition of temperature of the room.

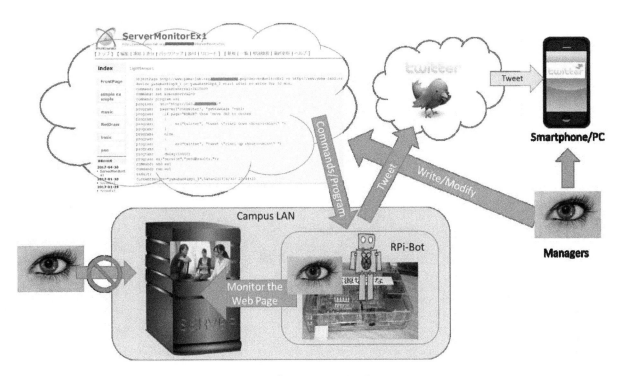

Figure 7: Web server monitoring system

ServerMonitorEx1

http://www.yama-lab.org/?ServerMonitorEx1

[トップ] 　[編集 | 凍結 | 差分 | バックアップ | 添付 | リロード] 　[新規 | 一覧 | 単語検索 | 最終更新 | ヘルプ]

---

index

FrontPage

simple ex ample

music

NetDraw

basic

pen

最新の20件

2017-04-30
• ServerMonitorE x1
2017-01-30
• SerialEx2
2017-01-29
• SerialEx1

LightSensor1

```
objectPage http://www.yama-lab.org/.php?ServerMonitorEx1 or http://www.yama-lab2.or
device yamaRasPiDp9_1 or yamaRasPiDp9_2 start after no write for 10 min.
command: set readInterval=3600000
command: set execInterval=0
command: program ex1
program:    url="http://163./"
program:    page=ex("connector", "getRawPage "+url)
program:       if page="ERROR" then 'move ch0 to center
program:       {
program:            ex("twitter", "tweet \"rinri down <hour>:<min>\" ")
program:       }
program:       else
program:       {
program:            ex("twitter", "tweet \"rinri up <hour>:<min>\" ")
program:       }
program:    delay(10000)
program: ex("service","sendResults.");
command: end ex1
command: run ex1
result:
currentDevice="yamaRasPiDp1_1",Date=2017/4/30/ 23:44:21
```

Figure 8: The program of the Web server monitoring system.

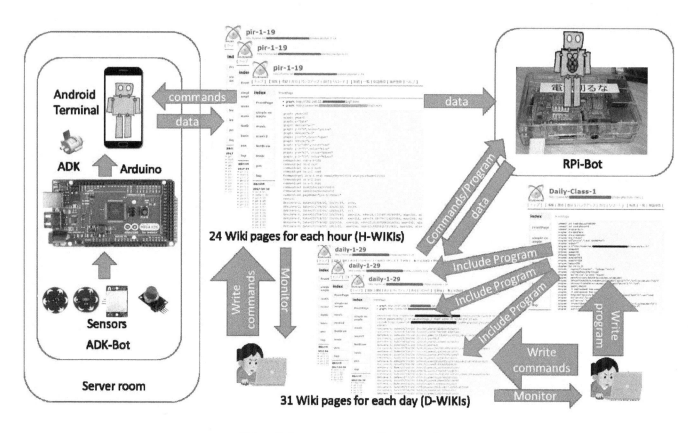

Figure 9: Server room monitoring system.

5 HELP FROM MY BOTS

We are using the Web server monitoring system for a half year and using the room server monitoring system for one and a half year. They are meeting our expectations.

Figure 10 shows the tweets which is tweeted by the RPi-Bot of the Web server monitoring system. The tweets alerted us that the Web server was down. We could see the Web server went down between 2:55 and 3:56 of March 18. It was a weekend and we were at home at that time. However, we went to the campus and fixed the problem.

Figure 11 and Figure 12 show the graphs of data in the server room. The graphs were generated by the server room monitoring system.

Figure 11 shows temperature, brightness, human motion and air pollution level in the server room during the day of April 27, 2017. The manager can see the graph by clicking the link to the graph page of the D-WIKI. On that date we can see that there was no temperature problem during the day. We believe someone entered the server room about noon because brightness of the room increased at that time. However, PIR-level, the

human motion level, did not increase at the same time. This means that someone did not come close to the ADK-Bot.

Figure 12 shows the graph of the H-WIKI which is corresponding to the hour that seems someone enter the server room of the day of Figure 8. The manager can know the detail time of the changes by seeing the D-Wiki page and the graph.

Fortunately, there was no air conditioner trouble after the deployment of the server room monitoring system, so we could not test that aspect of the system.

6 ALTERNATIVE MONITORING SOLUTIONS

6.1 Webalizer

Webalizer[10] is a fast, free web server log file analysis program. It is popular tool for visualizing usage of a Web server. Webalizer is installed in the Web server which is the target of the visualization. So, the manager can't see visualized usage of the server from the outside of the network if the server is not accessible from the outside. On the other hand, our monitoring system provides managers the ability to monitor the target server from the outside.

Figure 10: Tweets that show the Web server was down

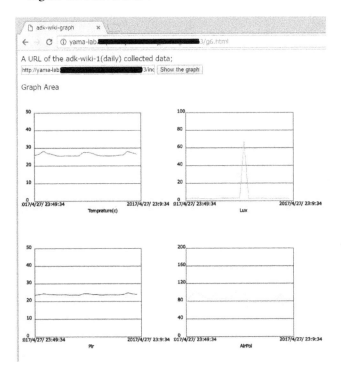

Figure 11: Transitions of temperature, brightness, human motion and air pollution level in the server room during the day of April 27, 2017.

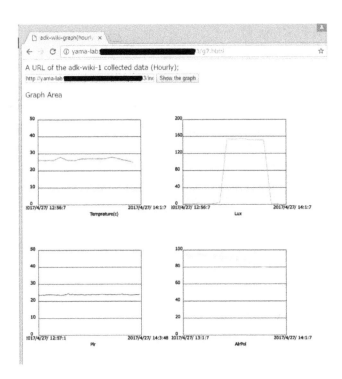

Figure 12: Transitions of temperature, brightness, human motion and air pollution level in the server room during the hour which seems someone enter the server room.

6.2 New Relic

New Relic[11] is a popular commercial server monitoring service. New Relic can monitor almost all servers whether they are accessible from outside the network or not. The user of the New Relic can monitor the data at the New Relic's Web server. However, the monitoring program for New Relic has to be installed in the target server. On the other hand, our monitoring system allows managers to monitor the target server without installing a program on the target server.

7 CONCLUSION

We have shown our monitoring method, which uses a little help from our bots. We have also shown our results from using these bot monitoring systems.

Our bots helped to enhance the reliability of the target server and the target server room. Our bots also helped reduce our work load and mental stress.

There are several opportunities to improve our monitoring method, such as enhancing the security and enhancing the reliability. We would like to report our progress next time.

ACKNOWLEDGMENTS

A part of this research was supported by JSPS KAKENHI Grant Number JP16K00197. We also thank students who helped us to develop monitoring systems.

REFERENCES

[1] Puri, R. 2003. Bots & Botnet: An Overview," SANS InfoSec Reading Room, http://www.sans.org/rr/whitepapers/malicious/, Dec., 2003.

[2] Masuya, M., Yamanoue, T., Kubota, S. 2006. An Experience of Monitoring University Network Security Using a Commercial Service and DIY Monitoring. In Proceedings of the 34th Annual ACM SIGUCCS Conference on User Services (Edmonton, Alberta, Canada. 5-8 Nov. 2006). ACM, New York, NY, 225-230. DOI=http://doi.acm.org/10.1145/1181216.1181267

[3] Mattauch, T., Hatoum, R., Pettit, H. 2012. Building a call center in 2 days: how a world class support center responds to crisis. In Proceedings of the 40th Annual ACM SIGUCCS Conference on User Services (Memphis, Tennessee, USA. 15-19 Oct. 2012). ACM, New York, NY, 97-100. DOI=http://doi.acm.org/10.1145/2382456.2382478

[4] Yamanoue, T., Oda, K., Shimozono. K. 2012. Capturing Malicious Bots using a Beneficial Bot and Wiki, In Proceedings of the 40th annual ACM SIGUCCS conference on User services (Memphis, Tennessee, USA. 15-19 Oct. 2012). ACM, New York, NY, 91-96. DOI=https://doi.org/10.1145/2382456.2382477

[5] Takashi Yamanoue, Kentaro Oda, Koichi Shimozono. A Malicious Bot Capturing System using a Beneficial Bot and Wiki, Journal of Information Processing(JIP), vol.21, No.2, pp.237-245(2013).

[6] Yamanoue, T., Oda, K., Shimozono. K. 2013. An Inter-Wiki Page Data Processor for a M2M System, In Proceedings of the 4th International Conference on E-Service and Knowledge Management (ESKM 2013), Advanced Applied Informatics (IIAIAAI), 2013 IIAI International Conference on.(Matsue, Shimane, Japan, 31 Aug- 4 Sep. 2013) IEEE, Los Alamitos, CA. 45-50. DOI= https://doi.org/10.1109/IIAI-AAI.2013.48

[7] Yamanoue, T., Oda, K., Shimozono. K. 2014. Experimental Implementation of a M2M System Controlled by a Wiki Network, In Applied Computing and Information Technology,Studies in Computational Intelligence, Springer, Vol.553, 121-136.

[8] Yamanoue, T., Fuse, I., Okabe, S., Nakamura, A., Nakanishi, M., Fukada, S., Tagawa, T., Tatsumi, T., Murata, I, Uehara, T., Yamada, T., Ueda, H. 2014. Computer Ethics Video Clips for University Students in Japan from 2003 until 2013, In Proceedings of the 38th Annual International Computer Software & Applications Conference (COMPSAC2013/ADMNET WS) , (Västerås, Sweden, 21-25 Jul. 2014). IEEE, NJ, 96-101.

[9] Yamanoue, T., Nakamichi, N., Kaneko, K., 2017. Enhancing Campus Cyber Security through a Class with Combination of Computer Ethics Videos and Logical Thinking. In SIGUCCS'16 Proceedings of the ACM on SIGUCCS Annual Conference (Denver, Colorado, USA, 6-9 Nov. 2016). ACM, New York, NY. 117-123. DOI=http://doi.acm.org/10.1145/2974927.2974939

[10] Webalizer, http://www.webalizer.org, as of 4 May, 2017

[11] New Relic,https://newrelic.com/, as of 4 May, 2017

Is Imaging Down?

Developing and Supporting a Large Scale Laptop Checkout Program

Sean Griffin
University of Wisconsin-Madison
1210 W. Dayton St
Madison, WI 53706, USA
sean.griffin@wisc.edu

Alex Davis
University of Wisconsin-Madison
1210 W. Dayton St
Madison, WI 53706, USA
alex.davis@wisc.edu

ABSTRACT[1]

The University of Wisconsin-Madison offers a free three-day laptop checkout service to students and staff. There are approximately 1,000 laptops available for checkout from any one of our eighteen campus locations which can be brought home free of charge; we are one of the largest and most generous laptop lending programs in the country.

The laptops we lend are laptops that as a standard configuration are dual-bootable, with both OS X and Windows installed. Additionally, the standard configuration also includes a limited number of free and campus licensed software. Laptops are cleaned between checkouts and reverted to a clean and consistent state with all extraneous files, history, and personal information removed. These laptops are expected to have patched and reasonably up to date operating systems and software for security and compatibility reasons. With a program of this size, keeping it running smoothly has, at times, proven difficult.

Maintaining this type of program presents service challenges. We require staff with varying experience levels to expend minimal effort on quickly and reliably cleaning, rebuilding, and updating two operating systems for up to 300 machines across campuses, daily. This paper provides a general overview of our laptop checkout program, discusses our current imaging workflow, and explores some of the decisions, challenges, and trade-offs we had to make to get us to where we are today.

---

[1] Produces the permission block, and copyright information

SIGUCCS '17, October 1–4, 2017, Seattle, WA, USA
© 2017 Association for Computing Machinery.
ACM ISBN 978-1-4503-4919-2/17/10...$15.00
https://doi.org/10.1145/3123458.3123476

KEYWORDS

Imaging; Mac, OS X; macOS; Windows; Dual-Boot; MDT; Microsoft Deployment Toolkit DeployStudio; Equipment Checkout; Laptops

1 INTRODUCTION

1.1 InfoLabs Overview

The University of Wisconsin-Madison offers a program called "InfoLabs" that provides hardware, software, and other technology resources to students so that they can meet their technology needs outside of the classroom. These InfoLabs are general access computer lab spaces spread across the campus and offer collaboration spaces, workstations, scanning services, printing services, and access to campus-licensed software. In addition to roughly 1,000 desktops, these InfoLabs also offer laptops and a variety of other hardware for checkout through a custom built Equipment Checkout System (ECS). Students have the opportunity to borrow and take home equipment, including laptops, for up to three days at a time, up to 20 times per semester, at no cost. There are currently about 1,000 laptops in total that are in circulation and they are used heavily. As a result, the InfoLabs are required to handle a combined total of about 5,000 checkouts per month.

1.2 InfoLab Operations

The InfoLab program is used to fund and coordinates items such as branding, software and hardware purchasing, pay-for-print services, and equipment check out. However, the libraries, residence halls, and academic departments hosting the physical InfoLab spaces are largely responsible for the staffing and day-to-day operations of these labs. Managing the InfoLab computers, particularly the laptop checkout system, presents a variety of challenges, which have led to a corresponding evolution of interesting solutions to meet these challenges. Presently, much of the administration of the InfoLab spaces is handled centrally by the UW-Madison Division of Information Technology (DoIT), but this was not always the case.

2 A BRIEF HISTORY OF IMAGING

2.1 The Wild West

2.1.1 Desktops. Prior to 2010, the InfoLab desktops were a mixture of single-boot Dell Optiplexes and Apple iMacs.

Separate images were created and maintained at each of the labs for each type of system. Master machines were manually set up and configured with all desired software, and then a thick image was pulled from the master machine and deployed to all of the other machines. Over the years, a number of different technologies were used to image and secure the machines; these included Carbon Copy Cloner, Radmind, and DeployStudio for OS X and PC-RDist, Ghost, Altiris, and Deep Freeze for Windows.

2.1.2 Laptops. The laptops available for checkout were managed in a fashion similar to the desktops, with each InfoLab again creating their own image. However, since we were transitioning from an exclusively Dell laptop environment to an environment with various models of Apple MacBook during 2006, two of the lab managers chose to collaborate. The collaboration resulted in creating a good system of scripts for dual-boot imaging and use. The managers developed new images for each OS once a semester and made those images available for other lab managers to download and use on their own machines. This collaborative process made things a bit less chaotic than the desktops process but the lab managers still had to figure out how to integrate the images into whatever deployment method they were using at the time.

2.1.3 No Sheriff in Town. This distributed system had some obvious drawbacks; the people creating the images had varying levels of skill, experience, and interest in image creation, and many of them did not really have the time available to dedicate to the task. The result of the poorly designed system was a student user experience that varied a great deal from lab to lab; software that worked perfectly in one lab might be broken, an incompatible version, or not installed at all in other locations. There was inconsistency in how frequently software and operating systems were being patched; it varied from never in some labs to at best somewhat infrequently in others. The biggest issue however, was that creating and maintaining images was extraordinarily time consuming, especially as the effort was being duplicated in each lab.

2.2 Early Consolidation

In 2010, the InfoLabs program administrators asked DoIT to create a common imaging infrastructure, and to maintain common images for the InfoLab desktops and laptops. Ideally, this would greatly reduce the effort that was being duplicated across labs and provide a more consistent experience across labs for lab patrons.

2.2.1 Combined Imaging System Requirements. As a result of the request, a team composed of DoIT technologists and InfoLabs staff was created to identify a list of requirements for a centralized imaging service. Their findings/recommendations included:

Ability to Handle Imaging Load
- Up to 300 laptops were being imaged daily as part of the checkout program, peaking in the late afternoon/early evening when most laptops were returned.

- Labs machines had to be imaged off-hours in relatively short windows of time near the beginning of the fall semester. The system needed to be able to simultaneously image around 70 lab machines each night to allow us to get all our desktops imaged within the desired timeframe.

Ability to Image Quickly
- Laptops require outlets, network jacks, and physical desk space to image, meaning in some locations it is not practical to image more than five at a time. Such a lab open 10 hours per day could image at most 25 laptops assuming optimal spacing of the returns for a process that takes two hours. For three-day check-outs, that would limit the total circulation to around 75. Since some labs had more than 100 laptops, imaging times of much more than an hour would create bottlenecks.

Designed for Dual Boot
- Our intention going forward was to standardize on dual-boot images on Apple hardware.
- The option to deploy half the image to get a viable Windows or OS X only machine was also desirable.

Bare-Metal Restore
- Machines frequently had failed hard drives replaced. Laptops were occasionally returned in unexpected states, with their hard drives repartitioned. Sometimes machines were unplugged halfway through imaging.

Zero or One-touch Imaging
- With upwards of 50 laptops being checked in, imaged, and checked back out every day in some of the busier locations, any extra steps associated with imaging would be a source of error and an unacceptable drain of staff time.
- Lab machines needed to image overnight when the labs were closed, ideally with no staff involvement and a working lab in the morning.

2.2.2 And in the Darkness Bind Them. The decision was made to standardize on DeployStudio as the software to use for imaging. DeployStudio is a free product that allows creating, deploying, and configuring images on Apple hardware. DeployStudio has as server component that connects to a network repository containing images, scripts, packages, workflows, and desired computer configurations. Administrators use the "DeployStudio Admin" client to connect to the DeployStudio server to create and manipulate workflows and stage computers. Lab machines boot a custom OS X recovery partition created with the "DeployStudio Assistant" client, which automatically starts "DeployStudio Runtime", the application that runs through the workflows and executes the specified steps.

Since it generally does not make sense to allow BSDP (NetBoot's extension of DHCP) to cross subnets, each lab needed its own NetBoot server. Mac Minis with NetBoot preconfigured were distributed to each lab. As long as those were being distributed, it made sense at the time to additionally use each NetBoot server as a local DeployStudio server, with DoIT pushing out workflows, scripts, and images to each as necessary, limiting overall cross-campus imaging traffic.

For the image itself, DoIT planned to eventually develop a centralized thin-imaging solution, but that would have to wait a semester. Back-to-School was approaching and efforts were focused on including a number of other necessary but unrelated operating system and user authentication changes into the initial consolidated image. DoIT created a thick image for each OS on the desktops and a similar but pared down set for the laptops.

The results were wonderful! Students were presented with a consistent dual-boot image regardless of which lab they visited and the individual lab managers did not have to each spend upwards of two weeks developing and testing their own images. For the next three years, DoIT distributed these manually created thick images, updating them yearly for the desktops and approximately once a semester for the laptops.

2.2.3 Only a Stopgap. Unfortunately, there were still some problems, especially regarding the Windows half of the operating system. The system was not as hardware agnostic as desired. Windows images created for one model of iMac or MacBook Pro often did not have the necessary drivers for another, to say nothing of trying to use it on Dell. Distributing changes to the various labs' NetBoot/DeployStudio servers took a fair amount of work, some of which could be done centrally and some of which required the local lab managers to take action, resulting in some inconsistency of versions of the images being deployed. The only way to update software and patch the OSes was to create and pull a new image, which was quite time consuming, so newly imaged machines were frequently 6 months or a year out of date, making them less secure and annoying users with update prompts.

Separately, DoIT was interested in a system that would allow technicians working on faculty and staff machines to deploy basic up-to-date Windows and OS X images with a variety of customizations and software load-outs and was uninterested in maintaining a separate, distinct imaging service to do so.

An opportunity was seen to accommodate the needs of both our InfoLabs and desktop support customers with one system, and a thin-imaging solution using a combination of DeployStudio and Microsoft Deployment Toolkit (MDT) was born.

3 THE CONSTRUCTION OF AN IMAGING SERVICE

3.1 Centralized Hardware

With the distributed DeployStudio servers, it would have been difficult to keep software versions consistent, as every change would need to be replicated across a dozen DeployStudio servers around campus. We realized that the best way to allow the frequent changes necessary for a constantly updated thin-imaging system was to consolidate on a single DeployStudio server using a single central repository. We also needed a location for the deployment share that would be used for MDT imaging. Space was initially provisioned and central network

shares created for these using our existing campus shared file storage services.

3.2 DeployStudio

3.2.1 NetBoot. The NetBoot image at each location was updated to one that pointed back to the new central DoIT DeployStudio server. Each lab continued to run their own NetBoot server, but now once imaging starts, everything runs from a central location. The computers are pre-staged with serials and names in DeployStudio and set to start the appropriate workflow automatically once they connect. To kick off imaging, staff need only connect the machine to a network and hold down the 'n' key while booting.

3.2.2 Partitioning. The first major step of the workflows is to partition the hard drive. The number of partitions depends on the machine and its intended use. Workflows manually run by technicians on machines that would be single-boot only get one partition. Lab machines running automated workflows get two or three depending on whether we want the Windows PE environment used for Windows imaging to persist after imaging has completed.

3.2.3 OS X Imaging. Deploying an OS X thin-image in DeployStudio was not a major departure from what we had been doing previously. Instead of capturing an entire completed thick image, we just capture the base install for each version of OS X for re-deployment. All our workflows use these same base images, which we update occasionally when new updates for OS X are released. This can be completed independently of the software and configurations installed by the rest of the workflow.

3.2.4 WinPE Imaging. When using thick images, we just needed to restore a monolithic Windows image to a partition. This could be done natively in DeployStudio. With thin-imaging, we needed a way to restore a generic OS X image, install some software on top of that, and then allow MDT to repeat that same process for Windows. Therefore, instead of a regular Windows image, we restore an image that boots into Windows Preinstallation Environment (WinPE) from which MDT can continue the imaging process.

3.2.5 OS X Software Installation and Configuration. Once the base OSes are deployed, Deploy Studio runs a variety of scripts which install and configure software, tweak the default user profile, and alter various system preferences. For the InfoLab laptops, this is quite extensive, as this is the only place they are configured before being checked out. For the desktops and for staff machines, some of this configuration is delayed until after imaging is completed, where it can be handled using other enterprise management tools like IBM BigFix.

3.3 MDT

MDT is a free set of scripts and tools for deploying Windows images created by Microsoft. It uses the Microsoft Assessment and Deployment Kit as a base, and allows the creation of task sequences to automate the process of installing or updating Windows, running sysprep, injecting drivers, running installers, etc. One of the sets of scripts uses a deployment strategy called Lite Touch. It allows a user to image a machine with the desired task sequence after clicking through a few dialog boxes. These can be made "Zero Touch" deployments with no required user interaction with the appropriate custom settings and parameters.

3.3.1 Windows Imaging Toolkit. MDT will automatically create bootable WinPE ISO files that will kick off the LiteTouch script. We edit these slightly to instead run a custom program that we have created called Windows Imaging Toolkit (WIT). After Deploy Studio has finished configuring OS X, computers are booted to the WinPE partition and run WIT. For automated one-touch imaging in the InfoLabs, WIT will automatically look up the desired task sequence, computer name, and a few other things from information stored in the computer database that DeployStudio uses, and then start LiteTouch with the appropriate credentials and parameters so that no interaction is required. For those requiring additional customizations, such as our technicians imaging machines individually for faculty and staff, options are provided to repartition the disk, select the desired deployment volume, and select from various MDT task sequences available to them. Many of these task sequences then further require them to specify the OS to deploy, Active Directory joining options, and the specific desired basket of applications to install once LiteTouch has started.

3.3.2 Windows Installation. Much like with OS X, we deploy a basic Windows base image. Although MDT will happily use a standard Windows installation disk for deployment, we quickly started capturing and using base WIMs with Microsoft Office and recent Windows updates included, as those were universally desired and sped things up a bit. Once MDT has finished running the Windows installer in WinPE, it boots from the Windows drive to allow the Windows installation to finish. After Windows is fully installed, MDT logs in automatically as the "Administrator" account and will run various scripts to further customize the deployment.

3.3.3 Boot Camp Installation. In order to deploy Windows drivers to the iMacs and MacBooks, we also need to run a Boot Camp installer during MDT. Of course, Boot Camp is not intended to be used in a scripted, Zero Touch manner, so that comes with its own problems. There are different versions of the Boot Camp installer for different models of Macs, so we have a wrapper that detects the computer model, and based on that, selects the correct version of the Boot Camp installer to run.

3.3.4 Other Software Installation. For software installations, we utilize the same file server that holds the imaging systems. There is a directory for batch scripts and installers, which we import to MDT's Applications section. Using MDT's CustomSettings.ini, we can specify different sets of default applications. InfoLabs desktops and loaner laptops proceed automatically using only these default applications. Technicians are presented with a screen of checkboxes where they can select additional software beyond the defaults for the type of deployment they specified.

3.4 Difficulties, Considerations, and Tribulations

Booting from DeployStudio into WinPE is not always as easy as it may seem, especially with the advent of the Unified Extensible Firmware Interface (UEFI). Legacy MBR-bootable NTFS WinPE images cannot always be blessed on newer machines that want to use UEFI and cannot read an NTFS partition. FAT32 UEFI-bootable WinPE partitions do not work on older machines with firmware that does not fully support UEFI. Making the Windows installer happy with either of those requires knowing whether you want a Hybrid-MBR or a Protective MBR and in some cases converting from one to the other as part of imaging.

System Integrity Protection (SIP), introduced by Apple in OS X 10.11, adds another layer of difficulty to this as it limits some of the things that you can do to the file system while SIP is enabled. We tend to disable it as one of the first steps in our DeployStudio workflows, but that doesn't take effect until the next boot. This makes for some interesting juggling of things to make sure the steps that require SIP to be disabled don't happen until after the machine is rebooted and DeployStudio is running its finalize scripts while booted into the deployed OS.

The Boot Camp installer often hangs on any driver installers that get stuck. If we were running Boot Camp manually, we could just click through some error screens and proceed without any trouble, but we need a no-touch solution and thus have had to unpack the Boot Camp installer a few times to replace or remove problem drivers.

4 NO PLAN SURVIVES CONTACT WITH THE ENEMY

4.1 New Hardware Required

Using the campus' existing centralized file sharing infrastructure made it easy to quickly provision space and roll out the new system. However, it quickly became apparent that it was not up to the task. There were a number of outages where network connections were dropped or where the network shares were entirely unavailable. Our everyday laptop imaging load was taking down the shared file hosting service for all of campus, and troubleshooting was requiring a significant amount of staff time. New dedicated hardware was procured to host these network shares that would be able to handle the load.

4.2 Working on BigFix's Schedule

With software deployment no longer tied to OS deployment, we now had more options for when that software deployment should actually occur. Instead of deploying the software as an imaging step, it could now be deployed asynchronously, after imaging proper had completed using group policy, IBM BigFix, and other enterprise management tools.

Since we were already creating content in BigFix to keep the various software packages up to date, it seemed to make sense to remove as much software from the imaging process as possible and to let BigFix handle all of the installation. This worked fine for DoIT technicians who were installing a relatively small number of fairly simple packages, but we started to discover problems with using it for the InfoLab desktops. We were seeing some inconsistencies with installed software, with the increased frequency of updates sometimes leading to buggy versions or botched scripts. The Mac images were particularly bad about missing software, as the machines had to be booted into OS X in order for BigFix to install OS X software, and that was generally only the case when they were being used by students.

We have since moved more of the installers back into DeployStudio and MDT, tolerating some duplication of effort and confusion over where things are actually getting installed in exchange for more consistent installations. It is an ongoing challenge to find the right balance.

4.3 Need for Speed

Still InfoLab managers were always asking for more speed. Some locations did not have gigabit Ethernet yet, so anything we could do to reduce downloads could result in significant speed increases. One of the biggest changes we made was rsyncing the OS X image. Rsync is a free file copying utility that inspects the partition and restores it to the state of a network image at a file level, rather than completely restoring the image byte by byte. This saved us 10 to 30 minutes of imaging time when OS X was still there, which could add up to a couple hours over multiple batches of imaging each day. However, we soon realized that rsync was slower than a full restore when we updated the image each month, and does not work especially well when the expected partitions are not there or when we want to repartition the drives to change the relative sizes of the OS X and Windows partitions. We have a script in the Laptop imaging workflow that determines whether they should fully rebuild or just keep the existing partitions and rsync OS X based on the existence of the desired partitions and various version tag files we embed in the images.

Keeping the partitions intact had other advantages as well. As would be expected, our other largest downloads were the Windows and WinPE images. On most machines, we deploy WinPE to the Windows partition, and then MDT wipes that partition it was booted off of to install Windows from a WIM located on the network file server. On the laptops, to avoid downloading WinPE every time, we sacrifice a couple gigabytes of hard drive space on each system and leave it there as a third partition. We give up a little more storage space and keep a cached copy of the Windows WIM and Boot Camp installer on the laptops as well. This WIM needs to be re-cached monthly as we update it, but cuts out roughly another 10 minutes off the time it takes to image.

4.4 Software Snags

We learned that running scripts to install the software packages one at a time took considerably longer than just restoring an image with the software already installed. While we had made desktop support technicians happy with full thin-imaging, the InfoLab managers were a little disappointed with the system.

Laptops could take as much as three hours to image. During peak return times, laptops would stack up and be unusable while they waited for other laptops to finish. With programs like SAS and Adobe Creative Cloud each taking over an hour to install, desktops could take over 6 hours to image. As more and more people clamored for a return to the old system, we thought there had to be a way to have both up-to-date systems and fast imaging times.

In the end, the solution we came up with was in-fact to return to thick imaging for the InfoLabs, while leaving the technician workflows as-is. This time, however, we were armed with the tools necessary to easily keep these thick images up to date. We converted our InfoLab laptop and desktop imaging workflows into image generator workflows, with an automated image-capture step at the end. Now, each month we could just update software install scripts, run the generator, and have a new up-to-date thick image ready for testing. Some configuration still had to be done on a per-computer basis during imaging, but we had mostly cut out the software install times. When we decided that updating our installers once a month was taking too much time for the DoIT team, we found ways to speed that up as well. Primarily, we leveraged Ninite to pull the latest installers for our set of software, and simply put those in the right place.

4.5 Putting it All Together

With all of that settled, we solidified our update process. Windows updates were disabled during imaging, and beyond when we received complaints about update prompts. Removing the Windows update step saved about half an hour. We are only comfortable with this because of the image generation process. Once a month, after patch Tuesday, we capture updated thin images for technicians, then use those to capture updated thick images for the InfoLabs. This takes a little extra effort from DoIT, but nowhere near as much as the original thick imaging methods.

After a brief period of testing the new laptop images, and making them available to InfoLab managers, they are put into production. We can be sure that software is in a working condition because it is frozen for the next month, and imaging times are much more manageable, hovering around an hour per computer.

Client Driven Change Management

Juliana Perry
Bryn Mawr College
101 N. Merion Ave.
Bryn Mawr, PA, 19010
jperry02@brynmawr.edu

Melissa Cresswell
Bryn Mawr College
101 N. Merion Ave.
Bryn Mawr, PA, 19010
mcresswell@brynmawr.edu

ABSTRACT

In this paper, we describe a client-driven approach to managing a change from Zimbra to Microsoft Office 365 for email and calendar.

CCS CONCEPTS

• *Information systems~Email* • *Social and professional topics~Project management techniques* • *Social and professional topics~Project staffing* • *Social and professional topics~Software selection and adaptation* • *Social and professional topics~Cultural characteristics* • *General and reference~General conference proceedings* • *Applied computing~Business-IT alignment* • *Applied computing~IT governance*

KEYWORDS

Change management; project management; lessons learned; communication; training; implementation; email; calendar; Office 365

1 INTRODUCTION

Change is hard on any campus, especially when your community has high expectations for services and the change is to a core service used daily by most. Bryn Mawr College was faced with a board mandate to move email and calendar to a hosted service from an in-house Zimbra installation that had served us well for many years but which we were clearly outgrowing in terms of capacity and functionality needs. We knew that we needed buy-in from our administration and from the community as a whole to select the best platform for the college and to make a successful transition. We elected a client-driven discovery process, followed by an implementation, communication, and user education approach designed to enable our clients to succeed.

2 Project Timeline

Spring 2015: Project announcement and launch
Summer 2015: Discovery with staff
Fall 2015: Finalize requirements and wish list
November 30 2015: Announced selection of Microsoft Office 365
Winter-Spring 2016: Community reminders and learning opportunities[1]
May 20-21 2016: Cutover to new platform
Summer-Fall 2016: Post-launch communication and education

3 Discovery

The mandate to move to a hosted service limited our choices of email platforms, in that we did not have to explore in-house solutions thoroughly. We also determined early on that hosting Zimbra or other open source options in the cloud would not be cost effective for our institution. This meant that the only mature platforms available at our time of selection were Google Apps for Education and Microsoft Office 365. Most of our peer institutions had switched to one of these two options, affirming them as reasonable choices. We spoke to a number of colleagues about their experiences with the migration and with ongoing service. Speaking with IT staff members at other institutions who had made the transition recently was invaluable.

Discovery in our own community took a number of forms, from surveys to open forums to stakeholder focus groups and individual interviews. The initial announcement of the project included an explanation for why it was necessary, a website with a FAQ and our project values[2], and an open question/comment form. While the comment form, as predicted, elicited a wide range of input and opinions (from fairly detailed discussions of experiences with the products under consideration, to wish lists, to the concise "Gmail bruh"), it was helpful to get a sense of community interests and engagement in the process.

We knew from anecdotal comments and support tickets that most of our power users were staff members. We conducted a series of staff focus groups targeting the President's Office and Division Heads; Admissions, Development, and Alumnae Office; power users in administrative offices; and academic department administrators. This resulted in a detailed list of required functionality and desired features.

Support tickets and anecdotes suggested that faculty use was less varied and simpler than that of administrators, but we wanted to be certain that this was true and that we were accounting for the full range of use cases. We identified a representative list of faculty members that ranged across disciplines (STEM to Social Work), technology use and skills, and point in academic career (adjuncts to tenured professors) and then scheduled interviews of no more than an hour with these faculty members or their suggested alternate. We also held a group discussion with our faculty Committee on Libraries, Information, and Computing.

We hosted several open forums, attended mostly by staff and a few faculty members. These were great opportunities to connect with community members concerned about the impact of the transition and to address those concerns, as well as to collect further needs and wants.

Surveys and the initial comment form turned out to be the best way to get information from students about their use of email. We invited them to the open forums and focus groups but interest levels were not high enough to lure them away from their other commitments despite offers of free lunch. Getting significant time with students, especially with graduate students who do not live on campus, was a challenge.

All of these interactions served as further reminders to our community that the transition was happening. They made our community feel included in the process rather than that IT was doing something to them without consultation. And we gained ambassadors who would bring those reminders (and hopefully, feelings of inclusion) back to their colleagues who could not or would not attend the meetings.

4 Communicating the Decision

Our discovery process led to the determination that Microsoft Office 365 was the best fit for our campus. Primary reasons for this choice included the overall feature set, and concern about Google IP addresses typically being banned in mainland China, from where a number of our international students come.

Our project website, live since the announcement of the project, was updated to include a FAQ about the decision as well as the announcement. The decision was also announced via an email to the campus.

We had identified Google products, at least those available for personal as opposed to business use, as being more widely known in the community and anticipated pushback for that reason. We also noted a variety of pre-existing opinions about Google and Microsoft as companies, based on past experience or widely held public perceptions. Transparency as to why we had selected the less familiar and perhaps more often maligned product was key. We did, however, choose to remove the open comment form after our discovery phase, feeling that more structured feedback through the conscious choice to email the Help Desk with comments would be more productive heading into implementation. Frank, honest communication[3] helped the community understand our choice, and we got far less pushback than expected.

5 Communicating Prior to Launch

Emails to the campus community about the project were minimal until shortly before launch and designed to provide reminders

without oversaturating the campus. Further details were made available in our established Library and Information Technology Services (LITS) blog and sent to the project website via RSS feed. Our goal was to communicate early, through existing channels (rather than relying on traffic to a new site), often enough (but not too often!), and with transparency.

Following the announcement of the decision after Thanksgiving break, we spent the spring periodically reminding the community of our launch date, when they would have opportunities to learn about the new platform through classes, and sharing videos and online learning options for those away for the summer. The implementation team tried very hard to minimize actions for end users—most only had to download any needed Zimbra Briefcase files and task lists, though there were later complications with calendar data migration.

Some constituencies required extra attention. The timing of our launch and provisioning of incoming student accounts meant that they might experience Zimbra briefly before the cutover and then have to adjust to a new system. LITS, Communications, and Admissions crafted a separate message and video to explain this to incoming students. As Bryn Mawr College provides email to retirees and emeriti, we sent them a postal letter about the announcement since not everyone in this group checks email frequently.

We also took the opportunity to have some fun while reminding the community about the change, and April Fools' Day was the perfect opportunity! Our outreach team created a message and video explaining that e-mail would be replaced by "Bananagrams."[4] The humor helped reinforce the reminder as people shared the video.

"Spotlight Series" messages shortly before launch covered a key topic about the new platform each week, helping the community prepare to be up and running after cutover.

> #1: Office Here, Office There, Office Everywhere![5]
> #2: More File Storage for All![6]
> #3: Hello Outlook Web App![7]
> #4: Tools for Calendar Ninjas[8]
> #5: Improved Mobile Experience[9]
> #6: Organizing Your Inbox[10]
> #7: OneDrive for Business[11]
> #8: Office Online[12]

6 The Outreach and Education Approach

Our education plan worked in tandem with our communication plan to prepare community members to get up and running with Office 365 quickly and confidently. We held pre-launch talks and demos to provide familiarity–mostly at pre-existing staff education opportunities to guarantee an audience. Hands-on classes on core topics such as inbox management, calendars, and collaborative work with OneDrive began day-of launch. Videos and other online modules provided self-paced learning opportunities for those off campus or otherwise inclined to learn on their own. Small group consultations were available by appointment after launch, mostly for staff with specific questions about translating business processes to the new platform.

Documentation (in-house or selected from Microsoft or other sources) was an additional resource for self-paced learning. We publicized these learning opportunities online, via email, and in print brochures ahead of launch, over the summer, and early in the fall semester.

Office 365 Learning Opportunities[13]
New Learning Opportunities for Office 365 & More[14]
Fall Lineup of Learning Opportunities for Office 365[15]

A key to our success in managing this change was clear, consistent messaging. A combined communication, outreach, and education plan and team enabled tightly coordinated offerings and a thoroughly integrated approach. Agile planning and lock-step collaboration with our Help Desk and Desktop Support teams meant that our communication and education efforts were informed by the day-to-day client experience. Outreach and education staff with Help Desk cross-training reinforced our commitment to a user-centered approach and strengthened the communications-education-support feedback loop.

7 Launch

Cutting over to the new system all at once was deemed best given our size, support staffing, and the warnings from peers and vendors that coexistence of systems was a very painful state—a warning certainly validated by an inevitably rough but necessary pilot experience for LITS staff. Nearly all members of the community would experience the change at the same time, and we had to prepare for that.

A phrase frequently uttered throughout planning launch was "the army of too much help." We added a staff member from March through October to help produce educational materials and provide support. Documentation was ready to go on launch day (and we carefully swapped out documentation regarding the old platform during our outage) so that people eager to return to email immediately after the outage could get started.

A fairly late addition to the plan, but an extremely helpful one, was for professional support staff members to make house calls to each of their supported areas on our first business day with Office 365. This increased community members' confidence that they could get up and running and receive help if needed, allowed us to solve many problems immediately, and helped us gather accurate details to troubleshoot issues that were not immediately resolvable.

A final important part of day one was our lunchtime huddle which allowed the relevant teams to discuss problems and get some much needed nourishment.

Post-launch outreach was scheduled through October, and included tips at key intervals. We began with the basics of email and calendar use and then moved to searching and other more advanced skills like inbox management. We also included topics that arose as we piloted and launched, such as navigating specific problems with recurring calendar events.

8 What We'd Do Differently

Looking back, we would have conducted a broader (but not longer!) pilot covering more user types. Using dual email systems was painful, but including some student and perhaps even simulated prospective student and emeriti users would have brought some significant pain points to light sooner. We would have also done some more in-depth discovery with executive assistants, especially regarding calendar use. There were some edge cases, especially with recurring events, that we could have been more prepared to communicate about if we had identified them more clearly.

Knowing what we now know about what it is like to manage a cloud service used by our entire campus, we are continuing to improve our policies around change management for production services. We knew that changes to the service would be more sudden and less controlled, but are still working out the best way to roll out new Office 365 services as they mature, and how to manage support for them.

9 What We Didn't Expect

Shared calendars could not be configured in the same way in Office 365 as they were in Zimbra, and communicating about the nature of the problem and the frustrating solutions available to us (usually manual deletion and re-creation of select items) was a challenge.

That being said, our thorough communication plan increased our community's tolerance of change and the aforementioned difficulties more than we had expected based on our previous experience making changes to core services.

10 What We Will Do Again

A number of techniques honed or developed for this project will be used in other projects with a similar scale.

The thorough, inclusive, and community oriented discovery process bought us good will, ambassadors in support of the change, and resulted in a high quality list of requirements. We gained a lot by planning communications from project announcement through launch—the vendors who reviewed our change management plan could not find anything to contribute except additional educational resources.

A carefully considered joint education and communication plan was vital to increasing community member confidence before, during, and after launch. The small group consultations were particularly useful in addressing specific problems and allowing the education and outreach team to take on some support questions that were more about business processes or educational needs, reducing the load on the Help Desk and Desktop Support staff. Knowledge sharing between education and support staff during the approach to launch was also extremely beneficial—support staff knew the odd things people did with Zimbra and what educators might need to translate for them. Future projects may involve a Desktop Support Technician more deeply in education work. Video tutorials were comparatively time-consuming to produce, but allowed for a contemporary and engaging multimedia approach that garnered positive feedback and even enthusiasm from the community.

Extra staffing was a key to success for a small project team with many other responsibilities. Our eight month temporary Outreach and Education Associate enabled us to produce more video and documentation materials specific to our community where vendor-provided documentation was minimal or where materials specific to our transition would help. Additionally, a dedicated project manager whose other duties were temporarily redistributed was well positioned to make sure that change management and implementation planning were in sync and that any problems were caught and addressed quickly.

Finally, our campus really runs on interpersonal relationships. Spending lots of time throughout the project simply talking with community members was key—the in-person interviews and open forums, house calls during launch, and thorough follow-up on even the thorniest of issues helped our community feel included in and supported by the process. This approach assured that we were listening to our users even if we selected a different product than they expected, or if we could not resolve a problem immediately. The resources invested to increase trust during this project will continue to serve us well in future projects with a significant change management component, provided we continue to prioritize client-driven discovery, support and education, and relationship building.

ACKNOWLEDGEMENTS

We thank the entire project team for their invaluable contributions to successful change management, and we thank Amy Pearlman for discussions that helped to shape this paper.

REFERENCES

[1]   http://lits.blogs.brynmawr.edu/category/email-project/page/3
[2]   http://email.blogs.brynmawr.edu/
[3]   http://email.blogs.brynmawr.edu/frequently-asked-questions/#decision
[4]   https://www.brynmawr.edu/news/bryn-mawr-college-launches-new-messaging-service-bunches-benefits-realized
[5]   http://lits.blogs.brynmawr.edu/5862
[6]   http://lits.blogs.brynmawr.edu/5939
[7]   http://lits.blogs.brynmawr.edu/5979
[8]   http://lits.blogs.brynmawr.edu/6021
[9]   http://lits.blogs.brynmawr.edu/6075
[10] http://lits.blogs.brynmawr.edu/6098
[11] http://lits.blogs.brynmawr.edu/6158
[12] http://lits.blogs.brynmawr.edu/6220
[13] http://lits.blogs.brynmawr.edu/6136
[14] http://lits.blogs.brynmawr.edu/6391
[15] http://lits.blogs.brynmawr.edu/6551

What's Your Story?

Casey Davis

Arizona State University   University Technology Office

P.O. Box 870101

Temple, AZ 85257-0101

Casey.Davis.1@asu.edu

ABSTRACT

Getting participants, let alone instructional designers, excited and engaged about creating and facilitating training for faculty and staff is a challenge. Instead of leading with required number of training and looking at average attendance, start with a story. Humans are hardwired for stories. We all want to be the hero, or work alongside the hero of the story. This session will examine how to identify your training department's story, cultivate it, and ultimately make the story a shared narrative for everyone on the team or in the department. Based upon cognitive research, best practices, and experiential knowledge and skills, participants will leave equipped with methods and approaches to uniting and revitalizing their training program. These methods and approaches include gamification, extended narratives, and blended styles of training that help technology departments integrate their training teams seamlessly into the daily operations and functions of their larger organizations.

KEYWORDS

Change leadership, project management, storytelling.

1 INTRODUCTION

Getting participants, let alone instructional designers, excited and engaged about creating and facilitating training for faculty and staff is a challenge. [8] Instead of leading with required number of training and looking at average attendance, start with a story. Humans are hardwired for stories. We all want to be the hero, or work alongside the hero of the story. This session will examine how to identify your training department's story, cultivate it, and ultimately make the story a shared narrative for everyone on the team or in the department.

SIGUCCS '17, October 1–4, 2017, Seattle, WA, USA

© 2017 Association for Computing Machinery.

ACM ISBN 978-1-4503-4919-2/17/10...$15.00

https://doi.org/10.1145/3123458.3123485

Based upon cognitive research, best practices, and experiential knowledge and skills, participants will leave equipped with methods and approaches to uniting and revitalizing their training program. These methods and approaches include gamification, extended narratives, and blended styles of training that help technology departments integrate their training teams seamlessly into the daily operations and functions of their larger organizations.

2 OVERVIEW AND PROCESS

Training is not something that most professionals flock to. Filling seats in workshops and trainings is a Herculean task to say the least. Engaging participants is entirely another matter. Achieving both of these goals is something akin to the Holy Grail of training and support for the majority of university technology offices. Most faculty and staff members attend technology training for one of two reasons. The majority of participants enroll in and attend technology training because their position with the school requires it. There are a few, however, that attend out of a desire to learn a new skill.

But, even when a small percentage of participants are intrinsically motivated to attend trainings, there is still the challenge of getting more people to attend trainings and to authentically engage them once there.[1] Achieving this provides a greater return on investment for everyone involved. At the heart of this challenge, and its solution, lies the power of story. The elemental and ancient power of story is the key to re-invigorating your training department.

Cognitive science and field research in psychology, sociology, education, and business continue to affirm the fact that by our very nature, humans are hardwired for story. We are narrative beings. In fact, history shows that the realm of stories and storytelling was once prominent in education and training. It is time for us to reclaim our birthright.[2] It is time for us to share our story and ask others to add to it with their own.

Infusing stories into your trainings and into your training department is something of a layered approach, each of which will be reviewed individually.[3] Afterwards, a summative perspective will examine how these three approaches can be intertwined to fortify your training department as well as cultivate innovation as well.

The three approaches are: (1) identifying your department's story, (2) guiding participants to mesh their stories with their departments', and (3) exploring with participants the expanding stories as they unfold during each training. While these three approaches seem fairly simple, they do require fairly precise and delicate application. These approaches and suggested implementation follows.[3]

In sharing your department's story with workshop participants as well as the larger whole of the university, the story must be identified and known by individuals working in the department. In other words, your training and support department must know its own story before it can invite individuals from other departments to join their stories with yours. Without knowing your story, there is no way to share or expand it.

Having your training and support team know and add to its story is essential. By identifying your training and support department's story, a shared identity and narrative arises. This provides a shared commonality where bridges can be constructed and strengthened. In order to identify the training and support department's story, two areas are crucial. One is the vision statement of the university as well as your department's vision statement.

Both of these pieces serve as powerful and essential guides in not only identifying, but cultivating, your team's narrative. The university's mission and vision statements provide measurements to provide direction and guidance in crafting the team's narrative. This direction is narrowed and honed through the application of the mission and vision statement of your university's technology office. Rather than limiting the scope and perspective of your team's narrative, these statements provide milestones for the path of your story without dictating the precise direction and actions.

The team's vision and mission statements support the departments, which likewise supports the university's statements. In essence, the training and support team has the knowledge and skills, but needs the precise focus that comes from these two mission and vision statements. These statements provide beginning answers to the questions of "What to do?" and "What's the plan?" Both of these questions are incumbent upon each other, forming something like a feedback loop.

The university's mission and vision statements give a high altitude perspective of what it wants to achieve as a whole and when it proposes to have these objectives met. Taken a step further, the University's Technology Office adds another layer of focus and precision to the direction and expectation. While neither of these statements identify or explain how these goals are to be achieved, they do provide an outline for actions. This is where you and your team are called to create your own stories, adding their own voices to it.

Utilizing these statements at the university and department levels, your team has an outline to guide their actions and points of view. Establishing, cultivating, and even refining your team's evolving narrative to provide additional clarity and focus is essential for success. These statements are foundations in the formation of your team's narrative.

From this understanding arises the questions of what does this look like in practice, and how is it effectively implemented with any fidelity to the process. Given the fact that this change will appear and unfold differently with each context, there are some fundamental guides and processes which can assist leaders to facilitate this shift in understanding and perspective.[6]

1. What's the big idea...?
   Every great story begins with an amazing, sometimes outlandish idea. For example, Columbus knew that he could reach the Orient by sailing West. Stephen King wondered what rabies was like from the animal's point of view. As a result of these seemingly hair-brained ideas, we are lucky to have knowledge of the Americas and the best-selling novel and subsequent movie, *Cujo*. While our epiphanies may neither be as earth shattering nor personally profitable, they are important nonetheless. The main idea, the topic, the theme of your team's story while directed by the mission and vision statements, is developed and defined by the individuals of the team. In my department, a renewed focus on delivering high quality training informed by client suggestions and requests has helped us refine our idea. Meeting and cultivating the popular demand for training, as well as responding to specific requests for training drives the team's vision and purpose.

2. Team-wide *Choose Your Own Adventure*
   The world is your oyster...kind of. Using the beacons of the university's and department's vision and mission statements, it is incumbent that as a team you identify what the goals of the training and support team are, and what measurements will be used in order to track and analyze progress at regular intervals. Now that the team has identified its main idea and theme of its narrative, the time comes to identify actions and measurements. Planning is essential. It is crucial to match and align the team's actions and goals so that they are precisely aligned and articulated. In a certain essence, the team has chosen its adventure. There is a caveat which is crucial in succeeding in the chosen adventure. With any plan, especially in its execution, there must be a measure of flexibility that keeps the plan organic, kinetic, and fresh no matter how long it takes to achieve the objective. In fact, ignoring this does more to set up your endeavor for failure than anything else. Flexibility is the key to success.

3. Sharing Your Story
   In sharing your story, the team is open and generous in sharing the team's story with workshop participants. With this sharing comes an invitation.

   This invitation is not a simple welcome to participants to listen to the team's story. No. While it is similar, this invitation is unique and frightening; it is different. This invitation asks the participants to open their stories.

   Under the guidance of instructional designers/trainers, the participants are invited to merge and meld their own stories with that of the training and support team. In a sense, a connective web of individual and collective stories grows throughout the larger organization. This is a powerful sense of networking in our age of over connectivity.

In essence, sharing your team's or department's story with workshop participants melds your story with theirs, looking to the larger story of the university's mission and vision statement. This helps to maintain the human aspect of shared stories while broadening its scope to include a greater number of individuals.

3 PRACTICES AND EXAMPLES

This practice of using storytelling not only to train, but to cultivate transformation has been useful for my own professional practices is a few different scenarios. These instances have occurred in both the public and private sectors.

3.1 In the Classroom

The earliest of these was as a middle school teacher. Over the 15 years as a public, charter, and parochial school teacher of Social Studies and Science, allowed amble opportunity for experimenting and adapting this technique. In almost any subject area, students want to honestly know the importance of what they are learning in their individual lives.

Stories got the students' attention like nothing else. More importantly, when the stories were shared, when it wasn't just about the teacher, students become more engaged and active.

Once students are guided into seeing that they are not only an important part of the story, but contributors as well, they evolve into the owners and authors of the story.

Taking this approach led to not just an increase in student achievement, but also an increase in student engagement during classes. Perhaps more importantly, students began pursuing their academic and intellectual interests. This self-directed learning is a primary goal of classroom learning.[7]

Working as a Senior Curriculum Manager for the Humanities for a smaller sized educational company, I was tasked with bringing together two disparate teams into a single working unit. Added to this, one of the teams had not had any direct oversight for months, and were almost a year behind on their production.

3.2 In Business

The more traditional approaches to team building and product management were not effective. Without deadlines moved, or additional funds provided, it was up to me to get the teams combined and moving in the same direction to meet production goals.

Once again, stories came to the forefront of the situation. Refocusing my developers' efforts on developing the next chapter of the shared story for the department, as well as the company, helped get the products delivered on time and meeting expectations.

3.3 At the University

While making deadlines and achieving goals was important, something more valuable was achieved. This group of individuals melded into a team with a shared vision and context. They were able to take a job and make it into a pursuit of professional passion, producing the best product available.

Currently, our Training and Support Team is tasked with developing a departmental wide training for new hires and current employees to cultivate a culture of service meshing with the vision and values statements of the university. For any large entity, this is a challenge. With hundreds of employees in the University Technology Office, this task seemed daunting at first.

However, incorporating the storytelling, or narrative approach to training provided not only a framework, but also a focus for designing and developing the training package for employees. By creating a narrative focus with storytelling, employees of the department will be able to identify, internalize, and incorporate the university's, department's, and their respective team goals with their own professional and personal goals.[9]

Showing the articulation of these visions and values statements, and linking individual actions in a cause and effect manner to them, employees will not only be able to see where they fit in within the "big picture," but also how they contribute to the overall narrative structure of the department, and university as well.

4 SUMMARY AND CONCLUSION

Focusing on identifying all the different stories swirling around when training commences can be intoxicating and confusing. Training is not only the sharing of information and skills, but also the co-mingling of stories. It is the braiding of different strands together, combining to create a single cord which connects us all in our perspective and actions professionally.

For this approach to cultivating innovation and growth within your department, one fundamental fact exists. Every member of the training and development team must know the shared story of the department, and the significant role they play in it. Without these two crucial aspects identified and understood/appreciated by the members of the training and development team, then the team's story can neither expand nor combine with another team's and department's stories. It becomes as dead as Latin, fodder for academic discourse and study.

The greatest challenge to this approach within your team and department is the same dilemma theater and cinema has grappled with for centuries. Simply, getting the audience to "buy-in" to the story as it unfolds. But this approach to training and team building presents a unique bend on this situation. In the training situation, the team understands that the perspective they are adopting is one which cannot necessarily be quantified or physically grasped at any given moment in time. Yet, in accepting this point of view, the team willingly becomes participants in expanding the story by sharing it with others via workshops and classes. While the team's and subsequently the department's story is neither fictitious nor fantastical, it is totally believable and is only limited by the innovation and determination of the team.

This is where leadership plays perhaps it greatest role in the entire process. As with most change leadership instances, it is not enough to implement. Engagement with the process through personal practice is a must for full "buy-in" from the team. In other words, the leaders of the team and even the department must juggle two roles. Leaders must fulfill the roles of actors in the narrative as well as directors of the overall story. This is a difficult responsibility to say the least. However, it is not impossible.

Anyone in a leadership position, official or unofficial, needs to approach their situation as storyteller and participant by taking cues from the fictional character Gandalf from Tolkien's fiction, made popular by Sir Ian McKellan in Peter Jackson's movies. In the larger narrative, Gandalf knew what the end objective was. He shepherded the other characters on the mission, without forcing or coercing them. The sagacious guide was also part and parcel of the band of heroes with his own role to play, and challenges to overcome.

Looking again to Gandalf, leaders can see that leading from the front, progressing shoulder to shoulder with the team, is the surest way to promote this approach to training and development. Leading this particular change from this vantage point provides the others in the team an exemplar of how they need to approach training workshops and classes in order to expand the team's narrative.

By identifying your team's narrative, its place in the larger story, and each member's role and contribution to the continuing story, training departments become a major player in cultivating change in the larger context. Using the department's and university's vision and mission statements to identify and cultivate your team's story is the surest way to make this fantastic point of view practical fact. Taking a storytelling, narrative approach to training and development allows trainers, designers, and workshop participants to write their own plot within the context of the larger story, and recognize the significance of their contributions.

ACKNOWLEDGMENTS

This work was made possible by the support of Arizona State University's University Technology Office, especially Deborah Whitten, Assistant Vice President, and Paul Stoll, Director of Training and Support Services.

REFERENCES

1. Simmons, Annette. Whoever Tells the Best Story Wins: How to Use Your Stories to Communicate Power and Impact. 2nd ed. (NYC: AMACOM), 2015.

2. The Story Factor: Inspiration, Influence, and Persuasion Through the Art of Storytelling, Revised ed. (NYC: Perseus Books), 2006.

3. Forman, Janis. Storytelling in Business: The Authentic and Fluent Organization. (Stanford, CA: Stanford University Press), 2013.

4. Guber, Peter. Tell to Win: Connect, Persuade, and Triumph with the Hidden Power of Story. (NYC: Random House), 2011.

5. Pollack, John. Shortcut: How Analogies Reveal Connections, Spark, and Sell Our Greatest Ideas. (NYC: Penguin Random House), 2015.

6. Gottschall, Jonathan. The Storytelling Animal: How Stories Make Us Human. (Boston, MA: Houghton Mifflin Harcourt), 2015.

7. Smith, Paul. Lead with a Story: A Guide to Crafting Business Narratives that Captivate, Convince, and Inspire. (NYC: AMACOM), 2012.

8. Sachs, Jonah. Winning the Story Wars: Why Those Who Tell – and Live – the Best Stories Will Rule the Future. (Boston, MA: Harvard Business Review Press), 2012.

9. Armstrong, David A. Managing by Storying Around: A New Method of Leadership. (NYC: Armstrong International), 1992.

Connecting Students to Life Beyond the Campus Walls: How I Developed a Training Program to Prepare Students for Life in the "Real World"

Robert G. Fricke
Whitman College
Technology Services
345 Boyer Ave.
Walla Walla, WA, USA
frickerg@whitman.edu

ABSTRACT

This paper will discuss the process in which I, along with the help of student staff and other full-time staff, developed a program that not only trained our student staff for positions at Whitman College Technology Services (WCTS) but aided them in translating and turning that experience into life beyond the walls of the college campus. It will highlight how we went from no formal training to developing our current model which uses an online, multi-tiered training system within Canvas LMS. Other components of the program include connecting with other full-time staff within WCTS as well as other departments on the campus to create workshops that include resume writing and interview skills.[1]

CCS CONCEPTS

Applied Computing → **Education**; Computer Managed Instruction • **Social and professional topics** → Management of computing and information systems → Software management → Software selection and adaptation

KEYWORDS

Student; Employees; Student Employee; Training; Resume; Workshop; Develop; Employee training; Program development; Training program; Canvas; LMS; Badges; Badging

SIGUCCS '17, October 1-4, 2017, Seattle, WA, USA
© 2017 Association for Computing Machinery.
ACM ISBN 978-1-4503-4919-2/17/10... $15.00
https://doi.org/10.1145/3123458.3123468

1 INTRODUCTION

Whitman College is a small liberal arts college located in rural Eastern Washington State in the secluded small town of Walla Walla. The student population of Whitman is about 1,500 students with a faculty and staff population of roughly 600. The college is completely undergraduate, with its most popular degrees being in the sciences. Founded in 1882 as a seminary school in remembrance of its namesake, Marcus Whitman – a missionary – Whitman has molded itself into one of the leading non-sectarian liberal arts colleges in the nation.

Technology Services at Whitman is staffed by 26 full-time employees and a student staff of 35. Under the Chief Information Officer (CIO), the department is split into 5 groups: Client Services, Instructional and Learning Technology, Enterprise Technology, Information Security, and Technology Infrastructure. Client Services, which is the focus of this paper, consists of a director, two hardware technicians, a Help Desk Supervisor/Consultant, a Desktop Systems Application Administrator/Consultant, and 20 student staff.

2 STUDENT CONSULTANTS

2.1 A Quick History

By the time I was hired at Whitman College in November of 2009, I had been in the technology field for about five years. I had gotten my start as a Help Desk Technician at a small bank. The tech world was not where I had planned I would end up. I was a 2003 graduate of Washington State University with a Bachelors of Education. I had planned to work in the Kindergarten to Eighth grade realm but those plans fell apart when I did my student teaching. I kept that passion of teaching but knew that elementary teaching was not for me. After graduation, I fell back into banking – a job that I had throughout college – and eventually landed a position within the bank's IT department. I was hired for my customer service skills and my first-hand knowledge of the systems that IT supported. A relocation to another part of the state is when I got into technology support in education. I was employed by an Educational Service District (ESD) in north-eastern Oregon and was tech support for two small rural school districts. A year into that position, I found the position at Whitman College.

The student consultant role in the Client Services group of Whitman College Technology Services (WCTS) has evolved over time. Previous to my arrival at Whitman in 2009, consultants were used primarily to monitor the general-use computer labs on campus. This mainly meant that they sat in a small office adjacent to the computer lab and made sure that printers were stocked and computers were booting. Student Consultants were rarely allowed to work the main Help Desk and it was primarily staffed by full-time WCTS staff members from all groups, not just Client Services. Having to work the Help Desk was a bone of contention for some of the full-time staff but was a mandate of the then Chief Technology Officer (CTO).

2.2 A Change in Management

Skip ahead to 2011. The Chief Technology Officer had announced her retirement at the end of the current fiscal year. My co-Desktop Support Consultant had put in his letter of resignation effective the end of March. He also had the role of managing the student consultants under the Client Services umbrella. Talks began to give management control of the student staff back to the previous manager who was now the Director of Instructional Technology (DIT). Taking a chance, I emailed both the CTO and DIT and threw out an offer to take over the role of managing the student staff. They both agreed and affective April 1, 2011, I was the newly minted manager of the Client Services student staff.

2.3 Observation

Taking over the position so late in the school year did not allow for much change to happen. I took this time to begin my observations of the roles that the student consultants had at WCTS.

Training for the student staff was lacking to non-existent. Nothing was formally in place and it was a system of older student staff members "passing" their information down to the new student staff. This resulted in large gaps of knowledge, inconsistent training, and bad habits being passed down.

The positions that student consultants had within Client Services at the time were Supply Runner, Library Technician, Lab Technician, Help Desk, and Student Manager. The Lab Technician had mostly been eliminated by the time I had taken over as manager. The Lab Technician consisted of a student sitting in a small office off of each of the campus' three academic computer labs. Their position was to maintain and clean the labs, make sure computers booted correctly, printing was working, and answer the occasional question from a student. It was a chair-warmer position that was not needed. I completely eliminated the position and rolled some of the responsibilities to the Supply Runner position.

The Library Technician, much like the Lab Technician, sat in a small office. They were there to answer questions about campus printing, assist with setting up printer drivers on students' computers, and check out laptops to students to use in the library. The small, closet-like office was located behind some stacks of the library and had no signage – it was hard to find and rarely visited.

The Supply Runner position consisted of stocking toner, paper, and other supplies in the labs around campus. They checked in with the Help Desk and would visit each lab within their hour shift.

Help Desk students were few. This was relegated to the most senior of student consultants and usually meant a student manager. Shifts were generally an hour at a time with most shifts being handled by full-time WCTS staff.

Student Managers, consisted of two students. Usually seniors, their role seemed unclear and more of a badge of honor than anything else.

3 REORGANIZING AND TRAINING

3.1 Minor Adjustments

Along with this period of observation came some restructuring of positions and evaluating costs. The final hold-out of the Lab Technician positions was eliminated. The position was not necessary as students in the lab were not utilizing the technicians enough to justify paying someone to be in the lab until 10pm most evenings. Each lab has a phone in them with posted numbers to reach the Help Desk during regular business hours or the Library Technicians in the evening if assistance is needed. Supply Runners could handle the majority of the duties the Lab Technicians did: tidying up the lab, checking computers, replacing paper and toner in the printers.

The largest complaint of full-time staff having to cover the Help Desk was the amount of time it took them away from their other job duties. This was especially true for those that worked on the opposite side of campus from the Help Desk. My plan was to make the Help Desk completely staffed by student employees.

The Help Desk was also awkwardly placed behind the main door to the office (Fig. 1).

Figure 1: **Help Desk location behind the main door**

Clients standing at the desk would risk being hit by the door if they did not move. I relocated the desk to the wall directly across from the door to give it more of a lobby feel and to avoid potential traffic jams at the door (Fig. 2).

Figure 2: **Help Desk relocated across from the front door. Accessible desk added.**

No real adjustments were made to the Library Technician position. However, I worked with the full-time Library staff to get some signage to help students with finding the office (Fig. 3). This helped some but it highlighted the poor location of the office. Tech questions were still being directed at the Library's Circulation Desk especially with the main printers being located at the desk's edge. Library staff were continuously redirecting students to the office that noone knew existed, even with the new signage in place.

Figure 3: **The door to the Library Technician office with new sign.**

3.2 More Changes

In 2012, the new CIO worked with the Director of the Library to form a working group of Technology Services staff, which included myself, two other WCTS staff, and the Librarians in an attempt to create collaboration between the departments on campus. Our mandate was to find opportunities where both departments could work together for a common campus good. As a group, we decided that finding a project with noticeable exposure to the entire campus would be a good place to start. We decided to focus on the Technology Support Office presence in the library. It was determined that a more centrally located desk would be of better benefit not only to the library staff but also to the entire campus. We decided that the Reference Librarian Desk would be a great option as it would be easy to reconfigure and the librarians that worked that desk could easily do the same functions from their current offices that

circumnavigated the desk. In the fall of 2012, the newly-minted Library Tech Desk was opened for business. We did not anticipate the amount of new traffic that would come, and the new desk highlighted how few students used our services before. The largest indicator was the amount of Junior and Senior level students that came to the desk to get our campus printing system installed on their personal laptops – something they did not realize they could before. This change also brought to light that more training was needed for the Library Tech Desk staff. Student staff needed to know how to install printers and how to answer other basic troubleshooting questions about connecting to wireless networks and installing site-licensed software.

3.3 Formalizing Training

It was time for a plan to formalize training. I came up with some goals to accomplish with the training not just for the Library Tech Desk duties but the student consultant experience as a whole. My goals: create a tiered system of training, create a system of consistent/standardized training that all would get, create a program that would create workforce-ready staff, create a work experience that would be resume worthy, treat and use the student staff like full-time staff. Training for all three groups of my students needed to happen but this was going to be a daunting task for me alone to handle. I put out a call for action in late fall of 2012. I formed a group with five student consultants and myself and in November we began developing a program. I presented my idea and vision and then paired up the student staff to create lists of areas where training would be essential to their positions. The student staff came back with a list of topics and sub-topics that was 7 pages long! The list consisted of topics such as Microsoft Word and GoPrint to Customer Service and Networking. The list was long and extensive and needed to be pared down. Next, we needed to figure out how the material would be taught. Would this be readings, in-person classes, online? How would we measure understanding of the topics presented? Do we need to incentivize the training? If so, how?

One idea for material presentation was utilizing Lynda.com. Topics were researched in their database and free trials were used but it ultimately came down to money. Whitman has a single license for Lynda.com and to expand that was going to be too much money. We finally settled on a combination of written materials that would be housed in our online wiki (Confluence) and self-created exams that would be distributed and collected within the campus LMS, CLEo (Sakai). Exams would be graded and progress would be tracked and documented by myself on a Google spreadsheet.

Incentivizing the training was going to be tricky. Budgets were tight so monetary incentive was not an option. Around that time, Educause had a webinar discussing badging. Badging is a system of giving a "badge" to indicate or acknowledge mastery in a given area. The working group liked the idea of them and felt it could be a way to "gamify" training and give the consultants a way of showing off what they have learned as well as making it a sort of challenge to see who gets their badges first or who has the most. The badges would not all necessarily need to be tied to a learning module. Some badges could be fun or ways to acknowledge other accomplishments. Those that were dedicated to learning material could be broken up into levels and progress to higher levels of difficulty as the student consultant progressed in their job. We determined that the best structure would be to tie certain badges to specific jobs and the jobs themselves would become stepping stones to progress within the institution. All newly hired student staff would start as Supply Runners with the expectation that they would work on their trainings during downtimes on the job and have the training completed within a semester. Once completed, they could then move on to the Library Tech Desk trainings, and finally, if they expressed interest in and were a good match, they could be asked to move up to the Help Desk. The group came up with the following program:

Supply Runner badge requirements:

Scheduling Meeting – Attend the begin of the semester scheduling and information meeting

Who's Whom in Student Consultants – Get to know the other student consultants

Word Level 1 – Know and demonstrate the basics of Microsoft Word

Excel Level 1 – Know and demonstrate the basics of Microsoft Excel

Printer Maintenance – Know how to stock paper, change toner, and locate/remove paper jams

Web Helpdesk Level 1 – Know how to log in, know when and how to create a Problem Report quick ticket, know when and how to create a Toner Order quick ticket

Library Tech Desk badge requirements:

Word Level 2 – Know the pagination requirements for Honors Thesis submittal, know how to add page numbers on a landscape page so that the numbers align correctly when bound with portrait pages, know how to add and format a Table of Contents, know how to format a reference page

Excel Level 2 – Demonstrate the use of spark lines; create filters; create charts, graphs, and tables; format cells and numbers

Acrobat Pro – Know how to create PDF/A and check for compliance, create fillable PDF forms from scratch, print and/or save documents as PDF

Network Pro – Identify the various options for connecting to the network on campus, how to register and connect devices on the network, basic network troubleshooting on PC and Macs

Whitmail Guru – Demonstrate the ability to setup Whitmail (Google mail) on various devices using Google's connection method and IMAP, setup LDAP, demonstrate the basics of using Google Drive and its components, demonstrate how to manage listserves

Web Helpdesk Level 2 – Demonstrate laptop check out/in procedures, create a basic (non-Quick ticket) ticket, create a GoPrint quick ticket, create FAQs for Web Helpdesk

Who's Whom in WCTS – take a quiz to learn the full-time staff of WCTS and what their roles are within the organization, demonstrate knowledge of when/why one would contact them

Help Desk badge requirements:

Word Level 3 – Demonstrate the ability to create a Mail Merge document with included Excel data set and demonstrate how to use Track Changes

Excel Level 3 – Demonstrate the ability to calculate between sheets within a workbook, use programming formulas to insert text, use advanced formulas (logical: IF, AND, OR), create pivot tables, create a data set for use in Word Mail Merge

Phone Savvy – Demonstrate the proper way to answer the phone at the desk; how to transfer calls to others and/or to voicemail; access and setup voicemail; how to call phones on campus, locally, and long distance (including international)

Web Security – Demonstrate the proper routing of calls/tickets of suspected infected faculty and staff computers, how to identify SPAM and phishing emails, identify the components that make up a "securely configured" computer

Bomgar Pro – Demonstrate the use of Bomgar and how to walk a client through the connection process

Who's Whom on Campus – Identify individual staff and faculty members of the Whitman campus including President, Provost, and Division Administrative Assistants amongst many others

Fun and other non-required badges:

Gold Star Tech – 4 years of service with WCTS

Silver Star Tech – 3 years of service with WCTS

Bronze Star Tech – 2 years of service with WCTS

Best Dressed – nominated by student consultants

Summer 20** - specially designed each year for those that work during the summer months

Mad Props – given to consultants who receive kudos from faculty or staff

Shift Savior – nominated by student consultants to recognize those that cover shifts in a pinch

Non-Striker – given to those consultants who do not receive any strikes (demerits for attendance, etc) in a semester

Idea Maker – given to those student consultants that come up with an idea that is implemented for the betterment of all

Problem Solver – given to consultants that resolve especially difficult issues that are presented to them

Trivia Buff – given to those that attend a Trivia night with the boss

Flash Response – given to those consultants that respond to specially marked emails from the boss

Mentor – nominated by student consultants to recognize those consultants that play a mentoring role at work and life

Unjammer – given to those consultants that successfully remove a particularly troublesome or gnarly paper jam in a printer

Wiki Master – given to those consultants that contribute and/or clean-up the department wiki

Classroom Helper – given to those consultants that assist a faculty member in a smart classroom with a technical issue

Worker Bee – given to the consultant who worked the most hours in a semester

Computer Setup – given to those consultants that deliver and setup a computer workstation for a faculty or staff member

Shift Taker – given to those consultants that pick up the most shifts dropped by other consultants during a semester

As a group, we decided to use the badging company Credly.com, that Educause recommended, to create and distribute the badges. The account was free to setup and individual accounts were free too. Each consultant would have to create their own individual Credly.com accounts to be able to have badges assigned to them. Each topic we created for training, along with the miscellaneous topics, would need badges created. As a team, we worked together to create designs for each topic (Fig. 4).

Figure 4: Badge designs for Excel Level 2 and An Acrobat Pro

We came to find out, however, that getting them displayed so that all of the consultants could see them was not going to be an easy task and would require money. We decided, in the beginning, that we would run the program to get a "proof of concept" before going to my director for funding.

With the groundwork created, the hard work began. In late May of 2013, I banded together the students that were working with us over the summer to begin the creation of the various readings, videos, and quizzes that would be required to pull off the program. It was mandated that the program be up and fully functional by fall semester of 2013. That gave the group only 3 months to get this program fully implemented. We came together as a group and were able to accomplish the goal. Articles were created in the wiki, videos were created using Screenflow and Camtasia and uploaded to Vimeo.com, and quizzes were created and uploaded to CLEo (Sakai). The quizzes would be distributed via consultants' dropboxes within CLEo and a spreadsheet was created to track the progress of the consultants with their training.

3.4 Lessons Learned

Fast forward to the end of the 2013-14 school year. The first full year was successful, in the grand scheme of things, but could definitely use some improvements. Here are my first-year lessons learned:

1. Having a way to display the badges for all to see would be a great benefit. If you can't see them, then who cares?

2. Keeping track of and grading the progress of 20 consultants while continuing my other regular duties was too time consuming and cumbersome.

3. Keeping track of progress on spreadsheets was time consuming.

4. Having no set due dates for the training was a bad oversight. A blind, "get it done by the end of the semester" ended up with many not doing any until the last minute or until nagged.

With a successful first year, I felt it was time to ask for some money to implement the badges even more. With a Pro account on Credly.com, you are able to create a connection with their site to display badges on your own site. My director approved the funds for getting the account upgraded and I discussed with our Enterprise Development team director about getting the project on their plate. It just so happened that over the summer of 2014 we had a student that was interning with our Development group. He was very interested in coding and wanted a project to work on that he could use those skills. Our homegrown scheduling system for the student consultants was long overdue an overhaul and facelift and it was a prime candidate for him to work on during the summer. Together we discussed the pros and cons of the system (he, too, was familiar with it as he worked as one of my student consultants the past two years) and what I was looking for. We also discussed how to go about incorporating the badges into the newly designed site. He worked tirelessly on the project over the summer and had it fully up and running in the fall of 2014. The new design was sleek and streamlined with a pleasing palate (Fig. 5).

Figure 5: Newly designed S3 "My Shifts" page

Consultants could easily locate their scheduled shifts, give up shifts, and claim shifts. Each consultant has a profile page built in that includes their student picture, their email address, and their phone number (if they choose to supply it). Their profiles also display their badges as long as they have accepted them within Credly.com and their account email address matches their school one (Fig. 6).

Figure 6: **Example of a profile page within the newly designed S3**

Each consultant could now click on the name of another consultant on the schedule and see this information as well.

Now, it was time to figure out how to handle the grading and tracking of progress of the consultants' training. Doing it all by myself was too much to handle when faced with all of my other regular job duties. It came time to give the Student Managers more responsibility. As being my eyes and ears during the evening shifts, I felt it was appropriate that they oversaw the training of the consultants that worked in the library as well as the Supply Runners (as the majority of those shifts were in the evening as well). It was on them to assign due dates and follow up with the consultants as they progressed through their trainings. The expectation was that each group would have their currently assigned level of training done before final exams of the semester came. This would ensure that the newly trained consultants would have the opportunity to pick up more shifts during our scheduled AdHoc weeks around finals and over the breaks. By doing this, it freed up some of my time and allowed me to focus on the trainings of the Help Desk staff. However, the process of distributing the assignments, doing the assigned quizzes, turning them in, getting them graded, doing any necessary follow up, and assigning the badges was still cumbersome.

At the annual SIGUCCS conference in 2015 in St. Petersburg, Florida, Jessica Morger from the University of Wyoming did a presentation titled "Consistency and Convenience: Use of Canvas in Help Desk Staff Training". Her presentation gave me some great ideas but most specifically it introduced me to the Canvas learning management system. In her presentation, Jessica noted that one could get a free account from Canvas. After the conference, I came back to campus and started investigating Canvas even further to see if it would be a good fit.

What sold Canvas to me:

1. It was free. My campus does not currently use Canvas for its LMS so finding something that was cost effective and had robust features was essential

2. Multiple courses could be created within the service
3. Students could be assigned to specific courses
4. Assignments, readings, and quizzes can be created within the LMS without the need of individually assigning each to each student
5. Quizzes are automatically graded and tracked per student
6. Assignment due dates can be created

During the summer of 2016, the student staff were tasked with transitioning the material from wiki pages, spreadsheets, and CLEo to Canvas. One of the summer staff was a student manager so he was given the lead on the project. By the fall of 2016, Canvas was in place and our newly hired students started the new training format (Fig. 7). The returning student staff were also put into the system to look for any gaps or errors in the areas they were already trained. By the end of the 2016-17 school year, 3 student staff had completed the Help Desk course, and 6 had completed the Supply Runner training and the progressed and completed the Library Tech Desk training.

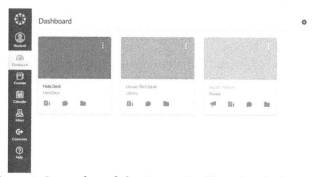

Figure 7: **Screenshot of the Canvas Dashboard with the 3 courses displayed**

During the implementation of Canvas, I was able to remove myself from the majority of the training of the consultants. Those duties were handed off to the Student Managers. These duties include, adding the newly hired staff to Canvas, adding current staff to any necessary courses, creating due dates for quizzes, following up with consultants on their progress, and assigning the necessary badges for each quiz or course completed. In addition, any consultant being trained at the Help Desk is partnered with a Student Manager to assist in their training and for the purposes of shadowing. Any newly hired student consultant, is also partnered up in the library with an experienced consultant to learn and become comfortable with the library desk as they worked on the training materials (Fig. 8)

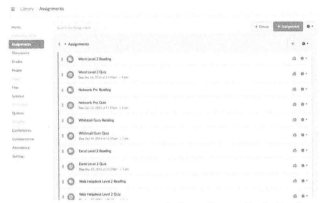

Figure 8: A listing of some of the Library Tech Desk readings and quizzes

Assessing this first year on Canvas, I have noticed the following:

1. Student Managers are more involved and are more leaders now than ever before
2. Student Consultants are being trained more consistently with fewer gaps in knowledge
3. Canvas has made follow up and tracking of training easier
4. There are a few gaps and room for improvement in the course content

Finally, we reach the summer of 2017. With a successful first year of Canvas implementation our working document of training is being tweaked. Content items such as Customer Service basics and Who Does What in WCTS are being created with the intent that all consultants will take them in the fall.

4 WORKSHOPS FOR STUDENT CONSULTANTS

From the beginning, it had always been my goal to create as many opportunities for the student consultants as I could to ready them for life beyond the campus walls. I felt that only giving them work experience wasn't enough. In the spring semester of 2015, I reached out to our campus Student Engagement Center. This office is our campus's equivalent to a Career Services Office. I worked with them to create a Resume Workshop for the students so that they could best translate the skills they were receiving by working for Technology Services into resume-ready bullet points. The workshop was held over the lunch hour on a Monday and Wednesday in early March with lunch being provided. Attendees only had to come to one or the other day, if they wished. The hope was to get the workshop in before they started applying for jobs or internships that summer. The workshop was a complete hit with all 20 available slots over the two days filled!

Building off of that success, I approached a colleague within WCTS about doing an Interview Skills Workshop the following spring. Together, we created content that explained interview etiquette, what to expect from an interview, what to do after the interview, and our own anecdotal experiences of being on both sides of the interview table. Each attendee was then given the opportunity to sign up for a mock interview with my colleague and I. Those that did the mock interviews were given feedback on what they did well and where they could improve. This workshop was not as well attended with only 7 coming but those that did come created great conversation and I felt it was worth doing again. Each spring, I plan to continue to provide these workshops for the student consultants. This last spring, February 2017, we provided the Resume Workshop again and had a total attendance of 13 students. We plan to have the Interview workshop again in early 2018 and alternate between the two going forward.

5 CONCLUSION

From the beginning, my plan was to have a training course that would be a working document for the student consultants. This would allow for changes to be easily implemented. New courses could be added if new positions were to be created. The world of technology is forever changing and services are being added and removed from campus every year. Being able to stay on top it makes managing and training the student consultants that much easier. Ultimately, my goal is to have the students leave us after 4 years and know that, whether they go into tech or not, they have skills that they can use and a reference they can put down on their resume. They are a part of the WCTS family for life and I try to keep in touch with all of them as best I can through Facebook (through a special group I created that connects past consultants with current ones) and text messages. I also post job openings within the Facebook group and make arrangements for meetups when I travel for work. It is and always will be my goal to make sure that those students that work for WCTS have every opportunity to excel once they connect to the outside world and leave the walls of campus.

Delivering Tomorrow's Workspace – Reimagining Application and Desktop Delivery Strategies

Muhammed Naazer Ashraf
Lehigh University
19 Memorial Drive West
Dept. of Mechanical Engineering
naazer@lehigh.edu

ABSTRACT

There has been increasing pressure now more than ever to eliminate and replace physical computing spaces with virtual environments. We will discuss the pros and cons of each solution from our experience, and why we felt that a combination of physical and virtual environments provides the ultimate benefits in advancing our teaching, learning, and research missions. It is important to understand all the delivery mechanisms available today and picking the right tool for the right job. When do you virtualize, when do you opt for server-hosted, when do you throw in GPU-accelerated workstations, and when do you offload to a high-performance computing cluster. It is important to understand the tools available to us and then carefully research and test how they can be best applied to a given scenario. Participants should walk away with real-world knowledge, skills and best practices in delivering high-performing computing labs.

CCS CONCEPTS

• **Computer system implementation** → **Microcomputers**; *personal computers, portable devices, workstations*

KEYWORDS

Virtualization; Microsoft; Remote Desktop Services; RDS; Citrix; XenApp; XenDesktop; Computer Labs; Engineering; Workspace; PVS; Provisioning Services; NVIDIA; GPU; GRID; Applications; Unidesk

1 INTRODUCTION

1.1 Lehigh University Overview

Lehigh University is a private research institution founded in 1865 and located in Bethlehem, Pennsylvania, USA. It boasts 600 faculty members, 1,100 support staff, and an enrollment of over 5,000 undergraduates and 1,500 graduate students. Library and computer services are combined in one integrated organizational unit known as Library & Technology Services (LTS). LTS owns and maintains over 500 classroom and lab PCs while also supporting nearly 2,300 departmental PCs.

1.2 Path to Prominence

Lehigh University revealed its 10-year plan, the "Path to Prominence," to the Lehigh community at the end of October 2016. It laid out an ambitious new framework on which Lehigh's future will be built. It is a vision that includes a series of sweeping, decisive steps that will see the university build on historic strengths and evolve into a more dynamic, impactful institution: an increase in student enrollment, renovations to numerous campus buildings, the construction of new academic and residential facilities, the addition of 100 faculty, an expansion in the area of health, and an addition of a new college. This expansion plan will serve as an opportunity to increase the university's visibility, both nationally and internationally, and play a key role in significant areas of education.

1.3 Software Story at Lehigh

Our Library & Technology Services group enlisted the help of an independent external consulting firm in the Spring of 2016 to conduct a client satisfaction survey to gather feedback on the quality of the services provided to the Lehigh University community. The results of this extensive survey were used to establish a baseline on current services and to help prioritize the continuous improvement efforts moving forward. The ultimate goal is to provide an excellent customer IT experience that supports the teaching, research, and business needs of Lehigh University. We noticed that the highest areas of dissatisfaction expressed by our students, staff, and faculty were:

1. "Availability of technology-enhanced spaces"
2. "Ease of downloading and installing licensed software"
3. "Availability of licensed software in classrooms and public sites"
4. "Selection of licensed software"

Drilling down into the results, we also noticed that the largest source of dissatisfaction for graduate students was access to licensed software. Our CIO and Directors immediately formed a few committees to address these pain points and the Software Services committee was born.

SIGUCCS '17, October 1–4, 2017, Seattle, WA, USA
© 2017 Association for Computing Machinery.
ACM ISBN 978-1-4503-4919-2/17/10 $15.00
https://doi.org/10.1145/3123458.3123480

It is useful to understand the current solutions that we had in place. The University had been offering three primary means of accessing our licensed software: LUIS (Lehigh University Install Software), our secure software download web portal (Fig. 1); physical public computing labs; and a VDI implementation with VMware Horizon and Microsoft Remote Desktop Services (Fig. 2).

LUIS was our main software portal and its vision was to serve as a one-stop shop for everyone's software needs. One of the biggest drawbacks, which was out of LTS's control, was the licensing of most of these applications. Nearly all licensed software had the stipulation that it could only be run on university-owned hardware. This precluded students being able to install it on their own personal devices. The other big drawback, owing to the licensing again, was that the software installers and serial numbers could not be shared with students. What this meant was the faculty members or LTS Consultants had to download and install the software for students even on university-owned hardware. The problems with this model were immediately evident, but it has still served as the primary means of accessing licensed software since 2012.

Figure 1: Lehigh University Install Software (LUIS) portal

The Virtual Public Site had evolved significantly since its announcement in 2011. Everyone loved the fact that they could now access software, albeit a small subset, from their personal devices. Feedback was very positive in the beginning, but usage began to dwindle as licensing once again reared its ugly face to spoil the day. We could only offer a small subset of our licensed applications as the vendors did not allow virtualization of their applications.

Figure 2: VMware Horizon Virtual Public Site

We have a little over 700 computers spread throughout the university in labs that serve as one of the primary modes of accessing our software. Usage of our physical labs has consistently been high for several reasons. One - they offer access to all our software. Two – they also serve as a central location for students to gather and get their work done. With the number of software titles growing over time, it started to place a burden on our Classroom Technology team that managed these labs. The desktop image has grown to a monolithic size, which has resulted in several incompatibilities and problems with some of the applications installed. The rising costs of maintaining the physical computers and replacing them every 3 years has become a pain-point with administration. The current trends in BYOD and the need for more active collaborative spaces is also placing increased pressure on our administration and the solutions are not so clear. We cannot immediately eliminate all public computing sites, but we recognize that something is going to need to change so we put a team together to look at our options.

We are now realizing that VDI technology is expensive in terms of both software licensing and infrastructure costs. What this team decided to focus on was to find a solution to deliver all the applications our students need, at any time, and from any device.

Our team narrowed down Citrix XenDesktop as a strong contender as it offered solutions that addressed our Public Site Computing dilemma, as well as securely delivering centrally-managed, on-demand applications to all our users, across any device, over any network condition.

Our leadership was looking for a solution to transform the way in which our technology was consumed. In particular, they were interested in the following:

1. Enhancing the student experience by allowing students the flexibility to work from any device, anywhere.
2. Virtualize classrooms and labs by centralizing and improving management of virtual applications and redesigning learning spaces.

3. Grow online and distance education initiatives to expand the reach of a Lehigh education by optimizing remote learning opportunities.

1.4 Computer Labs at Lehigh

Computer labs historically existed as a means for our University to provide students with a computer with a variety of applications they need to get their work done. Today, we find that 99% of our students come to Lehigh with at least one laptop or tablet device so the computer labs only exist as a way for students to access Lehigh software like Solidworks, Matlab, and ANSYS. There is also that expectation that if students require specialized software for a particular class, they will be able to go to a lab and find a computer to get their work done.

Applications are installed as part of a Windows 10 image and pushed out using a deployment tool like System Center Configuration Manager (SCCM). We are investigating SCCM and I encourage you to learn about that project in our "Scratching the Surface of Windows Server 2016 and System Center Configuration Manager" paper that will also be presented at the SIGUCCS 2017 conference. Our images keep growing larger as the applications keep getting larger and more complex. This is also beginning to cause conflicts and compatibility issues with some applications in our images.

The biggest challenges Lehigh University faces when it comes to effectively managing labs are the sheer number of applications that all our students need for their work, as well as the hundreds of thousands of dollars in lifecycle funds required to maintain these labs.

1.5 What Students Want

We have observed an interesting phenomenon that is happening with our current generation of students over the last several years. They consider themselves digital natives who are born with technology, and expect it to be available to them at all times. Work is no longer a place; it is an activity. They want to be able to go into the nearest building, coffee shop or favorite bench, sit with their friends, choose the nicest room, and generally work in the most productive environment. They also want to be able to use their personal laptops and tablet devices to access applications and not be tethered down to a particular computer or location. We believe Citrix XenDesktop will help deliver this workspace to our students.

2 How XenDesktop Works?

A XenDesktop deployment can be broken down into 5 layers: Users, Access, Resources, Control Management, and Hardware. These layers provide the flow of how Citrix manages and delivers a desktop or application to a user.

Users – this layer consists of one or more delivery groups. A delivery group is simply a group of users who have similar requirements often aligned with different departments. What is unique about the user layer is the flexibility. Users can use any device, from laptops to tablets to smartphones, as long as there is a Citrix Receiver client available for that device, which there is

for most platforms including Windows, Mac OS X, Linux, iOS, Android, Chrome, as well as HTML 5. In addition to any device, users can also access the environment from anywhere.

Access – this second layer defines how users will access the resources. The primary mechanism for this is the StoreFront, which provides the visible front end to the application and desktop store so users can subscribe to and launch their applications after successfully being authenticated.

Resources – make up the third layer. XenDesktop has several resource options available including applications, non-persistent desktops, persistent desktops, local desktops, shared desktops, remote PC access, and several more. Each one is applicable to a different use case.

Management & Control – This layer contains the delivery controller responsible for allocating, managing and maintaining the user, access, and resources layers. However, the administrative workflow responsible for installing, configuring, and deploying the environment is completely different from the workflow of supporting the environment. That is why the management and control layer include two management consoles: Studio and Director. Studio is used to setup and deploy the environment while Director is used to support the users.

Hardware – this is the physical representation of the overall solution. In comprises of the physical and virtual hosts used to deploy the solution. Citrix provides the flexibility of virtualizing on-premises using Citrix XenServer, VMware vSphere, or Microsoft Hyper-V. Cloud-based deployment options are also available on Citrix Cloud platform, Amazon AWS, and Microsoft Azure. XenDesktop also provides a hybrid deployment option where some resources are located on-premises while other resources are in the cloud.

2.1 Citrix Studio - Management

The hardware layer is defined within the Hosting section of Studio (Fig. 3). Citrix offers several different hosting platforms including XenServer, vSphere, Hyper-V, and cloud options, as shown in Fig. 4. The management and control layer is visible in the Controllers section of the console. The resource layer is defined by the different Catalogs in the Machine Catalogs (Fig. 5) section of Studio.

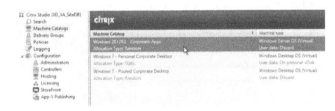

Figure 3: Citrix Studio Dashboard

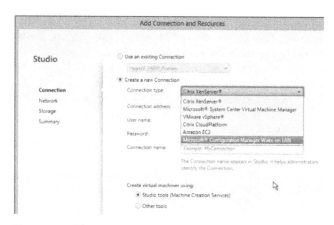

Figure 4: Adding Resources in Citrix Studio Dashboard

Figure 5: Machine Catalogs in Citrix Studio Dashboard

The user layer is defined as Delivery Groups within Studio. In Fig. 6 you can see four different deliver groups. The first one is for application delivery while the other three will deliver desktops to different groups within the organization.

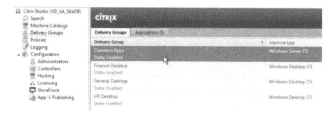

Figure 6: Delivery Groups in Citrix Studio Dashboard

2.2 Citrix Director - Support

The Citrix Director dashboard, as seen in Fig. 7, provides a high-level overview of the health of the environment. It provides visibility into failures, number of sessions, and details such as average logon durations. If we need to provide support to any users, we can simply type their name into a search box and Director displays a list of users and sessions available to them. If we drill down into a user session, we can see more details with the list of processes currently running, and gather insight into the user experience. See Fig. 8.

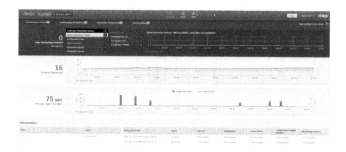

Figure 7: Citrix Director Overview Dashboard

Figure 8: Citrix Director Process Explorer Dashboard

3 KEY ENABLING TECHNOLOGIES

NVIDIA GRID, Unidesk, and Provisioning Services (PVS) are three of the key driving technologies that we are most excited about with the Citrix solution. We are confident that we are building a better workspace for our Lehigh students, which in turn will drive our teaching and learning missions.

Being able to deliver graphics capabilities from the data center that supports running applications like Solidworks, Siemens NX, and the Autodesk suite of applications has been a key factor in our consideration for this project. Citrix and NVIDIA were the pioneers when it came to delivering graphics-intensive applications and the GRID technology from NVIDIA was a key component.

3.1 NVIDIA GRID

NVIDIA GRID has brought the power of NVIDIA GPUs to virtual workstations, desktops, and applications. It provides the freedom and flexibility to deliver an immersive, high-quality user experience for everyone from designers to mobile professionals. NVIDIA GPUs and NVIDIA GRID software are now fully supported across VMware, Citrix, and Microsoft Hyper-V 2016-based data centers. The shared GPU feature enables higher user density per GPU while GPU-passthrough technology presents the entire GPU, which provides more power.

NVIDIA GRID supports Citrix XenDesktop and XenApp environments to power graphics-intensive applications from the data center to deliver to users a native PC-equivalent experience, which rivals that of a physical workstation.

3.2 Unidesk

Unidesk is the industry-leading application packaging and image management solution for virtual workspaces and is now integrated into XenDesktop & XenApp. Its patented layering technology offers a powerful solution to the traditional application virtualization solutions available. It simplifies application and image management in the XenDesktop and XenApp environments, while also accelerating application delivery and expanding the use cases for both solutions.

1. Applications can be packaged very quickly employing a standard install that does not require any specialized knowledge or tricks.
2. Completely eliminates app inter-dependencies.
3. Packaged apps are portable and cloud-ready

3.3 Provisioning Services (PVS)

PVS is a technology and feature that Citrix offers that we were blown away with. It offers a way to deliver a single image to multiple target devices that are diskless. These target devices can include both physical and virtual machines, thin-clients, laptops, desktops, or servers. The idea here is instead of booting into the local hard drive, you are PXE (Pre-boot Execution) booting to a PVS Server and downloading a virtual disk that contains the Operating System and the applications that are embedded in it. You are downloading this image for local execution on the target device. So nothing is being executed on the server, everything is being executed locally at the target device.

Citrix acquired PVS back in December 2006 from a company called Ardence at the time. It should be noted that at the time there was really no virtualization of any kind in production. Citrix acquired this product because it needed a more efficient way of managing its XenApp servers, which at the time was called Presentation Server. One of the biggest problems with these physical servers was scaling them. When you start having more servers, keeping the OS, patches, applications, and settings consistent across all these servers became an administrative nightmare. Making changes manually to each server became exponentially problematic.

The power of PVS is when it comes time to make an update to all the servers - you only need to update one virtual disk image and all your changes take effect as soon as you reboot. If you need to rollback changes, all you need to do is switch back that virtual disk to the one that was being streamed before that was working, and within a matter of minutes, you are up and running. It is a very elegant solution with multiple use-cases.

PVS centrally manages OS images and lets you leverage the full potential of the target devices. This is particularly useful in cases where VDI or application virtualization is not a good option, because you want to leverage the full power of the target device. Running ANSYS or MATLAB simulations on a high-end workstation is one use case, for instance. We will be able to stream a virtual disk image with those applications, which will then execute locally on the target device. This is a great alternative to traditional imaging methods and provides a very efficient way of managing large numbers of target devices from a central location.

This PVS technology can be applied to other resources such as file servers and even web servers. Some folks even go as far as saying that the PVS technology is the grandfather of virtualization because, if you think about it, you were literally separating the hardware from the software by not installing it on a local hard drive and having the flexibility of centrally managing it.

4 BUILDING THE ULTIMATE WORKSPACE

Lehigh University wants to provide the richest learning experience possible. We want to be able to turn any device and any location into a place of learning. The vision with the Citrix solution is to be able to deliver every application and service that a faculty, staff, or student would have available in a classroom or lab to anywhere in the world that they have a network connection, and on any device. The users will be just as enabled as they would have been sitting in that classroom with that application. Citrix will open up a lot of learning opportunities for students and take them beyond the scope of the classes they are enrolled in. Our hope is that it will also increase student engagement. When students have access to all of the applications they would have had sitting in lab or classroom from anywhere, they are going to use it more often. We believe Citrix will open up the opportunity for independent and exploratory learning in new ways that were not possible in the past.

Two of our most well-equipped physical labs are the Computer-Aided Design / Manufacturing / Engineering (CAD/CAM/CAE) labs in our Mechanical Engineering department. These labs have powerful HP Z-series workstations with professional graphics cards and large-screen displays. These labs are nearly always at capacity as both undergraduate and graduate engineering students utilize them. We discovered something very interesting when we surveyed these students before piloting the Citrix solution. When given the choice of being able to access all the software in this physical lab on their personal laptops, over 75% of the students answered that they would still prefer to come to the CAD/CAD/CAE labs to get their work done. At first, this did not make sense to us, as we were confident that the students would have preferred to stay away from the labs and work on their laptops. We then realized that the students were attracted to the space for several reasons and not just for use of the workstations. We will continue to solicit feedback during our pilot of XenDesktop and see if the original perception of the physical labs change.

The two primary CAD/CAM/CAE labs were designed with two different visions. The flagship site is shown in Fig. 9, where the computers are grouped in clusters of 3 or 4 workstations with plenty of table space and chairs to promote small group learning and discussion. The instructor and teaching assistants typically float around the large space and assist students with anything they need. The second site is designed in a more traditional sense with rows of computers with the instructor lecturing from the front of the classroom.

Figure 9: Computer lab with collaborative space design

The University has already made a substantial investment in physical PC lifecycle so we had agreed upon a phased approach toward desktop and application virtualization. In this model, we would try to supplement our physical workstations with application and desktop virtualization technology instead of replacing them.

The unique aspect in Engineering, in contrast to most other departments at Lehigh University, is nearly every lab was specialized in some way. Many of these workstations were "rolled down" from the CAD/CAM/CAE labs and still covered under the original 5-yr warranty. These workstations are running real-time data acquisition experiments where they were physically connected to specialized apparatus like high-speed cameras, lasers, transducers, electronic microscopes, and custom motion-controlled sensors. We have engaged the vendors at National Instruments, who make Labview, an application most commonly used for control and analysis in these types of experiments; however, they do not support any remote and virtualized computing. It is a physical limitation as these instruments need to communicate directly with the hardware and virtualization produces very unpredictable results, hence it is strongly unsupported. Several of these experimental scenarios are utilizing 10+ year old workstations that are carefully configured to run the required applications and nothing else. Here is where we feel installing the Citrix Receiver client or connecting to our RDS infrastructure will provide additional benefits of accessing more applications on these older workstations. We were very pleased with being able to run Windows 10 on nearly 10-yr old hardware.

The Citrix XenDesktop infrastructure has been improved with high-end NVIDIA GPUs like the Tesla M60 and leveraging NVIDIA's GRID technology to deliver virtualized graphics centrally from the datacenter. This will enable students who require graphics-intensive applications, such as those in engineering, to be able to seamlessly access all the software they require to get their work done.

4 NEXT STEPS

Our CIO was immediately on board with the recommendations of the team to move forward with the Citrix solution and carved out a budget to kick-start the pilot. At the time of this writing, we were preparing for our Fall pilot, where we decided to redesign an existing physical lab space with thin-clients, and offer the Citrix solution to the students in two engineering courses. The goal is to carefully monitor feedback and market the new solution as the primary mode of accessing software at Lehigh University.

While conducting interviews with research groups across engineering disciplines, we identified a potential problem with students that required high computing power. These students typically leverage workstations with over 64GB of memory and ran simulations for hours, days, and even weeks. We absolutely would not want to have these workloads running on our Citrix servers, as a few students would quickly monopolize the available resources. We needed a different method of delivering software for these special use-cases and we believe System Center Configuration Manager (SCCM, also known as ConfigMgr) is one solution.

This move to Citrix is going to be a paradigm shift in the way we have been installing, managing, and delivering applications so it was important that our team become familiar with the packaging and 'layering' techniques that seem to be direction where modern application virtualization is heading. We were familiar with a company called Unidesk that revolutionized desktop and application management with their patented layering technology that containerized desktop applications as virtual disks. Citrix acquired Unidesk in January 2017 and now integrates this technology in its XenDesktop & XenApp portfolio at no extra cost.

5 LOOKING INTO THE FUTURE

We are aware that both Microsoft and Citrix offer strong roadmaps for extending their deployments into the Azure cloud. This is tremendously beneficial as Lehigh University and other institutions are currently in discussions of how best to leverage the cloud for various services.

It is immensely valuable that we understand all our options keeping in mind the goals and original problems we were looking to solve. In an ideal world, there would be one solution that addresses all our needs. This, experience has shown, is rarely possible.

Our goal was to try and deliver the best workspace to our students. What we learned was that we needed to provide a few options in order to meet everyone's needs.

Next year we will have more data, statistics, and metrics to reevaluate and refocus our goals. We can then make a data-driven decision on assessing which model the students actually prefer with a stronger sense of certainty.

You can follow this project here: http://go.lehigh.edu/citrix

ACKNOWLEDGMENTS

I am grateful to my colleagues Timothy J. Foley and Gale D. Fritsche at Lehigh University for their tremendous support of my efforts and training.

Special thanks to my students Shiv Joshi, Jordan Geiger, and Jeevan Jain-Cocks who always made themselves available when I needed their assistance. It has been a privilege and honor to work with these individuals.

The following music was played (often loudly) during the writing of this paper: Dire Straits, Disturbed, Michael Jackson, U2, Taylor Swift, and Celine Dion.

Author Index

NOTES